Stephen D. Brookfield

Understanding and Facilitating Adult Learning

 Jossey-Bass Publishers

San Francisco • London • 1987

UNDERSTANDING AND FACILITATING ADULT LEARNING
A Comprehensive Analysis of Principles and Effective Practices
by Stephen D. Brookfield

Copyright © 1986 by: Jossey-Bass Inc., Publishers
433 California Street
San Francisco, California 94104

Published simultaneously in Great Britain
by the Open University Press
Walton Hall, Milton Keynes, England

Copyrighted in 1986 in Great Britain by Stephen D. Brookfield

Library of Congress Cataloging-in-Publication Data

Brookfield, Stephen D.
  Understanding and facilitating adult learning.

  Bibliography: p. 301
  Includes index.
  1. Adult education—United States—Case studies.
2. Continuing education—United States—Case studies.
I. Title.
LC5251.B76   1986   374'.973   85-23861
ISBN 0-87589-674-X (alk. paper)

Manufactured in the United States of America

The paper in this book meets the guidelines for
permanence and durability of the Committee on
Production Guidelines for Book Longevity of the
Council on Library Resources.

JACKET DESIGN BY WILLI BAUM

FIRST EDITION
     First printing: March 1986
     Second printing: December 1986
     Third printing: August 1987

Code 8605

A joint publication in
The Jossey-Bass
Higher Education Series
and
The Jossey-Bass
Management Series

❧ ❧ ❧ ❧

Consulting Editor
Adult and Continuing Education

Alan B. Knox
University of Wisconsin at Madison

Preface

❧ ❧ ❧ ❧

The facilitation of learning—assisting adults to make sense of and act upon the personal, social, occupational, and political environment in which they live—is an important, exhilirating, and profound activity, both for facilitators and for learners. It is also a highly complex psychosocial drama in which the personalities of the individuals involved, the contextual setting for the educational transaction, and the prevailing political climate crucially affect the nature and form of learning. Yet among theorists and practitioners of adult learning this complexity is frequently ignored. Instead, a kind of folk wisdom has emerged in which the facilitation of adult learning is seen as a nondirective, warmly satisfying encounter through which learners' needs are met. It is generally unacknowledged that such encounters might contain elements of conflicting purposes, contrasting personality styles, or challenges to learners to engage in an anxiety-producing reexamination of self or of previously unchallenged norms (organizational, behavioral, or moral).

Those engaged in helping adults to learn know that facilitating learning is often not a wholly fulfilling and bountiful experience in self-realization. A major purpose of this book is to examine critically the notion that facilitating learning is a smooth voyage along a storm-free river of increasing self-actualization that excludes elements of conflict, anxiety, self-doubt, or challenge.

Understanding and Facilitating Adult Learning explores the theory-practice disjunctions between theories-in-use (how practitioners attempt to assist adult learning in real life) and espoused theories (how the previously mentioned folk wisdom and clichés describe the process of facilitation). As a product of this exploration, I propose a new concept of facilitation that incorporates elements of challenge, confrontation, and critical analysis of self and society. This concept rejects the equation of facilitation with a nondirective attempt to serve as a resource person to learners who are essentially in total command of their learning activities. Instead it argues that facilitating learning is a transactional drama in which the personalities, philosophies, and priorities of the chief players (participants and facilitators) interact continuously to influence the nature, direction, and form of the subsequent learning.

The central goal of *Understanding and Facilitating Adult Learning* is to review a range of practice settings in which educators and trainers of adults attempt to facilitate learning and to identify elements of effective practice that illustrate the concept of facilitation outlined above. To this end I consider case studies of practice in several distinctive areas: higher education for adult students in colleges and universities, training programs and vocational education in business and industry, continuing professional education for various groups (doctors, lawyers, architects), community activist initiatives, informal resource and learning networks, health education, labor or union education, adult basic education (particularly adult literacy work), and the diverse arena of self-directed learning. In each of these areas of practice, I identify a number of principles of effective facilitation, explore the theory-practice disjunctions between espoused theories and theories-in-use, and examine the crucial influence of contextual factors on practice. Throughout the book I warn against adopting formulaeic responses to situations in which the personalities of learners and facilitators, conflicting purposes of administrators and facilitators, political climate of the time, or budgetary constraints alter fundamentally what is appropriate practice. Practitioners should always be encouraged to be skeptical of "quick fix" solutions that involve applying a standard reaction to widely varying situations. For this reason, I report on the experiences of facilitators who have improvised creatively in response to contextual constraints and elaborate on the broader implications and replicable aspects of particular practice efforts.

The audience for whom this book will be useful includes all those engaged in facilitating adult learning, whatever the context. In particular, the wide-ranging case studies of practice that are explored make the book useful for faculty, advisers, administrators, and counselors in colleges, polytechnics, and universities that include adults among their student body; organizers and teachers in adult and continuing education programs in schools, colleges, and universities; training directors and trainers in vocational, business, and industrial education; tutors and organizers in labor unions; teachers and administrators in the field of adult basic education; community workers in social and political action efforts; those engaged in continuing professional education for various occupational groups (lawyers, doctors, architects to name but three); health educators; and professors and students of adult learning. This is a very broad audience, and this breadth is reflected in the extensive and up-to-date bibliography of references to be found at the end of the book. The bibliography stands as the most complete and current collection of materials on facilitating learning in these diverse areas of practice available at the present time.

Overview of the Contents

The book opens with a review of effective practice in adult learning and an explanation of the concept of facilitation that informs the rest of the work. In this first chapter the focus is firmly on identifying elements of effective practice in facilitating learning. Six central principles are identified—voluntary participation, mutual respect, collaborative spirit, praxis, critical reflection, and self-direction—and the way these are implemented

in practice is discussed. Chapter Two reviews the general find-
ings of the last twenty-five years concerning adults as learners.
The works of writers such as Malcolm Knowles, Roby Kidd,
Alan Knox, and Robert Smith are discussed in full here.

The nature and form of self-directed learning—often
claimed to be the most distinctive of all learning styles in adulthood—is explored in Chapter Three. The research and theory in
the field of self-directed learning is reviewed, some criticisms of
the orthodox views are made, and a concept of self-directedness
focusing on critical awareness among learners is proposed. How
such self-directed learning might best be facilitated in various
organizational settings and the problems frequently faced by
facilitators in that effort are then explored in Chapter Four.

The concept of andragogy—currently the most influential
concept in the education and training of adults for most practitioners—is critically examined in Chapter Five. Case studies of
what is claimed as andragogical practice are reviewed, and
some of the key features and problems of this mode of practice
are highlighted. Chapter Six considers the role of the teacher of
adults and discusses the interrelationship between the role of
the teacher and that of the facilitator. Research concerning effective teaching practice is also presented in this chapter, and
the use of the discussion method as the pedagogical approach
most appropriate to adult learners is explored.

Chapters Seven and Eight are both concerned with understanding the range of settings in which adult learning occurs. In
Chapter Seven the emphasis is on informal settings, such as self-
directed learning, learning networks, and community action.
More formal and structured environments for learning, such as
business settings, colleges, and universities, are explored in
Chapter Eight.

Chapter Nine reviews the development of education and
training programs for adult learners that are based on the most
common model of program development, the institutional model. A central concern of this chapter is to scrutinize carefully
the theory-practice disjunctions between the tenets of this institutional model, which is frequently offered in textbooks of edu-

cational practice, and the real life experiences of program developers. The extent to which programmers develop creative, improvisational strategies to deal with contextually specific features of their programs is discussed, and the crucial distorting effect of context is emphasized. Some alternatives to this institutional model of program development are explored in Chapter Ten. Ideas from community education and self-directed learning are reviewed, and a model of flexible, participatory program development is presented. This chapter also discusses how practitioners set their priorities among differing claims on their resources, and how practitioners develop their own intuitively based theories of practice.

Chapter Eleven evaluates effective practice in facilitating learning and offers criteria by which good practice might be recognized. Chapter Twelve, the final chapter, proposes a philosophical rationale by which practitioners might judge whether or not they are exemplifying the model of critical facilitation suggested throughout this book.

Acknowledgments

Two colleagues at Teachers College have been particularly important to the writing of this book. Over the past three years I have been fortunate enough to work with Jack Mezirow in developing curricula and methods for training the educators of adults. Only he will recognize the considerable extent to which ideas, issues, concepts, and questions raised in the following pages have originated in, or been refined by, our discussions. His critically analytic questioning has been invaluable in helping me clarify my ideas and in suggesting directions for further analysis. Kimerly Miller, past program assistant in the Adult Education through Guided Independent Study (AEGIS) program at the college and currently an independent consultant in intercultural education and training, read and critiqued the manuscript. To her must go the credit for whatever sensitivity to issues of intercultural education are contained in the final manuscript. Finally, David and Sybil Brookfield have encouraged me to journey, both geographically and intellectually, in the field of the education and training of adults. Their support has been crucial to all stages of this project, and I am forever grateful for their understanding and encouragement.

New York, New York   Stephen D. Brookfield
January 1986

Contents

The Author

❧ ❧ ❧ ❧

Stephen D. Brookfield is associate professor of adult and continuing education and associate director of the Center for Adult Education at Teachers College, Columbia University, in New York City. He received his B.A. degree (1970) from Lanchester Polytechnic (Coventry) in modern studies, his M.A. degree (1974) from the University of Reading in sociology, and his Ph.D. degree (1980) from the University of Leicester in adult education. He also holds a postgraduate diploma in modern social and cultural studies (1971) from the University of London, Chelsea College, and a postgraduate diploma in adult education (1977) from the University of Nottingham.

Brookfield's main research activities have been in the fields of self-directed learning, community adult education, comparative adult education, qualitative research approaches to adult learning processes, program development and evaluation, and political and philosophical aspects of adult and continuing education. He has been national chair of the Adult Education Research Conference of North America (1985), a founding member of the International League for Social Commitment in Adult Education and of the British and North American Network for Adult Education, and a member of the national executive committee of the Association for Recurrent Education (United Kingdom). His books and monographs include *Independent Adult Learning* (1982), *Adult Learners, Adult Education and the Community* (1983), and *Self-Directed Learning: From Theory to Practice* (1985).

Brookfield has been a professor of adult education at the University of British Columbia in Vancouver, Canada, and was formerly research officer for the Advisory Council for Adult and Continuing Education of England and Wales. In this capacity he wrote a national report entitled *Distance Learning and Adult Students* (1983).

Understanding and Facilitating Adult Learning

❧ ❧ ❧ ❧

*A Comprehensive Analysis
of Principles
and Effective Practices*

~❦~ 1 ~❦~

Adult Learners

Motives for Learning and Implications for Practice

When adults teach and learn in one another's company, they find themselves engaging in a challenging, passionate, and creative activity. The acts of teaching and learning—and the creation and alteration of our beliefs, values, actions, relationships, and social forms that result from this—are ways in which we realize our humanity. The extent to which adults are engaged in a free exchange of ideas, beliefs, and practices is one gauge of whether a society is open, democratic, and healthy. If adults of widely differing class and ethnic groups are actively exploring ideas, beliefs, and practices, then we are likely to have a society in which creativity, diversity, and the continuous re-creation of social structures are the accepted norms. By contrast, societies in which inquiry, reflection, and exploration are the prerogative of a privileged minority are likely to be static, ossified, and hierarchical.

It would be easy for professional educators to translate the above argument into a declaration that a society can be considered healthy to the extent that it provides publicly funded learning opportunities for adults. This may be one indicator of a just society, but it is not the only one and it neglects the enormous amount of significant adult learning, individual and collective, that takes place outside formal educational settings. The

1

teaching-learning transactions undertaken by adults are complex and multifaceted, and they steadfastly refuse simple categorization. They occur in every setting imaginable, are conducted at different levels of significance to the learner, are oriented toward a variety of cognitive, affective, psychomotor, and political ends, and involve a range of formats and methods. We can argue that a T-group workshop for managers, a volunteer literacy effort, a staff development workshop for school principals, a course on collective bargaining for shop stewards, a tenants' action committee preparing a submission to a rent tribunal, a single parents' support group collectively exploring their experiences, and a men's or women's consciousness-raising group dealing with sexism, are all adult learning efforts.

In all these instances, several commonalities are observable. At a very basic level, of course, the participants involved are adults; that is, they have attained the legal and chronological status of adulthood. Second, they are engaged in a purposeful exploration of a field of knowledge or set of skills or in a collective reflection upon common experiences. Third, these explorations of knowledge, skills, and experiences take place in a group setting. Fourth, the participants in these explorations bring to the encounter a collection of experiences, skills, and knowledge that are going to influence how new ideas are received, how new skills are acquired, and how the experiences of others are interpreted. As Gagné (1971) has observed, every adult's stock of prior learning and experience coheres into a unique, idiosyncratic mediatory mechanism through which new experiences and knowledge are filtered. Hence, as educators we can never predict with total certainty how one adult (let alone a group) will respond to being presented with new ideas, interpretations, skill sets, experiences, or materials. Fifth, such prior learning and experience also comprise valuable curricular resources. In the examples of the teaching-learning transactions mentioned earlier, the topics discussed, themes explored, experiences interpreted, skills acquired, and knowledge investigated will be influenced by, and will draw upon, this prior learning and experience. The tenants, managers, school principals, shop stewards, single parents, and nonreaders will identify common problems, voice common concerns, specify skills in which they feel that they are deficient, and provide experiences upon which others in the group can reflect.

Finally, the transactions in these groups will be characterized by a respect for individual members that will be manifest in the procedures used. These groups will probably use discussion methods that will allow individual members' contributions to be jointly interpreted and explored; and, if the group leader is acting as a good facilitator, no one member will be cajoled, insulted, or intimidated by the pressure of majority opinion. Leadership of some of these groups will be rotational, and individual members will, at different times and for different purposes, assume temporary leadership of the group. Even where an appointed leader is present, it is likely that he or she will feel no sense of professional dereliction in surrendering "authority" to allow group members to voice concerns, change the curricular focus, and alter previously agreed-upon rules of group conduct. Integral to this climate of respect for individual members is an expectation that the teaching-learning process will be distinguished by a continual negotiation of objectives, methods, and evaluative criteria.

Participants in Learning

Judging by the number of journal articles, dissertations, and studies devoted to it, the topic of participation in adult learning is probably the most enduring research concern since investigations of this field began. There are endless analyses of typologies of participation, of motivational orientations (Boshier, 1971, 1972, 1973), and of attrition and dropouts. The literature on participation is voluminous; useful and comprehensive summaries of this literature are contained in Cross (1981), Darkenwald and Merriam (1982), and Long (1983a). Major national studies of participation are those of Johnstone and Rivera (1965), the National Institute of Adult Education (1970), the Advisory Council for Adult and Continuing Education (1982), Waniewicz (1976), Employment and Immigration Canada (1983), and Aslanian and Bricknell (1980). The U.S. Department of Education regularly reports figures on participation in adult education through the National Center for Education Statistics. The most recent of these reports estimated that over 21 million adults (13 percent of the total adult population) participated in adult education in 1981. This compares to British estimates of 4 percent of the total population (1970) and 10 percent (1982).

These figures vary significantly and raise one immediate concern, namely, the definition of "educational-providing agencies" that is adopted by the researchers concerned. On the whole, these studies adopt an operational, institutional definition of learning and education. In other words, adult education agencies are those bodies so named by the relevant government department of education. Excluded from such participation surveys, then, are informal voluntary societies, community action groups, staff development efforts in hospitals, universities, and high schools, training exercises in business and industry, education through social work agencies, labor education, and the entire range of self-directed learning efforts. The sampling frame for studies of participation tends to be the continuing and adult education programs offered by continuing education departments of universities, by local schools, and by community colleges (in the United States) and colleges of further education (in Britain). As reported elsewhere (Brookfield, 1983a), however, it is both naive and arrogant to assume that adult learning is restricted to settings and government agencies so named. If we regard adult learning as resulting from a transaction among adults in which experiences are interpreted, skills and knowledge acquired, and actions taken, then it is absurd to presume that this is restricted to formally designated centers of adult higher and continuing education. Rather, we should conceive adult learning to be a phenomenon and process that can take place in any setting. Indeed, it will often be the case that the most significant kinds of adult learning that are identified as such by adult learners themselves occur in settings not formally designated as adult educational ones. Such settings include families, community action groups, voluntary societies, support networks, work groups, and interpersonal relationships.

Underlying studies of participation, however, is a research

paradigm that views the adult learner as "an adult who is enrolled in any course of study, whether special or regular, to develop new skills or qualifications, or improve existing skills and qualifications" (National Advisory Council for Adult Education, 1980, p. 3) and that defines adult education as "courses and other educational activities, organized by a teacher or sponsoring agency, and taken by persons beyond compulsory school age" (National Center for Education Statistics, 1980, p. 1). As will be apparent from the examples discussed in the next section, such narrow notions of what constitutes adult learning and education reflect auditing procedures and administrative convenience rather than the complex, multifaceted reality of adult learning itself.

In terms of constructing a profile of the "typical" adult learner in formally organized education, the surveys of literature conducted by Cross (1981), Shipp and Mckenzie (1981), Darkenwald and Merriam (1982), Graham and others (1983), and Long (1983a) exhibit a remarkable congruence in their conclusion that the typical adult learner is a relatively affluent, well-educated, white, middle-class individual. Hence, the picture drawn by Johnstone and Rivera (1965) of adult learners as young, well-educated, white-collar workers of moderate incomes seems not to have changed in twenty years. Severely underrepresented, according to Cross (1981), are "the elderly, blacks, those who failed to graduate from high school, and those with annual incomes under $10,000" (p. 53). The major study by Aslanian and Bricknell (1980) found learners to be contrasted with nonlearners by being younger, better educated, more affluent, likely to be employed, and likely to be engaged in professional work.

As well as estimating the general proportion of the population engaged in education and training, many studies have focused on investigating specific variables such as sex, age, race, or educational attainment and their correlation to participation in formal education. Of perhaps greatest statistical significance is the general finding that it is previous educational attainment and participation that is the most statistically significant variable in determining future participation in formal education.

Anderson and Darkenwald's (1979) analysis of the 1975 data from the National Center for Education Statistics found that previous educational attainment was relatively independent of such other variables as income and occupation when taken as a predictor of participation in education in the future. The power of the previous educational attainment variable as a predictor of future participation in formal education courses is confirmed in a host of studies in Britain (National Institute of Adult Education, 1970; Hanna, 1964; Trenaman, 1957; Advisory Council for Adult and Continuing Education, 1982) and in America (Boaz, 1978; Carp, Peterson, and Roelfs, 1974; Johnstone and Rivera, 1965; Aslanian and Bricknell, 1980).

Simple conclusions to the effect that education is "addictive" or that "those who have education want more" are, however, misleading. It may be that previous educational attainment is statistically significant as a predictor of continuing participation in formal education, but statistical significance must not be understood separately from the social context in which such significance is discernible. Those who are poorly educated are, quite simply, apt to be poorer financially. They often belong to an ethnic minority group and are either unemployed or employed in low-paying occupations. Their poor educational attainment is not a cause but a result of their poverty. In Britain the two major reports on adult education by Alexander (Scottish Education Department, 1975) and Russell (H. M. Stationery Office, 1973) recognized that nonparticipants in further and higher education were working-class adults in low-paying jobs or unemployed. Major research reports on this category of "disadvantaged" adults have been conducted by Clyne (1973) and Niemi and Anderson (1970).

Viewing nonparticipants in education and training courses as disadvantaged is, of course, pernicious. It is easy to accept, almost without being aware of it, a stereotype of the nonparticipant in formal education as inadequate, deficient, and somehow unfulfilled. This view is fundamentally flawed, for two important reasons. First, to be disadvantaged is not an individual phenomenon, but a social product. When we repeatedly observe that the same ethnic groups, for example, are employed in low-paying occupations or that working-class families are the first to be unemployed when interest rates turn higher, it becomes clear that nonparticipation in education cannot be explained on the basis of individual inadequacies. Nonparticipation is a function of a cluster of cultural attitudes whereby formal education is perceived as irrelevant to the circumstances, life crises, and anxieties of working-class life. As C. W. Mills (1959) observed, personal troubles such as unemployment or divorce occur within an adult's immediate milieu and are often perceived as private matters generated by biographical circumstances. The individual adult may make no causal connection between a personal trauma and broader socioeconomic trends or political changes. He or she will see such tragedies as the result of personal inadequacy or individual fecklessness. In reality, it is evident that individual biographies are social products and that private troubles frequently reflect broader structural conditions. Those adults who come to this realization will perceive that their problems are shared by others. A consequence of this awareness is likely to be an understanding that alterations in individual destinies are inextricably linked to alterations in social structures. At some point, enough adults will realize that their "private" troubles are reflections of some broader structural contradiction and will come together in collective action to create more congenial structures. To Mills, the reestablishment of the severed connection between individual biography and social structures was the task of the sociologist. It also serves as a mission statement for a critical philosophical vision of facilitating learning.

Second, viewing nonparticipants in formal education as somehow disadvantaged may be premised upon the highly arrogant assumption that only participants in formal education are engaged in purposeful learning. As I have argued elsewhere (Brookfield, 1983a), however, "lifelong learning" is an empirical reality, not a political strategy, in that adults learn throughout the developmental stages of adulthood in response to life crises, for the innate joy of learning, and for specific task purposes. There is no need to advocate the introduction of lifelong *learning* since adults are continually engaged in purposeful learning in familial, interpersonal, community activist, recreational, and occupational settings. Much of this learning, such as building an intimate relationship, dealing with bereavement, or becoming aware of one's own sexism, is difficult to categorize in terms of formal course offerings, but that does not mean it is any less significant to the individuals involved. Parenthetically, it is interesting to observe that Tough (1979) has repeatedly found that adults contrast learning conducted in a self-directed mode unfavorably with that conducted in formally accredited educational institutions. It is as if they need external validation of their learning by a certified professional educator for it to be perceived by these same learners as educationally valid.

Third, it is salutary to reflect that, as a recent study demonstrates (Fingeret, 1983), adults whom educators perceive as deficient (for example, nonliterates) may not regard themselves, or be regarded by their peers, in this way. In interviews with illiterate adults in Syracuse, New York, Fingeret found that these individuals created networks with readers and that they saw themselves as interdependent, not inferior. These illiterate adults contributed a wide range of skills to their networks and were not viewed by others (or by themselves) as dependent. As Fingeret observes, this "nondeficit" approach to understanding adult illiteracy would not normally be adopted by middle-class educators, since they view illiteracy as inevitably correlated with a deficiency of some kind. Charnley and Jones (1979) also reveal that adults who do undertake literacy instruction are concerned with increasing their self-confidence, social skills, and self-image as much as with achieving the standardized measures of reading and writing success held by organizers of literacy programs.

It is clear, then, that figures of participation in formal courses sponsored by organizations such as schools, colleges, and universities in no way account for the sum total of purposeful adult learning. Rather, they are institutionally necessary measures that give useful information about specific settings for purposeful adult learning. They allow institutions of education to argue for budgetary increases on the basis of demonstrable achievement (that is, securing large numbers of participants).

But any book purporting to examine effective practice in the facilitation of learning has to acknowledge the multiplicity of settings for adult learning.

Moreover, it is naive to assume that simply because adults are under the direction of a teacher that learning is being facilitated. What is important to consider is the nature of the teaching-learning transaction itself and the extent to which features of mutual respect, negotiation, collaborativeness, and praxis are present. A mass lecture to an audience of adults in which there is no opportunity for discussion, no time for questions, no chance for collaborative exploration of differing viewpoints, and no attempt to make some links between the learners' experiences and the topic under discussion is poor practice. Simply because individuals who are chronologically adult are gathered together in a classroom does not mean that learning is automatically occurring. Teachers and trainers who coerce adults into attending classes, who abuse them publicly or in evaluative comments, who keep criteria of educational success private and require students to guess the covert agenda governing the educational encounter, and who manipulate adult learners in ways injurious to, and unperceived by, these learners are clearly not enhancing adult learning.

Principles of Effective Practice

Before proceeding to further discussion of facilitating learning, we should clarify the central principles of effective practice. These principles apply chiefly to teaching-learning transactions or to curriculum development and instructional design activities that support teaching-learning encounters and not to marketing, budgetary, or administrative tasks.

Let us consider, then, the following six principles of effective practice in facilitating learning:

• Participation in learning is voluntary; adults engage in learning as a result of their own volition. It may be that the circumstances prompting this learning are external to the learner (job loss, divorce, bereavement), but the decision to learn is the learner's. Hence, excluded are those settings in which adults are coerced, bullied, or intimidated into learning.

- Effective practice is characterized by a respect among participants for each other's self-worth. Foreign to facilitation are behaviors, practices, or statements that belittle others or that involve emotional or physical abuse. This does not mean that criticism should be absent from educational encounters. It does mean, though, that an attention to increasing adults' sense of self-worth underlies all facilitation efforts.

- Facilitation is collaborative. Facilitators and learners are engaged in a cooperative enterprise in which, at different times and for different purposes, leadership and facilitation roles will be assumed by different group members. This collaboration is seen in the diagnosis of needs in the setting of objectives, in curriculum development, in methodological aspects, and in generating evaluative criteria and indexes. This collaboration is also constant, so that the group process involves a continual renegotiation of activities and priorities in which competing claims are explored, discussed, and negotiated.

- Praxis is placed at the heart of effective facilitation. Learners and facilitators are involved in a continual process of activity, reflection upon activity, collaborative analysis of activity, new activity, further reflection and collaborative analysis, and so on. "Activity" can, of course, include cognitive activity; learning does not always require participants to "do" something in the sense of performing clearly observable acts. Exploring a wholly new way of interpreting one's work, personal relationships, or political allegiances would be an example of activity in this sense.

- Facilitation aims to foster in adults a spirit of critical reflection. Through educational encounters, learners come to appreciate that values, beliefs, behaviors, and ideologies are culturally transmitted and that they are provisional and relative. This awareness that the supposed givens of work conduct, relationships, and political allegiances are, in fact, culturally constructed means that adults will come to question many aspects of their professional, personal, and political lives.

- The aim of facilitation is the nurturing of self-directed, empowered adults. Such adults will see themselves as proactive, initiating individuals engaged in a continuous re-creation of their personal relationships, work worlds, and social circumstances rather than as reactive individuals, buffeted by uncontrollable forces of circumstance.

These six principles of facilitation have numerous implications for practice that will be discussed throughout this book. They are observable in many different settings, some of which are formally called "adult" or "continuing" education, some of which are designated as "training," and others that are recognized by other descriptions (networks, self-directed learning, community action, and so on). In general terms, though, a number of direct practice implications are immediately derivable from each principle.

Voluntary Participation. The fact that adults engage in an educational activity because of some innate desire for developing new skills, acquiring new knowledge, improving already assimilated competencies, or sharpening powers of self-insight has enormous implications for what facilitators can do. First and foremost, the educator has no need to spend a great deal of time and energy dealing with outright defiance, veiled opposition, or studied indifference among learners. Those who teach adults in the evening and children or adolescents during the day (as I did for a period) constantly refer to the difference in satisfaction and fulfillment derived from working with the two groups. Because adults' motivations to learn are high, the facilitator is prompted to expend a similarly high level of effort and ingenuity in designing educational experiences and in teaching. Adults' willingness to learn also means that they are less likely to resist participatory learning techniques such as discussion, role playing, games, small-group work, and collaborative analysis of personal experiences.

The voluntary nature of participation by adult learners also means that such participation can easily be withdrawn if learners feel that the activity does not meet their needs, does not make any particular sense, or is conducted at a level that is incomprehensible to them. The same holds true, of course, if learners feel that they are being treated in a humiliating or insulting manner. Facilitators thus have to pay close attention to curriculum development and educational process. Curricular themes for examination and topics to be discussed have to be grounded in adults' experiences, or at the very least there must be explicit connections made between unfamiliar concepts or bodies of knowledge and the current preoccupations or past experiences of learners. This can be done by selecting appropriate resource materials and by framing the investigation of new ideas, skills, or information in terms that are accessible to the learner, given his or her past experiences.

The importance of ensuring that new knowledge, concepts, skills, or frameworks of interpretation are presented to adult learners in a manner that is comprehensible in terms of their own experiences is a major reason for using participatory learning methods. A mass instructional technique such as a lecture may, as Bligh (1972) notes, be useful in presenting information in short, twenty-minute periods. As a host of research studies cited by Bligh indicate, however, the lecture is of little use if the educator or trainer is seeking to promote critical thinking or to encourage adults to be more flexible in their attitudes. A one-hour transmission of information in which there is no opportunity for questions, no small-group discussion of case-study applications of ideas, no "buzz group" activity, and no attempt to make connections between the audience members' experiences and the lecture's content is, therefore, poor facilitation. Educators who ignore the use of participatory techniques will find (unless they are stunningly charismatic performers) that their learners are physically absent in increasing numbers or are mentally absent in the sense of not being actively engaged with the ideas, skills, and knowledge being presented. As Chapter Nine will demonstrate, such mental absenteeism is a frequent feature of staff development efforts that do not build curricula on the concerns and experiences of learners and that use mass instructional techniques.

Mutual Respect. A fundamental feature of effective facilitation is to make participants feel that they are valued as separate, unique individuals deserving of respect. To behave in a manner disrespectful to others, to denigrate their contributions, or to embarrass them publicly through extended attention to their apparent failings are behaviors that are, in educational terms, disastrous. Educators who behave in this manner will be faced with a number of consequences. They will find participants leaving, they will be unable to generate the goodwill required to conduct effective participatory learning exercises, and they will find learners so intimidated by the prospect of public pillorying or private censure that they will be unable to learn. Many of the same consequences will result if educators allow learners to behave toward one another in hostile or combative ways. As Chapter Six demonstrates, successful educational experiences are generally characterized by the evolution of some form of group consensus regarding acceptable behaviors by participants.

Good facilitation, then, is characterized by a respect for participants' uniqueness, self-worth, and separateness. This does not mean, however, that educational encounters are characterized by some kind of universal bonhomie or false camaraderie under which fundamental differences are buried. Central to the effective facilitation of learning is the development of powers of critical reflection, and this means that adults will frequently be challenged by educators and fellow learners to consider alternative ways of thinking, behaving, working, and living. But this challenging of others' ideas and attitudes and this prompting of analysis of one's own behaviors and beliefs must occur in a setting where dissension or criticism of another does not imply some kind of personal denigration. As Brew (1965) has observed with regard to discussion groups, it is easy for educational encounters to degenerate into "numbers of people slamming shut their minds in one another's faces" (p. 325). Unless participants evolve what Bridges (1979) calls a "moral culture" governing educational interactions, then learners will react to being challenged or to being confronted with alternative and unfamiliar ways of thinking about their work, relationships, or beliefs with resistance and a dismissive mistrust.

One of the most daunting and difficult (but essential)

tasks of the facilitator, then, is to set a climate for learning (Knowles, 1980) and to assist in the development of a group culture in which adults can feel free to challenge one another and can feel comfortable with being challenged. Without such a climate or culture, teaching-learning encounters run the risk of becoming nothing more than exchanges of entrenched opinion and prejudice, with no element of challenge and no readiness to probe the assumptions underlying beliefs, behaviors, or values. It is useless to run a staff development workshop in which participants compliment each other, repeat the public norms of the organization, and confirm prejudices but never address fundamental differences in philosophy or practice. What *is* valuable, however, is the honest expression of differences, in an atmosphere where challenge and dissension are accepted as part of the educational process.

Collaborative Spirit. The existence of some kind of participatory and collaborative element is perhaps the most frequently cited difference between school education and the education of adults. In the former, standards, syllabi, materials, and evaluative criteria are generally externally defined according to local or national governmental regulations and requirements. In the latter, principally because formal accreditation or certification is not the aim of most adult education programs, there is often collaboration in assessing needs and generating objectives, methods of learning, and evaluative procedures. There is also an alternation of educational roles so that at different times various members of the adult learning group will assume responsibility for posing questions, identifying materials, suggesting priorities, and organizing aspects of the group process.

Such collaborative activities are, of course, grounded in the features of voluntary learning and respect for participants. Acknowledging the accumulated experiences of adults as valuable educational resources is frequently touted as a defining principle of adult education, but this can be achieved only through some collaborative medium. The distinct tradition in the facilitation of adult learning is that of adults meeting as equals in small groups to explore issues and concerns and then to take action as a result of these explorations. We can see this in the workers' education movement, the junto, community development initiatives such as the Antigonish movement (Coady, 1939), community action projects in Liverpool (Lovett, 1975) and Northern Ireland (Lovett, Clarke, and Kilmurray, 1983), the living room learning groups in British Columbia (Buttedahl, 1978), experiments using mass media such as the Canadian Farm Forum (Conger, 1974), BBC wireless discussion groups (Heywood, 1981; Perraton, 1978), and the Great Books program (Davis, 1961), as well as in the establishment of residential centers for community development such as the Highlander Folk School (Adams, 1975) and the Ulster People's College (Lovett, 1984). (For a more detailed discussion of these activities and the adult educational component therein, see Brookfield, 1983a.)

Action and Reflection. In the education and training of adults, the term *praxis* is closely associated with the ideas and literacy activities of the Brazilian educator, Paulo Freire. In several works (Freire, 1970a, 1970b, 1973, 1985), he discusses a number of specific techniques that were used to help South American illiterates acquire literacy skills. In developing these skills, learners would gradually become aware of forces and structures that were keeping them in a position of dependence. Central to this concept, however, is a process long ago recognized as fundamentally educational by such philosophers of education as Dewey (1916) and Neill (1960). This process centers on the need for educational activity to engage the learner in a continuous and alternating process of investigation and exploration, followed by action grounded in this exploration, followed by reflection on this action, followed by further investigation and exploration, followed by further action, and so on. This notion of praxis as alternating and continuous engagements by teachers and learners in exploration, action, and reflection is central to adult learning. It means that explorations of new ideas, skills, or bodies of knowledge do not take place in a vacuum but are set within the context of learners' past, current, and future experiences. In settings where skills are being learned, whether literacy skills, craft skills, or political advocacy techniques, this praxis is easily observable. Learners become acquainted with skills, apply these in real life settings, reflect with other learners on their experiences in these settings, redefine how these skills might be altered by context, reapply these in other real settings, and so on. This is the familiar mechanism of internships and field experience as used in numerous training settings.

In activities concerned primarily with changes in consciousness, attitudinal shifts, explorations of new interpretations of the world, or paradigm shifts of some kind, the same principle of praxis obtains. In these instances, the process is less easily observable as it occurs chiefly through the acquisition of new mental sets. Even here, however, it is hard to imagine anything other than the purest form of philosophical meditation or introspection occurring without the learner's renegotiating certain aspects of his or her relationships, social world, or work life. Adults do not acquire and internalize ideas, skills, knowledge, and insights in a context-free vacuum. They interpret these through the mediatory mechanisms they have developed, assign meaning to them, codify them according to categories they have evolved, and test them out in real life settings. In curriculum design, selection of materials, and use of educational methods, therefore, facilitators should anticipate, and build upon, this tendency of adult learners to interpret, understand, codify, and assign meaning to new ideas, insights, skills, and knowledge in the context of their own experiences.

Critical Reflection. That effective practice aims to foster an attitude of healthy skepticism is a prescriptively based notion, and, as such, it is disputed by some practitioners. They argue that facilitation means assisting adults to acquire skills, knowledge, ideas, and insights that have been defined by the learners themselves. This latter idea is said to exemplify a democratic, student-centered approach to learning, since it assigns to learners the responsibility for assessing needs, identifying educational aims and objectives, and generating evaluative criteria (which are usually based on learners' own sense of satisfaction).

Facilitating learning is, however, a collaborative enterprise, and this has implications for more formal settings where the role of "educator" can be clearly identified. In these settings the educator's values and priorities will influence the educational encounter, just as do those of the learners. It is my contention that learning is being effectively facilitated when the educator is prompting in learners a sense of the culturally constructed nature of knowledge, beliefs, values, and behaviors. But to develop this awareness, the facilitator must present alternative interpretations of learners' work lives, personal relationships, and views of the social and political world. This does not mean that the facilitator must try to convert or brainwash learners into accepting some new ideology. It does mean, though, that education must be distinguished from training. In training, a set of clearly identified skills are transmitted, and adults are required to assimilate these in the manner prescribed by the trainer, employing agency, or certification body. In education, by contrast, learners are encouraged to examine the assumptions underlying the acquisition of skills, to consider alternative purposes, and to place skill acquisition in some broader context.

This is very far from assuming, however, that learning cannot be facilitated effectively in training contexts. In the field of adult basic education, there are many instances in which educators have placed the acquisition of predefined skills in a context that encouraged learners to develop a critically questioning frame of mind. Such an attitude lies at the heart of Freirean methods and is exemplified in practical activities such as work with the elderly (Knott, 1983), community education (Aldred, 1984), work with college students (Finlay and Faith, 1979), the promotion of industrial democracy (Wilson, 1978) and work with immigrant women in industrial societies (Barndt, n.d.). Manuals of basic education (Rossman, Fisk, and Roehl, 1984) and studies of illiterates (Charnley and Jones, 1979) stress the development of a positive self-concept, the feeling of self-confidence, and the affirmation of self-esteem that result from coming to view the world differently through learning a language.

The point is that education is centrally concerned with the development of a critically aware frame of mind, not with the uncritical assimilation of previously defined skills or bodies of knowledge. Even within staff development or training activities that seem to be defined by organizational priorities, rather than by the learning benefits accruing to individuals, there is a realization that encouraging shopfloor workers, line managers, supervisors, and executives to challenge existing norms, practices, and structures is essential. Analyses of human resource development (Nadler, 1984), staff development manuals (Laird, 1978), investigations into conditions for corporate success (Peters and Waterman, 1982), and studies of effective learning within organizations (Argyris and Schön, 1978; Argyris, 1982) all stress the necessity for workers to be aware of underlying assumptions, norms, and uncritically accepted practices and to be encouraged to imagine alternative structures and practices. The eight lessons derived from an analysis of America's most successful companies include a willingness to experiment, an engagement in praxis, participatory involvement of all employees, and managers' acknowledgment of ambiguity (Peters and Waterman, 1982). Similarly, the concepts of double-loop learning and deuterolearning developed by Argyris and Schön (1978) focus on the ability of workers to become aware of underlying norms, policies, and objectives, to view these as relative and determined by context, and hence to be proactive in advocating change and innovation.

Self-Direction. The last principle of effective facilitation —that facilitators should assist adults to become self-directed learners—has now attained something of the status of an academic orthodoxy. As Kidd has written, "It has often been said that the purpose of adult education, or of any kind of education, is to make of the subject a continuing 'inner-directed,' self-operating learner" (1973, p. 47). This idea has been proposed by educators from Lindeman (1926) and Bryson (1936) to Rogers (1969) and Knowles (1975). It is one of adult education's most enduring articles of faith, and, like many revered tenets, its meaning has been distorted or skewed by those who choose to define it as they wish. As recent critical reexaminations have made clear (Brookfield, 1984c, 1985a), self-direction as a concept runs the risk of being denuded of context and of coming to be viewed solely as a technique in much the same way as programmed learning is now conceived.

The body of research, practice, and theoretical speculation on self-directed learning will be reviewed later in this book,
so an extended analysis at this point is inappropriate. It is important to say, however, that making adults self-directed learners does not simply mean assisting them to develop such skills as
how to retrieve information or locate resources. Self-direction
in learning is not a set of techniques that can be applied within
a context of objectives and evaluative criteria that are determined by others. At the heart of self-directedness is the adult's
assumption of control over setting educational goals and generating personally meaningful evaluative criteria. One cannot be a
fully self-directed learner if one is applying techniques of independent study within a context of goals and evaluative criteria
determined by an external authority. (The contradiction at the
heart of this idea is illustrated in a recent volume on the application of self-directed learning principles in a number of institutional contexts such as universities and hospitals. See Brookfield, 1985a.) Self-directed learning in adulthood, therefore, is
not merely learning how to apply techniques of resource loca-
tion or instructional design. It is, rather, a matter of learning
how to change our perspectives, shift our paradigms, and replace one way of interpreting the world by another.

As adults, we are generally enclosed within our own self-
histories. We assimilate and gradually integrate behaviors, ideas,
and values derived from others until they become so internalized that we define "ourselves" in terms of them. Unless an external source places before us alternative ways of thinking,
behaving, and living, we are comfortable with our familiar value
systems, beliefs, and behaviors. Teachers who rely on the same
exercises and notes for thirty years, managers who continue to
employ the same techniques of production organization, or programmers who run the same courses year after year are not
going to decide to change these practices simply of their own
volition. One task of the facilitator, therefore, is to present
learners with alternatives to their current ways of thinking, behaving, and living. Adults who engage in this kind of double-
loop learning in which they reflect critically on their assumptions and try to imagine alternatives are fully autonomous, self-

directed learners. Such adults are likely to be involved in a continual reinterpretation, renegotiation, and re-creation of their
personal relationships, work lives, and social structures.

Transactional Dialogues

It will be clear from the foregoing discussion, and from
descriptions of practice in later chapters, that there are two
common approaches to thinking about the facilitation of learning. One of these we might recognize as an *operational* approach.
In this approach, we regard as effective practice any activity in
which adults are being taught how to acquire certain skills and
knowledge, irrespective of content and context. If adults are
learning, and others are arranging the conditions of instruction,
then we are witnessing effective facilitation.

A contrasting approach to the facilitation of learning
views effective practice not just as helping adults acquire skills
and knowledge in a context- and content-free manner but as
containing some intrinsic features regarding the process and
content of teaching and learning. Hence, educational encounters
in which learners are abused or intimidated or racial prejudices
are encouraged would not be regarded as facilitation in its fullest sense. Neither would we regard as good practice those instances in which adult learners are reproduced in the image of
the facilitator, that is, when they mirror his or her ideas and beliefs exactly and demonstrate no capacity for critical reflection.
Finally, this approach would exclude activities in which the
learner is given no say in the method, aims, or content of the
teaching-learning transaction and in which any deviation from a
preset facilitator norm is met with exclusion from the educational activity.

This alternative approach is an *intrinsic* approach: It recognizes that education is value based and that facilitators should
therefore be explicit concerning the values on which their ideas
of good practice are based. The basis for this second approach is
that education is essentially a transactional encounter in which
learners and teachers are engaged in a continual process of negotiation of priorities, methods, and evaluative criteria. Viewing
teaching-learning encounters as transactional means that the

sole responsibility for determining curricula or for selecting appropriate methods does not rest either with the educator or with the participants. If the first obtains, then we have an authoritarian style and a one-way transmission of knowledge and skills that exemplifies all the worst aspects of the banking system of education (Freire, 1970a) or what Lindeman (1926) called the additive process, whereby the teacher receives from students precisely what has already been imparted from the teacher's academic repository, and the educator retains total control over the goals, content, and evaluative criteria of the educational activity. If the second approach prevails and curricula, methods, and evaluative criteria become determined solely by what learners say they want, then we run the risk that a service rationale (Lawson, 1979) or a "cafeteria" approach (Monette, 1977, 1979) will govern what passes for education. If the educator simply meets those needs articulated by groups and individuals, he or she may function as little more than an administrator, publicist, and budget specialist. Skills of administration, marketing, and financial management are certainly important in order to create the conditions under which teaching and learning can occur. We should be careful, however, of confusing the exercise of those skills with the sum total of what it means to be an effective facilitator.

Accepting the felt needs rationale and giving learners what they say they want mean that the facilitator has abdicated responsibility for contributing to the debate about normative standards, values, and criteria in training and education. To say one is meeting felt learner needs sounds humanistic, learner centered, and admirably democratic, yet to do so without allowing one's own ideas, experience, insights, and knowledge as an educator to contribute to the educational process makes the facilitator a service manager, not a fully participating contributor. It also condemns learners to staying within their own paradigms of thinking, feeling, and behaving. Since it is very difficult to generate alternative ways of thinking about, and behaving in, the world entirely as a result of one's own efforts, an important task of the facilitator is to present to learners diverse ways of thinking and acting.

One of the greatest myths that has sprung from an acceptance of the felt needs rationale is the belief that learning is always joyful, a bountiful release of latent potential in which the learner is stimulated, exhilirated, and fulfilled. This often happens. But it is also often the case that the most significant learning we undergo as adults results from some external event or stimulus that causes us to engage in an anxiety-producing and uncomfortable reassessment of aspects of our personal, occupational, and recreational lives. This external stimulus may be a calamitous event, such as being fired, experiencing the death of a parent, sibling, or spouse, going to war, or coping with a divorce. The learning in which we are forced to engage as a result of these events may be unsought and may have many painful aspects. Nonetheless, we may regard such learning as highly significant, precisely because it caused us to question our ways of thinking and behaving in our personal relationships, occupational lives, or social activities. Such questioning is initially uncomfortable and may be resisted, but it will often be the cause of our deciding to change some aspect of our lives. As anybody who has renegotiated an intimate relationship, who has confronted a parent, or who has attempted to change the patterns of relationships and activities in the workplace knows, to question the validity of the assumptions under which he or she has been living and to try to change the habitual activities and responses of oneself and others are not always joyous, releasing, and exhilirating experiences. We may conclude after this act of learning that the pain and anxiety were worthwhile, since they resulted in our living more fulfilling and stimulating lives. But as we are forced to undergo this reexamination of values, beliefs, behaviors, and assumptions about ourselves and those around us, we may find the activity to be an unsettling, painful struggle in which glimpses of insight alternate with confusion, uncertainty, and ambiguity.

The contribution of the facilitator to the teaching-learning transaction is somewhat of the order of the calamitous events mentioned earlier. It is not enough for educators and trainers to say to learners, "Do what you want, learn what you want, in whatever manner you wish, because you are the sole determinants of your educational destinies." This resembles a conversation in which one partner agrees with whatever the other says. Such conversations may be initially agreeable, but eventually one begins to suspect that the listener who responds to one's every comment and suggestion with enthusiastic agreement is not really listening at all. A conversation, after all, is also a transactional dialogue in which the comments and contributions of the participants build organically on each other's views and in which alternative viewpoints, differing interpretations, and criticism are elements essential to the encounter.

We may think of facilitation in much the same way, as a transactional dialogue between participants (teachers and learners) who bring to the encounter experiences, attitudinal sets, and alternative ways of looking at their personal, professional, political, and recreational worlds, along with a multitude of differing purposes, orientations, and expectations. The particular function of the facilitator is to challenge learners with alternative ways of interpreting their experience and to present to them ideas and behaviors that cause them to examine critically their values, ways of acting, and the assumptions by which they live.

We should note here that there is an enormous difference between facilitation and attempts at political or religious conversion in that in the latter activities the political or religious ideologues have predetermined the learning outcomes of the activity. They possess an ideology that they feel comprises the one true way of living in and thinking about the world, and views that do not coincide with these ideologies are deemed to be examples of bad faith, false consciousness, or wrong thinking. In effective facilitation, by contrast, the educator may hold beliefs about how people should think and act that he or she passionately espouses, but such beliefs are presented to learners for the same critical scrutiny and analysis that the participants apply to ideas of which the educator is personally critical. The end of the encounter, in other words, has not been preordained as the acceptance by participants of the facilitator's values and beliefs. Educators would be foolish to deny that they possess their own beliefs or to pretend that they are blank pages on which philosophies and values are yet to be written.

However, while they present their own ideas to learners as part of the teaching-learning transaction, they invite criticism and analytical scrutiny of these ideas by participants, and they are open to revising them as a result of this dialogue with learners. Political and religious ideologues do not seek to learn from the people they are attempting to convert, and neither do they encourage critical and sceptical scrutiny of their views. Since they believe themselves to be in possession of some universal and divinely ordained truth, there is no need for them to learn from others, and criticism appears irrelevant.

As we proceed through the following pages, examples of this transactional approach to facilitating learning in a number of different settings will be discussed. Such an approach may appear immediately applicable to liberal arts discussion groups, but its relevance to labor education, to community action, or to training in business and industry may appear somewhat obscure. As will be seen, however, these and other settings offer numerous documented examples of how teachers and learners as participants in a transactional dialogue have negotiated goals, methods, curricula, and evaluative criteria. In these examples we will see that facilitators are not blank ciphers through whom the demands and wishes of learners are uncritically transmitted, but neither are they authoritarian ideologues who prescribe curricula and methods that are to be considered as rigidly fixed and immutable. In an effective teaching-learning transaction all participants learn, no one member is regarded as having a monopoly on insight, and dissension and criticism are regarded as inevitable and desirable elements of the process.

❧ 2 ❧

Understanding
How Adults Learn

There can be few intellectual quests that, for educators and trainers of adults, assume so much significance and yet contain so little promise of successful completion as the search for a general theory of adult learning. Kidd (1973) has compared such a quest to the search for Eldorado, and reviews such as those of Dubin and Okun (1973) and Lasker and Moore (1980) confirm that individual learning behaviors are so idiosyncratic as to cast considerable doubt on any general assertions made about adults as learners. Learning activities and learning styles vary so much with physiology, culture, and personality that generalized statements about the nature of adult learning have very low predictive power. The most that Dubin and Okun (1973) will say in their review of eight schools of learning theory is that different elements of the theories of these schools can help to explain certain limited phenomena. It is all the more surprising, therefore, to hear confident generalizations regarding the characteristics of adult learning pour forth from the lips of graduate students and those presenting research papers.

According to Simpson (1980), the two distinguishing characteristics of adult learning most frequently advanced by theorists are the adult's autonomy of direction in the act of learning and the use of personal experience as a learning resource. In Chapter Three the first of these characteristics—the exercise of autonomous self-direction in learning—is proposed as the distinguishing characteristic of adult learning. It is important to recognize, however, that self-direction in learning is not an empirically verifiable concomitant of adulthood. There are many individuals who are chronologically adult but who show a marked disinclination to behave in anything approaching a self-directed manner in many areas of their lives. Self-directedness is rather being advanced as a prescriptively defining characteristic of adulthood. Hence, for an act of learning to be characteristically adult, it will have to exhibit some aspect of self-directedness. But before examining further the nature and form of self-directedness, let us consider the range of theoretical perspectives that have been elaborated with regard to adult learning.

Principles of Adult Learning

To specify generic principles of learning is an activity full of intellectual pitfalls. Even if we leave aside the variables of physiology, personality, and cultural background, we still have to consider the implications of those developmental theories that hold that adults function in very different ways when responding to the societal and personal imperatives required of them in young adulthood, midlife, and old age. This suggests that the generic concept of adulthood is so broad and oversimplified as to be of limited use as a research construct. Nonetheless, in the last twenty-five years a number of respected theorists have made an attempt to identify generalizable principles of adult learning in their quest to build a theory of adult learning that would aid practice.

The earliest of these attempts was that of Gibb (1960), who presented the following principles of adult learning as the basis for a "functional" theory: Learning must be problem centered, learning must be experience centered, experience must be meaningful to the learner, the learner must be free to look at experience, goals must be set and pursued by the learner, and the learner must have feedback about progress toward goals. As with other specifications of principles of adult learning, however, what Gibb actually offers is a mix of pedagogic procedures and learning theory.

Following on from Gibb, Miller (1964) identified six crucial conditions for learning premised on the belief that at the higher levels of human development in adulthood cognitive models of learning, rather than behaviorist ones, were necessary. Thus, Miller argued that students must be adequately motivated to change behavior, they must be aware of the inadequacy of present behaviors, they must have a clear picture of the behavior required, they must have the opportunity to practice required behaviors, they must obtain reinforcement of correct behavior, and they must have a sequence of appropriate materials. Despite Miller's emphasis on cognition, however, the conditions he specifies actually appear to fit the behaviorist paradigm.

In his review of theories of learning and their applicability to adulthood, Kidd (1973) identified the concepts (rather than the principles) that he felt informed the efforts of researchers into adult learning. These concepts were derived from the changing conditions of the adult's life-span, role changes required by changing societal imperatives, the egalitarian nature of adult student-teacher relationships, the greater differentiation (compared to children) of the organs and functions of adults, the self-directing nature of the adult, the physical, cultural, and emotional meaning of time, and attitudes surrounding aging and the prospect of death.

Gibb, Miller, and Kidd all based their arguments concerning the nature of adult learning on speculative grounds. Knox (1977), however, produced a widely referenced study of adult development and learning in which he offered a number of broad observations concerning adult learning. In Knox's view, for example, adults learn continually and informally as they adjust to role changes and other adaptations. Adults' learning achievements are, however, thought to be modified by individual characteristics. The learning context of the physical, social, and personal characteristics surrounding the learning act, as well as the content and pace of learning, also affect the learning achievement.

Knox also concludes that adults tend to underestimate their abilities and, by overemphasizing school experience and interests, often perform below their capacity. Longitudinal studies show a retention of, and sometimes increases in, learning abilities during adulthood, though cross-sectional studies tend to contradict this finding. Fluid intelligence decreases and crystallized intelligence increases in adulthood, and adults are able to learn as well in their forties and fifties as in their twenties and thirties, when and if they can control the pace of learning. Knox found the level of formal education to be associated much more with learning ability than with age, and recency of participation in formal education to be correlated with more effective learning. This finding, incidentally, was supported by earlier studies of Knox and Sjorgen (1965) and Knox, Grotelueschen, and Sjorgen (1968).

Other findings from Knox's survey were that effective learning entailed an active search for meaning in which new tasks were somehow related to earlier activities. Knox found that short-term memory held stable until late adulthood and that long-term memory apparently improved with age. In terms of the mechanics of learning, practice was deemed to be initially important for the reinforcement of learning. Prior learning experiences had the potential to enhance or interfere with new learning. Older adults were able to learn most effectively when they set their own pace, when they took periodic breaks, and when learning episodes were distributed according to a rationale dictated by content. Knox found learning transfer to decrease with age, though his findings on problem-solving abilities were ambiguous, with a decline according to cross-sectional studies and a holding steady (until age seventy) with longitudinal studies. The same difference was evident in studies undertaken of critical thinking. Task complexity and creativity were found to reflect individual differences and to be related only marginally to age. Knox concluded his summary in an optimistic vein, declaring that individual differences in learning were mostly unrelated to age and that "almost any adult can learn anything they want to, given time, persistence, and assistance" (Knox, 1977, p. 469).

One of the most ambitious attempts to identify the cardinal principles of adult learning and to put these to practical use is that of Brundage and Mackeracher (1980). These writers identify thirty-six learning principles and draw from each principle facilitating and planning implications. For example, Brundage and Mackeracher believe that adults are able to learn throughout their lifetimes. Their past experience can be a help or hindrance to learning. It is through such experience, however, that individuals construct the meanings and value frameworks that in turn determine how they code new stimuli and information. Brundage and Mackeracher declare that past experience needs to be respected by teachers and that it can be directly applied to current situations for good educative effect. Those adults with positive self-concepts are thought to be more responsive to learning. Environments that reinforce the self-concepts of adults, that are supportive of change, and that value the status of learner will produce the greatest amount of learning. These writers judge adults to be strongly motivated to learn in areas relevant to their current developmental tasks, social roles, life crises, and transition periods. The development of skills requires adults to have a clear perception of desired behaviors. Reinterpreting past experience is time consuming and requires a redefinition of values and meanings.

In Brundage and Mackeracher's view, voluntary participation in education and training is likely to create a nonthreatening climate of instruction that will result in a greater amount of learning. Learning will be further enhanced by regular feedback on progress, and positive feedback will act as a reinforcer for the pursuit of more learning. They think that a certain degree of arousal is necessary for learning to occur, whereas stress acts as a major block to learning. Brundage and Mackeracher also think adults learn best when they can control the pace of their learning and when they enjoy good health. However, because each individual will have an idiosyncratic learning style, it is dangerous to prescribe one mode of learning for all adults. Typical points of personally significant transition occur at the ages of twenty, forty, and sixty, and adults are said to be most responsive to learning programs that are related to these transitions. Collaborative modes of teaching and learning will enhance the self-concepts of those involved and result in more meaningful and effective learning. A blend of learning for autonomous mastery of life with participation in groups is said to provide the greatest satisfaction for the learner.

As a result of a career-long exploration of the development of adults' learning-to-learn capacities, Smith (1982a) has identified six general observations concerning the nature of learning: It is lifelong, it is personal, it involves change, it is partially a function of human development, it pertains to experience, and it is partially intuitive. Adult learners, however, also exhibit four essential characteristics. First, they have multiple roles and responsibilities, and this results in a different orientation to learning from that of children and adolescents. For example, they wish to make good educational use of the finite time they invest in education, they often take responsibility for identifying what they wish to learn, and they have a partially or fully formed self-concept. Second, adults have accumulated many life experiences, and these result in distinct preferences for modes of learning and learning environments, such modes and environments comprising the essentials of individual learning styles. Third, adults pass through a number of developmental phases in the physical, psychological, and social spheres, and the transitions from one phase to another provide for the reinterpretation and rearrangement of past experience. Finally, Smith argues, adults experience anxiety and ambivalence in their orientation to learning. In particular, attempts to become more autonomous and self-directed are likely to involve threatening elements. Anxiety and stress may also be the result of job pressure, relational problems with significant others (lovers, spouses, parents, children, close friends) or of the adult's recalling the anxiety produced by earlier schooling experiences.

These four characteristics of adult learners—their special orientation to learning, their experiential base, their particular developmental changes and tasks, and their anxiety regarding learning—generate, according to Smith, certain conditions for learning. Adults learn best when they feel the need to learn and when they have a sense of responsibility for what, why, and how they learn. Adults use experience as a resource in learning so the learning content and process must bear a perceived and meaningful relationship to past experience. What is to be learned should be related to the individual's developmental changes and life tasks. The learning method used will foster, to different degrees, the adult's exercise of autonomy. Adults will, however, generally learn best in an atmosphere that is nonthreatening and supportive of experimentation and in which different learning styles are recognized.

Darkenwald and Merriam (1982) present a list of eight principles of learning derived from learning process research that they believe can serve as guidelines for effective facilitation. They surmise that adults' readiness to learn depends on the amount of their previous learning, that intrinsic motivation produces more pervasive and permanent learning, that positive reinforcement is effective, that the material to be learned should be presented in some organized fashion, that learning is enhanced by repetition, that meaningful tasks and material are more fully and easily learned, that active participation in learning improves retention, and that environmental factors affect learning.

The specification of principles of adult learning undertaken by Gibb, Miller, Kidd, Knox, Brundage and Mackeracher, Smith, and Darkenwald and Merriam can be summarized as follows: Adults learn throughout their lives, with the negotiations of the transitional stages in the life-span being the immediate causes and motives for much of this learning. They exhibit diverse learning styles—strategies for coding information, cognitive procedures, mental sets—and learn in different ways, at different times, for different purposes. As a rule, however, they like their learning activities to be problem centered and to be meaningful to their life situation, and they want the learning outcomes to have some immediacy of application. The past experiences of adults affect their current learning, sometimes serving as an enhancement, sometimes as a hindrance. Effective learning is also linked to the adult's subscription to a self-concept of himself or herself as a learner. Finally, adults exhibit a tendency toward self-directedness in their learning.

Such conclusions constitute a catechism familiar to educators and trainers of adults, as well as to learning theorists. They support Simpson's (1980) contention referred to at the outset of this chapter that adult learning theorists most commonly emphasize the experiential dimension of adult learning and stress the self-directedness of adults. Self-directedness is seen both as an empirically observable trait and as a propensity that should be encouraged. We should note, however, that the samples for the studies on which these generalizations concerning the nature of adult learning are based are culturally specific. To this extent, the research on adult learning is no different from that on its childhood equivalent, where, as a massive comparative study of primary school quality recently acknowledged, "With less than 5 percent of the world's school population, the United States accounts for the majority of the world's empirical research on education" (Heynemman and Loxley, 1983, p. 1164).

In research into adult learning, moreover, the adults who form the sampling frames are for the most part ethnically homogeneous; that is, they are Caucasian Americans. They are also drawn chiefly from middle-class or upwardly mobile working-class families, since this is the foremost clientele of continuing education programs. To base a comprehensive theory of adult learning on observations of white, middle-class Americans in continuing or extension education classes in the post–Second World War era is conceptually and empirically naive. It is, admittedly, cumbersome to preface every comment regarding adult learning theory with a caveat concerning the cultural and class specificity of one's sample and, hence, the limited generalizability of one's conclusions. Nonetheless, we fall far too frequently into the mistake of declaring that research reveals that adults, in a generic sense, learn in a certain way.

The eagerness to construct an empirically verifiable theory of adult learning is inextricably bound up with the quest for professional identity on the part of adult educators. As much as we would like to believe that the conduct and dissemination of research are motivated by an intellectually altruistic search for truth, it must be recognized that the definition of research "problems" and the selection of appropriate topics for investigation often reflect wider societal or professional imperatives. In this case, the reality is that the discovery of a set of learning behaviors that are unmistakably adult would be a cause for substantial professional celebration. If we could discover certain empirically verifiable differences in learning styles between children (as a generic category) and adults (as a generic category), then we could lay claim to a substantive area for research that would be unchallengeably the property of educators and trainers of adults. Such a claim would provide us with a professional identity. It would ease the sense of insecurity and defensiveness that frequently assails educators and trainers of adults in all settings when faced with the accusation that they are practicing a nondiscipline. The discovery of an empirically discrete domain of adult learning would grant to us an intellectual and professional raison d'etre.

Such a revelation is unlikely to transpire for some considerable time, and it may be that the most empirically attestable claim that can be made on behalf of adult learning styles concerns their range and diversity. Certainly we should be wary of claiming too high a level of generalizability for theories and concepts of adult learning derived from studies of white Americans in the lower-middle, middle, and upper classes. How can we write confidently of adult learning style in any generic sense when we know little (other than anecdotally) of the cognitive operations of, for example, Asian peasants, African tribespeople, or Chinese cooperative laborers? Even within North American culture the empirical accuracy of generalizations about adult learning principles is highly questionable in that we have few studies of the learning styles of Native Americans, white working-class adults, Hispanics, blacks, or orientals.

Applying New Research Instruments

The body of research literature discussed in the preceding section is one characterized by a mixture of speculation and empirically observed features of adult learning. The studies cited use a variety of methodological approaches and survey different samples, with the result that baseline comparisons are extremely hard to make. In recent years a number of researchers and practitioners have sought to synthesize the findings of this body of research into some framework of central adult learning principles. These central principles have then been converted into various research instruments that their designers believe can be applied to examining the extent to which principles of adult learning are being exemplified in any given practice setting. Two of these instruments—the Principles of Adult Learning Scale (PALS) and the Andragogy in Practice Inventory (API)—were designed to test the presence of effective facilitation in practice rather than to provide empirical measures of forms of adult learning. In other words, both these instruments can be used to determine whether or not (in the eyes of the designers of these instruments) teachers or programmers are behaving as effective facilitators.

The PALS was devised by Conti (1978, 1979, 1983, 1985) to measure the extent to which practitioners supported the collaborative mode of teaching-learning that is usually cited by writers in the field as an exemplification of good practice. Conti surveyed a number of highly regarded theorists, including Freire (1970b), Lindeman (1926), Houle (1972), Knox (1976), Kidd (1973), Knowles (1984), and Bergevin (1967), to discover what they held to be the basic assumptions of adult learning. Not surprisingly, his findings are similar to those identified by the theorists reviewed in the present chapter and to the central principles of effective facilitation identified in Chapter One. Hence, Conti found these writers to argue that "the curriculum should be learner centered, that learning episodes should capitalize on the learner's experience, that adults are self-directed, that the learner should participate in needs diagnosis, goals formation, and outcomes evaluation, that adults are problem centered, and that the teacher should serve as a facilitator rather than as a repository of facts" (1983, p. 63).

For his doctoral dissertation, Conti determined "to develop and validate an instrument capable of measuring the degree to which adult education practitioners accept and adhere to the adult learning principles that are congruent with the collaborative teaching-learning mode" (1979, p. 164). Drawing on Flanders's (1970) Interaction Analysis Categories that were established to assess student initiating actions, Conti constructed a five-point Likert scale to record practitioner responses on a number of items that were based on collaborative principles but "reworded in behavioral terms compatible with realistic experiences of practitioners" (Conti, 1979, p. 165). For each of the items said to describe actions congruent with the collaborative mode, a separate item was included to describe practice antithetical to the collaborative mode. The PALS instrument was tested for construct, content, and criterion-related validity by two juries of adult education professors and fifty-seven practitioners in six separate programs. Testing for reliability was undertaken in phase two of the field testing by twice administering the scale to twenty-three adult basic education practitioners in Chicago and comparing the congruence of the scores. The outcome of the study was a forty-four-item rating scale that Conti believes can be used to assess the effectiveness of collaborative modes in producing significant learning gains or to identify themes and topics around which in-service training activities could be designed for staff development.

Since its initial framing, Conti (1983) reports that the PALS has been used in numerous training workshops and that it has formed the basis for three research studies. Dinges (1980) used the instrument to study 265 Illinois ABE teachers in a staff development needs assessment, Pearson (1980) administered PALS to 99 midwestern training directors to investigate the relationship between managerial style and the adoption of collaborative modes of facilitation, and Douglass (1982) used it to examine the relationship of professional training in educating adults to the degree of support granted to the collaborative mode by 204 hospital educators and cooperative extension educators in the state of Washington. In addition, scores have been collected from 153 Texas practitioners in adult basic and allied health education. Not surprisingly, perhaps, the research of Pearson (1980) and Douglass (1982) indicates that the chief variable positively correlated with the adoption of a collaborative approach in management training, hospital education, and cooperative extension is the amount of previous formal education (specifically training in adult education) undertaken by these practitioners. It seems, from these studies at least, that those who are trained as educators of adults do indeed incorporate collaborative principles into their subsequent professional activities. After Conti's presentation of the PALS research at a recent conference of university adult educators in Britain (Conti, 1984), we can expect some cross-cultural validation of this instrument through comparative analyses of educators' use of the collaborative mode in Britain and North America.

Turning to the API, which was devised by Suanmali (1981) on the basis of Mezirow's (1981) interpretation of andragogy and his specification of a charter for andragogy, we find that it is a ten-item inventory of educator practices. To help adults enhance their capability to function as self-directed learners, the educator must (Suanmali, 1981, pp. 31-32):

1. progressively decrease the learner's dependency on the educators;
2. help the learner to understand how to use learning resources—especially the experiences of others, including the educator, and how to engage others in reciprocal learning relations;
3. assist the learner to define his/her learning needs—both in terms of immediate awareness and of understanding the cultural and psychological assumptions influencing his/her perceptions of needs;
4. assist learners to assume increasing responsibility for defining their learning objectives, planning their own learning programs and evaluating their progress;
5. organize what is to be learned in relationship to his/her current personal problems, concerns and levels of understanding;
6. foster learner decision-making—select learner-relevant learning experiences which require choosing, expand the learner's range of options, facilitate taking the perspectives of others who have alternative ways of understanding;
7. encourage the use of criteria for judging which

        are increasingly inclusive and differentiating in awareness, self-reflexive and integrative of experience;

8. facilitate problem-posing and problem-solving, including problems associated with the implementation of individual and collective action; recognition of relationship between personal problems and public issues;

9. reinforce the self-concept of the learner as a learner and doer by providing for progressive mastery; supportive climate with feedback to encourage provisional efforts to change and to take risks; avoidance of competitive judgment of performance; appropriate use of mutual support groups;

10. emphasize experiential, participative and projective instructional methods; appropriate use of modelling and learning contracts;

This instrument was examined by 147 members of the American Commission of Professors of Adult Education. The professors interviewed displayed a remarkable degree of agreement concerning the extent to which the practices identified above were indicative of good andragogical practice.

    Finally, James (1983) and Manley (1984) have conducted small-scale Delphi (or modified Delphi) investigations of what practitioners and professors of adult education regard as exemplary principles of practice that facilitate adult learning. Manley's review of the literature and her survey of eighteen members of the American Commission of Professors of Adult Education yield a familiar cluster of categories. The professors surveyed agree that adult learning is best facilitated when learners are engaged as participants in the design of learning, when they are encouraged to be self-directed, when the educator functions as a facilitator rather than didactic instructor, when individual learners' needs and learning styles are taken into account, when a climate conducive to learning is established, when learners' past experiences are utilized in the classroom, and when learning activities are deemed to have some direct relevance or utility to the learners' circumstances.

In a more ambitious study, similar to Conti's researches, James (1983) devised the following set of basic principles of adult learning after a team of researchers had undertaken a search of articles, research reports, dissertations, and textbooks on adult learning (p. 132):

1. Adults maintain the ability to learn.
2. Adults are a highly diversified group of individuals with widely differing preferences, needs, backgrounds, and skills.
3. Adults experience a gradual decline in physical/sensory capabilities.
4. Experience of the learner is a major resource in learning situations.
5. Self-concept moves from dependency to independency as individuals grow in responsibilities, experience and confidence.
6. Adults tend to be life-centered in their orientation to learning.
7. Adults are motivated to learn by a variety of factors.
8. Active learner participation in the learning process contributes to learning.
9. A comfortable supportive environment is a key to successful learning.

All nine principles were validated by a jury of national adult education leaders, and from these principles a questionnaire was constructed comprising forty-five statements (from four to six statements for each of the nine principles identified). The questionnaire was then administered to educators in five settings: hospital patient education, university extension programs, community colleges, business and industry, and agricultural extension. Some interesting differentials emerged in the study. Hospital patient educators, university extension instructors, community college instructors, and agricultural extension instructors all perceived themselves as implementing all the principles identified "frequently," while business and industry personnel perceived themselves as implementing principles one, two, and eight "sometimes" but the others "frequently." An interesting difference was also revealed regarding the principle ranked highest by these practitioners. In hospitals, universities, community colleges, and agricultural extension, principle nine—"a comfortable, supportive environment is a key to successful learning"—was ranked as the most important. In business and industry, however, principle three—"adults experience a gradual decline in physical/sensory capabilities"—was ranked highest. In contrast to the findings of Conti's PALS research, the principle referring most explicitly to collaborative modes of teaching and learning (principle eight) was ranked relatively low by instructors in all five settings (James, 1983, p. 134). In Chapter Ten in particular, a number of studies of how practitioners do or do not conform to principles of good practice in real life program development settings will be examined. For the present it is enough to say that the foregoing instruments all represent contributions toward building a body of research on principles of good practice. The next chapter takes one particular aspect of the principles previously discussed—that of the adult's assumption of self-direction in learning—and examines the validity of this concept as an operational aim to be pursued in teaching-learning transactions. It also considers critically the research on which ideas about self-direction in adult learning are based, and it proposes a reinterpretation of this concept to take into account the extent to which self-directed adults exhibit an empowered autonomy in their learning activities.

Exploring
Self-Directedness
in Learning

Defining Self-Directed Learning

The development of self-directed learning capacities is perhaps the most frequently articulated aim of educators and trainers of adults. This self-directedness is usually defined in terms of externally observable learning activities or behaviors rather than in terms of internal, mental dispositions. In the most commonly cited definition, that of Knowles (1975), self-directed learning is defined as a process in which individuals take the initiative in designing learning experiences, diagnosing needs, locating resources, and evaluating learning. In a similar way, Tough (1966, 1967) has defined self-teaching as the assumption of responsibility by the learner for planning and directing the course of learning. Studies of autonomous learners tend to stress the technical aspects of learning activities as the defining characteristics of autonomy. Moore (1980) defines the autonomous learner as one who identifies learning needs, generates learning goals, and evolves evaluative criteria. Research such as that of Penland (1977) on self-initiated learning and that using the Self-Directed Learning Readiness Scale (SDLRS) (Guglielmino, 1977) also define self-directedness in terms of learners' ability independently to plan, conduct, and evaluate their learning activities.

Field Dependence and Independence. If we examine the notion of self-directed learning in cognitive terms rather than in terms of exhibited behaviors, however, the concept that seems to hold the greatest promise for yielding some insights is that of field independence. As characterized by Witkin (1949, 1950), field independent learners are analytical, socially independent, inner-directed, individualistic, and possessed of a strong sense of self-identity. Field dependent learners, in contrast, are extrinsically oriented, responsive to external reinforcement, aware of context, view things holistically, and are cognizant of the effects that their learning has on others. Field dependents make greater use of mediators in learning and experience greater difficulty in learning material in the absence of an imposed structure for learning than do field independent learners.

As reported in the literature (Witkin and Berry, 1975; Holtzman, 1982), field independent learners are apparently more likely to be found in open, democratic societies that emphasize self-control and autonomy. Field dependent learners, however, are comfortable in more highly regulated settings or those where the norms are well defined and unchanging. They are characteristically found in cultures that stress clear role definition, social control, strict child-rearing practices, and respect for authority. Hence, by implication, a field independent style of learning is deemed to be somehow more democratic—and, hence, more laudable—than field dependency. Field dependent learners are said to be found in Mexican and Native American cultures, whereas white American and Northern European cultures support field independent functions.

It has also been suggested that field independent styles of learning are more characteristic of mature adulthood than are field dependent ones. Holtzman (1982) writes that such personality attributes as self-concept, articulateness of body image (degree of detailed clarity and boundaries), and method of impulse regulation (self-control) form an interrelated cluster that includes field independence. Such psychological differentiation is felt by Holtzman to be closely tied to the developmental change from undifferentiated early childhood and adolescent states to more highly differentiated adult states. Even (1982) points out that adult education philosophy tends to view the development of self-directedness as its reason for being. She believes that adult education philosophy favors the field independent cognitive style and that educators and trainers of adults have been biasing learning approaches toward field independent students.

This assumption of the innate superiority of field independent learning styles does, however, come into conflict with the characteristics and concepts of facilitation as outlined in this book. As discussed earlier self-directed learning is equated with the exhibition of critical reflection on the part of adults. Such critical reflection is marked by an awareness of the contextuality and contingency of knowledge and by an appreciation of the culturally constructed nature of value frameworks, social codes, and belief systems. But these capacities are precisely those said to be possessed by field dependent learners. Hence, we have to rethink very critically the notion that the single-mindedness, planning capability, and goal orientation characteristic of field independent learning are somehow superior to the field dependent's awareness of contextuality. Even (1982) is one analyst who is careful to make no value judgments concerning the innate merits of these two styles. As she points out, there is no correlation between learning style and intelligence level. To most educators, however, findings such as those that field dependents favor traditional social roles, are found more often in non-Western, preindustrial cultures, and are poor at analytical problem solving will be interpreted unequivocally. Field independence—the single-minded pursuit of specified learning goals—will be regarded as unquestionably the preferred learning style.

The research of Thiel (1984) is instructive on this point. Thiel surveyed thirty adults drawn from French-speaking associations in Quebec. All these individuals met Brookfield's (1981a) criteria of successful independent learners. They were recognized as expert in their fields of interest as measured by peer acclaim, and they had been pursuing a learning activity not related to their jobs for at least four years. These adults were independent or self-directed in their learning in that they were pursuing their learning outside the formal educational environment. Thiel administered a version of the Kolb (1980) Adaptive Style Inventory that had been translated into colloquial French by a jury composed of adult educators, translators, and individuals familiar both with Kolb's experiential learning model and with vernacular French as spoken by the thirty adults surveyed.

In terms of the preceding discussion of field independence and dependence, it is fascinating to note that Thiel's adult learners were placed most frequently within the accommodator category. The characteristics of accommodators are somewhat analogous to those of field dependent learners. Accommodators prefer to use trial and error methods or some variant of active experimentation in their investigation of concrete experience. They excel in situations that require them to adapt to specific and immediate circumstances, and they rely heavily on others for information rather than on their own analytic ability. Thiel points out that his sample members learned successfully without employing abstract conceptualization abilities. These findings support my own research (Brookfield, 1980, 1981a), in which the successful independent learners surveyed reported that learning networks of fellow enthusiasts—networks in which knowledge was transmitted through oral encounters—were their most important resources in developing their expertise. Not only were these networks congenial settings in which information could be shared, but they also provided the independent learners with an evaluative arena. These adults would measure their skill development against that of other individuals generally recognized as exemplary. These learning networks also provided the occasion and the context for successful learners to function as skill models and resource consultants to neophyte enthusiasts.

It is significant that my studies and Thiel's—both of which have concentrated exclusively on *successful* self-directed learners—report that the characteristics of learning conducive to success are most emphatically *not* those traditionally associated with field independent learning styles. Compare this to the traditional view that field independent styles and successful self-directed learning are closely linked as reported by Pratt (1984). Pratt writes that his review of research on field independent and dependent learning styles caused him to conclude that "a picture emerges of individuals with strong tendencies toward FD [field dependency] being less self-directing in their learning, wanting more structure and guidance from an instructor, and not preferring the independence that may be required in collaborative modes of education, unless there is sufficient structure and guidance provided" (p. 151).

My work on successful self-directed learning, along with Thiel's, is thus a timely reminder of the limitations of the analytical constructs of learning styles that are developed in classroom settings with children, adolescents, and undergraduates and are then applied to the study of adult self-directed learning. In my work and Thiel's, successful self-directed learners appear to exhibit those characteristics that are associated with field dependent learners and accommodators. Their learning activities are explicitly placed within a social context, and they cite other people as the most important learning resource. Peers and fellow learners provide information, serve as skill models, and act as reinforcers of learning and as counselors in times of crisis. The observable skill levels of fellow learners provide an easily verifiable evaluative index for those developing their expertise in informal settings. Successful self-directed learners appear to be highly aware of context in the sense of placing their learning within a social setting in which advice, information, and the skill modeling provided by other learners are crucial conditions for self-directed learning.

Evidently, then, a great deal more research and reflection is needed before we can say with any confidence that self-directed learners exhibit some uniformly identifiable characteristics. Certainly, the constructs of Witkin and Kolb cannot be simply and uncritically superimposed on self-directed learning activities. If anything, superimposition of these categories leads to confusion and ambiguity rather than to clarity of understanding. To be sure, we could modify the Kolb and Witkin constructs to bring within their analytical orbit the phenomenon of self-directed adult learning. It would be far more fruitful, however, for researchers to develop new constructs and categories based on an inductive analysis of emergent characteristics of adult self-directed learning.

Comparisons of successful self-directed learners' reported insights into their own learning with the adult learning principles identified in the literature reveal several significant disjunctions. Danis and Tremblay (1985) criticize the view predominant in much literature on adult learning that the learning process is cyclical and that adults' learning is generally focused on problem solving. They state as a general learning principle that "self-taught adults proceed in a heuristic manner within a learning approach which they organize around intentions, redefine and specify without following any predetermined patterns" (p. 131). These adults report that random, accidental events are often significant in suggesting new learning paths, a finding also noted in my study of successful independent learners (Brookfield, 1980). These successful learners were found to contradict the mode of learning on which many institutionally organized education and training programs are premised.

Danis and Tremblay also report that their learners "do not describe their learning process in terms of management nor do they seem to follow the linear, predetermined steps of planning and evaluation" (p. 131). These learners were also found to branch out into related fields of interest in an unplanned way and to place at the heart of their activities the creation of a learning network of peers, both of which findings were first noted in my research (Brookfield, 1980). The link made by many theorists between the performance of developmental tasks or roles and adults' deciding to learn is not borne out in either my studies or those of Danis and Tremblay. These studies emphasize instead the pleasure and joy that resulted from the act of learning and the tendency of the adults involved to prompt others to engage in learning as a result of the exhiliration that they themselves had experienced. This passion and its animating effect of encouraging others to engage in learning are noted in all studies of successful independent learners. The work of Brookfield, Thiel, and Danis and Tremblay thus contradicts many of the learning principles that are proposed in the literature as generalizable to all adults. It is evident that we lack accurate studies of the range of learning styles observable with different learners in different settings. Until such studies accumulate to the point where we can say with some certainty what the typical styles of learning in certain situations are, we should be wary of proposing universally applicable, general models of teaching or program development to be used with adults.

Self-Directed Learning and Self-Education. A fundamental problem with the term *self-directed learning* results from the gerundive nature of the word *learning.* As Verner (1964) and Little (1979) have argued, the term *learning* gives rise to considerable confusion when it is used by different writers both as a noun and as a verb. Verner and Little both argue that the word should be used only as a noun to describe an internal change in consciousness, that is, an alteration in the state of the central nervous system. Hence, the term *learning* would be reserved for the phenomenon of internal mental change whether that be characterized as a flash of gestalt insight, double-loop learning, or a rearrangement of neural paths. Such internal phenomena would be discernible externally in the form of permanent behavioral change, and it would be by observing such change that we would reason that learning had occurred.

This semantic confusion can be seen to have profound implications for our understanding of the processes of learning and education and their interrelationship. Although the word *learning* functions colloquially as both a noun and verb, it is its use as a verb that has been adopted by writers in the field of self-directed learning. And because the verb *learning* is used to describe a range of activities, it has become equivalent to the *act* of learning. We talk of someone being engaged in learning if they set learning goals, consult assistants, locate and use books and articles, and devise evaluative indexes. To talk of self-directed learning, in this sense, is not to describe a particular kind of internal change in consciousness, but to refer to the activity of acquiring skills and knowledge with a minimum of professional assistance.

The term *education,* Verner (1964) and Little (1979) argue, should be reserved for describing the process of managing external conditions that facilitate the internal change called learning. By this definition, an educator would be one who deliberately manages external conditions of instruction in order to produce desired internal mental rearrangements. Hence, an adult who sets learning goals, locates appropriate resources, devises learning strategies, and is responsible for evaluating the progress made toward the attainment of those goals would be engaged in self-education or self-directed education rather than self-directed learning.

According to Verner and Little, then, the processes and activities described by most writers on self-directed learning should really be called self-education. Tough (1966, 1967) did indeed favor the term *self-teaching* at the outset of his research and viewed the adults in his sample as responsible for managing the tasks of teaching normally undertaken by an external educator. In this sense he was very close to Verner and Little. Since that time, however, he has come to favor the terms *learning projects* (Tough, 1979) and *major learning efforts* (Tough, 1978), both of which involve an emphasis on the activities associated with learning.

In an earlier work (Brookfield, 1983a), I used the term *self-directed learning* in its active sense. In specifying the characteristics of adult learning in the community, I argued that such learning must be deliberate and purposeful (though not always marked by closely specified goals), occur outside of designated educational institutions, receive no institutional accreditation, and be voluntary and self-generating. For the purposes of the present work, however, it is useful to distinguish between two forms of self-direction. First, there are various techniques of self-directed learning; these include specifying goals, identifying resources, implementing strategies, and evaluating progress. This collection of techniques for seeking out and processing information is what Verner and Little refer to as self-education. Second, self-directed learning can refer to a particular internal change of consciousness. Put briefly, self-directed learning in this second sense occurs when learners come to regard knowledge as relative and contextual, to view the value frameworks and moral codes informing their behaviors as cultural constructs, and to use this altered perspective to contemplate ways in which they can transform their personal and social worlds.

Self-Directed Learning and Independence. Formulations

of self-directed learning that stress the autonomous or independent nature of such learning to the exclusion of external assistants or stimuli fall foul of a dangerous yet common misconception. In speaking of the self-directed learner, it is all too easy to presume that such an adult is wholly in control of the learning adventure. Indeed, such individual hegemony over learning is sometimes posited as the chief characteristic of self-directed learning.

It is evident, however, that no act of learning is fully self-directed if this is taken to mean that the learner is so self-reliant that he or she can exclude all external sources or stimuli. Acts of contemplative introspection or certain forms of meditation may come close to this state of intellectual self-sufficiency. However, all other forms of cognitive activity involve interaction with external stimuli. This argument has been fully discussed elsewhere (Brookfield, 1983a), and it is enough to say here that the self-directed learner is not, in Moore's words, "an intellectual Robinson Crusoe, castaway and shut off in self-sufficiency" (1973, p. 669). In the pursuit of skills, knowledge, and insight adults will come into contact with books, magazines, computer programs, and so forth; all of these are devised by humans for the purpose of facilitating skill development or knowledge acquisition. Although the writers of these books, magazines, and programs are not physically present to the learner, they nonetheless partly control his or her cognitive operations.

From another point of view (and, it must be admitted, somewhat confusingly), it is possible to argue that we are all independent learners in that our mental strategies for processing and coding the information that our nervous systems receive are entirely idiosyncratic. An adult's past experiences and the previous learning that has taken him or her to a certain point will perform a mediatory function with regard to new stimuli. As I have written elsewhere, "All learners perceive and codify stimuli in an individual, idiosyncratic fashion, and to that extent all learning activities are characterized by a degree of independence" (Brookfield, 1983a, p. 24).

There is also a danger in overemphasizing the need for

adults to establish beforehand the purpose and intent of their learning activities. Although a degree of direction and deliberation is an essential condition in self-directed education, it is possible for adults to embark on an intellectual voyage without knowing their final destination. There are many adults engaged in what may be regarded as purposeful self-education who nevertheless do not specify intermediate and final learning goals for themselves. An adult may embark on an independent exploration of a field of knowledge (for example, learning how to play a guitar) with no real knowledge of how to devise learning activities that will result in the development of a certain level of skill. As that adult becomes aware of the standards and operations intrinsic to that skill or knowledge area (for example, what constitutes good technique, how to improvise within certain keys, how to tune an instrument by ear), then he or she can begin to set manageable short- and long-term learning objectives. One can develop such facility, however, only after becoming acquainted with what Peters (1965) calls the *grammar* of the activity, that is, the internal criteria, operations, and procedures inherent in a subject area or skill set.

One final point on this relationship between self-direction and independence. The techniques of self-directed learning can be applied in a number of contexts for a range of purposes. These contexts are, for the most part, subject free. We can become self-directed (in terms of setting goals, locating resources, implementing strategies, and evaluating progress) in our attempts to ride a bike, to master Fascist or Communist theory, to develop an appreciation of Mozart, or to play the guitar. These examples, however, all place the conduct of a self-directed learning project within predefined frameworks. We can conceive of becoming a better bike rider, Fascist, Communist, or guitarist when we inhabit a certain paradigm of expectations, options, and familiar possibilities. In this kind of self-directed learning we are operating within self-imposed limits. We are trapped in our own history in that we cannot logically conceive of alternative frameworks. How can we engage in self-directed learning in areas completely outside our experience? It is hard to imagine an adult's deciding to engage in paradigm shifting, perspective transformation, or the replacing of one meaning system with another purely on his or her own volition. What will induce this exploration of alternative perceptions and meanings is some kind of external event or imperative. This could be a calamitous circumstance of some kind (for example, bereavement, war, divorce, or job loss), or it could be the result of another individual's prompting the adult to engage in the very painful process of analyzing critically his or her state of being and the assumptions underlying that state.

A New Orthodoxy?

A major theme of the previous chapter was the manner in which the search for characteristics unique to adult learners has become a quest for a professional identity for adult educators, as much as for the intellectual insights that search might yield. The phenomenon of self-directed learning has, in recent years, seemed to offer the best hope for researchers engaged on this quest. In particular, the work of Tough (1966, 1967) has been seized upon by adult learning theorists and researchers as comprising a rich vein for exploration. Since the mid 1960s, for example, there have been over fifty follow-up studies to Tough's initial survey of the self-teaching projects of forty graduates of the University of Toronto. There is a real danger, however, that a concept that seems to possess a high degree of explanatory power will become debased through too frequent and arbitrary use. If we invoke self-directedness every time we are asked to explain what is distinctive about facilitating learning, then we are succumbing to a new, uncritically accepted, academic orthodoxy.

In an earlier work (Brookfield, 1983a, p. 44) I suggested that a spirit of self-critical scrutiny should infuse the research efforts of those who, like myself, had spent some time investigating the efforts of self-directed learners. Since that time some critical papers (Brookfield, 1984c; Brockett, 1984a) on the subject have been published, as well as a sourcebook of readings (Brookfield, 1985a) that contains accounts of attempts to introduce self-directedness into various adult learning settings and the contradictions encountered in those efforts.

Samples Not Diverse Enough. The middle-class nature of the groups of adults assembled as samples of self-teachers, self-directed learners, or autonomous learners is one of the strikingly consistent features of research studies in this area. As noted, Tough's initial study (1967) surveyed the self-teaching projects of forty college graduates, and his later samples (1968, 1979, 1982) have been drawn primarily from educationally advantaged populations. Groups surveyed by other researchers include professional men, pharmacists, teachers, graduate students, parish ministers, university and college administrators, degreed engineers, and nurses. Thus, if we take these studies to comprise the research universe for investigations into self-directed learning, our resultant generalizations will have a marked culture- and class-specific level of generalizability. We certainly cannot claim for these groups any kind of statistical representativeness in terms of the total American or Canadian population. The great majority of individuals in these samples have attained an educational level well above the average. To assume that the behaviors exhibited by these educationally advantaged adults will be displayed by adults from a range of different class and ethnic backgrounds is, to say the least, highly questionable.

Indeed, to talk of the adult's propensity for self-directed learning on the basis of research into a sample comprised chiefly of middle-class Americans is a dangerous act of intellectual ethnocentrism. Very few researchers have chosen to investigate the self-directed learning activities of working-class adults in America. (Those who have include Brockett, 1983b; Booth, 1979; Leann and Sisco, 1981; Armstrong, 1971; and Johnson, Levine, and Rosenthal, 1977.) Conspicuous by their absence are studies of self-directed learning among blacks, Puerto Ricans, Hispanics, Asian Americans, or Native Americans, although Wenden (1982) has surveyed self-directed learning of language by immigrants.

The fact that the majority of studies in this field have been conducted with samples of advantaged, white, middle-class Americans does not invalidate these research exercises. They are valuable and instructive investigations of the learning activities of a certain populace, and their authors usually issue any number of caveats regarding the limited nature of the samples and the dangers of arbitrary generalization. Such warnings have tended not to be heeded, however, and we are now at the stage where it is conventional wisdom that adults are self-directed learners. The patent absurdity of claiming that adults (as a generic category) are self-directed learners is obvious to anyone who reflects on the cultural and class specificity of the samples from which such generalized statements are drawn. The self-directedness of adult learners is in real danger of becoming an academic orthodoxy, and we should be careful to repeat long and loudly that self-directedness as an empirical descriptor and self-directedness as a prescriptive aim are two entirely different things. While we may seek to use the latter as a guide for our practitioner efforts, we should be wary of claiming the former to be attestable truth.

Methodolatory. In a provocative essay, Gouldner (1967) coined the term *methodolatory* to describe the process by which researchers develop a slavish and uncritical adherence to a particular research mode irrespective of the success of that mode in producing new knowledge or in suggesting new concepts and hypotheses. The most serious consequence of this unthinking subscription to certain research techniques is the manner in which the framing and conduct of research become determined by a prior commitment to methodology. Thus, the definition of an important, relevant, or profound problem becomes a statement as to which phenomena, events, or behaviors are susceptible to investigation through a particular methodology. Instead of framing a research problem as one to be investigated because, on its own merits, it is significant, researchers assign significance according to whether or not that problem is amenable to investigation within the dominant methodological paradigm of the day.

Research into self-directed learning has been characterized by the use of structured interview schedules, questionnaires, prompt sheets, and measurement scales, the majority of them modified versions of the schedules, prompt sheets, and questionnaires devised by Tough and his researchers. More recently, a new wave of dissertations has been completed using the SDLRS (Guglielmino, 1977). This emphasis on quasi-quantitative instruments has had several consequences. The first of these is that such instruments become self-defining in respect to the learning activities they uncover. If unequivocal, quantitative measures of learning are sought by the researcher, it is likely that subjects will, perhaps unwittingly, concentrate on recalling learning projects that appear to meet the interviewer's expectations as reflected in the research methodology. Hence, the finding that learning projects most commonly originate in the learner's being assigned an action goal (Tough, 1968), usually of a vocational nature, may be the result of researchers' presenting examples of easily identified psychomotor skills projects when discussing "typical" learning projects with their subjects at the outset of an interview. It is much easier for an adult to recall the assistants consulted, the time spent, the goal-setting procedure used, and the nonhuman materials that were most helpful if that individual is describing the process by which a car was repaired or a basement rewired. But external, behavioral indexes of learning (number of hours spent, number of assistants consulted, number of books read) become much harder to obtain and more ambiguous in nature if we seek, for example, to explore an individual's development of esthetic appreciation, raising of political consciousness, or development of interpersonal sensitivity.

A second consequence of adopting formalized measures of self-directed learning, administering an interview in a standardized fashion, or presenting a self-completion questionnaire to subjects is that of intimidating those learners unused to such investigative hardware. Working-class adults, members of ethnic minorities, or recently arrived immigrant groups who are confronted with a battery of scales, prompt sheets, or questionnaires will likely be suspicious of such devices in that they commonly associate them with welfare offices. Also, as Brockett (1984a) has pointed out in respect to the SDLRS, that scale is suited to measuring readiness for self-directed learning among adults who have an average or above-average level of formal educational attainment and who rely on books and journals for information. With adults of low formal attainment or with those who have explored knowledge and skill areas using fellow learners as the primary source of information, the SDLRS is a questionable measure of readiness for learning.

Studies of self-directed learning have generally relied on structured interview schedules and precoded categories of response into which subjects' perceptions concerning their learning are fitted. Lists of self-directed learning projects, definitions of major learning efforts, lists of individuals who typically assist in the conduct of self-directed learning, lists of reasons for starting learning projects, various prompt sheets—all these have been presented to self-directed learners in an attempt to elicit information about their learning efforts.

But the use of these standardized instruments with groups of working-class adults or with learners from certain ethnic minorities will cause these individuals to regard the researcher with suspicion. This is hardly likely to foster the atmosphere of trust and reciprocity necessary to an authentic research encounter in which the subject states as truthfully and accurately as possible the details concerning the planning and execution of a learning project. In my own research into successful independent learning, I used an open-ended, conversational style of interviewing. Interviews were conducted in subjects' homes, they were allowed to see and approve all records of the interview (notes and transcripts), the questions asked related to specific features of the interviewees' learning efforts rather than to general themes, and the interview agenda was largely determined according to the subjects' areas of interest and their identification of significant aspects of their learning. An account of this attempt to overcome the culture-specific associations of interviews with interrogations can be found in Brookfield (1981a). Similar styles of interviewing used in recent adult education research are those of Fingeret (1983) and Holmes (1976).

A third result of applying strictly defined and tightly administered quantitative measures in the investigation of self-directed learning is the absence of attention to the quality of learning. It may be helpful in certain contexts to estimate the number of hours adults spend in conducting their own learning, but what about the quality or effectiveness of that learning?

While it is impossible for a researcher to study all aspects of a phenomenon, failing to investigate the quality of self-directed learning seriously weakens the arguments of those who claim that such learning is distinctively adult.

One crucial area for future research in this field, therefore, would be an attempt to estimate the congruence between adults' own judgments of the effectiveness of their self-directed learning activities and the effectiveness of those activities as measured by some objective measure. Relying solely on self-reported estimates of the success, quality, and effectiveness of self-directed learning is clearly questionable. Just as self-assigned ratings of social class tend to reflect adults' desire to place themselves in categories higher than those to which they would be assigned according to some objective measure, so adults are likely to claim for their learning efforts a degree of quality and effectiveness that might be unsupported by external assessment.

Unequivocal measures will, admittedly, be hard to find for all examples of learning projects conducted in a self-directed mode. How, for example, could we judge a person's immersion in the works of Blake, Mozart, or van Gogh in an attempt to raise her level of esthetic discrimination? In projects concerned with developing psychomotor skills, however, it would not be too difficult to devise valid and verifiable indexes by which to judge success. And even in hard-to-measure kinds of learning projects, there is one reasonable measure—judgment by experts—that might be applied. For example, learners' perceptions of their success in learning in affective or esthetic domains might be compared to the judgments of the success of that learning by experts in the area studied. In one of my own studies (Brookfield, 1980), I used judgment by experts as a criterion for deciding which adults might be included in a sample of successful independent learners.

Finally, on this question of determining the quality of learning, we should note that the literature on self-directed learning projects does not address the innate value or worth of differing learning activities. Clearly, however, the individual or societal benefits of learning how to wire a basement are not of the same order as those accruing from, say, a sustained and

committed perusal of Fascist doctrine. How we decide which
kind of learning is somehow more worthy is, of course, a philosophical question outside the realm of methodological discourse.
What is important to consider, however, is the implicit manner
in which research designs come to treat all learning projects as
possessing equal significance. In their internal characteristics,
their personal meaning to the adult concerned, and their wider
societal significance, however, projects can be very different. To
compare learning how to deal with divorce or bereavement with
learning how to repair a car is methodologically unsound. Similarly, organizing a political advocacy group is an activity of a
very different order from, say, becoming expert in Armenian
cuisine. The danger of emphasizing the mechanical aspects of
self-directed learning activities is that of coming to regard all
self-directed learning as exhibiting some kind of conceptual or
substantive unity. The examples quoted above show the absurdity of such a proposition.

Autonomy and Empowerment

To many practitioners, the term *self-directed learning*
conjures up images of isolated individuals busily engaged in
determining the form and content of their learning efforts and
controlling the execution of these efforts in an autonomous
manner. This notion of autonomy centers on the idea that the
learner is particularly skilled at setting objectives, locating resources, and designing learning strategies. It is a conception that
equates autonomy with methodological expertise. However, a
critique of this concept of autonomy has been mounted by
Strong (1977) and Chené (1983). To Strong, autonomous learning is not so much a matter of methodology as of decision making. The highest level of autonomy is realized when adults make
a conscious and informed choice among learning formats and
possible activities on how best to achieve their personal learning goals. Autonomy, then, is predicated upon "decision making
arrived at after consideration of all possibilities, based on sufficient knowledge, understanding, and skills of communication"
(1977, p. 10). It is not simply equivalent to learner control over

goals and methods of learning, since such control can be exercised without a full knowledge of alternative learning goals and possible learning activities.

The dangers of equating control over techniques of learning with autonomy have also been recognized by Chené, who concurs that "to be resourceful and to be independent do not equal the achievement of autonomy" (1983, p. 42). Like Strong, Chené argues that autonomy can only be exhibited once the norms and limits of the learning activity are known. She believes autonomy is possible only when learners have an awareness of the process of learning, an appreciation of the norms governing the standards and activities in the area explored, and an ability to make critical judgments on the basis of this knowledge. Hence, "it is only when the limits of possible choices are drawn and the ability to judge developed that adult learners can exercise autonomy over their learning" (p. 46).

The point made by these writers is a crucial one. If we conceive of self-direction solely in terms of a command of self-instructional techniques, we can then speak of self-directed learners who operate within fixed and uncritically assimilated frameworks of knowledge. From this viewpoint, one can become a superb technician of self-directed learning, in command of goal setting, instructional design, or evaluative procedures, and yet be unable to question the validity or worthwhileness of one's intellectual pursuit as compared to competing, alternative possibilities. We might think here of the self-directed party member or religious zealot who is completely unaware of alternative political doctrines or religious creeds but who *is* skilled in certain technical activities concerned with the design and management of self-instruction.

It is quite possible to exhibit the methodological attributes of self-directed learning in terms of designing and executing learning projects but to do so within a framework of narrow and unchallenged assumptions, expectations, and goals. Learning to be a good disciple, to be an efficient bureaucratic functionary, or to be an exemplary political party member are all examples of projects in which the techniques of self-directed learning may be evident. In none of these projects, however, is there exhibited critical thought concerning other alternatives, options, or possibilities.

The concept of self-directed learning advanced within this book is very different from this technicist one. At its heart is the notion of autonomy, which is defined as the possession of an understanding and awareness of a range of alternative possibilities. Hence, self-directed learning is predicated upon adults' awareness of their separateness and their consciousness of their personal power. When they come to view their personal and social worlds as contingent and therefore accessible to individual and collective interventions, then the internal disposition necessary for self-directed action exists. When adults take action to acquire skills and knowledge in order to effect these interventions, then they are exemplifying principles of self-directed learning. They are realizing their autonomy in the act of learning and investing that act with a sense of personal meaning.

Self-directed learning as the mode of learning characteristic of an adult who is in the process of realizing his or her adulthood is concerned as much with an internal change of consciousness as with the external management of instructional events. This consciousness involves an appreciation of the contextuality of knowledge and an awareness of the culturally constructed form of the value frameworks, belief systems, and moral codes that influence behavior and the creation of social structures. The most complete form of self-directed learning occurs when process and reflection are married in the adult's pursuit of meaning. As we have said, it is possible to be a technically skilled self-directed learner in one's attempt to be a good party member, employee, or graduate student. The norms or assumptions underlying what it means to be a "good" functionary in any of these settings need never be questioned. All that would be required for an activity to be a technically correct example of self-directed learning would be that the individual concerned was effective in designing a successful learning program with a minimum of external assistance.

The most fully adult form of self-directed learning, however, is one in which critical reflection on the contingent aspects of reality, the exploration of alternative perspectives and meaning systems, and the alteration of personal and social circum-stances are all present. The external technical and the internal reflective dimensions of self-directed learning are fused when adults come to appreciate the culturally constructed nature of knowledge and values and when they act on the basis of that appreciation to reinterpret and recreate their personal and social worlds. In such a praxis of thought and action is manifested a fully adult form of self-directed learning.

❦ 4 ❧

Facilitating
Self-Directed
Learning

In this chapter and the next our attention is focused on helping
adults to learn. The current chapter is concerned chiefly with
the facilitation of self-directed learning, that is, with assisting
adults to free themselves from externally imposed direction in
their learning and with encouraging them to become proactive,
initiating individuals in reshaping their personal, work, political,
and recreational lives.

In one sense, the distinction often drawn between assisting adults to become self-directed learners and working with
groups of learners is specious. Ultimately, it is individuals who
learn, not groups. The settings for such learning do, of course,
vary, so that we can speak of learning in an individual mode or
learning in a group mode (Brookfield, 1983a). However, even
when one is a member of a learning group, one does not transfer
part of one's consciousness to the group. There is no group
mind, no separate entity that is learning over and above the individual learning undertaken by each group member.

It is important, though, to distinguish individual from
group modes because they involve different kinds of learning,
different learning styles, and different kinds of behaviors on the
part of facilitators. When facilitators provide individual counseling, negotiate individual learning contracts, and help learners become aware of their individual learning styles, they are using

methods and attempting to achieve objectives that are distinctive enough to be considered on their own terms, separate from the activities involved in working with groups of learners. Facilitators who work with groups are aware that the dynamics of group processes (such as the ways in which isolates emerge, status hierarchies develop, or interpersonal competition is apparent) can both enhance and be inimical to the learning of participants. The learning engaged in by individuals when they are in groups and that occurring when they work in a more personal, self-directed way with facilitators are sufficiently different in process and focus to allow us to make a useful and valid distinction between them.

It is important to state firmly and repeatedly, however, that self-directed learning through the individual mode is in no sense superior to the learning that occurs within groups, or vice versa. In most teaching-learning transactions we can see a mix of these two modes, and such a mix is generally the most effective process for enhancing adult learning. Through individual reflection and personal interaction with a facilitator, adult learners are able to become more aware of their unique learning styles and to develop a sense of direct control over the method and direction of learning. Through developing such a sense of their uniqueness and of their ability to control aspects of the teaching-learning interaction, learners will find that their personal investment in, as well as their motivation for, learning is enhanced.

It is generally unwise, however, to presume that this form of individualized self-directed learning should be viewed as a fully educational teaching-learning transaction. The dynamics of group process are such as to encourage the collaborative exploration of experiences, the collective interpretation of learners' individual realities, and the recognition of elements of themselves, and their lives, in others. The recognition of oneself in the accounts of others in a group, along with the validation of one's own experience that this serves to inculcate, is an often-repeated theme in literature related to the women's movement. In a different way to that pertaining to individualized work between learner and facilitator, groups can act as motivators for further learning. As adults find their experiences echoed in the accounts of others, and as they react to, support, and build upon the contributions of various group members, enthusiasm and genuine engagement in the encounter begin to develop. Readers will no doubt be able to recall many instances when, as participants or leaders, they have experienced a sense of mounting excitement, anticipation, and real exhiliration as group members recognized their own lives in others' accounts, when they realized that another member's insights had caused them to reinterpret their own experiences, or when several members arrived at the same point of realization after an extended period of analysis, conflict, reinterpretation, and apparent frustration.

But the aim of facilitation—to make of adults self-directed, critically aware individuals capable of imagining and then realizing alternative ways of thinking and living—remains unchanged, whether we use an individual mode or a group activity. The point is that the two modes, individual and group, exhibit features that allow for different approaches to this general objective. No doubt the most satisfying educational experience, for learners and educators alike, occurs when the sense of individual control brought on by becoming aware of one's unique learning style and by negotiating individual curricula and objectives is married to an involvement in an ongoing learning group in which one's ideas, experiences, and achievements are subjected to collective exploration and interpretation by group members.

Role of Facilitators

The concept of facilitation is relatively new, though the activities inherent to it have been discussed in educational writings over the last century or so. The notion that educators should function as enablers or facilitators of learning is derived chiefly from the works of humanistic psychotherapists and counselors, and the first name that comes to mind here is that of Carl Rogers. Educators and trainers regularly declare themselves to be facilitators of learning, rather than teachers or instructors, and the term has now entered the mainstream of educational literature (Knox, 1974; Cross, 1981; Brundage and

Mackeracher, 1980; Brockett, 1983a; Knowles, 1975; Knowles and Associates, 1984; Peterson, 1983).

Facilitators of learning see themselves as resources for learning, rather than as didactic instructors who have all the answers. They stress that they are engaged in a democratic, student-centered enhancement of individual learning and that responsibility for setting the direction and methods of learning rests as much with the learner as with the educator. Facilitators are usually described as being in a "helping relationship" (Brill, 1978). Such a relationship is said to offer "exciting possibilities for the development of creative, adaptive, autonomous persons" (Rogers, 1961, p. 38), and the elements central to such relationships are said to be trust, mutuality, and purposeful interaction (Eisenberg and Delaney, 1977). Various writers have specified the educational skills appropriate to facilitators. Tough (1979, p. 183) identifies four characteristics of "ideal" helpers:

- They are warm, loving, caring, and accepting of the learners.
- They have a high regard for learners' self-planning competencies and do not wish to trespass on these.
- They view themselves as participating in a dialogue between equals with learners.
- They are open to change and new experiences and seek to learn from their helping activities.

The summary of adult learning principles undertaken by Brundage and Mackeracher (1980), and discussed in Chapter Two, draws a number of facilitating implications derived from these: Teachers should be sensitive to learners' self-concepts, learners' past experiences should be recognized as providing educational material, teachers should be willing to share their experiences with learners, and they should be open to learners' suggestions. Teachers of older adults should allow more time for reflection by learners, and there should be a general atmosphere of flexibility, regard for learners, and openness. If the teacher specifies clear learning objectives and provides regular reinforcement of success, this will reduce learners' anxieties considerably. Teachers should be aware of different learning styles and have a range of appropriate teaching styles at their disposal. A balance of independence and group interaction should be pursued. Throughout their analysis, Brundage and Mackeracher constantly stress how important it is that teachers be flexible, responsive to learner needs, ready to use learners' experiences in teaching activities, and willing to value learner dignity in an unconditional way. These conclusions are similar to those of Brockett (1983a), who seeks to specify roles and skills based on models of helper behaviors in the field of counseling. He identifies three broad skill domains—attending, responding, and understanding—that are important to teachers who wish to develop collaborative, interactive patterns of teaching and learning. In particular, he thinks that the exercise of such skills is important for the teacher's fostering of self-directedness among adult learners.

One important element in facilitating learning is helping learners become aware of their own idiosyncratic learning styles. A degree of self-knowledge regarding the way one typically sets out to plan intermediate and final learning objectives, what kinds of resources are best suited to one's learning style, what strategies one employs to make sense of abstract concepts, and how one approaches learning new psychomotor skills can all help an adult determine which educational method is best suited to his or her own style of learning. In recent years, in fact, a growing number of educators and trainers have become interested in this area of *mathetics,* or how adults learn how to learn. R. M. Smith, for example, has spent the last two decades developing a theory and practical repertoire of training exercises premised on the idea that it is as important to teach adults how to learn as it is to specify particular curricular domains for learning. He advocates that educators become sensitive to this idea and include a "learning-how-to-learn" orientation for new instructors and learners at the outset of a program, so that they can use their newly acquired awareness of their own learning styles to gain as much insight, knowledge, and analytical capacity from the subsequent course as possible (Smith and Haverkamp, 1977; Haverkamp, 1983). Learning-how-to-learn orientation courses presume that there are identifiable skills of learning that are generic and replicable. Hence, "learning how to learn involves possessing, or acquiring, the knowledge and skill to learn effectively in whatever learning situation one encounters" (Smith, 1982b, p. 204).

Smith uses the term *training* to refer to the educator's attempts to inculcate an awareness in adult learners of their learning styles. He regards a diagnosis of learning styles as a central activity in training for learning how to learn. In the design of training for learning how to learn, however, Smith admits that he contradicts a central principle of facilitation as it is usually conceived. He advocates that training participants (the adults who will be engaged in learning how to learn) should *not* be involved in designing training exercises. He thinks that metalearning—that is, the act of reflecting on one's learning style—is too complex an activity to be left to anyone other than a trained educator.

In his chief work on learning how to learn as applied learning theory, Smith (1982a) outlines a number of training exercises for facilitators who want to assist adults to become more self-reflective about their learning styles. He describes workshops and materials for learning how to learn in three modes: self-directed learning, collaborative learning, and institutional learning. But he advises against calling workshops on these topics by such titles as "Becoming a Self-Directed Learner" or "Learning How to Participate in Discussions." He feels that it is better to advertize such courses as "Bright Ideas for Learning" or to use other titles that do not present the learner with the reality of engaging in metalearning. The level of complexity involved in asking adults to reflect on their own learning style is felt to be too intimidating for students initially.

A number of adult educators have developed courses in learning how to learn concurrently with Smith's exploration of this concept. As Smith (1983) himself acknowledges, the greatest activity in this area has been initiated by European educators such as Gibbs (1981) and Harri-Augstein and Thomas (1983). In English adult education, there are at least three experiments in organizing learning-how-to-learn courses for adult students that have been documented in recent years (Brookfield, 1978b; Hutchinson and Hutchinson, 1979; Macdonald, 1982).

As is evident from discussions earlier in this volume, self-directed learning is, in the world of adult learning research and theory at least, an idea that has come of age. Not only do a number of researchers claim that adults spend between 500 and 700 hours each year in self-directed learning, but they also maintain that much of this learning is enjoyable and effective, not haphazard and serendipitous as some professional educators would have us believe. These findings have given considerable comfort to deschooling theorists, who argue that communities contain enough knowledge banks, skill models, consultants, and natural learning webs to make the abolition of formal schooling a real possibility. Over the last two decades, moreover, a number of initiatives to create new, open, and flexible institutional paths for adult learning have emerged. The concept of open learning (Mackenzie, Postgate, and Scupham, 1975) has recently become fashionable, and the establishment of the Open University in Milton Keynes, England, has inspired a number of smaller-scale analogues, such as the Open Learning Institute in British Columbia. Many institutions of higher education have also recognized that the knowledge and skills gained by adults through work and community activities might qualify for formal course credit. Thomas Edison College in Trenton, New Jersey, and Empire State College have been leaders in assisting adults to document prior experiential learning.

It is evident, then, that the last twenty years have witnessed a mounting challenge to our stereotypical views of the nature and extent of adult learning and the appropriate roles for professional educators. The ability and readiness of many adults to carry out self-directed learning projects have become generally accepted. Along with this development, a number of energetic practitioners have begun to explore ways of bridging the gap between the world of formal education and the activities of self-directed learners. At times, we have come close to accepting an academic orthodoxy according to which all adults are natural, self-directed learners, and the task of the facilitator is simply to release this boundless capacity that lies dormant in all adults. Those practitioners who have tried to liberate the genie of self-directed learning from within the bodies and minds of adult learners are aware, however, that this view is extremely oversimplified. Far from acquiescing in the joyful release of latent talents for self-directed learning, many learners within formal courses, classes, and programs have stubbornly resisted the efforts of educators to transfer control over learning to them. Some are visibly intimidated by being asked to design their own learning plans, others feel resentful of what they perceive as faculty laziness in not providing strong leadership, still others are confused by facilitators who urge that learners be self-directed but at the same time retain control over the criteria by which learners' efforts are judged.

In this section a number of different institutional initiatives to assist adult learners become more self-directed in their learning will be examined. It is important to realize, however, that in all these case studies the institutional context strongly influences the extent to which real self-directedness in learning is possible. Within most formal educational contexts, full self-directedness on the part of learners is likely to be an unattainable, if seductive, chimera. The realities of curricular imperatives, grading policies, and institutionally devised evaluative criteria, as well as the difficulty of convincing administrators and skeptical faculty of education of the validity of a learning activity conducted in a self-directed mode mean that total self-direction is precluded. It is also important to remember that adults will be at different levels of readiness for self-directed learning, so that educators will need to spend different amounts of time assisting different learners. Finally, it is crucial that we do not blindly accept the orthodox view that self-direction is the preferred mode of learning in all cases for all adults. Given the complexity of adult learning styles, motives, and orientations to learning discussed in Chapter Two, it is clearly unrealistic to claim for the self-directed learning style (or indeed any learning style) some form of commonality across the spectrum of adult learners and settings for learning.

A recent collection of case studies of attempts to apply principles of self-directed learning in graduate adult education, the health professions, cultural institutions, and community settings identifies a number of constraints and contradictions that make this application somewhat problematic (Brookfield,

1985a). Essentially, a number of contextual variables seem re-peatedly to skew, distort, or otherwise alter the neat applica-tion of self-directed learning principles:

First, faculty are often untrained in this mode of educa-tion. They may be philosophically committed to the notion of empowering learners by encouraging them to take a measure of control over learning, but unsure how to deal with the real life complexities, role conflicts, and ambiguities that inevitably occur.

Second, learners are at different stages of readiness for this kind of activity. Some have experience in other contexts of working in a self-directed manner and respond eagerly when asked to plan, conduct, and evaluate their learning activities. Others, however, are threatened and intimidated by the pros-pect, and urging them to become self-directed actually serves as a block to, rather than an enhancement of, their learning. Often added to this confusion is resentment at what is seen as educa-tors' abdications of their leadership roles.

Third, institutional givens and unalterable structural fac-tors (grading policies, admission criteria, semester hours, pre-determined syllabi, available resources, and evaluative criteria) frequently make attempts to encourage a measure of self-directedness in learners not only difficult but almost farcical.

Fourth, working in this mode is so time consuming that many educators will prefer to work with standard curricula, learning formats, and evaluative procedures. This is particularly the case with younger, untenured faculty, who may well see the time needed for individualized assistance to self-directed learn-ers as a threat to their own research and, hence, to their profes-sional security and advancement.

Fifth, the amount and degree of contact between facilita-tor and learner required in self-directed modes mean that it is important for these individuals to be compatible. At the same time, however, the individuals who subscribe to the idea of self-directed learning may have very different reasons for doing so. Some may be attracted to this mode because of its flexibility, others because of the opportunity they perceive for closely structured activities. Some may be excited about the liberating potential inherent in this mode of education and the opportunity it gives adults to exercise a measure of control over their personal lives. Others may be attracted to it because of its essentially solitary nature and because they will not have to deal with the social pressures of peer learning situations.

Finally, there are no reliable instruments to screen applicants for their readiness for self-directed learning. The Guglielmino Scale (1977) is, as Brockett (1984a) points out, suitable only for those who are already literate and have been successful in their previous learning. With individuals unused to formal educational experiences, it is almost impossible to predict with any confidence their future success in self-directed learning activities. Hence, adults may be admitted to programs in which self-directed learning principles are applied, on the basis of their own declarations and documentation of self-directed learning capacities, only to find themselves threatened by the educator's refusal to chart every step of their learning path for them.

Experiments in Self-Directed Learning

As Campbell (1984) and others have acknowledged, adult learners are "the new majority" of students on university campuses throughout the world. Chapter Eight will document some of the implications for institutional practices deriving from this change in the nature of the student clientele—new approaches to advising and counseling, altered pedagogic practices, and the formal recognition of experiential learning, to name but three. Of particular interest, however, is the way in which some universities have adapted what they see as *the adult* mode of learning—self-directed learning—in their curriculum development, learning formats, and evaluative procedures. Over the last twenty years there have been many examples of university, college, and polytechnic programs that purport to be organized according to principles of self-directed learning and that claim to have the fostering of adults' powers and capacities of self-direction as their fundamental aim.

With the establishment of the Open University in England in 1969, and the work of the American Commission on Non-

Traditional Study in the early 1970s, it became evident that institutions of higher education were entering a new era in which flexibility of access, curriculum, and learning format were to be of the utmost importance. As documented by Valley (1972), Ruyle and Geiselman (1974), and Houle (1973), the growth of external degree programs such as those of the University Without Walls, open universities, and Empire State College represent an attempt by university administrators to adapt their institutions to the circumstances and concerns of adult students. In this section we will examine (1) those higher education institutions that have altered undergraduate and graduate curricula and methods to incorporate principles of self-directed learning and (2) graduate programs in adult education such as those at Teachers College, Syracuse University, St. Francis Xavier University (Antigonish, Nova Scotia), and the Ontario Institute for Studies in Education that have reorganized aspects of their training of adult educators according to what are proposed as essentially self-directed learning principles.

In an OECD-sponsored review of higher education initiatives in Germany (Knoll, 1979), America (White, 1979), Britain (Squires, 1979), Denmark (Severinsen, 1979), and Eastern Europe (Grant, 1979), the attempt to individualize learning was recognized as a major development in higher education observable in all these countries. The following case studies illustrate the variety of approaches that have been adopted in this attempt to incorporate aspects of self-directed learning into traditional institutions of higher education.

In 1974 the School for Independent Study was established at the North East London Polytechnic with the intention of allowing students to undertake diploma in higher education and baccalaureate degrees through the mechanism of self-directed learning. The student body that the school wished to attract to this experiment was intended to be very different from the traditional group of college age students drawn from middle-class families. Instead, the school set out deliberately to attract adult learners with working-class backgrounds. As reported in several studies of the school's operations (Burgess, 1977; Percy and Ramsden, 1980; Stephenson, 1981, 1983), the following assumptions and practices were paramount:

- Knowledge is not fixed and established, waiting for students' assimilation; hence, it is important for adults to identify the knowledge they need in order to explore the issues they have raised. This means that learners must be encouraged to challenge accepted wisdom and to feel no sense of failure at experiencing the "error" phase of trail and error activities.
- The purpose of education is to assist learners to become independent, that is, "able to cope with the unfamiliar without dependence upon traditional solutions or on other people" (Stephenson, 1981, p. 146).
- It is important, therefore, to allow learners to negotiate their own appropriate programs of study, with faculty serving as resources and agents of external scrutiny.
- Negotiating learning activities is best accomplished through a learning contract method in which objectives, relevant resources, specific activities, and evaluative procedures are outlined.
- Faculty assist learners by identifying resources, linking learners to these resources, clarifying options, and encouraging the formation of peer learning networks when appropriate.

In comments on the experience of offering diploma and baccalaureate degrees through independent study in an institution where the majority of students are pursuing traditional, single-subject degree courses, faculty at the School for Independent Study identified a number of problem areas. Percy and Ramsden (1980) report an early evaluation study that revealed differences in emphasis among tutors regarding the methods by which learner self-direction might be encouraged. Some were worried by an overreaction against traditional methods and the acceptance of a form of anti-intellectualism whereby personal development, unrelated to cognitive improvement, was felt to be a sufficient justification for work done in the school. Differences were also revealed in attitudes to the competing validity claims of learners' self-assessment, peer assessment, and external assessment by staff and external examiners. There was some concern regarding the acceptance of the logic of self-assessment in institutions where external standards of competence are generally specified as evidence of successful learning. Finally, disagreement was recorded concerning the relative importance that ought to be assigned to differing tutor roles. In particular, there was a conflict between being wholly supportive of learner-defined goals and evaluative criteria, on the one hand, and being prepared to offer clear and firm direction over what the lecturer felt was ultimately in the learner's best interests, on the other.

Stephenson (1981) calls attention to an institutional difficulty of some significance, namely, the amount of time faculty must spend explaining the rationale for self-directed learning to faculty within other departments in which independent study learners are temporarily involved. He points out that "our staff and students must constantly conduct dialogue with everyone else about the ways in which our work is totally different" and that "this activity rapidly becomes wearing and eventually frustrating. It takes up a great deal of energy which could be put to other purposes" (p. 158). A consequence of this is that students may decide to withdraw from independent study or to transfer to more conventional programs of study.

This raises the general point that those involved in self-directed learning programs within traditional institutions of higher education must be prepared to spend time educating administrators and other faculty regarding the rationale and operational procedures of this mode of learning. Such a programmatic initiative is far more likely to succeed if it is publicly endorsed by the head of the institution and if those involved in the self-directed program regularly communicate with colleagues in other areas regarding the organization and philosophy of that program. Conflict, confusion, and ambiguity are bound to exist in some degree, however, and those attempting to introduce self-directed learning principles need to be alert to the public relations dimension of their efforts and must be ready to explain, clarify, and inform colleagues about their activities. Stephenson offers the hope "that over the years the accumulated experience of hundreds of successful relationships between individual students and tutors will gradually erode these traditional barriers" (1981, p. 158).

Accounts of other experiments in this area, some of which now are fully accepted and institutionalized as part of the "normal" program in higher education institutions, are readily available. For the past thirteen years Holland College in Nova Scotia has conducted skill training for adults by means of learning contracts (Coffin, 1983). At Loretto Heights College in Colorado, the University Without Walls program allows adults to undertake a bachelor of arts degree program through a course of individualized study. The program uses learning contracts, personalized evaluation, and academic credit for prior experiential learning within the context of a degree organized for adult students. Learners enroll in courses, but the sequence and curricular choices are different for each individual (Greenberg, 1980). In the physical sciences Hills (1976) describes the use of a self-teaching system in a course on chemical bonding at the University of Surrey, the application of self-testing in an electrical engineering program at the same institution, and the use of self-teaching courses in audiovisual communication for biology and chemistry teachers at Concordia University in Montreal. From a review of these case studies he concludes that first- and second-year undergraduates in the physical and applied sciences can use self-teaching—"where the student actively takes responsibility for his own progress, that is, progress toward becoming a self-directed individual" (p. 10)—as a valid and effective instructional alternative to the more traditionally accepted lecture method.

Within the world of graduate adult education, a number of master's and doctoral programs in adult education, particularly in North America, have consciously employed techniques of self-directed learning in their training of future adult educators, as well as for in-service development of professionals. At Teachers College in New York City, for example, the Adult Education through Guided Independent Study (AEGIS) program uses self-directed learning principles as the core of a doctoral program in adult education. Bauer (1985a, 1985b) has recorded the chief features of the program:

- Attendance at monthly seminars (Saturdays) for six hours of discussion of the course's reading materials and reflection on theory-practice disjunctions in adult education.

- A strong reliance on learning contracts that are negotiated by faculty and participants to determine the form and purpose of the participants' course work completed during the core courses in the program. These contracts are individually negotiated during a special intensive summer course devoted solely to contract negotiation. Participants plan learning contracts for each of the core courses they will take in the second year of their studies with the faculty members who will be teaching those courses.

- Acknowledgment and accreditation of previous professional learning through the mechanism of a "professional seminar" in which participants complete a learning contract relating their prior professional experience to the concepts and issues of adult education. This theme is pursued further in course seminars, where the bulk of the time is spent in participants' exploring and collaboratively interpreting the manner in which contextual variables alter the simple replication of textbook constructs and models of practice in real life adult education settings.

- The formation by participants (at the strong and repeated instigation and encouragement of the faculty) of peer learning networks. Network members regularly organize conference calls, monthly preseminar evening meetings, and post-seminar reflection groups to continue the exploration of theory-practice disjunctions that are a feature of the AEGIS course seminars.

- The use of pass-fail as the grading mechanism in the course. Because participants are not in competition with each other, there is an atmosphere of collegiality and collaborativeness among participants and faculty. Those participants who do not meet the conditions of work that they contracted to undertake or who do not satisfy the evaluative criteria they have themselves negotiated are asked to undertake revisions to their work until it meets the conditions of the contract. Alternatively, they can request a renegotiation of their contract. When a dispute remains as the course ends, the participant is awarded an incomplete grade, rather than being failed. He or she then undertakes to complete the contract work in the subsequent semester.

- Faculty serve as resource persons and as discussion animators. Since all participants have three to five years of experience as adult and continuing education practitioners (organizers, learners, administrators, counselors, and teachers),
they do not need to receive instruction in basic techniques
of adult education; rather, they are encouraged to engage in
a critical analysis of the validity of adult education concepts
and practice injunctions contained in literature through a
collaborative exploration and interpretation of practitioner
experiences. This reservoir of experience makes it possible,
for example, to explore the ethical dilemmas experienced by
educators and to ground such explorations in the actual experiences of participants. The manner in which adult education programs are psychosocial dramas directly affected by
contextual factors, such as the personalities of the principals
involved or the political climate of the culture and the institution, is also much more effectively explored when the participants have considerable experience of this than when
they are attending courses designed to train them for future
roles as adult educators. Because there is no clear divide between the experience levels of faculty and participants, this
transition to fulfilling the roles of resource person, discussion animator, and prompter of critical analysis of theory-
practice disjunctions is easier for faculty to manage than in
courses where participants are novice adult educators.

In an interview-based research project on this use of self-
directed learning principles as the raison d'etre of adult education doctoral study, Bauer (1985b) raises three problem areas
reported by faculty and learners. First, despite various screen-
ing procedures to gauge their capacity for, and previous experience of, working in a self-directed mode, participants enter the
program with differing levels of self-directedness. Particularly
traumatic for many participants is the realization that what
they have perceived as evidence of self-direction in their professional lives (the ability, perhaps, to develop a highly successful,
innovative adult education program) does not necessarily transfer to a capacity for self-direction in the academic sphere. Participants regularly overestimate their self-organizational capaci-

ties and experience threats to their self-image as successful professionals when they find they are unable to meet the deadlines, objectives, and evaluative criteria they have themselves negotiated in their learning contracts. To be unable to complete a contract successfully and on time is perceived as evidence of uncharacteristic and extremely discomforting failure. To be asked to do revisions to an assignment because it does not meet the conditions of the contract is frequently interpreted as a sign of inadequacy. The realization that professional organizational success as a dean, director, or training manager does not translate directly into academic achievement can be profoundly threatening to participants' self-esteem.

A second problem area concerns the constraining effect of institutional contextual variables on the program. Because of the timing of course offerings at Teachers College, the comprehensive certification examination that all doctoral students must pass, and the requirements of the Ed.D. dissertation, limitations are necessarily placed on the degree of self-direction open to participants. Participants are moved through the two years of course work as cohorts, and their course offerings are prescribed for them by faculty. One advantage of this system is that collaborative peer networks develop quickly. Additionally, AEGIS participants are able to complete the course work required for doctoral candidates at Teachers College and to make progress with their dissertation research in a much shorter period of time (two years) than is normal at this level of work. The disadvantage is that participants cannot exercise choice in course selection, and they cannot lighten a particular semester's course load when personal or professional crises arise.

Finally, the AEGIS program is reported by its faculty members (of whom I am currently one) to present challenges to them not normally found in more traditional modes of doctoral study. It is essential that they give immediate and sustained reaction to participants' work since these adults are on campus only one Saturday in each month. Additionally, the negotiation and advisement on completion of a large number of highly individualized learning contracts are extremely energy and time consuming. Bauer (1985a) reports that these time demands "can be especially threatening for an untenured professor, since research and publication are vital in reappointment and tenure decisions" (p. 48), and she speculates on the possibility of reduced professorial life-spans for those who work in programs attempting to incorporate principles of self-directed learning.

At Syracuse University in upstate New York, an AEGIS-style graduate adult education program is run at the master's degree level. Called the Weekend Scholar program, it involves "a teaching and learning process whereby learners and instructors negotiate a learning contract establishing each individual's goals, strategies, and evaluation criteria for the particular subject matter under study" (Brockett and Hiemstra, 1985, p. 34). As with the AEGIS program, participants meet for course seminars on weekends, and it is taken for granted that these adults "have the ability to assume a high degree of self-direction in meeting program expectations while maintaining professional and personal responsibilities" (p. 34). Brockett and Hiemstra report that learners exhibit more positive attitudes about learning, the instructional process, and the program generally than had originally been anticipated. As with the Teachers College AEGIS program, participants' membership in a stable cohort of learners prompts them to form learning networks and peer self-help groups and allows them to achieve a collaborativeness and cohesion that are generally not found in graduate education programs. The master's degree in adult education at St. Francis Xavier University in Nova Scotia has been offered for a number of years in a self-directed learning format. At the Ontario Institute for Studies in Education (Toronto), courses within the graduate adult education program on "Self-Guided Learning and Change" and "Personal Change Paths" encourage learners to analyze and explore their own self-directed learning experiences.

Formal research on the use of learning contracts as an aid to self-directedness within educational institutions is still sparse. In the field of graduate adult education, however, we have the studies of Kasworm (1982) and Caffarella and Caffarella (1983). In studies of two graduate student cohorts in a course in "Methods and Techniques in Adult Education," Kasworm reported how her use of learning contracts and individualized curricula was perceived by course members. By having participants complete the Self-Directed Learning Readiness Scale at the beginning and end of the course, by doing a content analysis of observational diaries kept by the facilitator and selected students, and by having students complete evaluations of themselves as self-directed learners, Kasworm found that students for the most part evaluated the course favorably and that they had an increased awareness of themselves as self-directed learners. Approximately one-quarter of the participants did state, however, that they found the course to be difficult and that they would not choose another course using the self-directed format. A majority of students, particularly in the first half of the course, also expressed some anxiety or displeasure at the lack of external direction, fear that they would fail to fulfill the learning contract, and lack of confidence in risk taking within the self-directed format. The crucial variable regarding success in the self-directed mode (as identified by participants themselves) was the ability to use peer learning resources. This was particularly the case with students who lacked confidence in risk taking, and it underscores the suggestion made in Chapter Three concerning the social and collaborative nature of self-directed learning.

In a larger survey of 163 graduate students in departments of adult education at six American universities, Caffarrella and Caffarella (1983) used a triangulated approach to see what effect the use of learning contracts within graduate adult education programs would have on students' perceptions of their readiness and competencies for self-directed learning, their continuous learning activities, and their teaching styles. They found that readiness for self-directed learning did not alter as a result of using contracts in graduate courses and that the use of learning contracts had an effect on only three of twelve self-directed learning competencies identified—translating needs into objectives, identifying resources appropriate to achievement of those objectives, and selecting effective learning strategies. Learners exhibited a strong philosophical commitment to the idea of using learning contracts and reported that they had changed their own teaching styles to encourage self-direction on the part of their students. These learners said that they had become better at time management, at goal setting, and at combining different methods of learning.

The application of self-directed learning techniques has recently become popular within the fields of health, medical, and nursing education. One of the best documented case studies comes from McMaster University in Hamilton, Ontario. In the McMaster M.D. program, students combine membership in a small tutorial group with extensive self-directed learning activities, such as individual biomedical problem solving, negotiated learning contracts, and discussion with other group members on how to assist and then evaluate each other's activities. In descriptions of the course (Neufeld and Barrows, 1974; Sibley, 1978) and in a study of participants' experiences (Ferrier, Marrin, and Seidman, 1981), learners admitted to feeling a high level of anxiety over the lack of a defined core curriculum but thought that the self-directed mode had prepared them for real life professional problem solving. They also thought that it had given them a better grasp of fundamentals than they would have received from the more traditional methods at other schools.

Learning contracts and individualized curricula are now familiar in many nursing education programs (Buzzell and Roman, 1981; Martens, 1981; Wiley, 1983; Ash, 1985). In her analysis of the application of self-directed learning principles to the health professions, Ash (1985) documents her involvement with a nursing orientation program at the Memorial Sloan-Kettering Cancer Center, a program that uses self-instructional modules, selected readings, individual consultancy, videotapes, and clinical simulations. She notes that the initial reaction of nursing students to being asked to work within this mode is one of anxiety and confusion. The readiness of learners to work in this manner varies significantly, and some are able to meet the requirements of demonstrable learning much more quickly than others. There is a greater variation in the time needed to learn than is typically the case in lecture-based, progressively sequenced courses where students are taken in lockstep through a series of previously prescribed stages and activities.

Cultural institutions such as libraries, museums, art galleries, and botanical gardens are environments in which, according to Carr (1985), invitations are extended to individual learners to explore artifacts enshrining various interpretations of private and public experience. Museums (Chadwick, 1980) and public libraries (Dadswell, 1978; Burge, 1983) have both been proposed as sites for centers of assistance to self-directed learners who wish to explore areas of interest independently. Dadswell points out that large numbers of community members view the public library as a neutral community resource—unlike adult and continuing education centers, which are imbued with associations of elitism, authority, and irrelevance for those adults whose school experience was alienating and demeaning. Major reports such as those of the British government on adult education (H. M. Stationery Office, 1973; Advisory Council for Adult and Continuing Education, 1982) and the American Commission on Non-Traditional Study (Gould, 1973) have urged that libraries become centers for independent learning and that they advise adult learners on how best to pursue independent learning projects.

Such a mission was at the heart of the Adult Independent Learning Project in which eleven large American public libraries established a learners' advisory service for self-directed learners who wished to study outside of the formal educational system. In reports on the service's effectiveness Dale (1979, 1980) described how learners' advisers helped adults diagnose their learning needs, frame specific objectives, locate appropriate resources, choose from among different learning strategies, and assess their progress. The experience of this project indicates to me that public libraries should assign one member of the library staff to assist novices in various areas of interest and newcomers to library usage to learn how to judge the level at which books are written and how to read selectively so that their individual needs are satisfied (Brookfield, 1983a). This adviser might be permanently on hand, might travel from small library to small library at advertised times, or might hold weekly "new interests" clinics at which learners could contact the adviser for assistance on a walk-in basis.

Some libraries have in fact become sites for educational advisory services (Butler, 1984; Payne, 1985) and educational brokering services (Thresher, 1979). A natural way for libraries to assist self-directed learning would be for them to become the sponsoring and housing agency of skill exchanges. Learners in these exchanges would contract with each other to barter skills, and the library would contain the directory of skill models. Peer matching services, in which learners establish a *parrainage* (Goldschmid, 1981) system of exploring areas of interest collaboratively, could also be sited in libraries. Neither of these initiatives would require extensive financing, simply the willingness of a member of the library staff or perhaps a volunteer to keep the directories up to date and to distribute them to inquirers. Since adults use libraries as neutral community resources and knowledge banks, there would be no need for an extensive and costly campaign to attract individuals to the library. There is little doubt that as interactive computer technologies develop and become less expensive, it will become possible for many adults to tap into the skill exchange or peer-matching services simply by calling up the file on a personal computer that is tied into some mainframe community resources computer.

Self-Directed Learning: Central Themes

From this review of attempts to introduce techniques of self-directed learning into a number of formal and informal institutional settings, five themes clearly emerge.

The Centrality of Learning Contracts. The chief mechanism used as an enhancement of self-direction is the learning contract. In adult education (Knowles, 1984), higher education (Berte, 1975), training settings (Galbraith and Gilley, 1984), and religious education (Sawyers, 1985), contracts have been proposed as the most effective technique for assisting students to diagnose their learning needs, plan learning activities, identify and select resources that are relevant and appropriate, and become skilled at self-evaluation. The ability to write contracts is a learned skill, and facilitators must spend considerable time helping students to focus on realistic and manageable activities.

Contract planning requires particular skills of both the facilitator and learner, and it cannot be assumed that learners possess this innate ability. A preparation for contract planning and writing is therefore generally necessary, particularly if the learner has not been involved in this activity before. Perhaps courses in "planning learning through contracts" should be required of learners new to programs using this method so that faculty do not have to engage in extended instruction in the techniques of working within this mode while simultaneously trying to negotiate a contract for an actual piece of work.

Preparation for Self-Directed Learning. Notwithstanding the research cited in Chapter Three concerning adults' apparent capacity to conduct self-directed learning, it is evident that when techniques of self-directed learning are used as an alternative means for satisfying curriculum requirements and achieving specified competencies, both learners and teachers will be faced with frequent ambiguity, uncertainty, and problems both of planning and directing learning. Before programs using such principles are established, therefore, an induction period of some kind is essential for future teachers. During this period, they might participate in a workshop or clinic in which they would be asked to role play the kinds of skills that they will need in dealing with learners. Alternatively, the workshop might involve a series of problem-focused cases in which faculty would be asked to respond to typical problematic situations. These situations might involve learners who are unable to convert a general interest in a topic into a set of specific activities, learners who contract to undertake certain work and then are unable to complete it, learners who present their teachers with regular requests for revisions, or learners who find that the resources they had assumed would be available for the successful completion of the contract have suddenly been denied.

It is just as important that learners be prepared for the shock of being asked to take control over aspects of their learning. Particularly in institutions where other departments and program areas conform to a more traditional mode, learners will often find it unsettling, inconvenient, and annoying to be asked to work as self-directed learning partners in some kind of negotiated learning project. Notwithstanding the fact that learners may ultimately express satisfaction with this experience, initially, at least, there may be substantial resistance. It is crucial, then, that learners be eased into this mode through an induction course, and faculty must make explicit from the outset the rationale behind the adoption of these techniques. In the Teachers College AEGIS program, for example, new cohorts of participants attend a weekend orientation to self-directed doctoral study; they are asked to provide evidence of their self-directed learning capabilities both in the admission interview and in their written application; and they are sent the AEGIS mission statement emphasizing self-directedness before starting the program. Moreover, they are eased into this mode over two semesters; it is not until the end of their first year of study that they are asked to negotiate the assignments for their courses through a series of learning contracts.

Peer Learning Groups. Almost without exception those who have been involved in introducing self-directed learning techniques into formal institutions report that, far from being involved in an isolated, single-minded pursuit of individualized objectives, self-directed learners rely heavily on peer learning groups for support, information exchange, stimulus through new ideas, and locating relevant resources. As with the research into self-directed learning in informal settings, those involved in this activity place a premium on membership in a peer learning network. Faculty, therefore, must encourage learners to form such groups as soon as feasible. In the Teachers College AEGIS program this begins at the first weekend orientation, where learners are encouraged to group into regional clusters as a prelude to forming local support groups.

Time Commitment. Altering a program to incorporate self-directed learning principles requires an adjustment on the part of faculty, learners, and administrators concerning the amounts of time that can realistically be expected of all concerned to result in productive and personally significant learning. It is much more economic of time to rely on institutionally prescribed curricula, delivered through lectures and tested in examinations. Any departure from this requires learners and teachers to engage in an extended exploration of curricular concerns, diagnosis and explication of felt (by the learner) and prescribed (by the educator) needs, and negotiation of a mutually agreeable learning plan. Faculty engaged in developing programs in which self-directed learning techniques are to be applied must ensure that senior administrators at their institutions are aware and supportive of these altered time requirements. This has enormous implications for promotion and reappointment of faculty, since the institutions concerned will have to be willing to give less weight to the traditional criterion for career advancement (scholarly publishing). Otherwise, faculty working within self-directed programs in these traditional institutions may find themselves hoist on the petard of their own enthusiasm. The time spent in assisting learners to conceive, negotiate, execute, and evaluate individualized learning contracts is time that cannot be devoted to the more traditional scholarly and publishing activities. Unless administrators recognize the successful conduct of self-directed learning formats as a criterion of career advancement, faculty will be penalized for their commitment to helping learners become self-directed at the expense of time for research, scholarly pursuits, and publishing.

Perceived Benefits. Despite the initial frustration, ambiguity, and resentment felt by learners who are asked to depart from their normal pattern of teacher dependence and to take control over aspects of their learning, the majority of learners and facilitators end up approving the introduction of techniques of self-directed learning. This is perhaps particularly so for learners who speak of the "liberating" aspects of being told that their judgments concerning appropriate learning activities are as valid as those of their instructors. They see their learning as more personally significant when they have a personal investment in its organization and conduct and when it is explicitly and deliberately grounded in their own concerns and circumstances.

Individual and Institution: Some Conflicts

In many formal educational institutions, in training and human resource development schemes run within business and industry, in community action projects, in medical, health, and nursing education, and in cultural institutions such as libraries and museums, educators are explicitly putting into practice what they believe to be self-directed learning principles. The rationale most frequently cited for these practices is that of placing control over learning in the hands of learners. It is claimed that learners will be able to exercise autonomous control over their learning through the alteration of programs to conform to these principles. Such a claim is revolutionary in its substance and implications. It is also unsubstantiated by empirical experience. In all the case studies of self-directed learning that we have discussed, there is a tension evident between the institution's mandate to produce qualified or technically competent persons according to some external criterion and the individuals' own attempts to prescribe for themselves what they wish to learn. This has been vividly manifest in my own attempt to practice self-directed learning within the context of the Teachers College AEGIS program, as well as in my earlier attempts to encourage self-directed learning among community members in England (Brookfield, 1985a). Time and again, learners have squarely confronted me with the uncomfortable and unsettling reality that by my suggesting alternatives to what they proposed, or in my challenging the validity of certain learning paths they chose to pursue, I was thereby acting in educational bad faith and contradicting the principles of effective facilitation.

In the terms in which it is stated, this criticism is entirely valid. But to facilitate self-directed learning by ceding control for defining learning goals entirely to learners, with the facilitator serving purely as a resource person, does not allow the educator an active, initiating, constructivist role in the educational process. Recall that in Chapter Three self-directed learning was defined as an internal change in the consciousness of the adult after he or she has engaged in a critical analysis of a range of alternative possibilities, some of which might have been conceived by that person, others of which were probably suggested by the educator.

It is important, therefore, for those involved in facilitating self-directed learning to clarify that this activity requires the facilitator to challenge the learner, place before him or her alternative possibilities, and suggest action options that might initially be met with suspicion or some other form of resistance by the learner. Much of the frustration felt by adults who are told that they will be working as self-directed learners must come from this ambiguity concerning the form that self-directed learning activities are supposed to take. Faculty, tutors, instructors, and facilitators must be open and honest with learners concerning the constraints, limitations, and contradictions inherent in working in a self-directed mode within an educational institution that is established for purposes of public certification and accreditation. Unless learners are told that self-directed learning does not mean that they are free to pursue any and every activity in whatever way they choose but that it involves an active, interventionist role on the part of the facilitator, then those learners can legitimately claim that the facilitator is contradicting the spirit and principles of self-directed learning when he or she challenges the value or appropriateness of an activity proposed by a learner.

It is more honest, and much simpler, to acknowledge that self-directed learning activities, like other forms of teaching-learning, will inevitably assume a transactional character and that both facilitators and learners will find themselves actively engaged. It may be that these educational encounters place a much greater emphasis on encouraging learners to be the originators of learning activities that they themselves will conduct and that the format for these encounters will most commonly be that of a dyadic interaction between facilitator and learner, but it is still an interactional encounter. Apart from activities undertaken by adults entirely outside formal educational institutions, and without the benefit of contact with fellow learners, no self-directed learning activity can avoid this interactional dimension.

As in all interactional encounters, tensions will frequently arise when the expectations of those involved do not match. There is likely to be a constant tension between the learner's preference and the institution's mandate. This tension is implicitly acknowledged in the almost universal adoption of learning contracts as the chief mediatory mechanism through which self-directed learning is conceived and planned. Use of a contract implies a process of negotiation between parties of contrasting and sometimes conflicting preferences. If this interactional, negotiating stance is made explicit to learners as they enter institutionally sponsored programs of self-directed learning, then those learners will feel less betrayed when facilitators challenge or suggest alternatives to their wishes.

It is also important to recognize that advocating self-directed learning is, in institutional terms, a highly political act. Granting control to learners is not something that can easily be done within institutional limits. Faculty cannot engage in limited empowerment of learners; indeed, limited empowerment is a self-negating concept. It is contradictory to empower learners within spheres of action that have been previously defined by the educator. The act of taking control over learning is one that will, at various times, entail challenges to prevailing institutional forms. It will inevitably involve learners in setting aside various aspects of institutionally prescribed curricula and operational procedures and criticizing them for their irrelevance, autocratic nature, or perpetuation of inequity. To urge that learners become self-directed and then to complain that these same learners are rejecting institutionally approved curricula or that they are adopting alternative programs and methods is highly inconsistent. Attempting to limit the exercise of learner control to institutionally convenient activities, while at the same time claiming to be engaged in practicing fully autonomous self-directed learning, is a contradiction in terms.

In all the aforementioned case studies, the idea of fully empowering learners to take control over the evaluative standards by which professional competence is ascertained, or encouraging them to dismiss faculty whom they find unhelpful, elitist, or ideologically distasteful, is very far from the minds of those urging the use of self-direction. And yet it is precisely this kind of challenge to prevailing institutional forms and mores that is the logical outcome and manifestation of programs in which learners are urged to become fully self-directed. As Heaney's (1983) account of the Universidad Popular in Chicago illustrates, "A fatal contradiction is embedded in any attempt to undertake liberatory education within the confines of estab-

lished educational bureaucracies. To the extent that such efforts succeed, they fail'' (p. 62). The same comment might be
applied to self-directed learning; hence, when learners attempt
to take full control over the formats, curricula, and evaluative
criteria governing their learning within formal educational institutions, they are likely, sooner or later, to come into direct confrontation with the managers of those institutions.

The variety and form of these confrontations, and the
compromises that sometimes result, have been documented by
Cunningham (1982). Discussing Knowles's (1975) concept of
self-directed learning, she asks, "To what extent can learners be
in charge of goal setting, methodological choice, and evaluation
when traditional institutions maintain ultimate control of these
functions?" (p. 82). Cunningham argues that the learner is often
granted an illusion of power in terms of self-directedness but
that the institutional forms, procedures, and criteria generally
prevail. In contrast to Heaney's (1983) criticism of the incorpo-
ration of adult education principles into established educational
institutions, and the blurring of the proactive role of the learner
he sees resulting from this, Cunningham takes a more pragmatic
view. She maintains that when philosophy consistently and consciously informs educational practice, adult educators have to
realize that their philosophies are competing with other philosophies and conceptions of appropriate practice. She writes that
"in the area of practice the educator must negotiate philosophy.
Choices are made as to what can be deleted or altered with the
least damage to the intended outcomes. It is not problematic
that inconsistencies occur when a thoughtfully conceived system of values is put into practice" (Cunningham, 1982, p. 85).

Facilitators choosing to work within existing educational
institutions that have as their rationale the certification and accreditation of learners according to institutionally set standards
must expect to encounter ambiguity, contradiction, and compromise in their efforts to promote self-directed learning. To
some, the price of compromise with institutional expectations
will be too great to pay, given the limited benefits that accrue
to learners when only a relatively small measure of self-directedness is introduced into programs. Others will continue to de-

velop a high tolerance for ambiguity and inhabit what has been called the limbo of the informal adult educator (Brookfield, 1983a). They will pay a price in their professional and personal lives for this activity, but they will draw sustenance from other educators who are dealing with the same contradictions and compromises. They will also experience the exhiliration and euphoria exhibited by those whose attempts to conceive, plan, and conduct their own learning result in significant changes in their self-esteem and an increased sense of their self-worth and individual capacity. As one account of a professional adult educator working from within an established educational institution to support the self-directed learning of adults maintains, "The tale is not one primarily of overwork, however, or of acting on the defensive against predatory budget pruners. Attempts to help adult learners make their lives more personally meaningful tell a tale of pleasure and satisfaction. The expressions of genuine appreciation offered by adults for whom my efforts produced some kind of joy in learning more than compensated for the institutional neglect" (Brookfield, 1985a, p. 84).

⁓ 5 ⁓

Andragogy

Alternative Interpretations and Applications

The concept of andragogy can be interpreted in several ways. To some it is an empirical descriptor of adult learning styles, to others it is a conceptual anchor from which a set of appropriately "adult" teaching behaviors can be derived, and to still others it serves as an exhortatory, prescriptive rallying cry. This last group seeks to combat what it sees as the use with adult learners of overly didactic modes of teaching and program planning, such as those commonly found in school-based, child education.

Andragogy is also now, for many educators and trainers of adults, a badge of identity. Such individuals frequently describe themselves as "andragogues," declare that their practice exemplifies andragogical principles, and believe that the concept represents a professionally accurate summary of the unique characteristics of adult education practice. Cross (1981) notes that andragogy has been much more successful than most theories in gaining the attention of practitioners, and she credits Knowles with sparking debate on educators' assumptions regarding adult learning processes and with "setting forth a plan for critique and test in an otherwise barren field" (p. 225).

Some of these critiques will be considered presently. For the moment, it is important to note that at the time of writing, this concept is the single most popular idea in the education and training of adults, in part because and for the way in which it grants to educators of adults a sense of their distinct professional identity. Indeed, Jarvis (1984) writes that the theory of andragogy has "acquired the status of an established doctrine in adult education, but without being grounded in sufficient empirical research to justify its dominant position" (p. 32).

The writer most closely associated with the term is Knowles. In tracing the conceptual and linguistic roots of the term, Knowles (1980, 1984) cites a number of Germanic, French-Canadian, and Yugoslavian sources. His correspondence with Merriam-Webster dictionaries reveals that Webster's can find no previous use of the term in English (Knowles, 1980). As I have recently pointed out (Brookfield, 1984a), however, the first use of the term was that of Eduard Lindeman, who undertook (with Martha Anderson) an interpretative translation of a number of writings about the folk high school system in Germany. In their monograph *Education Through Experience,* Anderson and Lindeman (1927) declared andragogy to be "the true method of adult learning" (p. 3) and viewed the attainment of adulthood as marked by a growing awareness of self and by a readiness to make existential choices. The adult learning process was regarded as "an effort toward self-mastery" (p. 3).

Andragogy is described by Knowles (1980), however, as "simply another model of assumptions about learners to be used alongside the pedagogical model of assumptions" (p. 43). He does not present andragogy as an empirically based theory of learning painstakingly derived from a series of experiments resulting in generalizations of increasing levels of sophistication, abstraction, and applicability. And, in fact, the concept should be treated exactly for what Knowles claims it to be—a set of assumptions. Attempts to erect a massive theoretical edifice concerning the nature of adult learning on the foundations of a set of empirically unproved assumptions are misconceived.

The four assumptions of andragogy (already familiar, no doubt, to many readers of this book) are as follows (Knowles, 1980, pp. 43–44):

1. Adults both desire and enact a tendency toward self-directedness as they mature, though they may be dependent in certain situations.
2. Adults' experiences are a rich resource for learning. Adults learn more effectively through experiential techniques of education such as discussion or problem-solving.
3. Adults are aware of specific learning needs generated by real life tasks or problems. Adult education programs, therefore, should be organized around 'life application' categories and sequenced according to learners' readiness to learn.
4. Adults are competency based learners in that they wish to apply newly acquired skills or knowledge to their immediate circumstances. Adults are, therefore, "performance-centered" in their orientation to learning.

At the conceptual core of andragogy is the first of these characteristics, that is, the idea that the attainment of adulthood is concomitant on adults' coming to perceive themselves as self-directing individuals. This self-concept of a self-directing personality is founded in the adult's assumption of such social roles as worker, spouse, parent, and citizen. Knowles declares that "the psychological definition of adulthood is the point at which individuals perceive themselves to be essentially self-directing" (p. 46). He believes, however, that this tendency to self-directedness is not generally transferred to educational settings by adults. The task of the facilitator of learning, therefore, is to create an educational program and setting in which adult students can develop their latent self-directed learning skills.

There is some confusion, however, as to whether or not self-direction is being presented as an empirically verifiable indicator of adulthood. In other words, to what extent does the attainment of a certain chronological age mark an automatic transition from a dependent to an independent self-concept and to the exhibition of self-directed behaviors? Knowles has declared andragogy to be an assumption, and it might be best for us to view self-directedness as a prescriptively based concept. This would mean that we could stipulate that the attainment of adulthood (in the sense of maturity) can only be considered to have occurred if and when an individual behaves in a self-directed manner. In this approach, self-directedness would not be considered an empirically innate characteristic of adulthood, since many adults pursue lives in which self-directed behaviors are noticeably absent. Their attainment of a certain chronological age is most emphatically *not* accompanied by the exhibition of self-directedness. However, to describe those adults who do exhibit such behaviors, we would use the term *mature*. Adult education would then become education devoted to the nurturing of the prescribed characteristics of adult (in the sense of mature) behaviors. This is a much more complicated notion than that of adult education as the imparting of skills and knowledge to individuals who have attained a certain chronological age. "Adult" education would become that education concerned with the enhancement of the prescriptively desired conditions of adulthood.

In his critique of andragogy Elias (1979) points out that Erikson and Piaget both found elements of self-directedness in children's learning. But my own concern is less with the putative presence of self-directedness in children than with the visible lack of self-directedness (in terms of individual autonomy) discernible in many cultures. Thus, Freire's ideas are premised on the assumption that many Third World adults inhabit a culture of silence in which alternatives to their accepted circumstances are never presented, generated, or contemplated. Such adults belong to the intellectual equivalent of the culture of poverty outlined by Lewis (1961). When we contemplate totalitarian regimes, whether of the left or right, we find that self-directedness, as manifested in a desire and ability continuously to recreate the circumstances of one's own existence, is mark-

edly absent from the lives of most subjects living under such regimes. Indeed, were self-directedness an empirically undeniable
aspect of adulthood, then the continued existence of a totalitarian regime would be inconceivable. If adults were innately
self-directed in the sense of having an undeniable drive toward
autonomy, then they would be impelled by this drive to challenge such regimes and to create alternatives through which
they could express their independence.

There are also many who believe that even adults in contemporary democracies lack self-directedness. The Frankfurt
School of social critics, for example, documented the fear of
freedom characteristic of those living in twentieth-century
democratic, industrial societies. According to Fromm (1942),
the unwillingness of individuals to confront the fact of their
separateness and to embrace their aloneness as the precondition of productive relationships resulted in a flight into political
dogmas and religious creeds. Hence, the rise of Fascist regimes
and of totalitarian Communist societies.

There are good grounds, therefore, for maintaining that
self-directedness—that is, autonomous control over aspects of
work life, personal relationships, societal structures, and educational pursuits—is an empirical rarity. A review of cultures
throughout the world reveals that most social structures are
rigid and hierarchical and that they place a primacy on the sub-
jugation of individual options. This is not altogether surprising,
however, since most people appear to accept the security provided by the apparent stability of such structures. Indeed, in the
last century Durkheim ([1897] 1952) identified the dissolution
of normative codes and behaviors as the cause of an increase in
suicide, mental breakdown, and other pathological symptoms.
It was not uncommon for individuals presented with the realization that there were no divinely ordained, objective givens in
terms of immutable values or fixed moral codes to become neu-
rotic. The logical outcome of his reasoning is that societies that
provide options for the continual redefinition of self and personal change are unhealthy societies.

We must conclude, therefore, that while self-directedness
is a desirable condition of human existence it is seldom found in

any abundance. Its rarity, however, in no sense weakens the view that the enhancement of self-directedness is the proper purpose of education; instead, it provides a compelling reason why educators should pursue this end with unflagging zeal.

Is Andragogy a Proven Theory?

Recent critiques by Day and Baskett (1982), Pratt (1984), and Hartree (1984) have helped to clarify the extent to which andragogy can be considered an empirically accurate construct, a verifiable theory of adult learning, or a philosophically based prescriptive concept. Pratt argues that the concept is essentially prescriptive in that it specifies desirable learner roles and instructional characteristics. He criticizes the "dangerously subtle" (p. 149) use of language involved in moving from a philosophically based concept to an apparently empirically valid theory of adult learning held to apply across variations in context, goals, subject matter, and types of learners.

The potential for confusing an essentially prescriptive concept with an apparently descriptive model is also identified by Hartree (1984), who believes that the assumptions underlying andragogical theory are shaky and that it is unclear whether andragogy is to become a theory of teaching, a theory of adult learning, or a collection of practice injunctions. She allies herself with McKenzie (1977) in seeing andragogy as an essentially philosophical construct that has come to prescribe elements of "good" practice in the field. To Day and Baskett andragogy should be understood not as a theory of adult learning but as "an educational ideology rooted in an inquiry-based learning and teaching paradigm" (1982, p. 150).

That andragogy has come to be viewed by professional educators as a set of practice injunctions is supported by the work of Suanmali (1981). Adapting the charter for andragogy outlined by Mezirow (1981), Suanmali developed the already-mentioned API that was scrutinized by 147 members of the Commission of Professors of Adult Education. These professors exhibited a remarkably high level of agreement concerning the importance of andragogical practice in facilitating self-directed adult learning. Thus, while Hartree (1984) argued that the internal conceptual contradictions and ambiguities of andragogy meant that adult education was still "a discipline in search of a theory" (p. 209). Suanmali reached a more optimistic conclusion. To her, the study indicated "a consensus regarding the major concepts used in the andragogical process" and suggested that "despite various perspectives among adult educators there exists a unique body of knowledge in the field of adult education" (1981, p. 149). We can say, then, that the concept of andragogy is one that has great emotional appeal to those involved in facilitating adult learning. It is learner centered; it suggests all kinds of humanistically desirable and democratic practices; and it separates educators and trainers of adults from their counterparts in childhood, secondary, and higher education.

But the criticisms raised by Elias (1979), Day and Baskett (1982), Houle (1972), Pratt (1984), and Hartree (1984) suggest that we should consider very carefully whether or not we wish to adopt the badge of andragogue as equivalent to that of educator and trainer of adults. Pratt (1984) warns of the danger of "ideological andragogues" (p. 152) who elevate what are prescriptive injunctions into unchallangeable, empirically based generalizations. In their different ways, Pratt, Cross, Hartree, and Jarvis all warn of the danger that an uncritically accepted, academic orthodoxy may emerge in the field of adult learning. This orthodoxy, stated briefly, takes the andragogical injunction that adults are self-directed as its starting point. From this apparently empirically verifiable principle, it derives a set of practice injunctions for facilitators of self-directed learning projects. Because adults are seen as naturally self-directing, there is no need for us to teach them anything. As facilitators, we become resource persons whose function is to assist adult learners to execute the learning efforts they have designed for themselves.

As noted throughout this book, this orthodoxy is appealing and comforting to many educators. It provides a sense of professional identity in that it makes clear distinctions between the characteristics of adult learners and those of child learners.

It is also comforting because it removes from the facilitator the need to make difficult, value-based choices concerning curricula and appropriate educational programs. Adult learning is seen as a wholly joyous experience, a flowering of latent potential. There is no sense that significant, personally meaningful learning might involve painful reassessments of the self or the confrontation of uncomfortable psychological, familial, or political realities. It will be argued at points throughout this book, however, that facilitators are professionally bound not always to take learners' expressions of learning wants and needs as the sole criteria for all curriculum development and instructional design. At times facilitators will be called upon to prompt adults to confront painful facts and realities about their personal and work lives and about the social structures in which those lives are rooted. To take learners' definitions of need as always determining appropriate practice is to cast the facilitator as a technician within a consumer mode. It is to remove from the facilitator all professional judgment and to turn him or her into a "knee-jerk" satisfier of consumer needs. Education thus becomes one giant department store in which facilitators are providers of whatever learners (consumers) believe will make them happy.

There are many instances when educational and training programs are of necessity, and quite legitimately, established to meet expressed and articulated learner needs. It would be a foolish programmer who steadfastly refused to take into account learners' definitions of need when deciding which programs to sponsor and which topics to explore. Not only would such a program probably fail in strictly financial terms, it would also contradict one of the central tenets of effective facilitation, that of building curricula, methods, and evaluative criteria on learners' expressed concerns. For a facilitator completely to ignore learner needs and expressions of preference is arrogant and unrealistic. But it is just as misguided for a facilitator to completely repress his or her own ideas concerning worthwhile curricula or effective methods and to allow learners complete control over these.

The point is that facilitating learning is a transactional encounter in which learner desires and educator priorities will inevitably interact and influence each other. In most educational programs there will be some curricular areas and programmatic activities that represent a direct response to the expressed needs of learners, others that reflect the educator's view of what ought to be minimally present in any education or training program. If the balance between learners' concerns and expressed needs and facilitators' contributions in curricular and methodological spheres is too greatly disturbed, we are likely to see a tilting to one or another extreme. When this happens, the program will either become an educational supermarket, where customers are served with whatever curricular whim takes their fancy at a particular time, or it will offer narrowly focused, elitist courses and activities and attract learners whose preferences and prejudices match those of the programmer.

To what extent, then, can facilitators derive from the concept of andragogy a set of well-grounded principles of good practice? Much as with any concept that purports to account for real life happenings, it contains some elements that have relevance and accuracy and some elements that must be viewed with scepticism. The characterization of adult learners as moving inexorably toward self-direction has already been discussed at length, and some criticisms of the cultural- and class-specific nature of that idea have been advanced. The second assumption of andragogy as set forth by Knowles (1980)—that adults possess a reservoir of experiences that affect how they perceive the world and that represent an important source of material for curriculum development and learning activities—seems well grounded. To me, it is this second assumption of andragogy that can arguably lay claim to be viewed as a "given" in the literature of adult learning. Indeed, the development of critical reflection on experiences, along with the collaborative interpretation and exchange of such experiences, is proposed throughout this book as one of the most significant forms of adult learning in which individuals can engage.

It is aspects of the final two assumptions of andragogy— that educational programs should be organized around life-application sequences and that learning experiences should be organized around competency development categories—that need to be scrutinized very carefully regarding their general applicability. These two assumptions can easily lead to a technological interpretation of learning that is highly reductionist. Underlying these tenets is a view of learning that could lead practitioners to equate the sum total of adult learning with instrumental learning; that is, learning how to perform at an improved level of competence in some predefined skill domain. This behavioristically inclined, competency-based view of learning can lead practitioners to neglect the complexity and multifaceted nature of learning. It may cause them to neglect, for example, the reflective domain of learning that accounts for most significant personal learning. It underestimates the large amount of learning undertaken by adults for its innate fascination and for the joy and fulfillment it provides. The research of Brookfield (1980), Thiel (1984), and Danis and Tremblay (1985) all demonstrate how much of adults' most joyful and personally meaningful learning is undertaken with no specific goal in mind. It is unrelated to life tasks and instead represents a means by which adults can define themselves. Houle (1961) described these adults as "learning oriented," in that they were continually inquiring into new knowledge and skill domains, whether or not these were related to some immediate life application. In this writer's own research into independent learners who had become recognized as experts in a particular field, this approach to learning was pithily summarized by one of them in the following way: "It's like breathing, a part of my life. I can only see it getting wider, not narrower. It's just a continuous thing that gets bigger and bigger seemingly" (Brookfield, 1981a, p. 20).

Three attempts to use the concept of andragogy as a guide to constructing a model of effective educational practice for use with adults are represented in the work of Ingalls (1973), Godbey (1978), and the Nottingham Andragogy Group (1983). Ingalls (1973) outlines a series of exercises and techniques designed to help staff trainers in social service agencies apply the concept to their work. In andragogy workshops for the training of trainers, Godbey offers his *Applied Andragogy*

(1978) manual as an aid to "satisfying praxis" (p. 12) and provides advice on how a mix of methods can be used in accordance with andragogical principles.

The Nottingham Andragogy Group (1983) expresses dissatisfaction with some aspects of Knowles's conceptualization of andragogy and redefines it as an attempt to assist adults to become the originators of their own thinking and feeling. It relates the concepts and methods of Freire to andragogical principles and offers a set of assumptions regarding andragogy that differ somewhat from those of Knowles. To the Nottingham group, andragogy regards adults as social beings, products of history and culture; that is, adults are contextually located. In adulthood individuals acquire the capacity to think creatively and critically by integrating affective and cognitive dimensions of learning in group and individual settings. An andragogical approach is one in which adults are encouraged to think critically rather than to accept others' thinking. To this extent, the Nottingham group's reinterpretation of andragogy as the development of critical awareness is very close to the mode of facilitating learning presented in this book.

In its discussion of methods the Nottingham group includes directive and expository modes such as lectures, films, T-groups, and programmed instruction but stipulates that the procedures, curricula, and evaluative criteria be collaboratively determined. The group does admit, however, that what it labels the discovery method would be used more extensively as the group gained confidence. Twelve salient features are identified as essential to the andragogic process: a nonprescriptive attitude, issue-centered curricula, problem posing, praxis, continuous negotiation, shared responsibility for learning, valuing process, dialogue, equality, openness, mutual respect, and integrated thinking and learning. The group even goes so far as to offer six stages of andragogic course structure, and it describes andragogical procedures in recruitment, publicity, and course development.

The evaluative procedures discussed by the Nottingham group are of particular interest. The group readily acknowledges the importance of evaluation but admits that the subjectivity of the phenomenon to be evaluated—the development of

critical awareness—poses a major difficulty where the application of traditional criteria are concerned. Four areas are open to
evaluation, however, all of them concerned with aspects of
praxis. Changing relationships among group members can be
charted through examining the style and content of verbal exchanges. The sharing of power and responsibility for managing
the group process can be observed. Individuals can reflect on
their developing feelings of control over learning. Finally, all
group members can reflect on the ever changing nature of the
group's progress. Evaluation thus becomes but one aspect of the
continuous negotiation and appraisal already identified as a
salient feature of andragogy. It is both collaborative and formative. The group declares that evaluation "must be an integral
and continuous activity within each stage of the andragogic process and should involve all participants equally" (Nottingham
Andragogy Group, 1983, p. 45). This is one of the very few
documented attempts to develop an evaluative framework
grounded in and responsive to identified features of the adult
education enterprise. It will be considered further in Chapter
Eleven.

Andragogy in Practice: Case Studies

Given the popularity of the concept with practitioners
noted by Cross (1981), many contemporary educators and
trainers are probably consciously adopting andragogical principles in their work. This likelihood is reinforced by the already
mentioned research of Pearson (1980) and Douglass (1982), in
which collaborative approaches to organizing teaching and
learning activities were associated with previous training in
adult education. In a recent work on this topic, Knowles and
Associates (1984) identify seven components of andragogical
practice that they feel are replicable in a variety of programs in
almost every kind of institution throughout the world (pp.
14-18):

- Facilitators must establish a physical and psychological climate conducive to learning. This is
  achieved physically by circular seating arrange-

ments and psychologically by creating a climate of mutual respect among all participants, by emphasizing collaborative modes of learning, by establishing an atmosphere of mutual trust, by offering to be supportive, and by emphasizing that learning is pleasant. Such a caring, respectful, helping, and accepting climate is said by Knowles to be "a climate of humanness" (1984, p. 17).

- Facilitators must involve learners in mutual planning of methods and curricular directions. People will make firm commitments to activities in which they feel they have played a participatory, contributory role.
- Facilitators must involve participants in diagnosing their own learning needs.
- Facilitators must encourage learners to formulate their own learning objectives.
- Facilitators must encourage learners to identify resources and to devise strategies for using such resources to accomplish their objectives.
- Facilitators must help learners to carry out their learning plans.
- Facilitators must involve learners in evaluating their learning, principally through the use of qualitative evaluative modes.

Examples of initiatives in which educators have claimed to apply these principles are available in a wide variety of fields, including counseling, HRD in business and industry, and higher education and professional education.

Counseling. Petersen, Adkins, Scott, and Tzuk (1981) conducted an experiment in andragogical counseling at Concordia University in Montreal by establishing a workshop for adult undergraduate students at the university. The organizers adopted the problem-centered orientation to work that Knowles argues is endemic to adult learning. In a series of workshop sessions, facilitators served as models of problem solvers and employed role playing to illustrate applications of the problem-solving process. Participants reportedly participated in group analyses, team presentations, case studies, and small-group discussions of how they engaged in problem identification, how they gathered resources, and how they generated alternative courses of action. They also discussed their decision-making processes and their evaluation efforts. On the basis of a problem-solving inventory and self-reports, the sponsors concluded that the workshop changed individuals' attitudes about their problem-solving ability. Participants reported increased self-confidence regarding their ability to undertake problem solving and said they considered more information and were better able to evaluate consequences during decision making. The authors concluded that "problem-solving training seems to be a viable and attractive approach to designing adult counseling based on life-span development and andragogical principles" (p. 162).

HRD in Business and Industry. Claims for the adoption of andragogical principles for training in business and industry are found in Ingalls (1973), Knowles and Associates (1984), Knowles (1984), Daloisio and Firestone (1983), Thorne and Marshall (1976), Margolis (1984), Fabian and Mink (1984), Lloyds Bank of California (1984), Sullivan (1984), Green (1984), and Sinclair and Skerman (1984). Ingalls (1973) discusses how to apply andragogy in management and administration, how to build andragogical training support systems in organizations, and how to conduct a trainer's workshop in andragogy. This workshop, an effort to train trainers, was pilot tested with U.S. Department of Health, Education, and Welfare employees across the United States and crystallized into a workshop for thirty-five to forty participants that used a small-group format with groups of eight to ten individuals. The salient features of these workshops are as follows:

• Climate setting is achieved by beginning workshops with a social hour, by using the first session for participants to interview each other in pairs, then in fours, and by then requiring groups of four to combine into groups of eight (family groups) in which all participants outline their expectations for the workshop. Each of these family groups is then asked to come up with a group name that summarizes its shared intentions and identity and to perform a short skit to introduce itself to the other three groups.

- Participants' involvement in diagnosing their learning needs is achieved by asking the same groups to record on flip charts a list of members' interests. These are then hung on the walls to serve as benchmarks to be referred to during the coming weeks.
- Participants' translation of needs into objectives is achieved by asking the groups to realign their members into design groups. The workshop director presents to the whole workshop the steps of andragogy, trying to tie expressed needs to these steps and then asking workshop participants to express (through a show of hands) their interest in each of these steps. As people select their areas, they are assured that they can either change groups during the workshop or opt for independent study. Design groups (D-groups) are then formed; their task is to design an exercise that will be presented to the whole workshop at the end of the week. This exercise is to deal with the particular andragogical process area chosen by that group's members. D-group members have the chance to meet again in their family groups in the early stages of the workshop in order to compare their experiences of working in D-groups.
- Participants' continuous and active involvement in learning activities is ensured by their engagement in D-group design of workshop-wide activities on the andragogical process, which are due for presentation on the last day. In observations of these groups' past activities, Ingalls records that "the implementation phase was characterized by great enthusiasm, humor, and energy in the total community" and that "the level of involvement was intense and absorbing as [the] tension built up over four days was released in creative activity" (1973, p. 123).
- Participatory evaluation occurs on the last day of the workshop and has been reported to be highly subjective but very

favorable. Even in workshops with residual conflict, Ingalls claimed that there was general approval of the experiential learning format.

In his own application of andragogy to human resource development, Knowles (1984) argues that when learning tasks are complicated (as in learning to become a more effective manager), humanistic theories of learning and the use of self-directed learning projects are appropriate. In human resource development activities within firms, factories, businesses, and organizations generally, Knowles offers the following practice injunctions concerning the introduction of andragogical principles:

- *Climate setting.* An atmosphere of "adultness" within organizations can be fostered by granting the personnel department a central role in the organizational system and by using interlinked work groups, or project task forces, somewhat along the lines of quality circles. Additionally, those organizations in which HRD is granted high status, is treated financially as a capital investment (and not as an operating cost), and in which participants in HRD programs receive job emoluments will raise participants' expectations and motivation for learning.
- *Creating a mechanism for mutual planning.* HRD programs should have planning councils or task forces that possess executive power and in which responsibilities are shared.
- *Diagnosing learning needs.* Knowles explicitly admits that "there are 'givens' in every situation—such as minimal organizational requirements and that we have to live with them" (1984, p. 124). Within the framework of these constraints, however, he urges the use of self-assessment techniques so that employees can use tools and procedures supplied by the educator to make judgments concerning their own levels of performance.
- *Formulating program objectives.* Learners within organizations should be able to formulate objectives as part of the training process and should have the freedom to change and renegotiate these as the training program progresses.

- *Designing learning activities.* Entrants into training programs should participate in learning-to-learn orientations in which they collaboratively explore the resources available to them in other training group members.
- *Conducting learning.* Knowles urges that organizational developers concentrate their energies on teaching human resource developers to become familiar with andragogical principles.
- *Evaluating the program.* Knowles sees the Kirkpatrick hierarchy of evaluation (discussed in Chapter Eleven) as the most relevant to andragogical evaluation. To the four stages of this hierarchy is added a stage in which learners are encouraged to reexamine their ideas concerning desired competencies. This repetition of the diagnosis stage, in which learners become critically aware of the accuracy of their self-diagnosed learning needs, is somewhat similar to Argyris's (1982) notion of double-loop learning. Knowles advocates qualitative modes of evaluation in which the perceptions of participants concerning their activities and the system within which they work are the focus of the evaluation. He sees these as well suited to andragogical evaluation within organizational human resource development.

A number of organizations claim to use all or some of these principles in their training activities. The Westinghouse Executive Forum (Knowles, 1984) is a training program for new general managers in which some andragogical principles are adopted. Six task forces of managers meet to explore how training exercises that deal with the six areas of functional performance required of general managers might be best used. The findings of these six task forces determine the basic curriculum for the resultant workshops. Four assumptions are proposed as undergirding all management training efforts for new general managers. First, participants in the courses will by definition be high achievers, experienced decision makers, and self-starters. Second, each individual participant will have greater experience than others in certain specific areas. Third, each participant will need strengthening in certain areas not required by others. And, finally, most useful to participants will be a supportive environment and resources that will help them assess their needs and plan a program of continuing self-development.

The curriculum of these training workshops is built around the competencies identified by the six task forces, and Westinghouse managers serve as role models in terms of attitudes, values, philosophy, and sense of priorities. General managers are involved in determining course content, making presentations, and participating in the program. Knowles describes how the corporation devised a series of learning unit modules in four areas of competency development and notes that 100 Westinghouse executives attended an orientation seminar designed to help them perform as resource people for self-directed learning. The actual training exercises include an orientation to the course in which the assumptions of the course are made clear and participants are split into small groups for group-building exercises, content units that use such techniques as group discussions, small-group exercises, case problems, role playing, games, and other experiential learning approaches, and the construction by each participant of a personal development plan to be followed during the unit. On the final day of the workshops participants review their personal development plans and arrange times and places to meet for follow-up clinics. Evaluative reports of participants' activities after they have returned to the workplace emphasize their use of participatory decision making in the workplace, their increased willingness to delegate authority, and their generation of a variety of self-directed learning projects. Also claimed is a change in corporate culture regarding training activities: "There have been several reports, too, of evidence of a better understanding by management of the role and process of training—and increased support of it" (Knowles, 1984, p. 209).

Sullivan (1984) has described how Commercial Union Automation Services, a Boston-based insurance company, established an education center to help its employees learn data-processing procedures in a self-directed way. The center uses self-programmed instruction courses, audiocassettes, courses, and workshops, and managers undergo a training session in understanding self-directed learning and individualized needs assessments. Employees are told when they first attend the education center that "if you are able to carry out your functions competently as a result of the training, then your manager will recognize this and consider it in growth appraisals. If you fail to take advantage of the resources offered, then you will not become competent, not progress, and probably not be with us in the future" (p. 75). The threat to these learners (not that thinly veiled) that they will be sacked if they fail to learn is in obvious contradiction to the principles of effective facilitation mentioned earlier in this book. The fear of losing one's livelihood is, of course, a very effective motivator for prompting an adult to acquire a particular qualification, undergo a training course, or acquire a new skill. However, the collaborative peer learning mode emphasized so strongly as endemic to andragogy will be particularly difficult, if not impossible, to achieve if employees are told that those who learn will be rewarded and those who do not learn will be fired. It is also evident that the criteria used to judge a good training exercise are closely tied to work productivity and leave little room for the learner to acquire critical awareness and self-directed capacities or to explore a range of alternative behaviors, concepts, and feelings.

Higher Education and Professional Education. In a course that I currently offer on "Adult Education for Social Action," an attempt is deliberately made to inject some collaborative, participatory elements into a graduate adult education activity. The course opens with the construction of an inventory of participants' learning needs in the field of social action, and group members then assign themselves to small planning groups that work on class activities for those sessions in which their topic will be explored. The pass-fail option is the chief grading mechanism used, and participants submit self-assessment portfolios at the end of the course. Learning contracts are used to determine the format of the chief paper required for the course.

During the first two evenings, participants clarify their interests in adult education for social action, identify their learning needs in this area, and list the previous experiences they have had in the field and the resources they can bring to the group. These individual interests, needs, and resources are synthesized and published for the whole group, and the third session is devoted to negotiating, as a group, the provisional allocation of time for the rest of the semester. At this session participants also sign up for membership in planning groups for each of the topic areas that they have determined will be explored in the course. These small groups have complete responsibility for managing the sessions, and the role of the faculty member is that of consultant on planning and resource person. Hence, if requested, I can supply supplementary readings, react to role plays, simulations, or case studies that the groups are considering using, and suggest outside speakers and other resources that might be useful to them. Sometimes the groups use me, sometimes they do not. My help is available, but groups are not penalized if they choose not to consult me.

Groups choose to use a variety of participatory techniques—role plays, films, simulations, case studies, debates—and time is allowed for these groups to meet during class. My role is to create a climate in which participatory learning can take place and then to act as resource person in the manner indicated. A climate for participatory learning is created partly by my personal conduct (trying to be open, friendly, self-deprecating, and humorous) and partly by honoring the commitment to cede control for planning sessions to course members. There is no point in declaring that the course will be participatory and then subtly hinting at what I feel ought to be favored directions. I indicate my biases whenever possible but follow such statements with repeated assurances that those course members who have conflicting biases will not be punished for them.

Learners' achievements are assessed through two mechanisms. First, all participants complete a "participant self-assessment portfolio" that documents their involvement in, and contribution to, the course activities. These portfolios include examples of resources individuals have located for their groups, accounts of tasks they have carried out for the benefit of their planning groups, descriptions of their roles in group exercises, and accounts of their participation in class discussions. As faculty person, I undertake to complete my own assessment of each participant's contribution on a "participant involvement" form that is given to him or her at the end of the class. On the basis of these two data sources, a grade is awarded for the 30 percent of the course assessed through class participation.

For the remaining 70 percent of the course grade, participants complete a negotiated term paper. The paper is provisionally agreed on by the fifth meeting of the class, after negotiations between faculty member and participants, and is handed in by the tenth meeting. Papers are generally returned to participants with further questions and comments to which they are asked to respond. In this way writing papers becomes a continuing dialogue between learners and facilitator. If they are enrolled on a pass-fail basis, then they are awarded an incomplete grade if the work needs further revision; the incomplete is removed once the paper has been resubmitted. The negotiated term paper is on any topic the learner wishes to pursue, provided that its relevance to adult education for social action can be demonstrated. A modified learning contract is used whereby participants submit early in the course a statement of what they intend to explore in their paper. This statement comprises a provisional title for the paper, a full statement of its overall purpose, a description of the specific focus of the paper, an outline of the chief resources to be used, and a description of the evaluative criteria participants will apply in judging the worth of their papers. The completed paper is expected to include a self-assessment section in which participants judge the worth of their efforts and the extent to which their criteria of accomplishment have been met.

For those course members who are unfamiliar with the content area of the course, a number of possible options for papers are presented, including case studies, analyses of thinkers' ideas, program designs, and explorations of particular issues. It is emphasized repeatedly that these are simply fallback positions. It is clearly unrealistic, however, to assume that all participants will be able to identify on their own a topic related to adult education for social action.

Particularly revealing in the participants' evaluative comments on this experience is their frustration with my downplaying of the traditional, didactic instructional role. In the evaluations of the spring 1985 course on "Adult Education for Social Action," for example, typical comments under the category of "What could be improved?" were as follows:

> "Some additional input from instructor could provide insights into issues."
> "More chance to hear Stephen's thoughts on a number of important issues."
> "Reduce the amount of time listening to group reports and increase S. B.'s involvement."
> "Question a bit the relevance and value of self-assessment and participation portfolio. You be the judge."
> "A little more comment on student's oral presentations."
> "More readings, more intervention needed by instructor."
> "More sharing of instructor's knowledge and experiences in form of a lecture."

Two interpretations might be made of these comments. The first is that course members wished me as facilitator to be more challenging and confrontational and less accepting of their contributions; in other words, to perform as a role model of the critical facilitator. But this first interpretation seems to me overly charitable. My own belief is that participants were uncomfortable with being required to assume a degree of responsibility for designing their curriculum, negotiating their assessed piece of work, and judging the worth of their efforts. In both the self-assessment of their own negotiated papers and in the participant portfolio that they were asked to organize and submit, course members were visibly disturbed by the prospect of taking responsibility for generating the criteria by which their efforts were to be judged.

According to andragogical tenets, this, strictly speaking, should not happen. Instead, the adult's tendency toward an independent self-concept should ensure that participants experience this requirement to assume some control as a liberating activity, freeing them from the shackles of a didactic, authoritarian form of education. That this is most definitely not always the case illustrates just how effectively facilitators and participants have been socialized into the traditional forms of education. Facilitators who attempt to encourage collaborative modes in which a genuine effort is made to prompt learners to take control over their learning run the very real risk of being perceived by those learners either as unwilling to undertake their pedagogic responsibilities in a fully professional manner or as refusing to inform learners of the real rules of the game. According to this latter interpretation, facilitators make a show of encouraging collaborative control among members of the learning group, while in reality keeping covert the "real," "true," or "official" criteria by which learners' efforts are to be judged. Faced with these reactions and interpretations from participants, it is not surprising if facilitators revert quickly and easily to more traditional instructional roles. It is much easier, after all, simply to pose questions to which learners are supposed to supply the missing, correct answers. It takes a great deal of willpower, together with a strongly felt and well-articulated rationale for the critical facilitation role, not to succumb when a group visits upon a facilitator the identity of resident expert and fount of wisdom.

Andragogical approaches are now commonly found in higher education settings, particularly where adults comprise a large majority of the student body. To this extent we do not need to advocate their introduction, since this seems already to have been accomplished. It is equally obvious, however, that considerable work is still needed to prepare faculty for working in this mode, to gain institutional support and recognition of those who use such approaches, and to discover how best to initiate learners into this mode of working. Many adults return to the world of education anticipating that their higher educational experiences will parallel those of their elementary and secondary education. For them to be asked to assume a collaborative role with a previously unquestioned authority figure or to share responsibility for identifying learning needs and planning learning can be an extremely intimidating and anxiety-provoking experience. Some attempts to ease the transition from passive to collaborative modes are discussed in the "Return to

Study," "New Opportunities," and "Fresh Horizons" programs described in Brookfield (1981d).

Community Action Learning Groups

What have been characterized as andragogical approaches are at the heart of many community action initiatives, particularly if andragogy is reconceptualized in the manner of the Nottingham Andragogy Group's (1983) integration of Freirean principles with andragogical tenets. Although andragogy has been principally associated with classroom, student-centered exercises, it is evident that many of the assumptions underlying community development, community action, and participatory research are similar to those informing andragogy. Central to the idea of andragogy are four features that are also at the heart of community action initiatives: (1) Adults work best when they are in collaborative groups; (2) success comes when adults begin to exert control over their personal and social environments and thus begin to see themselves not as controlled by external and unchallengeable forces, but as initiating, proactive beings capable of creating their personal and social worlds rather than simply living passively within them; (3) the focus of activities is determined by adults' perceptions of relevance rather than being externally imposed; and (4) adults learn best when they engage in action, reflection, further action, and further reflection.

These principles bear a strong resemblance to the injunctions of participatory researchers (Hall, 1979; Conchelos and Kassam, 1981) to turn research exercises into activities in which the distinctions between researchers and subjects are blurred, to select topics for research according to subjects' definitions of importance, and to make data collection and data analysis a collaborative exercise in which all are involved in exploring and interpreting the multiple realities of subjects' perceptions. In participatory research, projects are conceived, designed, and conducted by the community for the benefit of all community members. Along with the projects labeled "participatory research" in the Third World (Hall, 1975) and with rural native communities, Latin American immigrant groups, and native people in Toronto (Participatory Research Group, 1980), most other community action initiatives have adopted the collaborative and critically proactive approaches also espoused by participatory researchers. These principles and practices inform the efforts of activists such as Coady, Horton, and Lovett (Brookfield, 1983a); taken together, initiatives such as these comprise an impressive body of community action projects.

In participatory research projects, as well as in community action efforts, certain principles of practice are repeatedly found:

- The medium of learning and action is the small group.
- Essential to the success of efforts is the development of collaborative solidarity among group members. This does not mean that dissension is silenced or divergence stifled; rather, group members are able to accept conflict, secure in the knowledge that their peers regard their continued presence in the group as vital to its success.
- The focus of the group's actions is determined after full discussion of participants' needs and full negotiation of all needs, including those of any formal "educators" present.
- As adults undertake the actions they have collaboratively agreed on, they develop an awareness of their collective power. This awareness is also felt when these adults renegotiate aspects of their personal, occupational, and recreational lives.
- A successful initiative is one in which action and analysis alternate. Concentrating solely on action allows no time for the group to check its progress or alter previously agreed-upon objectives. But if the members of the group engage solely in analysis, they will never come to recognize their individual and collective power. Empowerment is impossible without alternating action and reflection.

The literature available on community action projects is voluminous, and its extent has been indicated elsewhere (Brookfield, 1983a) and will be discussed in Chapter Seven. The connections between andragogy and community problem solving have been explored by McCullough (1978), and the centrality of collaborative process to community education is discussed at length by Minzey and LeTarte (1979) and Warden (1979). For purposes of the present discussion, however, a project known personally to me will be examined.

The material in this section is drawn chiefly from a recent study of attempts by four church-related organizations to use group-related methods to assist adults to reflect critically on their life circumstances and to become knowledgeable and confident enough to engage in collective social action. The study, conducted by Tan (1984), identified three kinds of learning—skills or task-related learning, critical learning, and interactional learning—that seem to correspond closely to Habermas's (1971) three modes of knowing (the technical, the emancipatory, and the communicative). Two of the four initiatives reviewed by Tan are particularly illuminating—the South Bronx People for Change program (SBPFC) and the St. Mary's Reflection Groups.

The SBPFC program was established in 1979 as a nonsectarian, nonprofit community organization designed to assist the residents of the South Bronx organize for community action that would help them reclaim their rapidly deteriorating neighborhoods. It employs six full-time staff members who organize and train parish neighborhood groups. They focus on developing community leadership skills among residents, assisting groups in their attempts to hold public meetings on community issues, and prompting social analysis among adults in the area. These staff members, who are mostly black or Hispanic residents of the South Bronx, work with approximately 100 active participants and 400 less active participants. Central to the SBPFC program are three practice elements:

- *Community organizing skills.* These include how to survey the neighborhood, how to identify problems, and how to develop strategies for action (raising consciousness, organizing forums for community animators, organizing teams and task forces, and understanding lobbyist and advocacy tactics).
- *Social and power analysis.* This includes prompting residents

to consider their individual and collective circumstances in a critical light. It is similar to Freire's idea of assisting people to engage in problem posing. When people begin to ask critical questions concerning the focuses of decision-making power in their neighborhoods, they also begin to speculate on the possibility of assuming this power themselves.

• *Integrating faith and social action.* The rationale for critical analysis and for people to assume the responsibility for changing their neighborhoods, work conditions, and personal lives is examined as an implementation of Judeo-Christian traditions and teachings.

In this triad of purposes we find the praxis of acting, reflecting, and placing new action within an elaborated rationale that is highly characteristic of both andragogy and some community animation activities. The nurturing of critical awareness and analytical skills takes place within the context of developing particular community-organizing techniques, and both of these activities, in turn, are interpreted according to an overall rationale (in this case a religious one). The SBPFC program does not hold leadership courses as such; rather it uses events such as the annual unity conference, reflection days, organizing meetings, and community research projects as means for developing individuals' skills.

When a particular project is conceived by a local group, staff from the SBPFC will involve themselves in organizing meetings, workshops, and training sessions. All group sessions for whatever purpose begin with a climate-setting exercise, perhaps the saying of a prayer, the reading of a scriptural passage, or a brief period of reflection. The chief learning method used in training sessions is that of discussion. Large-scale social issues such as "housing" are reconceptualized within the realm of learners' experiences, so that the group might consider the situation of one particular building. Participants are encouraged to ask questions such as, "Who owns the building?" "Why would the owner allow it to be burned down?" Through storytelling, drawings, role playing, and discussion, participants explore their relationships to each other and to other community residents.

At each stage of a group's activities, its members allocate time for evaluative reflection on their accomplishments and activities. One example of significant community mobilization was the gathering of 3,000 signatures on a petition having to do with crime and police action by a committee formed after the unity conference of 1982. Accompanied by 100 people, the committee met with the police commissioner of New York at police headquarters, and three commitments were obtained from the commissioner on policing activities. In another instance, a petition drive solicited support from local politicians, and the formation of a committee to meet with representatives of the Metropolitan Transportation Authority resulted in that authority's committing $30,000 to reopen an elevated subway station that had been gutted by fire. Finally, the unity conference of 1983 identified voter registration as a key issue, and this led to the organization of block parties, church bazaars, and church services at which new voters were registered. Groups are now regularly engaged in organizing tenants, pressing for apartment repairs and the restoration of electricity and water, and securing more frequent and visible police patrols.

As Tan points out, however, "The greatest and most encouraging outcome for the staff is to witness the changes taking place in people's self-worth, confidence, and having the sense of being able to act and articulate their concerns" (1984, p. 61). He quotes one of the SBPFC organizers on the excitement arising from this process: "All these people, just getting up and really being, you know, prophets, . . . being participants in some sort of action, demanding for their rights, demanding for answers to their problems, . . . and really speaking out on injustices. . . . I mean, it's most exciting for me. I mean, sometimes I get the chills just seeing them up there" (Tan, 1984, p. 61).

In the second of the initiatives, this one on the Lower East Side, the participants involved are more concerned with analysis and reflection than with securing changes in the fabric of their community. Since 1977 parishioners of St. Mary's

Church have met in small groups in one another's homes to reflect on the religious, social, and political circumstances of their lives. Called Reflection Groups, their intent is to make participants more aware of their life situation through discussions and reflections on social justice issues.

The groups are led by "animadores," that is, volunteer lay leaders who are given special training by staff members working for the church. Animadores attend weekly training sessions and meet weekly with groups for discussion. Tan's description of training sessions for animadores is as follows: "The Friday training and reflection sessions for the 'animadores' are held in the church hall or conference room. If there are any newcomers they are introduced to the group and are made to feel welcome by an applause. Whenever there are more than 20 participants the group is divided into smaller groups of around 10 people, to enhance . . . interaction. The sitting arrangement is in circular formation. The overall atmosphere and informality is being created so that the participants could enjoy the session" (1984, p. 123).

The techniques for training animadores to function as facilitators appear strongly andragogical. At the heart of these techniques is the use of role play exercises that confront animadores with the typical situations that they will meet as discussion leaders. Animadores learn how to involve hesitant group members in collaborative discussion, how to deal with overly talkative participants, how to encourage silent members, and how to react to expressions of hostility or indifference through role playing these situations and having their behaviors observed and then analyzed by other group members. For those times when animadores are facilitating groups that contain large numbers of illiterates, the use of pictures to stimulate discussion and analysis is explored.

A central function of the Reflection Groups at St. Mary's is to commit members to take some form of action, usually on a personal level, in between group meetings. Participants' experiences with these actions then become the starting point for discussion at the next meeting. Whenever these groups join together to participate in marches and demonstrations or to petition public authorities, they meet afterward to evaluate their activities, to consider the chief problems they encountered, and to try to generate solutions. Tan quotes examples of groups that pressed the New York City Community Relations program to move cars from a children's playground and gathered information about a proposed co-op building before holding a protest meeting at city hall that prevented these plans from being implemented.

The SBPFC program and the St. Mary's Reflection Groups exemplify andragogical principles of practice in the following ways:

- Learners' concerns—the problems and circumstances in their neighborhoods—are the focus of the curricula of the groups.
- Active, participatory learning modes are used throughout; role playing, case studies, group discussions, and simulations are particularly common.
- Action alternates with reflection in an andragogical praxis; groups are oriented toward making changes in the lives of their members and securing changes in their neighborhoods, and at the same time they are encouraged to engage in analysis and reflection.
- The overall rationale of the activities of these groups is to develop among participants an awareness of their capacities for critical awareness, for changing their personal and social lives, and for becoming self-directed, empowered adults.

Conclusion

The concept of andragogy has undoubtedly become influential in determining how practitioners conceive of the effective facilitation of adult learning, and any discussion of this practice must therefore take the concept seriously. What has become clear from the case studies discussed, however, is that the concept is not at all as fixed or immutable as some practitioners might believe. In their different ways Lindeman, Knowles, and the Nottingham Andragogy Group have all offered markedly divergent interpretations of the concept. Lindeman seems to suggest that the concept refers to the way in which educators might assist adults to confront the anxiety that accompanies the transition to adulthood. Knowles offers a set of injunctions concerning how facilitators might base their practice on some assumptions regarding adult learning processes. The Nottingham Andragogy Group views andragogy as a process through which adults become critically aware of the assumptions they have uncritically accepted as governing their conduct and through which they attempt to re-create their lives.

This conceptual confusion, much like that surrounding attempts to develop a theory of adult learning, is likely to persist for some considerable time. Indeed, the divergence of interpretations of andragogy may be thought of as reflecting the diversity of philosophies and ideological orientations held by those who see themselves as educators and trainers of adults. The notion of collaboration between participants in an adult learning group, along with the idea that teaching-learning is a transactional encounter, seem to be at the core of the concept; and that is why effective techniques of facilitation are often so close to andragogical injunctions. As Davenport and Davenport (1984) point out, however, andragogy has been variously classified as a theory of adult education, a theory of adult learning, a theory of the technology of adult learning, a method of adult education, a technique of adult education, and a set of assumptions. The term is most closely associated with Knowles's ideas, and critiques of andragogy—for example, those of Houle (1972), Elias (1979), Day and Baskett (1982), Pratt (1984), and Hartree (1984)—have generally focused their attention on discussions of Knowles's works. It is undeniable, however, that these critiques have paled into insignificance in comparison to the conceptual sway that andragogy now exercises in the minds of facilitators of adult learning.

In my view, which concurs with that expressed by Knowles (1980, p. 43), the concept is a set of assumptions concerning adult learning processes from which we can derive a number of injunctions concerning appropriate teaching methods. In terms of the principles of effective practice identified at the outset of this book, it is clear that the role of past experience in affecting how adults interpret their current personal and social worlds is central both to andragogy and to effective facilitation. It is also clear that the collaborative element is endemic both to andragogy and to effective facilitation.

On three counts, however, various extravagant interpretations have been made of Knowles's ideas. First, as Chapters Three and Four have noted, there has been a too ready acceptance of the idea that a drive toward self-directedness is an innate characteristic of adulthood, readily apparent in all teaching-learning transactions. Second, the notion that adult learning efforts are generally problem-centered sequences in which adults seek immediately applicable knowledge must also be questioned. In particular, the work of Brookfield (1980), Thiel (1984), and Danis and Tremblay (1985) on characteristics of successful self-directed learners has shown that some important adult learning is most emphatically *not* problem centered; rather it is often a free-flowing exploration of an area of knowledge undertaken for the innate fascination of that activity. Third, the idea that adults always seek immediate application of learning within competency development categories is also a doubtful one. In particular, some of the learning that adults themselves regard as being their most significant personal learning cannot be classified as the development of immediately applicable competencies. In adults' attempts to create meaning out of job change, divorce, bereavement, and the renegotiation of intimate relationships, just to give a few examples, we can see learning activities that have as their focus the development of self-awareness and self-insight rather than the development of performance-based competencies.

We should not conclude this discussion of andragogy without considering just how realistically andragogy can claim to be an approach to teaching adults grounded in unique features of adult learning and, hence, an approach to be sharply distinguished from pedagogy. It is my view that what are called pedagogy and andragogy are both appropriate, at different times and for different purposes, with children, adolescents, young adults, the middle aged, and the elderly. Such a belief was expressed by Knowles (1980, p. 43) who wrote of pedagogical and andragogical models that they "are probably most useful when seen not as dichotomous but rather as two ends of a spectrum, with a realistic assumption in a given situation falling in between the two ends." As anyone who has observed the activities of English primary schools (for children aged five to eleven) or who has read John Dewey on the education of children will realize, andragogical approaches that urge teachers to base curricula on learners' experiences and interests are nothing new in the educational field. Moreover, learning is far too complex an activity for anyone to say with any real confidence that a particular approach is always likely to produce the most effective results with a particular category of learners, irrespective of the form, focus, or nature of that learning. Learning can be instrumental, skill or knowledge oriented, or self-analytical and can occur (sometimes simultaneously) within psychomotor, cognitive, affective, or reflective domains. Once we realize that every learning group contains a configuration of idiosyncratic personalities, all with differing past experiences and current orientations, all at different levels of readiness for learning, and all possessing individually developed learning styles, we will become extremely wary of prescribing any standardized approach to facilitating learning. Neat practice injunctions (whether pedagogical or andragogical) are appealing for their apparent simplicity and replicability. The act of facilitating learning, however, is one that is sufficiently complex and challenging as to make us suspicious of any prepackaged collections of practice injunctions.

❧ 6 ❧

The Facilitator's Role
in Adult Learning

The concept of the facilitator of learning now exercises something of a conceptual stranglehold on our notions of correct educational practice, and to talk of the role of the teacher, or of teaching as a function, is unfashionable and distasteful to some educators of adults. Such talk calls to mind authoritarian classrooms, heavily didactic procedures, and overly directive instructors. Teaching is an activity inevitably associated by many with the world of elementary and secondary schooling; it conjures up images of an individual standing at the head of rows of desks and talking at a captive audience. Because educators and trainers of adults are usually at pains to contrast the emotionally congenial aspect of their practice with what they regard as the rigid and conformist nature of schooling, they frequently avoid using the term *teacher*. This is partly why the terms *facilitator* and *resource person* are in such favor.

As the previous chapters point out, however, it is all too easy to see the job of the facilitator as one concerned solely with assisting adults to meet those educational needs that they themselves perceive and express as meaningful and important. Educators who profess to be facilitators and not teachers are generally at pains to stress the democratic and student-centered nature of their practice. In their terms, facilitators do not direct; rather, they assist adults to attain a state of self-actualization or to become fully functioning persons. Similarly, a resource person is usually not seen as someone whose task is to

123

suggest alternatives, point up contradictions, draw attention to relationships of dependence, or prompt painful, critical scrutinies of assumptions, value frameworks, or behaviors. Instead, a resource person is often seen as someone who assists adults to locate individuals and material resources in order that they may complete learning efforts that they, as learners, have defined. This view emphasizes the primacy of the learner, grants a substantial measure of control to learners, and places learning directly in the context of learners' own experiences.

The problem with accepting this as the sum total of the educator's responsibility is that it assumes a high degree of self-knowledge and critical awareness on the part of adult learners. To act as a resource person to adults who are unaware of belief systems, bodies of knowledge, or behavioral possibilities other than those that they have uncritically assimilated since childhood is to condemn such adults to remaining within existing paradigms of thought and action. It is misconceived to talk of the self-directedness of learners who are unaware of alternative ways of thinking, perceiving, or behaving. Such learners can indeed express felt needs to educators, but such needs often will be perceived and articulated from within a narrow and constrained paradigm. The felt need of a drug addict is for greater, cheaper, and purer quantities of the chosen drug. The felt need of an insecure lover may be for greater and more uncritical amounts of approval from the partner. The felt need of the domineering parent may be to assert authority over children who are trying to express their independence.

In all these situations it is possible to detect what might be called "real" educational needs. The drug addict needs to be weaned away from physical and psychological dependency. The lover needs to develop a sense of separateness and inner strength. The parent needs to recognize the child as a separate and growing being. We call these real needs because each individual will become more fully adult if such needs are fulfilled. In this belief is contained the explicit judgment that some states of being are better than others.

As educators, then, we cannot always accept adults' definitions of needs as the operational criterion for our development of curriculum, design of programs, or evaluation of success. There are occasions when we may feel impelled to prompt adults to consider alternatives to their present ways of thinking and living. Adults caught within constrained relationships, unsatisfactory jobs, and closed political systems often cannot imagine other ways of conducting relationships, earning a living, or being a citizen. The task of the teacher of adults is to help them to realize that the bodies of knowledge, accepted truths, commonly held values, and customary behaviors comprising their worlds are contextual and culturally constructed. Through being prompted to analyze their own behaviors and to consider alternative ideas and values, adults can come to an awareness of the essential contingency of their worlds. Such an awareness is the necessary prelude to their taking action to alter their personal and collective circumstances.

The teacher of adults, then, is not always engaged in a warm and wholly satisfying attempt to assist adults in their innate drive to achieve self-actualization. Analyzing assumptions, challenging previously accepted and internalized beliefs and values, considering the validity of alternative behaviors or social forms—all these acts are at times uncomfortable and all involve pain. A facilitator who accepts adults' definitions of need can avoid this pain and be involved in an apparently creative, unthreatening, and satisfying encounter. But teaching involves presenting alternatives, questioning givens, and scrutinizing the self. The outcome of these activities may be a more satisfactory level of self-insight, but these experiences may induce pain and feelings of insecurity. As teachers, we are charged with not always accepting definitions of felt needs as our operating educational criteria. We are also charged with the imperative of assisting adults to contemplate alternatives, to come to see the world as malleable, to be critically reflective, and to perceive themselves as proactive beings.

This kind of teaching is to be sharply differentiated from that in which children are the learners. The pain and insecurity induced by a challenging of beliefs and behaviors can be more easily accepted in adulthood than in childhood. Children or adolescents may reject the notion of the world as contingent and malleable. They seek a degree of security and safety in their family structures and a degree of stability in their role models. It is in adulthood that the propensity for critical scrutiny exists, and it is in analyzing and reflecting upon the contingency of the world that adults realize their adulthood. Teaching that is centered on prompting an awareness of the contextuality and contingency of beliefs and behaviors is, therefore, a uniquely adult form of teaching.

It will often be the case, of course, that adult learners will react quite negatively to a teacher's attempts to make them more critically reflective. In such cases, teachers should respect the learner's individuality and remember that adult education is a collaborative, transactional encounter in which objectives, methods, and evaluation should be negotiated by all concerned. The danger arises when the teacher is unaware of any philosophical rationale underlying his or her activities, not when that rationale is contested by some learners. Teachers who are proselytizing ideologues are really not teachers at all; they measure their success solely by the extent to which learners come to think like them, not by the learner's development of a genuinely questioning and critical outlook. Deviation from the "party line" of the teacher's received truth is equated with intellectual incompetence.

Models for Teaching Adults

The teacher new to the education of adults will find no shortage of practical handbooks designed to help him or her work with adult classes. Typical of such handbooks are *How to Teach Adults* (Adult Education Association of the USA, 1955); *How Adults Can Learn More—Faster* (Warren, 1961); *Tested Techniques for Teachers of Adults* (National Association for Public Continuing and Adult Education, 1972); *When You're Teaching Adults* (National Association for Public Continuing and Adult Education, 1959); *The Second Treasury of Techniques for Teaching Adults* (Warren, 1970); *Guide to Teaching Techniques for Adult Classes* (Snyder and Ulmer, 1972); *You Can Be a Successful Teacher of Adults* (National Association for

Public Continuing and Adult Education, 1974); *Teaching Adults* (Dickinson, 1973); *Teaching Adults in Continuing Education* (Bock, 1979); *The Easy-to-Use Concise Teaching Handbook for Part-Time Non-Teachers* (Coren, 1983); and *How to Teach Adults* (Draves, 1984). These handbooks generally provide some brief elaboration of adult learners' characteristics and then proceed to cover the range of techniques that might be used in teaching adult classes. Other general references on methods of teaching adults, all of which ground pedagogic principles in a more extended analysis of research into the conditions of adult learning, are Stephens and Roderick (1971), Knox (1980), Bergevin, Morris, and Smith (1963), Bergevin, McKinley, and Smith (1964), and Robinson (1979). These analyses tend to emphasize two conditions for effective teaching: that the teaching-learning transaction be built upon adult learning patterns (Bradford, 1965) and that adult teachers have at their disposal a spectrum of styles (Leahy, 1977).

Educators of adults who have considered the concept of teaching tend to stress its pluralistic nature. Bryson (1936) urged that the teacher of adults entice students to engage in further learning, inculcate principles of rational skepticism, and take on the role of leader. In his discussion of inculcating a rational skepticism, Bryson comes close to the concept of facilitation advocated in the present work. Bryson advised teachers to assist adults "to stand firmly against the winds of doctrine" (p. 64) and declared that "a constant and stubborn effort to help those students who work with him to acquire a more alert attitude toward their already accepted and verbalized beliefs, and toward all new things offered them, is the hallmark of a fit teacher for grown men and women" (p. 65). As a consequence of encouraging such skepticism, however, the teacher was likely to encounter the dislike and ridicule of society and its leaders. Because rational skepticism served as a corrective to the simplistic solutions and propaganda offered by political leaders, teachers who encouraged this attitude would open themselves to public criticism.

Lawson (1983) and Barton (1964) have both offered analyses of teaching that emphasize its pluralistic nature. Barton proposes "ordered pluralism" as an action plan for teaching, and Lawson declares that there are numerous valid objectives, methods, and subjects in adult teaching. Apps (1979) identifies a range of possible teacher roles—trainer, conditioner, counselor, model, resource, guide—that can be performed in individual, group, or community settings. Ruddock (1980) recognizes eight major roles for teachers of adults—resource person, expositor, demonstrator, promulgator of values, taskmaster, assessor, helper, and group manager. Hostler (1982) and Lenz (1982) both view the teaching of adults as an art. In Hostler's words, teaching can never be reduced to a set of comprehensive rules that can be routinely applied in various situations. Miller (1964), however, protests against arbitrary use of this artistic metaphor to describe the teaching process. He argues that "no artist ever became successful without an enormous amount of rigorous training in his art and continual submission to very tough criticism from his peers and mentors" (p. 4).

However, to emphasize either the plurality of teaching methods or the essentially artistic nature of teaching is to obscure the central question of what should be the purpose of teaching. There may indeed be a plurality of methods available for the achievement of a particular goal, and the pursuit of that goal and the use of these methods may indeed require art. But this does not remove the necessity of developing a clear philosophical rationale to guide practice. If we are to say that teaching involves activities other than merely satisfying learners' declared needs and wants, then we must specify the criteria we have adopted to judge whether or not a particular activity is an instance of true, correct, or proper teaching of adults.

Learning Styles and Teacher Behaviors

Research into the teaching of adults has concentrated on four themes: (1) the awareness by teachers of adults of the need for a style of teaching different from that used with children, (2) the pedagogic implications that can be derived from analyses of adult learning theory, (3) the factors contributing to instructional effectiveness most commonly identified, and (4) learners' perceptions of the qualities of successful teachers. For example, Beder and Darkenwald (1982) surveyed 173 public school and college teachers who taught adults and preadults and recorded an awareness among teachers of the differing learning styles of these two groups. Adult learners were perceived as more motivated, serious, and self-directed than preadult students, and teachers were prone to adjust their teaching methods in response to this. They took account of adult learners' prior experiences and reduced the controlling and structuring behaviors used with preadults. These differences, however, were not large, and Beder and Darkenwald concluded that "they do not warrant the inference that classroom practices differ sharply as a function of age" (p. 153).

Gorham (1984) reported a similar perception of adult students as essentially different from preadults among the 115 university, community college, and public school teachers she surveyed. These individuals also claimed to be less directive and structured when teaching adults than when teaching preadults and to provide more emotional support to adult learners. In her follow-up analysis of 15 teachers whose classroom behaviors were observed, however, she did not find that these perceptions of the uniqueness of adult learners were reflected in altered teaching behaviors. For example, teachers of adults were as directive with these learners as with preadults, although the direction would take subtler forms. And while teachers were willing to make alterations in classroom management within a set paradigm of appropriate teaching behaviors, they were not willing to generate a new paradigm to govern their interactions with adults.

Discussions of the chief findings of adult learning theorists regarding characteristically adult styles of learning, and the implications of these for the teaching of adults, have been undertaken by Dubin and Okun (1973), Mackie (1981), Even (1982), and Moore (1982). Dubin and Okun's review could offer no conclusions regarding the appropriate teaching behaviors to be used with adults, since they could find no one theory of learning that seemed to possess a high level of explanatory power where adults' learning styles were concerned.

Mackie (1981), more optimistic regarding a possible synthesis of research, outlined ten pedagogic principles derived from a review of writings by behaviorist, cognitive, and personality theorists (these principles were also recognized by Williams, 1980, and used in his training of adult tutors for teaching roles): the learner must be motivated to learn, the learning format should allow for individual differences in ability and style, new learning should build on the learner's current knowledge and attitudes, learning should be reinforced, opportunities for practice should be available, the learner should be an active participant, material to be learned should be organized into manageable units, guidance should be given in developing new responses, new skills and knowledge should be generalizable, and the material to be learned should be meaningful to the learner (Mackie, 1981).

Even (1982) has drawn attention to the discrepancies that may arise when field independent teachers are working with field dependent learners (or vice versa). Since field independent learners do not require either a great deal of structure or a friendly and caring atmosphere, teachers who exhibit this style will not emphasize group process and will be unworried by a lack of clear structure in their teaching. But such an approach will be markedly unpalatable to certain field dependent learners. A review of the Adaptive Style Inventory constructed by Kolb (1980) and its relevance for adult teaching styles has been undertaken by Moore (1982). Moore matched the Kolb inventory with Brostrom's (1979) Training Style Inventory (TSI) and concluded that certain of the learning styles identified by Kolb called for certain of the teaching styles outlined by Brostrom. Hence, diverger learners were best suited to humanistic teaching styles, accommodators were best served by functionalist teachers, converger learners responded to a structuralist teaching style, and assimilators benefited most from a behaviorist teacher.

It is clear, then, as Dubin and Okun, Mackie, Even, and Moore all acknowledge, that a great deal more thought needs to be devoted to the question of appropriate teaching behaviors in groups containing adults with widely varying styles of learning. Universal prescriptions concerning *the* method that is applicable to all situations are not helpful and ignore the existence of multiability, multiethnic groups of learners who exhibit a broad diversity of learning styles.

The characteristics of successful teachers have occupied the attention of a number of researchers. Pratt (1979b, 1981) developed an instrument to measure appropriate adult instructional processes with 146 adult students in a range of settings (business, community colleges, and universities). Five clusters of valued characteristics deemed appropriate as role components for a teacher of adults were identified: developing adult-to-adult working relationships, developing understanding of and responsibility for instruction, dealing with closure and ending (summarizing learning accomplishments and indicating future learning), establishing role clarity and credibility, and guarding the contract (keeping instruction within the agreed boundaries). In a review of research on teacher effectiveness, Pratt (1981) deplored the simplistic search for qualities that all teachers should possess. Such a search is doomed to failure given the enormous complexity of adult learning and teaching interactions. Wilson (1979), however, devised a model that might be used to recognize the competencies necessary for successful performance of an adult teaching role. He proposed five broad categories of competence; thus, the teacher should be a content resource person, a learning guide, a program developer, an institutional representative, and in command of expressive competencies. According to Wilson, his model provides a theoretical base by which instructional competencies appropriate to adult learners can be identified.

The final cluster of research studies having to do with the teaching of adults—that of learners' perceptions of valued teacher behaviors—forms an interesting counterpoint to the research on instructor effectiveness just discussed. Solomon and Miller (1961) identified a number of variables of good teaching after interviews with teachers and a review of research. These variables were then used by Solomon, Bezdek, and Rosenberg (1963) to study twenty-four teachers of evening courses in American government whose behavior was recorded on tape, as well as by students and trained observers. Profiles of effectiveness were constructed, and these suggested that precision and clarity in presenting information, along with high teacher animation (generation of excitement, use of humor), were the qualities that contributed most to increases in factual knowledge, to growth in comprehensive understanding, and to high learner evaluations.

McKeachie (1970) reviewed the literature on psychological characteristics and instructional methods regarding adult learners and offered a number of broad conclusions. Sociable learners were found to perform better in discussion classes; field independent learners, not surprisingly, preferred modes of independent study; learners of high intelligence developed their critical thinking skills best when allowed to participate in classes, and highly motivated learners did well in independent study. Interestingly enough, however, independent study did not strengthen learner independence; it merely served to confirm that characteristic.

Three recent studies of adult teachers' styles have built upon these earlier studies and reviews to explore the connection between adults' learning styles and preferred teacher behaviors. In a recent administration of PALS, Conti (1984) measured teacher behavior in a collaborative teaching mode. The scale was administered to twenty-nine teachers in southern Texas who worked with General Educational Development (exam) (GED), ESL, and basic education students. GED students were found to learn more in a traditional teacher-centered environment, whereas basic education students and ESL learners responded better to participatory teaching practices and the development of a warm and supportive classroom environment. Zerges (1984) surveyed 248 continuing education students enrolled in business courses to explore the link between student personality type and valued instructor behaviors. These students rated, in order of importance, the following instructor behaviors as the most valued: competent knowledge of up-to-date materials, clear statement of expectations and objectives, sequential organization, and prompt and fair evaluation. The favored interpersonal qualities of instructors (responsiveness, animation, humor, friendliness) were regarded as less valuable than the behaviors already mentioned.

Finally, Schmidt (1984) investigated the learning styles of adult students returning to the University of Wisconsin at Madison. These adults were found to prefer working independently, though under teacher direction. They did not like competitive class activities, and they did not especially wish to develop warm social relations with their instructors or peers. They viewed course membership as providing an opportunity for reflecting on the relationship between theory and practice. Classroom encounters were seen as comfortable settings for the testing of new ideas and the challenging of the viewpoints of peers and teachers. A supportive social environment was not deemed to be particularly important.

Teaching Adults: Exemplary Practices

In view of the admonitions of the researchers just discussed to avoid characterizations of the "good" teacher, an attempt to outline exemplary practices in teaching adults may seem absurd. But characteristics of good teachers of adults are offered by a number of writers. Apps (1981) lists eight exemplary instructor characteristics derived from a review of humanistic psychology. Thus, exemplary instructors are concerned about learners, are knowledgeable in their subject, relate theory to practice and their field to other fields, appear confident, are open to different approaches, present an authentic personality in the class, are willing to go beyond class objectives, and are able to create a good atmosphere for learning.

Exemplary characteristics of teachers of adults offered by other writers are that they like people and act intelligently toward them; they are courteous, good humored, tactful, fair, energetic, articulate, imaginative, and adaptable (Stephens and Roderick, 1971). Heath (1980) profiles five role models of successful teachers of adults as measured by positive student evaluations. She does not offer a set of exemplary qualities held by all such teachers, but she does observe that the five teachers surveyed shared similar attitudes toward their work. All were said to possess great sensitivity, warmth, and genuine regard for their students. To Draves (1984) teachers of adults should love their subject, be desirous of sharing the intellectual joys that studying that subject brings, and be knowledgeable. He identifies general skills and talents that are necessary for good teaching and are replicable in different contexts. Good teachers should be good listeners, they should instill confidence in insecure learners, they should avoid punitive actions, they should establish a supportive learning climate, and they should use humor.

Despite the evident dangers of specifying too closely any general principles of method, a number of educators have been as ready to do this as others have been to offer sets of exemplary teaching skills. Although we may question the empirical validity of such claims, they do have the virtue of helping to concentrate teachers' minds on the rationale underlying their practices.

In his analysis of the types of interactions occurring within adult classes, Jensen (1963) outlined a total of twenty-nine guiding principles for adult instruction. He identified certain sociopsychological conditions for effective formal instruction; these centered chiefly on the need to establish a group climate that would encourage problem solving and task interactions. Jensen advised teachers to spark disagreement among group members as a way of discouraging patterns of dependency and to grant to adults' experiences a full measure of credibility. Hendrickson (1966) places a similar stress on collaborative patterns of teaching-learning in his specification of ten principles of good teaching. Among other things, such teaching recognizes the importance of emotional atmosphere to learning, it encourages involvement on the part of learners, it provides frequent evidence of success to learners, it uses adults as a prime teaching resource, and it takes into account factors of fatigue and motivation unique to adult learners. Finally, Apps (1981) offers eight exemplary teaching principles for teachers working with adults returning to college. Teachers are advised to know the biographies of their students, to use learners' experiences as class content, to integrate theory with practice, to provide a climate conducive to learning, to offer variety in format and technique, to provide feedback, to help learners acquire resources, and to be available to learners for out-of-class contacts.

Such advice as has been offered, then, is silent on the question of curriculum. Good adult teaching is generally seen as the ability to set a certain emotional climate, to use learners' experiences as educational resources, to provide plenty of evaluative information to students, and to encourage collaboration and participation. Jensen deals with the development of critical and analytic capacities, but he does not identify the curricular components for producing such abilities. Thus, process skills are strongly emphasized over command of any particular content area. The criteria of success regarding good teacher performances relate to techniques of effective group management rather than to the prompting of critical awareness on the part of learners.

Discussion Method Irreplaceable

It is to achieve this goal of encouraging adults to undertake intellectually challenging and personally precarious ventures in a nonthreatening setting that has caused teachers of adults to devote so much attention to the discussion method. A peer learning group can exhibit undesirable tendencies, such as the exclusion and silencing of deviant opinions, but it can also be a powerful support for adults who wish to experiment with ideas, opinions, and alternative interpretations and to test these out in the company of others engaged in a similar quest. As therapy groups of all kinds have illustrated, adults are prepared to admit to doubts, anxieties, and inadequacies, provided that they feel themselves to be in the presence of peers who will listen to their testimonies in a supportive, nonjudgmental manner.

It is also in the context of such groups that some of the most challenging and exciting personal adventures in learning occur. Groups can act not only as powerful motivators to, and reinforcers of, learning; they can also provide the occasion and setting for vigorous debate and exploration of vividly contrasting positions. There is a limit to the extent to which any individual can engage in self-scrutiny without the stimulus that fellow learners can supply. Lectures, demonstrations, independent study, and programmed learning are all useful techniques by means of which information can be assimilated and a grasp of fundamentals can be acquired. But it is when one's nascent, inchoate ideas and concepts are tested out in the company of others that a certain creative tension comes into play.

This creative tension can be inhibited, however, by economic factors. Emphasizing process to the total exclusion of either curricular content or a fundamental rationale is a position that few would explicitly advocate but into which it is all too easy to fall given the need to maintain high enrollment levels. Teachers may be so concerned to ensure that learners' experience of adult education is satisfying and pleasant that they downplay the more intellectually demanding and challenging aspects of a subject for fear of threatening learners to the point where they will leave the group. Adults will often be quite unwilling, for example, to consider the contextuality of their situations and to view their beliefs, behaviors, and values as culturally created and provisional. Such an activity can be personally threatening and disturbing, and teachers may well (with good reason) presume that adults are not prepared to pay to belong to a class in which they are challenged to examine their most fundamental beliefs.

Nevertheless, teachers of adults cannot simply function as process managers, resource persons, and technicians of learning. What teachers must strive to do, and what is perhaps the most difficult of all pedagogic balances to strike, is to prompt adults to consider alternatives and to encourage them to scrutinize their own values and behaviors, without making this scrutiny such a disturbing and personally threatening experience as to become a block to learning. There is no point in a teacher rigorously pursuing the critical examination of group members' dearly held beliefs, if that process is so anxiety producing for participants that they feel they must leave the group to protect their self-esteem.

Shor (1980) has identified a number of roles for the discussion leader—convener, facilitator, advocate for missing perspectives, adversary of oppressive behavior in class, lecturer, recorder, mediator, clearinghouse, and librarian. Drawing heavily on Freire's thought, Shor regards the teaching function as "an animation of consciousness" focused upon learners' "extraordinarily experiencing the ordinary" (p. 93). Critical teaching is seen as a way of assisting adults to escape from immersion in mass culture. The liberatory classroom becomes a "separate zone for consciousness change" (p. 99), with the ideal outcome being the "withering away of the teacher" (p. 100). The teacher assumes an oscillating stance, at times "provoking conceptual literacy in the critical study of a subject area" (p. 101), at other times retreating from discussion to allow the group members to come to their own points of critical consciousness. The overall function of the teacher is to provoke students' separation from mass culture and then to assist in a critically aware reentry into that culture.

Emphasis on the unique suitability of the discussion method for the development of adult learners' critical faculties recurs throughout the history of adult education. In an early handbook of adult education, Essert (1948) claimed that membership in a discussion group was a substitute for the spirit and form of the neighborly *gemeinschaft* community that had been lost in the process of urbanization. In the writings of Lindeman (1926, 1930) the discussion group is regarded as the pedagogic setting uniquely suited to adult education because it allows for collaborative reflection on the meaning of group members' experiences. Lindeman also believed (1945) that in the postwar era the neighborhood discussion group was essential for political literacy. Such groups provided the finest available medium for the discussion of controversial issues. They combatted propaganda, allowed for the development of flexible modes of thought, and encouraged the development of natural leadership.

In other countries the discussion method has been accorded a similar status as the adult education method par excellence. The Danish folk high schools, the Swedish study circles, and the Canadian Farm Forum experiment are all examples of mass educational initiatives that used the discussion method as their chief teaching medium. In Britain, the WEA and Extramural tutorial group (a noncredit, university-level class for adults) constitute a distinct tradition in adult education that still exerts considerable contemporary influence. Elsdon (1975) points out that discussion is the major tool used in the training of prospective educators of adults, and Paterson (1970b) notes that a declaration of the importance of discussion forms one of the chief articles of the catechism in which novices to liberal adult education are expected to verse themselves. Indeed, in practically every movement dear to the hearts of educators of adults the discussion group has constituted the methodological heart. The particular form of discussion, however, varies considerably in each of these initiatives. Hence, blithe declarations regarding the importance and value of discussion are meaningless, since they tell us nothing of the actual processes occurring in the groups concerned.

A review of discussion methods (Osinski, Ohliger, and McCarthy, 1972, p. 4) concludes that definitions of discussion are often static, arbitrary, trivial, replete with hidden agendas, and within the realm of fantasy. There does seem, however, to be a continuum of definitions of discussion characterized by the degree of teacher control exercised over content and process. At one end is an open, collaborative quest for meaning of the kind advocated by Lindeman (1930), Paterson (1970b), and Bridges (1979). At the other end is the idea of guided discussion, in which the direction of discussion is under control of the teacher (Bligh, 1972).

Two definitional features are central to most conceptualizations of discussion. First, discussion is seen as directed conversation on a topic of mutual interest (Brunner and others, 1959), as purposeful conversation and deliberation (Bergevin, Morris, and Smith, 1963), and as a conversation with a purpose (Brown, 1975). The second characteristic of discussion often mentioned is participation. Gulley (1965) declares that all or most members of a group must participate if there is to be a true discussion. Legge (1971) nominates as the first criterion of an ideal discussion that all members talk freely and easily.

Central to the notion of discussion are two features that may be either complementary or contradictory. Discussion sessions can be judged successful to the extent to which they pursue certain cognitive ends or to the extent to which all members offer verbal contributions of approximately equal length. In a critique of discussion behaviors (Brookfield, 1985b), I have examined the way in which discussion groups can become arenas of psychodynamic struggle and fields of emotional battle. Many adults were schooled in competitive settings in which the pursuit of knowledge was obscured by the quest for grades and examination success. It is hard for such individuals to accept openness of discourse and to tolerate diverse opinions. Since discussion sessions are invested with emotional significance, any disagreement may well be interpreted as a personal assault. Additionally, groups tend to place high value on cohesiveness and to exclude deviant opinions. But as Fawcett-Hill (1977) maintains, it is important that groups tolerate deviant opinions. Such divergence guards against intellectual stasis.

Bridges (1979) has specified certain epistemological underpinnings of discussion. All members (including leaders) should have respect for each other, and all should be skeptical of their own, as well as of others', authority. (This is close to Bryson's notion of rational skepticism as the desired outcome of adult teaching.) Bridges also prescribes a moral culture for group discussion; it includes six ethical principles that participants should accept as the tacit assumptions underlying their discourse: reasonableness (openness to divergent perspectives), peaceable orderliness, truthfulness, freedom, equality, and respect for persons. Discussions conforming to the epistemological principles and moral culture outlined by Bridges would be characterized by openness of content, membership, and learning outcomes. Participants would set aside their own prejudices to entertain imaginative speculation.

Paterson (1970b) proposes discussion as the educational activity par excellence. It is an educational end in itself, requiring no extrinsic justification. To Paterson, adults commit and discover their whole beings in the process of presenting for group consideration their interpretations of their experience. He writes that "to address others in discussion . . . is to bear witness to one's attempt to reconstruct one's experience meaningfully, and it is at the same time to invite others to share this reconstructed experience" (p. 37). In this way participation in open discussion becomes a characteristically human activity of the most intimate and fundamental kind. Since openness is an essential characteristic for discussion, the concept of guided discussion must be discarded. In Paterson's words, "True discussion cannot be directed, or even guided, for to attempt to do so is in effect to opt out of the discussion, to close one's consciousness to alternative interpretations of the phenomenon under discussion before these alternatives have ever been stated" (p. 47).

To participate in this authentic form of mutual address, in this collaborative search for meaning, requires personal courage and analytic ability of a high order. It requires adults to be willing to examine the cultural origins of many of their beliefs, to be aware of how many of the assumptions that inform their conduct have been acquired from external sources and authorities such as parents, schoolteachers, and peers, and hence to view their dearly held meaning systems as provisional and relative. In this sense to participate in discussion—in the collaborative externalization, exploration, and critical analysis of personally significant meaning systems—is to realize one's adulthood to its fullest extent.

Four conditions can be identified that, if they are met, are likely to increase the chance that productive discussions will occur. The first of these is for group members to devise an appropriate moral culture for group discussion. This requires the group to arrive at a set of procedural rules for achieving equity of participation. Second, discussion leaders can give some thought to the materials that are to form the substantive focus of group discussions. The questions to be discussed should not be too factual or too uncontroversial, and they should not be answerable in the course of preparatory reading by the group. Third, the leader should be well versed both in the subject matter to be covered during the discussion and in the principles of group dynamics. Only someone skilled at dealing with the problems caused by apparent isolates, pressures to silence deviants, and those adults who attempt to use the group as a means of bolstering their self-esteem can be said to be an effective discussion leader. Fourth, discussion participants should be prepared for discussion not only through the generation of a moral culture for discussion sessions but also through the development of reasoning skills (so that inconsistencies and ambiguities in argument can be detected) and the improvement of communication abilities (so that ideas can be accurately articulated). In providing a forum for the pursuit and realization of these reflective analytical skills, as well as in requiring participants to evolve a democratic, moral culture governing group discourse, the discussion method is uniquely suited to facilitating critical adult learning.

Although collaborative discussion is now seen as an effective mode of facilitating learning, the literature that deals with instructional methods is still based mainly on the work of Tyler (1949), and the task of teaching adults is frequently seen as a subcategory of the general task of program development. Teaching is relegated to step three or four in different models of program development, including those of Houle (1972), Knowles (1980), Verner (1964), Lauffer (1977), and Boyle (1981). In fact, teaching is generally not referred to as "teaching" at all, but rather as management of learning experiences, instructional management, or implementation of the instructional plan.

As will be argued further in Chapter Ten, however, this view is only one of a number of approaches to teaching adults. The Tylerian model of objectives-oriented program development in which learners acquire skills and knowledge specified in advance by the teacher and in which success is measured by learners' performance of predetermined behaviors is often constraining and overly restrictive. The model *does* have some utility, but chiefly in the area of psychomotor skill acquisition. Tyler developed his work to assist schoolchildren acquire specific, predetermined skills and knowledge of an unambiguous, technical kind. In some training contexts where it is a question of acquiring technical skills (in industrial or nursing settings, for example), the sequenced, objectives-oriented nature of the model is highly satisfactory.

The problem is that some facilitators of learning have

taken this model as the paradigm suitable for encouraging all kinds of adult learning. Much of the most significant adult learning, however, is of a nontechnical kind. It is concerned with the resolution of moral difficulties, with the development of self-insight, with acquiring the capacity to explore the world views of others, with reflection on experience, and with the evolution of personal ethical codes. One mode of teaching and learning highly suitable for these forms of learning is the discussion method. It is striking just how frequently the educational activities organized by adult learners themselves (rather than by professional educators) take this form.

For example, collaborative discussion is typically found in groups organized by single parents, the recently bereaved, divorcees, homosexuals, newly arrived immigrants, drug abusers, and feminists. These groups are composed of individuals who are seeking a reinforcement of their sense of self-worth. Their members are engaged in a redefinition of self and in a reinterpretation of their past actions and relationships from a newly realized psychological vantage point. They are also all seeking to set forth their experiences, to understand and explore others' experiences, and to heighten their self-awareness through this process of collaborative interpretation. The leadership of such groups is typically rotational. At different times, various individuals within these groups will take the responsibility for encouraging others to contribute to the discussion and will attempt some kind of analysis or interpretation of the experiences that have been voiced.

The adults in these groups are attempting to create new meaning systems. They are reinforcing each others' dormant, half-perceived feeling that there is some massive disjunction between their present ways of living and thinking, on the one hand, and the kind of existence they ideally envisage for themselves, on the other. At times these support and experience exchange groups transform themselves into activist groups that work to change oppressive external conditions. For some groups (such as feminist groups, homosexual support groups, and single-parent families) a common pattern will be a form of praxis in which analysis of common experiences alternates with public advocacy and demonstrations. The very act of participating in a public demonstration in support of gay rights or to demand changes in housing and welfare policies to benefit single parents will serve to strengthen and reinforce these adults' newly adopted and newly created identities. For groups of drug abusers, divorcees, newly arrived immigrants, or the recently bereaved, however, it will often be enough for members to meet regularly for support, for the presentation and analysis of typical problems, and for the gaining of practical assistance in negotiating the changed circumstances of their lives.

Teaching Outcomes

We have emphasized that the concept of facilitation should be broadened to include activities in which adults are encouraged to consider alternative ways of thinking and living and in which they are prompted to scrutinize critically the extent to which supposedly universal beliefs, values, and behaviors are in fact culturally constructed. But if we prompt adults to consider these questions, are we not really engaging in a form of amateur psychotherapy? Asking people to reflect on their experience, to consider the motivations underlying their actions, and to try to appreciate the way in which their behaviors are perceived by others sounds dangerously close to playing at therapist. This argument deserves to be taken seriously. There are many adults who suffer from clinically diagnosed conditions that range from schizophrenia to severe depression. For an educator to presume to treat them effectively is folly indeed.

There are, however, many adults who are troubled, frustrated with circumstances in their personal or occupational lives, insecure concerning their abilities, and seeking ways to develop more productive relationships with others. Such adults may be disturbed at certain aspects of their personal lives, but they are in no sense clinically "disturbed." There are very few readers of these words, I would venture, who are not disturbed at some aspect of their personal worlds or occupational lives, and it is precisely these adults who frequently form the clientele of adult classes. One of the great tragedies of contemporary life is the overprofessionalization of all aspects of human interaction. We are getting dangerously close to believing that we can engage in thoughtful self-reflection only if we are sanctioned by some professional to whom we pay a fee for the supervision of our self-reflection. Those who accept the argument that adults can undertake reflection on their past actions and current relationships only under the guidance of a skilled psychotherapist are doing nothing more than supporting the professional power and prestige of therapists.

One of the most valuable inquiries into methods of helping adults become critically reflective was initiated by Perry (1970) and pursued by Weathersby (1980), Weathersby and Tarule (1980), Boud (1981), and Cameron (1983). Instead of talking in a general way about the development in learners of critical awareness and the realization of the contextual, subjective aspects of the world, Perry sets forth nine intellectual stages, which he terms *positions*. These positions are not meant to be rigidly sequential, nor to be mutually contradictory. Additionally, they do not include all the intellectual orientations possible in adulthood since they are derived from a series of intensive interviews with undergraduate students at Harvard. They do provide a useful analytical structure, however, that can be applied to understanding the development of critical reflectivity in adults, without in any way presuming them to be inevitably followed in every case. Indeed, with his undergraduates Perry freely admits that students become frozen at different stages of passive detachment or dualist absolutism.

Put simply, Perry's nine positions represent a move from an initial dualist perspective in which the world is perceived as comprised of black and white, mutually exclusive polarities to one in which the individual has come to a realization of the contextuality and relativity of the world and has then gone on to make a conscious commitment to one of many possible identities. In their exploration of these ideas on ethical growth and intellectual development as they relate to adulthood, the Syracuse Rating Group (Cameron, 1983) has also distinguished nine stages in adults' intellectual and ethical development. The final stage of "developing commitments" is distinguished by an awareness of the effects that individual behaviors have on others and by a continuous search for new challenges. This search is undertaken with full knowledge that these challenges involve risks to one's self-esteem and that this final stage is never really "final" (in the sense that one achieves a static and unchanging life-style). In leading up to this final stage, adults typically pass through stages in which they begin to view knowledge as contextual and become able to take on the perspective of others. This recognition of the contingency of knowledge inevitably brings about an appreciation of the socially created nature of knowledge. Immediately prior to stage nine are those stages in which adults realize that only through making a commitment will a sense of individual meaning and responsibility for the creation of their personal worlds emerge.

As Boud (1981) has noted with regard to the Perry scheme, "It is [therefore] helpful for the teacher to have in mind that within the same class there will probably be students with radically different outlooks on what is taking place, who will be reacting in very different ways" (p. 31). An early application of the earlier stages of this framework to a sample of adult students at a community college identified dualist, multiplist, and relativist positions among the adults studied (Cameron, 1983). The study noted that faculty in community colleges typically teach content in the same manner, regardless of the intellectual development of class members, and that faculty need to be more flexible in their pedagogic roles to take account of the diversity of intellectual stages present in any class.

The Perry scheme represents an interesting area of future speculation for theorists of adult learning. Perry's contribution has been to posit an initial framework in which the transition from dualism to relativism to critically aware commitment has been clearly outlined. If these stages can be translated into specific outcomes, with sufficient flexibility of interpretation so that widely varying settings can be included, this might provide adult teachers with a means by which they could recognize the diversity of stages reached by different members of learning groups. Alternatively, and in a more inductive manner, the framework provides an analytical construct that one can apply to many different educational initiatives as a way of coming to understand the teaching-learning transactions occurring therein.

There is little doubt that didactic pedagogic procedures in which learners are viewed as receptive repositories eagerly awaiting the deposits of experts are not likely to result in the development of critically aware commitment as outlined by Perry. Rather than looking to concepts of teaching drawn from research on traditional teaching methods, therefore, it might be more fruitful to consult concepts and practices drawn from related fields such as community development or community action. The concept of the animateur (Kidd, 1971; Blondin, 1971) is one such idea, and UNESCO has explored the manner in which training schemes to develop animateurs might be established. At the very least, it is important to realize that between the authoritarian transmission of information to uncritically receptive automata and the nondirective, free-flowing realization of learner-defined activities lies a crucial facilitation role. Facilitators have to be as wary of supporting every inclination, preference, or demand of learners as they are of forcing these same learners to follow a lockstep sequence of previously prescribed educational activities. In both instances learners are liable to develop an uncritical stance toward their own personal and intellectual development; in the one case because their opinion is never challenged or questioned, in the other because they are given no choice or chance to voice an opinion. Either option denies the essentially transactional nature of teaching-learning, and both options pretend that challenge, creative confrontation, and (sometimes painful) self-scrutiny have no place in adult learning. Without these elements, learners may find their educational encounters initially comforting but they will sooner or later come to suspect that such encounters are not really educational at all. When this awareness finally dawns, the resultant withdrawal from participation will have the same significance and result from the same kind of frustration as that caused by the learner's being allowed no voice in the educational transaction.

❧ 7 ❧

Learning in Informal Settings

Adult learning takes place in a bewilderingly wide range of contexts. The central principles of effective facilitation discussed earlier, however, provide us with a conceptual basis for recognizing whether or not a group of adults is engaged in a fully transactional encounter, whatever the setting. We must now consider a number of these settings for adult learning and highlight the practice features that enable us to view these activities as educationally effective.

In a series of handbooks on adult learning issued in the United States (Ely, 1948; Knowles, 1960; Smith, Aker, and Kidd, 1970; Boone, Shearon, White, and Associates, 1980), in general foundations texts such as those of Darkenwald and Merriam (1982), Klevins (1982), and Jarvis (1983b), and in historical and contemporary reviews of practice such as those of Kelly (1970), Knowles (1977), Legge (1982), and Peterson and Associates (1979), the following are identified as settings, forms, or contexts for adult learning:

- women's education
- labor education
- adult basic education
- continuing professional education
- correctional education in prisons
- industrial training
- armed forces education
- health education
- community development
- mass media
- cooperative extension programs
- continuing education at universities
- voluntary organizations
- cultural institutions (libraries and museums)
- proprietary schools

- schools
- community colleges and colleges of further education
- workers' education
- self-directed learning

- correspondence colleges
- extension and extramural departments in universities
- adult education centers
- informal group learning

In addition to this (far from exhaustive) list of providing agencies, there are regularly identified in these same texts a number of special client groups or particular program areas:

- citizen education
- leisure education
- art and crafts
- parent education
- consumer education
- education for the handicapped
- community action

- education for the elderly
- intercultural education
- adult religious education
- human relations training
- educational brokering and counseling
- education for home and family life

To attempt a comprehensive survey of participation rates, programmatic offerings, and institutional contexts of these agencies, program areas, and special groups would be an encyclopedic enterprise well outside the scope of the present work. It would be useful at this point, however, to take a number of these settings and to cite instances of practice within them that exemplify the principles of effective facilitation as outlined earlier. In this chapter the emphasis is placed on exploring informal settings for learning such as learning networks, community action groups, and the range of noninstitutional settings in which self-directed learning takes place.

Self-Directed Learning

The decade of the 1970s, in the study of adult learning, was characterized by a plethora of research studies on self-directed learning and the popularization of the concept by Knowles (1975) and Tough (1967, 1978, 1979). We have had our attention as trainers and educators forced back onto the phenomenon of adult learning—how, when, and where adults learn—instead of concerning ourselves chiefly with the design of external instruction. There is now much less likelihood that educators will presume that valid and valuable adult learning can occur only in the presence of an accredited and professionally certified teacher. Knowles, Tough, and others have helped to dispel the false dichotomy whereby institutionally arranged learning is seen as rational, purposeful, and effective and self-directed learning in informal settings is viewed as serendipitous, ineffective, and of a lower order.

In the analysis of self-directed learning in Chapter Three the research findings in this area were carefully scrutinized. At this point it is enough to mention that self-directed learning— the attempts of adults to acquire skills, knowledge, and self-insight through educational experiences that they are responsible for arranging—has been studied in an enormous variety of adult learning populations. We have studies of college graduates (Tough, 1967, 1968), professional men (McCatty, 1973), pharmacists (Johns, 1974), teachers (Fair, 1973; Kelley, 1976; Strong, 1977; Miller, 1977), parish ministers (Allerton, 1974), college and university administrators (Benson, 1974), clergy (Morris, 1977), graduate students (Kasworm, 1982; Caffarella and Caffarella, 1983), degreed engineers (Rymell, 1981), and nurses (Savoie, 1980; Kathrein, 1982). These adults come from educationally advantaged backgrounds, but there have also been studies of working-class adults in America by Armstrong (1971), Johnson, Levine, and Rosenthal (1977), Booth (1979), and Leann and Sisco (1981). In Britain Elsey (1974) and Brookfield (1980) have researched the use made of informal learning networks by adults of low educational attainment.

The picture that emerges from this body of research is interesting, if not always consistent. According to Tough (1979), adults typically spend 700 hours per year engaged in purposeful learning. Nearly three-fourths of these purposeful learning activities (Tough uses the term *learning projects*) are planned by learners themselves. Even adults who show a marked reluctance to engage in learning, according to Tough, conduct at least two learning projects each year. The Organization for Economic Co-operation and Development (OECD) has published a report drawing on information submitted by the U.S. Department of Health, Education, and Welfare that concludes that self-directed learning accounts for approximately two-thirds of the total learning efforts of adults (Organization for Economic Coopera-tion and Development, 1979). Penland's (1977) study of a na-tional probability sample of 1,501 adults across the United States placed the figure of self-directed learning at a lower level than Tough's. It found that adults undertake approximately three projects each year involving 155.8 hours on the average. The importance of self-directed learning has been acknowledged in major reports conducted by Johnstone and Rivera (1965), the Scottish Education Department (1975), and the American Commission on Non-Traditional Study (Gould, 1973), all of which offer varying estimates of the amount of self-directed learning undertaken by adults.

The fact that adults are choosing to conceive, design, exe-cute, and evaluate self-directed learning activities and that many of them are apparently viewing this as the "natural" way to learn has enormous practical implications. In building curricula and choosing methods, facilitators must try to connect what adults see as a "natural" way of learning with more formal kinds of training and educational activities. We can see such at-tempts being made in the increasing use of learning contracts by educators in adult and higher education, in the development of courses on learning how to learn in which adults are taught to reflect on their own learning styles, in the development of edu-cational counseling and brokering services, in the attempts by public libraries to assist independent learners, and in the devel-opment of computer software packages for self-directed learn-ing activities.

Informal Learning Networks

In contrast to ABE, CPE, labor education, and the activi-ties of institutions of higher education, the adult learning that occurs within informal networks does not have certification or

accreditation as its end. Such networks are not usually affili-
ated with a formal educational institution, nor do they offer
courses leading to some form of qualification. Rather they are
groups of adults united by some common concern, some shared
status, or some agreed-upon purpose that exchange information,
ideas, skills, and knowledge among members and perform a number of functions having to do with problem solving and the creation of new modes of practice or new forms of knowledge.

As Sarason and Lorentz (1979) observe, the term *networking* has now become so fashionable that "the concept's
practical significance [may] get lost in slogans, labels, and horta-
tory proclamations about the need for more efficient and coor-
dinated use of available resources" (p. 3). According to Ferguson (1980), networks are the next stage in human evolution,
and Fisher (1983) has declared that for a social activist, government bureaucrat, human service worker, academic or social service director not to perform some network function is a professional dereliction of duty. Networks have been observed especially
among health professionals, but a recent categorization of 1,500
networks develops a typology of networks according to function and identifies seven categories: healing, sharing, using, valuing, learning, growing, and evolving (Lipnack and Stamps, 1982).

As mechanisms for learning, networks have a dimension
that is important to trainers and educators. A recent case study
of adult learning occuring within the Westchester Resource
Network in New York State (Thompson, 1984) found participants in the network to be self-confident, self-motivated, creatively curious, tolerant of ambiguity, and continuing learners.
Content-specific knowledge was acquired in the network on
such topics as crime, the problems of aging, ecology, new curriculum content for teachers, responsibilities and functions of local, county, and state departments, aspects of early adolescent
schooling, and how to effect changes in local ordinances. Major
educational functions of the network identified by participants
included the exchange of information, the development of
problem-solving techniques in concert with others, attitudinal
changes among members, the fostering of peer-group support,
the development of interpersonal communication skills, and the

use of connectional thinking in which adults became adept at making quick connections between diverse resources, bodies of knowledge, or problem-solving techniques. Members of this network also traced connections between the skills, knowledge, and attitudes developed through the network, on the one hand, and alterations in their work lives and personal relationships, on the other.

Although the terms *network* and *networking* may be currently fashionable and may be thought to refer to some purely contemporary development, most analysts of learning have long recognized that learning networks are important mechanisms through which adults acquire skills and change attitudes, become more insightful concerning their own behaviors, and explore alternative ways of living, thinking, and feeling. Today's theorists of "deschooling" (Illich, 1970; Reimer, 1971) concentrate on the construction of neighborhood learning webs and the use of local skill models as teachers. But these goals have been realized in practice by any number of initiatives in the history of adult education. Workingmen's self-help reading groups, various preunion workers' associations, lyceums, learning exchanges, free universities, and cooperatives are all examples of networks in which significant adult learning took place, both individually and as part of collective action. As noted by Knowles (1977), Henry Barnard's 1838 description of lyceums as free learning exchanges that were open to all and characterized by equality among members and by the rotation of teaching and learning roles among different participants sounds remarkably close to the descriptions of networks available in contemporary literature (Sarason and Lorenz, 1979; Sarason and others, 1977).

A number of contemporary examples of learning networks are particularly important to our discussion of the diverse practice settings in which adult learning occurs. There are, first, networks among educators and trainers themselves in which information is shared, problems are posed, skills are acquired, and initiatives for action are kindled. Beder, Darkenwald, and Valentine (1983), for example, have studied the self-planned professional learning engaged in by public school adult education directors in New Jersey. National networks such as the annual Adult Education Research Conference (AERC) in the United States are made up of researchers and educators who pay no fees and establish no administrative structures but meet solely for the purpose of a collaborative exploration of ideas and research related to adult education. Internationally, 1984 saw the launching of two important adult education networks: the International League for Social Commitment in Adult Education and the British and North America Network for Adult Education.

Second, there are learning networks in which educators are involved as animateurs who assist, stimulate, prompt, and support the activities of others. Examples of such learning exchanges have become easier to find in recent years. The *1981 National Directory of Free Universities and Learning Networks* in America lists 251 groups involving over 300,000 participants. The most famous of these, in Evanston, Illinois (Squires, 1974), reported in 1977 that over 30,000 participants had registered to exchange knowledge or skills in over 3,100 topic areas (Lewis and Kinishi, 1977). The Evanston exchange, known simply as TLE, has no affiliation with formal educational institutions, and fees are arranged by participants among themselves (some preferring to barter services rather than pay money). As well as putting adults who wish to exchange skills and knowledge in contact with each other, TLE has assisted in the development of other exchanges such as Each One-Teach One in Corona, New York, The Learning Connection in Uniondale, New York, and The People Index in Tallahassee, Florida (McElroy, 1980). As the titles of these organizations suggest, they all attempt to develop ways in which adults can teach, and learn from, one another in a collaborative atmosphere, at low cost, and with control over goals, methods, and evaluative criteria resting with the learners. TLE has also explored means by which exchanges could cooperate with public libraries and has been involved in a Fund for the Improvement of Postsecondary Education project on the dissemination of information about networks throughout the country.

The Free University movement (Draves, 1979, 1980)—a

national, noncredit adult education movement begun in the 1960s in the United States—also places control over methods, criteria, curricula, and modes of payment in the hands of learners. This means that classes are held in a number of varied settings, that credentials are outlawed, that the community is regarded as a learning environment, that knowledge and action are constantly linked (classes frequently engage in action projects and developmental activities), that process is valued over content, and that curricula are wholly the responsibility of participants (Draves, 1980). Regarding this last feature, Draves writes that "while out of ten crazy ideas, nine may be no good, that tenth idea may turn out to be something important to society. If we quash all ten ideas, which we would have to do because we don't know beforehand which idea will prove accurate, we quash creativity, imagination, and, in the end, all social progress" (p. 130).

Learning exchanges in England have been observed in the Centerprise project in East London (Rogers, 1979), in the New Communities project in Southampton (Fordham, Poulton, and Randle, 1979), and in the Attleborough experiment (Amison, 1982). These last two are different in form from the American learning exchanges, in that their formation has been prompted by professional educators (from Southampton University and the Norfolk Local Education Authority). As we will see in discussions of British university adult education throughout this book, there is a tradition in these institutions (often in collaboration with the WEA) of providing outreach to, or engaging in community action with, working-class learners in informal settings.

The third form of network includes those in which educators have played a deliberate role in directing or coordinating the network's operations. Educators in this third category do not serve simply as assistants to initiatives run primarily by others. Rather, in this category of networks they are the prime movers, even though they may emphasize collaborative formats of group discussion as the chief medium of educational transactions. Examples of this category of networks include study circles, the Great Books program, the Canadian Farm Forum, People Talking Back (the Canadian radio experiment involving discussion groups exploring political issues of the day), and various women's groups.

As reported by Titmus (1981), the annual enrollment in Swedish study circles represents over 60 percent of the Swedish adult population. Borgstrom and Olofsson (1983) estimate that 310,000 circles were in operation in 1980–81 and involved over three million participants. The Swedish study circles are run on collaborative lines with an equality of status among all participants; but, unlike learning exchanges, there is a greater fixity of curriculum. Indeed, the curriculum is specified beforehand and pursued by all members of the circle. A recent extension of the study circle idea to the United States is evident in New York State, where the Study Circle Consortium runs over 400 study circle groups in community agencies, hospitals, health centers, churches, libraries, businesses, and homes. These circles are established to discuss issues of public concern, to assist participants to develop a reasoned personal position on them, and to engender a spirit of increased commitment to political participation. They are seen, therefore, as a means of enhancing political literacy among the adult population (Kurland, 1979, 1982; Osborne, 1981). Issues such as nuclear disarmament, social welfare policy, educational priorities, and American foreign policy are the curricular stock-in-trade of such circles.

The mass media are commonly used to prompt the formation of local discussion groups. Although distance learning experiments are now common in universities such as the Open University (Britain), they have a much longer tradition in the education of adults. The Farm Forum experiment in Canada during the 1930s was an attempt to use radio broadcasts to stimulate the formation of local listening and discussion groups. These groups not only exchanged ideas on agricultural principles and practice but also engaged in community developmental activities. The Farm Forum motto of Read, Listen, Discuss, Act enshrined the notion of praxis before that term became fashionable, and the founder of the movement, Ned Corbett (then director of the Canadian Association for Adult Education), regarded some kind of group enterprise directed toward community action to be an integral measure of the success of local groups

(Conger, 1974). In purely quantitative terms, the forum was a major success, with estimates of the number of participants during the 1949-50 period ranging from 21,000 (Faris, 1975) to 30,000 (Kidd, 1963). The Farm Forum was proposed by UNESCO as a model of mass education ripe for replication in the Third World (Sim, 1954), and its influence is strongly evident in later Canadian radio discussion group efforts such as "Living Room Learning" (Buttedahl, 1978) and "People Talking Back" (Faris, 1975). Examples of similar experiments in the formation of local discussion groups through mass media of communication are the BBC Wireless Discussion Groups of the 1930s (Perraton, 1978; Heywood, 1981), and the Great Books discussion project in the 1950s in America (Davis, 1961). Bode (1960) reported that in 1960 New York University's Division of General Education alone had ninety-one Great Books discussion groups under its egis, with 1,500 learners meeting in each other's homes. The Learning Box scheme in Australia during the 1930s was an attempt by the universities of Western Australia and Sydney to facilitate learning through self-help groups scattered among the rural population (Watts, 1978).

More recently, the Department of Extramural Studies at the University of Manchester distributed a package of study notes to local discussion groups on the topic of television and the family (Luckham, 1983). Groups met in homes, schools, and clubs. Many of these were already existing women's church, and tenants' groups. I also worked to develop a Supporting Autonomous Adult Learning Groups scheme through an adult education center (Brookfield, 1979a, 1983a). In this latter instance, a package of resource materials for discussion was also provided, but the content of the package was determined by the group's members rather than as a result of some educator's initiative. The group was comprised of women who met in each other's homes every two weeks for leaderless discussions on matters of social concern. After stumbling on the existence of this group (by being invited to address it one evening on the effects of television), I offered to provide a package of materials to be distributed to group members before each leaderless discussion. This package included relevant statistical data, extracts

from major reports or studies, alternative explanations or interpretations of the phenomenon under discussion, and suggested
questions for discussion. It was delivered to members, and at no
time was I present at any of the subsequent discussions.

Finally, the growth of the women's movement during the
last fifteen years has prompted the formation of numerous consciousness-raising groups, along with groups designed to interpret and explore the common experiences of women or to create new forms of knowledge. As documented by Thompson
(1980, 1983), Westwood (1980), Keddie (1980), Hughes and
Kennedy (1983), Callaway (1981), and the International Council for Adult Education ("Women and Adult Education," 1980),
increasing numbers of women have been meeting "to validate
their own experience, generate their own knowledge, become
their own teachers, and take control of their own learning"
(Thompson, 1983). Some of these efforts, such as the Women's
Salon in my neighborhood in New York City, have no connection with educational institutions. Others, such as those sponsored by the Department of Adult Education at the University
of Southampton (Department of Adult Education, University
of Southampton, 1981; Thompson, 1983), meet under the egis
of university structures.

In such groups the emphasis is on participants "creating
their own knowledge" (Spender, 1980), "speaking for themselves" (Gayfer, 1980), and "re-visioning" themselves (Callaway, 1981). Members collaborate in questioning prevailing
modes of knowledge, in generating alternative frameworks of
interpretation, in creating new ways of thinking and living, and
in exploring each other's experiences. As described by Thompson (1981), Kellaway (1981), and Atkins (1981), leadership in
these groups is typically rotational, with different members, at
different times, assuming leadership roles. All members are
united in a common concern to question the values, assumptions, and behavioral stereotypes that they had previously uncritically assimilated. They are attempting to develop a sense of
self-worth derived from their own experiences rather than from
male-imposed criteria of personal worth. In their creation of
more authentic criteria against which their efforts and activities

can be judged, as well as in their exploration, interpretation, and re-creation of their personal and social worlds, the members of these groups are exemplifying transactional teaching-learning principles.

The attention of trainers and educators could profitably be turned to the phenomenon of learning networks much more frequently than is presently the case. Such exchanges are a reality among most professional groups, and Knox (1974) noted some years ago that networks of information and skill exchange are viewed by professionals as important mechanisms for the development of their professional expertise. Knox identified twelve features of exchange networks that can be used to assist the self-planned, continuing learning of health professionals or other professional groups. As he points out, exchange networks are useful mechanisms for information exchange, can be run cheaply, allow for an initial exploration of a new area with little professional risk attached, and need a minimum of staffing (principally a coordinator). With the development of microcomputers and various forms of interactive technologies, we can expect a corresponding increase in the amount and variety of networking activities among professional groups and other adult learners. As we witness the growing complexity of professional subspecializations in industrial societies, the functions of networks as vehicles for professional, personal, and political learning will become increasingly important. At various points throughout this book we will refer to ways facilitators can work to enhance the educational dimension of such activities.

Community Action

The final informal setting for adult learning to be discussed—that of community action initiatives—is so multifarious in its forms and purposes that a full treatment of this phenomenon would fill not one, but several books. My own previous practice and intellectual explorations have often been in this area (Brookfield, 1983a), and anthologies such as that of Butcher, Collis, Glen, and Sills (1980) illustrate the diversity of action case studies that are available to the interested observer.

Put at its simplest, practically every community action initiative—from parents pressing for day-care facilities or a safe street crossing, to villagers attempting to build an irrigation system, to tenants' groups presenting schemes for rent reform, to demonstrations against local industry's intentions to build a car park on public play space, to campaigns for a nuclear freeze—exhibits a strong educative dimension in that the adults involved are engaged in a continuous process of developing skills, acquiring knowledge, and reflecting on their experiences, mostly in collaboration with other adults.

Those educators who are employed by formal educational institutions tend not to have the time or opportunity to become extensively involved in community action initiatives. They are generally engaged in what has been called adult education for the community (Brookfield, 1983a) in which the demands of various client groups in the community are met by the organization and implementation of requested courses. Some have attempted to outline how the community might be used as an educative resource for adult learning in the tradition of the Mott Foundation's work, and examples of this include Whale's (1976) teaching model of "The Community as a Place to Learn," Hiemstra's (1982) description of the educative community, and Fletcher's (1980) paper on "Community Studies as Practical Adult Education." These writers all discuss how adult learning experiences might be planned in community settings through use of participant observation, the collection of oral histories, interviews with community members, and the locating of courses in such community settings as zoos, churches, parks, galleries, community centers, and factories.

What is often lacking in these proposals, however, is an appreciation of how educators can work with community action groups to enhance the educational dimension of their activities. This omission is probably not surprising considering that many action initiatives are politically contentious, and participants in a community group trying to change city hall policy may be in direct confrontation with the very officers who pay the salary of the educator. It is a brave individual who comes out of the political closet to declare his or her allegiance to a local political activist group. The educator working in this informal, community-based context is likely to inhabit an unsettling professional limbo in which institutional indifference alternates with criticism from local elected officials and in which a tolerance of ambiguity is an essential requirement if the educator is to keep his or her sanity.

Despite the personal and professional perils of this kind of work, however, many examples of successful facilitation of learning have been conducted in this area. Some of the most well known of these are the Antigonish movement (Coady, 1939; Lotz, 1977), the Highlander Folk School (Adams, 1975; Kennedy, 1981), and the Liverpool Educational Priority Area community development project (Lovett, 1975). Treatments of these initiatives are contained in Lovett (1980) and Brookfield (1983a), and a case-study documentation of Lovett's subsequent work in Northern Ireland is contained in Lovett, Clarke, and Kilmurray (1983). An interesting cross-cultural transference is observable in Lovett's latest initiative, the Ulster People's College, in that it is a deliberate attempt to establish in Belfast a residential center modeled along the lines of the Highlander Folk School in which activists, union organizers, and religious and lay leaders can come together to reflect collaboratively on important community issues and concerns. The Highlander Folk School itself, of course, was modelled after a Danish folk high school; and just as the form of the Ulster People's College was influenced by Lovett's visit to Highlander, so Highlander was influenced by Horton's trip to Denmark in 1931 in which he studied the folk high school system.

The practice thread that ties together the initiatives discussed above is that of placing adult learning within a context of some wider movement for social change or some community action initiative. In the Antigonish movement in Nova Scotia during the 1920s and 1930s, Jimmy Tompkins and Moses Coady of the extension department at St. Francis Xavier University worked with fishermen's groups, poultry farmers, and miners to set up credit unions, canneries, and cooperatives, as well as study groups. Coady believed that these adults were most concerned with economic needs and that education had thus to start with the economic dimension of life and be rooted in movements for economic reform. At the Highlander Folk School in Tennessee in the 1930s, Myles Horton, its founder, involved teachers and students at the school in the strike by non-unionized coal workers in Wilder against the local coal company. Horton was arrested and charged with "coming here and getting information and going back and teaching it" (Adams, 1972, p. 497), and from that time on the school allied its programs and curricula to the promotion of social change. Union workers and other activists came to figure prominently in the student body. In the 1950s, after the bureaucratization of the union movement blunted its concern for social change, Horton became involved in the civil rights movement, specifically with preparing blacks who could not read or write to take the voter registration test. Curriculum and materials were based on the experiences and concerns of the learners, instruction took place outside of formal school settings, and the teachers were black. The Citizenship School on Johns Island in South Carolina taught about 100,000 adults to read and write between 1957 and 1963 (Adams, 1972). The Highlander Research and Education Center in Knoxville, Tennessee, the contemporary incarnation of the Highlander Folk School, places its activities and curricula firmly in the context of working with activists, leaders, and groups in community development projects and workplace reform.

Some of the methods used in these projects bear directly on the principles of effective facilitation identified earlier. As writers on community problem solving have recognized, assisting community group members to articulate concerns, explore needs, devise action agendas, locate appropriate resources, and implement change are all strongly educational functions. McCullough (1978) has called this an andragogical approach to community problem solving, and Campbell (1980) argues that this form of education has advantages over many others since the groups are already in existence, participants are motivated, the curriculum is relevant to participants' lives, and group activities directly address the needs of those adults concerned.

Coady, Horton, and Lovett all emphasize practice elements that, in different ways, recall the ideas of John Dewey on problem solving and Paulo Freire on praxis. In a radio broadcast Coady declared that "an adult education programme, to produce results and affect the lives of the people, must result, in the first instance, in economic action on their part. . . . We must take the learner where he is. We build on the interests that are uppermost in his mind" (1979, p. 7). Workers would enter the villages or towns of fishermen, farmers, and miners, and a mass meeting would be held at which ideas for social and economic changes would be presented to participants. Networks of small study groups would be formed after this meeting at which study materials would be examined and problems identified and discussed. These groups were the prelude to direct action in the form of credit unions, cooperatives, and other social or economic reforms. St. Francis Xavier University also held conferences and courses for volunteer workers and local leaders.

In contrast to the community immersion often advocated by community workers and participatory researchers as a precursor to educational work, Coady believed in a more head-on approach. Work in a new community would begin with the mass meeting at which "intellectual dynamite" would be exploded, and an "intellectual bombing operation" would serve "to blast these minds into some real thinking" (Coady, 1939, pp. 30–32). This is in marked contrast to the Freirean approach (Freire, 1970b, 1973), in which literacy workers immerse themselves in a village, talking informally to inhabitants and gaining a sense of their daily concerns and meaning systems. Having derived some understanding of the village's outlook on the world, workers then ask probing questions in culture circles so that villagers might become aware of, and reflect upon, contradictions in their lives and beliefs. The Antigonish movement rested on a number of practical activities—mass meetings, living room study groups, kitchen meetings, community refresher courses—and the workers in the movement became extremely adept at obtaining funds to finance economic projects such as credit unions or processing plants. The overall focus of the movement was clearly economic; and, as Lotz (1973), Armstrong (1977), and Lovett (1980) have all recognized, it succeeded in engaging large numbers of workers in education linked to social action through the use of a variety of group-animating processes.

Unlike the Antigonish movement, the Highlander Folk School did not attempt to initiate social action but rather to identify emergent social movements and activist groups and to assist these with advice, resources, and the opportunity to explore experiences in residential workshops. As noted by Clark (1978), Lovett (1980), and Kennedy (1981), certain practice elements are representative of Highlander's approach. Education is achieved not only through working with existing groups but also through holding residential workshops where discussions and small-group work predominate. Curricula at workshops are devised by the participants themselves, are focused on their immediate concerns, and are meant to help participants explore collective solutions to problems. Most importantly, perhaps, workshops, discussions, and problem exploration occur in an already existing activist context. In an interview in 1976, Horton summarized his ideas on this process as follows: "It's the action that counts, not talking. You can analyze later on. When people get over that action, then you need to talk about it, to internalize it, discuss it. You need to try to get people to understand the importance of it. It takes too long the other way. You do it and then talk about it. You don't talk first or you talk yourself out of it" (quoted in Kennedy, 1981, p. 177).

One final important commonality of the initiatives already discussed is the rejection of the felt needs rationale. Coady's mass meetings in Nova Scotian towns were intended to create dissatisfaction with existing conditions, an awareness of prevailing inequalities, and the beginnings of a critical outlook concerning the possibility of community action and self-help in the economic and political spheres. Conti (1977) argues that both Freire and Horton believe education must be concerned with raising the consciousness of the oppressed so that they can take collective action to change society. Lovett, Clarke, and Kilmurray (1983, p. 75) also observe that "Highlander was not neutral. It had a radical ideological position and actively sought to provide, not only an explanation of how things were and how they got that way, but a 'vision' of what it might become and how this might be achieved." In a recent interview on his founding of the Ulster People's College, Lovett (1983, p. 5) declared that "people need to think, not only about the particular skills they need to deal with a particular problem, but about where they have got with their efforts, about what exactly they are trying to do, about the nature of the society in which they live. You don't do people any favours if you avoid raising those issues. Sometimes the situation requires very hard, frank analysis, in which people will have to engage in what is really a difficult intellectual journey—which may not be all that pleasant: like a lot of educational tasks there may be a lot of sweat involved in it. A lot of people have the idea that education should always be fun, and easy, but sometimes it has to challenge people, and it's hard." The examples of adult learning occurring within the context of community action initiatives in settings as diverse as those discussed (Nova Scotia, Tennessee, Liverpool, Northern Ireland) are thus united by this common vision of a society based upon principles of social justice, participatory control, and democratic decision-making processes.

Of particular relevance to discussions of this common vision of democratic justice are the twelve myths of community education that have been identified by Warden (1979), two of which—the "no conflict" and "no special interest" myths—are particularly relevant to this discussion. The "no conflict" myth assumes that there will be a congruence of desires and perceived needs when community members articulate their preferences for community change. The no special interest myth is held by those who see communities as warm, spontaneous groups, united by a spirit of communal brotherhood and sisterhood. Both of these myths are inaccurate and dangerous. They obscure the reality that communities are pluralistic and that the various interests present will frequently be in conflict. These myths also ignore fundamental social inequalities such as class and ethnic divisions. Those who find no conflicts in the communities in which they work are probably not addressing significant community issues. Baillie (1979) has also pointed out how the community educator's concern with process can betoken a neglect of the ends of such educative action. It is easy to let the establishment of mechanisms for consultation and communication, such as forums or community councils, become the end of community action and to allow ultimate purposes to be obscured.

I have argued elsewhere that "for an adult educator to make moral or ethical judgments regarding what should be taught and what kind of society should be encouraged is normal and inevitable" (Brookfield, 1983a, p. 89) and that a decision concerning which groups and causes an educator should assist "is a second order decision which will depend on the values, ethics, and moral stance of the educator" (p. 199). The literature of adult education is frequently so concerned with the development, application, and perfection of technique in areas such as needs assessment, objectives setting, and design of instruction and evaluation that ultimate purposes for education are neglected. Given the plethora of possible groups, causes, settings, and activities in which educators might involve themselves, it is crucial that they evolve a philosophical rationale comprising basic principles, purposes, and criteria to guide their efforts. Developing programs for adult learners is not simply an applied skill that exists independently of political or moral considerations. Educators and trainers are continually faced with choosing among conflicting priorities, and such choices are informed by educators' personal philosophies of education, as well as by the missions of their employing agencies. The phenomenon of priority setting by program developers will be discussed in Chapter Ten, and the beginnings of a rationale to guide trainers and educators in choosing among priorities is explored in Chapter Twelve.

❧ 8 ❧

Learning in Formal Settings

The purpose of this chapter is to review the kinds of structured environments in which adult learning occurs, generally under the direction of an educator or trainer who is working within an institutional base. The settings examined are those in which the majority of professional educators and trainers of adults work, and they therefore merit careful consideration. The chapter concludes with some comments regarding the contextual distortions commonly experienced while trying to facilitate learning within formal institutions.

Adult Literacy and Basic Education

In quantitative terms adult basic education is a major enterprise within the field of public education. In the United States it is estimated that 60 million Americans, or one-third of the adult population, are illiterate (Kozol, 1985). In fiscal year 1980–81 the federal appropriation for adult basic education was $100 million, and 1.8 million adults were enrolled in adult basic education (ABE) classes. The U.S. Adult Education Act of 1966 established a national program of ABE at much the same time that the British government set up the Adult Literacy Resources Unit with a budget of £1 million. National studies of adult literacy programs have been undertaken with funds from the U.S. Office of Education (Mezirow, Darkenwald, and Knox, 1975) and the National Institute of Adult Education in England and Wales (Jones and Charnley, 1978), and the Ford Foundation funded a major study of adult illiteracy in the United States in the 1970s (Hunter and Harman, 1979). On the Continent, the Common Market sponsored a series of case studies of the use of mass media in basic education in Britain, Denmark, France, the Canary Islands, and the Netherlands (Kaye and Harry, 1982). Strategies for the basic education of adults have appeared in Britain (Advisory Council for Adult and Continuing Education, 1979) and America (Rossman, Fisk, and Roehl, 1984), and at least one journal devoted to adult literacy and basic education has been established in recent years. There are, of course, various interpretations of what constitutes adult basic education and, in particular, adult literacy work. Those readers wishing to explore this area further are directed to the analyses of Drennan (1980), Cortwright and Brice (1970), Hargreaves (1980), Fingeret (1984), and the works cited earlier in this section.

Fundamental to much adult literacy work is the principle of voluntarism. Adults do, of course, attend formally sponsored literacy programs of their own volition. More importantly, however, adult literacy work is the sector of public education, both in Britain and the United States, where volunteers frequently serve as teachers and where professional educators are more likely to perform a supervisory and training role than to be wholly responsible for instruction. Literacy Volunteers of America, as their name implies, is concerned chiefly with deploying volunteers to help adults learn basic literacy skills. In Britain, the adult literacy project of the 1970s was premised on the notion of using a cadre of volunteers to work on a personal, one-to-one basis in the teaching of reading and writing skills. The professional educator, in both these instances, functions first as a trainer and then as a supervisor of volunteers. Analyses of educators' uses of volunteers in literacy and other work are found in Elsey and Gibbs (1981), Elsey, Hall, Hughes, and Laplace (1983), and Ilsley and Niemi (1981).

The use of volunteers as literacy teachers may make the teaching of literacy a more transactional encounter. There is less chance of the "deficit" approach to literacy teaching contaminating the activity, since learners are less likely to be intimidated by volunteers than by certified professional teachers. Volunteer literacy teaching is also characterized by an inductive approach to curriculum building and selection of methods, since volunteer tutors are encouraged to use their learners' real life experiences as curricular materials and to use active learning techniques rather than relying on general texts. This writer's mother, for example, used rifle catalogues as a teaching aid when she was working as a volunteer literacy tutor with an adult who had a passionate interest in guns. As noted by the National Institute for Adult Education (U.K.) survey of the impact of the adult literacy campaign in the 1970s (Jones and Charnley, 1978), most volunteer training schemes actively encouraged volunteers to develop their own materials in conjunction with their students.

Praxis is at the heart of much literacy work in that illiterates are encouraged to practice literacy skills in real life settings, to discuss these experiences with volunteer tutors, and then to reengage in a real life application of skills after this reflection. Various literacy workers have tried to adapt the methods of Freire in their work with illiterates in industrial societies, and a central concern in these efforts is to build a familiarity with, and confidence about, language using reflections on learners' active experiences with language. Moriarty and Wallerstein (1979) have adapted Freirean methods in English as a second language (ESL) work. They advocate the use of home visits, group walks in the neighborhood, analysis of learners' photographs, personal storytelling, songwriting, and humorous skits as teaching devices for making learners feel comfortable with their exploration of language and symbols.

Similar experiences are documented in Enright's (1975) description of Freirean methods in Northern Ireland, Heaney's (1983) documentation of the Universidad Popular in Chicago, and Brandt's (n.d.) account of using photographs, cartoons, drawings, and songs to tell the personal stories of immigrant women adapting to Canadian life and thereby becoming familiar with English. In the accounts of literacy and ESL work given by Moriarty and Wallerstein, Enright, Heaney, and Brandt, certain commonalities are apparent, all of which illustrate the principles of effective facilitation identified in Chapter One. Learners attend voluntarily; educators are frequently volunteers from the local community; the educational "content" is the life experiences of participants as reflected in stories, songs, photographs, drama, and cartoons; these materials are produced by the learners themselves, thereby ensuring that learning is activity based; and teaching and learning roles are shared, alternately, among group members.

An equally strong theme in these four accounts relates to the principles of effective facilitation that involve inculcating a spirit of critical inquiry in adults and assisting them to take control over their personal, social, and work lives. In the practice examples discussed in these accounts, learners' sense of control over the production of learning materials began to be reflected in actions outside the classroom. The immigrant women in Canada were encouraged to participate in their factory union as a result of learning English. At the Universidad Popular students' increasing control over curricula, the governing board, and the appointment and evaluation of teachers resulted in the withdrawal of funds by the City Colleges of Chicago. As Heaney (1983) writes, when adults truly take control over the educational structures governing them and when they create their own curricula and educational activities, they run the risk of exiling themselves from their institutional base.

Heaney also describes briefly three literacy projects aimed at placing the teaching of language within a context of learners' collective analysis of real life problems and active involvement in neighborhood struggles to change the conditions of marginal groups. The Liberacion Learning Center in South Florida, the Instituto del Progreso Latino in Chicago, and Project Literacy in San Francisco are all community-based experiments in education for Hispanic groups. These initiatives are characterized by the learners' increasing control over the structure and operations of language being placed within a context of exercising control over their individual lives and neighborhood conditions: They explore how language (especially that of bureaucratic officialdom) is used to oppress them. The Florida farmworkers learn language within culture circles (Freire, 1970b, 1973) in which they collectively analyze their work experiences and place their work in the context of national and international markets; in Chicago learners have created a collective governance structure; in San Francisco groups of learners meet twice weekly to discuss themes of work, popular culture, organization, and self-awareness.

These three practice initiatives reflect an orientation commonly found in adult literacy work; that is, the acquisition of language is viewed as a means of social and political empowerment, as much as a development of instrumental skills. This perspective owes much to the ideas of Freire, to be sure, but it is also a reflection of a much longer tradition of social concern in adult education. The fact that many illiterates are members of working-class groups or ethnic minorities and are in a condition of economic disadvantage (though they may belong to culturally vibrant groups) means that facilitators will often view literacy work as a means of assisting adults to develop the confidence, skill, and knowledge to come together in a collective effort to change their society. In contrast to most publicly funded adult educators, literacy workers frequently subscribe explicitly to this ethos of education for social and political transformation. Kozol's manifestos concerning adult illiteracy in the United States (1980, 1985) and the description by Hirshon (1983) of her work with Nicaraguan revolutionary *brigadistas* in the Sandinista literacy campaign are good examples of the revolutionary and crusading fervor endemic to much literacy work. In a recent overview of adult literacy education, Fingeret (1984) first notes that "education will not create additional jobs, solve the problems of crime and malnutrition, or make the world safe from terrorism. Social structures and social forces beyond the reach of literacy educators are at work maintaining the structures of social inequality" (p. 45). But she goes on to say that education can "provide tools and access to opportunities for working together with others to change those structures and, in the process, create rather than merely accept the future" (p. 45).

Continuing Professional Education

Continuing professional education (CPE) is a major growth area in the education and training of adults. As reported by Jarvis (1983b), Costello and Richardson (1982), Charters (1970), Frandson (1980), Hohmann (1980), and Houle (1980), a major responsibility of adult education or continuing education directors in universities, colleges, and within the professions themselves is coming to be seen as the provision of educational opportunities throughout a professional's life-span of work. In the major treatments of CPE in Britain (Jarvis, 1983b) and America (Houle, 1980; Stern, 1983), a number of goals for this provision are identified. These include helping professionals to master theoretical knowledge, to increase problem-solving capacities, to use practical knowledge, and to enhance their careers (Houle, 1980), all of which are described as performance characteristics. Pursuing these goals is said to make the learner a more effective professional. Houle also sees a related cluster of "collective identity characteristics" as a focus for CPE. These relate to professionals' development of a sense of belonging to discrete occupational groups and include providing formal training, credentialing, creating a professional subculture, seeking legal reinforcement, gaining public acceptance, developing ethical codes of practice, enhancing relations with other vocations, and clarifying professionals' relationships with users (Houle, 1980, pp. 49-73). Such goals can be considered as incidental outcomes of educational activities in that mastery of performance characteristics is likely to result in the development of a sense of collective professional identity.

According to Jarvis (1983b), the aims of CPE are to inculcate a professional ideology (especially in relation to understanding good practice and service), develop and enhance appropriate knowledge and skills, and prompt in the practitioner an increased sense of critical awareness. It is this last feature that is of particular relevance to the principles of effective practice identified in Chapter One. Jarvis maintains that "the aims of the educational process are about the learners rather than about the profession or the wider society" and that "the aims of professional education may not relate intrinsically to the needs of the profession nor to those of the wider society" (p. 41).

An interesting debate on Houle's ideas on CPE has been conducted by Woll (1984) and Knox (1984b). Woll characterizes Houle's view of CPE as an "empty ideal" and argues that many of the characteristics of the professionalization process identified by Houle are control mechanisms. To Woll, what is missing from Houle's view of CPE is "an articulation of the vision, the principles, the content of the ideal in the name of which control is to be exercised" (p. 174). Knox replies that Woll misunderstands the essentially transactional element of Houle's model and that Houle's characteristics are really "major ways in which professionals interact with their clientele, each other, and the larger society to achieve a balance of autonomy and control, to improve the quality of service" (p. 52).

Readers must make their own judgments concerning the validity of these opposing positions. What is undeniable, however, is that since Carlson (1977) lamented the lack of attention paid to CPE, a great deal of research and discussion has taken place. There are research studies such as those of Cervero and Rottet (1984) on analyzing the effectiveness of CPE for nurses, as well as studies on applying the principles of effective practice to CPE, particularly in the health and medical field (see Green, Grosswald, Suter, and Walthall, 1984; Austin, 1981; and Gonnella and Zeleznik, 1983). In addition, college presidents and university chancellors have begun to press their institutions to assist in the initial preparation and ongoing development of professional groups such as lawyers, dentists, accountants, pharmacists, nurses, real estate agents, and doctors. It is now not uncommon for presentations at research conferences to focus upon adult education processes occurring within such programs, and there has been a renewed concern among adult educators about the implications for their own practice of the professionalization of their field (Imhoff, 1980; C. D. Brown, 1984).

As well as that CPE provided within institutions of formal education, fields such as accounting, real estate, and pharmacy have established their own intraprofessional continuing education enterprises. In Britain the continuing education of accountants has been conducted almost entirely through commercial correspondence colleges. Professional educators do have a real contribution to make to these kinds of activities, principally in ensuring that principles of effective practice are employed. Such a contribution can take many forms. At a technical and process level, trainers and educators can ensure that participants are treated respectfully, that their experiences and accumulated reservoirs of skills are recognized, that curricula incorporate discussions of professionals' real life problems, concerns, and experiences, and that participatory methods and experiential learning techniques are used. These include discussion, T-group work, role playing, simulation, nominal group techniques, videotaping, microteaching, and small-group analysis of case studies. Professional groups such as doctors, pharmacists, dentists, nurses, and lawyers regularly encounter real life instances in which agonizing choices between different courses of action have to be made, serious ethical dilemmas are experienced, the neat prescriptions of textbooks and case histories are inappropriate, and contextual factors such as personality, political climate, or budgetary change significantly alter practice. In staff development exercises for such groups, it is much more meaningful to build curricula and organize workshops that take these experiences as their starting point, engage participants in a collaborative analysis and exploration of experiences, and encourage professionals to reflect continually on their interpretation of correct practice in actual work settings.

Trainers and educators can also ensure that participants in CPE programs develop some degree of critical awareness along the lines suggested by Jarvis (1983b). At the very least, CPE programs should include some attention to the ethical dimensions of appropriate practice (as indicated by Houle, 1980). Hence, educators can ensure that, through their consultancy work on curricula and methods or in their actual teaching, they assist professionals to consider the moral correctness and social justification of their activities. Interpretations of professional fairness will, of course, vary according to the ideological bent of educators, and some may choose to ignore such contentious curricular areas for fear of losing remunerative consultancies. It does not seem unduly idealistic, however, to expect educators to design exercises and help participants develop materials in which the ethical dilemmas of their own practice are explored with peers and subjected to a variety of interpretations.

Documented attempts to apply principles of effective facilitation in CPE are becoming increasingly common. Examples include Minkler and Cox's (1980) application of Freirean philosophy and methods to health care, Allan, Grosswald, and Means's (1984) discussion of facilitating the self-directed learning of health professionals, Knox's (1984a) discussion of strategies for strengthening continuing education for the health professions, the McMaster Medical School's training of doctors by means of self-directed learning techniques (Ferrier, Marrin, and Seidman, 1981; Neufeld and Barrows, 1974), the development of self-directed patient-management packages for 20,000 doctors in Britain (Harden, Stoane, Dunn, and Murray, 1979), and the application of andragogical principles to legal education (Bloch, 1982), social work education (Kilpatrick, Thompson, Jarrett, and Anderson, 1984; Farquharson, 1984), nursing education (Reed Ash, 1985), and English as a second language (De Paula, 1984).

Finally, it is important to note that the engagement of some participants in CPE is not always voluntary. When adults are forced to learn against their own inclinations and desires, the resulting resentment is likely to become a major block to any kind of meaningful learning. Consequently, participation in compulsory CPE might lead to increased statistics of adult participation but be characterized by the kind of mental absenteeism already discussed in Chapter One. A vigorous critique of mandatory continuing education has been mounted by writers such as Day (1980) and Rockhill (1981, 1983). Day has condemned compulsory adult education as "a repulsive idea [that is] antithetical to the ideals that the early adult education movement cherished" (1980, p. 5), and Rockhill feels mandatory continuing education (MCE) turns adult education into an agent of social control, limits individual freedom, and places efficiency above ethical considerations. Roby Kidd has lamented that the enthusiasm of some educators for MCE signaled that they were "pathetically pleased to be wanted, to be recognized even for the wrong reasons" (quoted in Brookfield, 1983a, p. 31), and he criticized the monetary greed that he felt underlay many CPE programs.

It is certainly true that Lindeman (1926) and Bryson

(1936) explicitly stated that adult education was inherently voluntary, and one of the earliest British adult education initiatives, the Workers' Educational Association (WEA), was based (and still is) on a network of local groups staffed by volunteers. Moreover, a review of research on MCE (Cunningham and Hawking, 1980) concludes that there is no correlation between MCE and improved practice. This is not surprising when we consider that the resentment caused by being ordered to learn new knowledge, upgrade existing skills, or attend professional development workshops is likely to act as a major block to effective learning. What stand, then, should educators and trainers of adults take concerning MCE? There is obviously an excellent case to be made for requiring professionals regularly to acquaint themselves with recent developments in legislation, clinical technique, or technological developments. No one wishes to hire lawyers who are ignorant of recent legislative changes or be under the knives of surgeons who are unaware of improved surgical techniques. Neither do we wish to be counseled by social workers who feel that poverty is solely the result of individual fecklessness or taught by teachers who believe corporal punishment is the best motivator for learning. Those readers who have found themselves the victims of professional incompetence, in whatever sphere, know how frustrating this can be, particularly if that incompetence is the result of the professional's inertia concerning professional development or of his or her outright refusal to keep abreast of recent developments.

It is also important that professionals be made aware of the potential for client abuse that is present in their refusal to undertake further professional learning after initial entry to their particular professional body. There is an obvious logic to the requirement that psychotherapists be in therapy themselves, since this allows them to reflect on their own professional practice by placing themselves regularly in the role of client. It might be interesting to require teachers and trainers of adults to participate as learners in an adult learning group, as I did as part of my graduate education. Viewing practice (both pedagogic and administrative) within my institution from a student's viewpoint alerted me to some of the most frustrating aspects of the adult education experience. This made me more cognizant of elements in my own practice that might appear to students to be intimidating or insensitive. Being required to assume a student role caused me to reflect on my own behaviors, expectations, and attitudes, and led to my altering the way in which I welcomed new learners to my classes. It also caused me to make my assumptions and expectations as clear as possible from the outset so that learners were in possession of full knowledge of my values and intentions.

There are good reasons, then, for requiring professionals to engage in regular periods of reflection on their experience, to explore others' accounts of how they managed ambiguities and contextual problems in their practice, and to expose themselves to new theoretical or technical advances in knowledge and practice. Indeed, it is for the right of workers to claim regular periods of paid educational leave that educators and activists have lobbied vigorously in Europe (Charnley, 1975). The Italian scheme of 150 hours per year of paid educational leave for workers is seen by Yarnit (1980a) as "a political advance for the Italian working class, as well as a purely educational gain" (p. 193) and is described as "highly subversive" (p. 192) of the interests of government and capital. To Titmus (1981) the scheme should also be seen in a sociopolitical context as a collective advancement of working-class conditions. Although the Italian workers study for middle-school certificates, both Titmus and Yarnit agree that the educational methods avoid a didactic, magisterial transmission of knowledge from teacher to taught and that they concentrate on "an interdisciplinary approach and collective management of learning, in which the starting point is the students' experience and group discussion plays an important part" (Titmus, 1981, p. 211). In the fight for workers' rights to enjoy periods of paid educational leave in Britain (Killeen and Bird, 1980) and on the Continent (Taylor, 1980; Charnley, 1975), then, we can see a political initiative that has resulted in educational experiments of considerable social significance.

That universities are increasingly involved in CPE is undeniable. In studies such as Fox's (1981) analysis of CPE program planning in six southern universities or Knox's (1982b) survey of university-based CPE in medicine, pharmacy, social work, education, and law, we can see how researchers are beginning to examine these activities as distinctive administrative case studies. As suggested earlier, trainers and educators can work to ensure that CPE initiatives exemplify principles of effective practice and alert professionals to the potential for client abuse in their practice, encourage the collaborative development of curricula based on learners' experiences, and develop in professionals a capacity for double-loop learning in which they become critically aware of the standards, norms, and expectations governing practice in their professional area. From the development of such critical awareness we can expect to observe a corresponding increase in professional practices that respect clients and condemn exploitative abuses.

Labor Education

Labor education (in Britain, trade union education) is by any standards a major educational activity. In Britain and the United States it has a long and respectable history. The first example in America of labor education as a separate enterprise was the establishment of the International Ladies Garment Workers Union at the turn of the century, and the first program for labor unions to be mounted by an institution of higher education was at the University of Wisconsin in 1926 (Mackenzie, 1980). In Britain working-class initiatives developed by workers for their own purposes were evident throughout the nineteenth century in the activities of the cooperative movement, the Chartists, workingmen's associations, and self-help reading circles (Kelly, 1970). As the twentieth century progressed, these became more organized in the form of workingmen's colleges, mechanics' institutes, the WEA, the Labour College, and workingmen's residential colleges such as Woodbroke and Fircroft.

Estimates of the amount and variety of educational activities sponsored by labor unions vary according to author, country, and classificatory scheme used. Legge (1982) notes that the

1977 annual report of the Trades Union Congress (TUC) in Britain estimated that 180,000 union members each year would be engaged in union-organized education by the 1980s. The TUC education committee runs a variety of courses for workplace representatives on matters such as safety, company finance, and work study. Twenty thousand places are estimated to be available each year for union members to attend courses, usually held at a local polytechnic or college of further education. The TUC training college has trained 900 union officers using specially designed, self-study materials, and individual unions (such as the General and Municipal Workers Union, the Association of Scientific, Technical, and Managerial Staff, the Transport and General Workers Union, and the National Union of Railwaymen) have established their own residential education centers to train their own officials.

Jennings (1981) estimates that in 1981 43,856 students were enrolled in courses offered by local universities, colleges, polytechnics, and WEA districts in conjunction with the TUC. The TUC pays the fees of these students, but the courses are generally taught by faculty from the public educational institution. Typical program areas are finance, health and safety, business management, and social studies. Some institutions have developed courses for particular labor unions, as has happened with the miners' education courses offered at Nottingham (Thornton and Bayliss, 1965) and Sheffield (Macfarlane, 1975). Jennings places the numbers involved in correspondence courses organized independently by the TUC for 1976–77 as 4,140. The British Broadcasting Company (BBC) also organized a trade union education program in 1975 in which a series of television programs were broadcast in conjunction with a TUC correspondence course and WEA-organized local discussion groups. The three major reports on adult education in Britain in recent years (H. M. Stationery Office, 1973; Scottish Education Department, 1975; Advisory Council for Adult and Continuing Education, 1982) all stress the need to support the provision of education by labor unions.

In the United States a major survey of lifelong education (Peterson and Associates, 1979) estimates that 500,000 workers are enrolled in apprenticeship programs jointly organized by management and labor. Seventy-five thousand trade unionists are said to be students in courses arranged by individual trade unions to assist them in performing the shop steward roles of handling grievance procedures and negotiating conditions of work. Organized labor has 21.5 million members spread among 200 unions, yet only one-fourth of these unions maintain education departments. Most programs are sponsored by the unions themselves or universities (Darkenwald and Merriam, 1982, p. 176). There are forty-one universities that have established labor studies programs (Turner, 1977), thirty-one institutions with labor studies majors (Dwyer, 1977), and "numerous" community colleges that offer a labor studies degree (Peterson and Associates, 1979). There are also 200 contracts available by which union members can attend college free of charge or at a subsidized rate (Charner, 1978).

Problems of accurate definition bedevil the study of labor education. Briefly, three terms are in common use, all of which describe different programs with different purposes. *Workers' education* is used in a general sense to refer to the development among workers of a sense of critical awareness regarding political, economic, philosophical, cultural, and sociological matters. This is the sense in which the term was used by Mansbridge (1944), and a recent essay by Confer (1984) employs the term to describe activities "designed to contribute to the awareness and effectiveness of workers as participants in the economic, political, cultural, and social systems" (p. 205). *Labor education* is generally used to refer to educational programs designed to help union representatives and members perform their union-related functions more effectively. Rogin (1970) views labor education as "the attempt to meet workers' educational needs as they arise from participation in unions. It is education directed toward action" (p. 301). *Labor studies* is a term that describes a new curricular area and field of academic specialization that is offered as a degree option in university programs. Subjects included in the broad areas of labor studies include sociology, social psychology of the workplace, organizational psychology, group dynamics in the workplace, leadership styles, management theory as related to negotiation, collective bargaining and the law, and political science.

Labor education programs—those created to assist union members and representatives in the performance of their union functions—are assigned a wide variety of functions. Burkitt (1982), in fact, classifies the TUC education policy in terms of the five educational functions identified by Liveright and Haygood (1969). As suggested by surveys of workplace training (Westbrook and Whitehouse, 1978) and the International Labor Office's (1975) handbook for workers' education, however, labor education programs tend to be highly instrumental and oriented toward the acquisition of specific skills through active modes of learning. Participants acquire skills in such areas as handling grievances, conducting committee meetings, collective bargaining, interpreting safety and health regulations, recruiting members, and explaining union policy and decisions to members.

As developed by Gray (1966), the International Labor Office (1975), Somerton (1979), and Burkitt (1982), labor education is seen in terms closer to that traditionally associated with workers' education. Gray (1966) notes that labor education programs have historically been concerned to raise the consciousness of union members concerning the class struggle in American society and to increase union solidarity. The International Labor Office handbook declares that "it is the vision of the social potential of these individual motives which justifies workers educational programmes" (1975, p. 10). As Burkitt points out, "The emphasis in trade union/workers education has a strong role element and stresses collective action for social change. These are not values emphasized in traditional adult education provision where the emphasis is on personal development and the use of leisure time for educational pursuits chosen by the individual" (Burkitt, 1982, p. 75).

Given the plethora of terms, functions, and providing agencies (universities, colleges, unions), it is difficult to make any generalizations concerning the extent to which this variety of activities exemplifies the transactional approaches outlined earlier. Some obvious connections are, however, immediately observable. For example, the majority of labor education programs are grounded in participants' real life tasks, concerns, and activities such as grievance handling, bargaining, and interpreting policy to members. There seems to be a genuine congruence between union members' concerns and interests and the curriculum of labor education as devised by the central union office. The Westbrook and Whitehouse (1978) survey of TUC workplace representative training shows just how close members' specifications of typical tasks are to the curriculum of labor education courses.

Second, active methods seem to be widely used. The surveys of Rogin (1970), Mackenzie (1980), and Confer (1984) all stress how discussion methods, role plays, simulations, case studies, and other participatory learning techniques are the stock-in-trade of many labor education courses. The notion of praxis (even if that term is not actually used) seems to be familiar to, and implemented by, many labor educators. What seems to be absent from some programs, however, is the development in adults of the capacity to be critically reflective of their own practice and the norms and procedures of their union activities, as well as those of the factory or business setting. Intimidation, abuse, and graft and corruption are by no means the sole prerogatives of management; and, in American unions perhaps more than in British, instances of criminal practice, bribery, and corruption are well documented. In British unions, the pervasiveness of socialist ideology means that union activists are much more likely to scrutinize the activities and decisions of national executive committees (NECs). Those NECs that do not, in word and deed, act in a spirit of solidarity and with due cognizance of the class struggle are likely to be publicly criticized by the grass-roots activists.

In the case studies of practice that will be referred to at later points in this work, we can see how alliances between labor unions and public educational institutions may result in precisely the form of effective facilitation that exemplifies principles of good practice. The development of industrial democracy in the Sheffield steel industry is described by Wilson (1978) as an application of Freirean methods of dialogic, collaborative education. Courses for coal miners in Britain (Fatchett, 1982; Macfarlane, 1975) have been said to enable miners to move into broader political and public affairs, to generate community involvement, and to increase participants' capacities for self-directedness. In the United States liberal arts curricula developed for workers are provided by the University of Pennsylvania and the State University of New York at Buffalo (Fried, 1980). At Wayne State University in Detroit student services, curricula, and delivery systems have been revised to assist blue-collar, working-class adults engage in higher education through the university's weekend college program (Feinstein and Angelo, 1977; Stack and Pascal, 1980). At the College of New Rochelle (Taaffee and Litwak, 1980) and Empire State College (Dwyer and Torgoff, 1980), both in New York, similar programmatic revisions and curricular alterations have created access points to higher education for municipal, service, clerical, and blue-collar union members.

But an important difference should be noted here between American labor education and European trade union education. In Europe, unions are much more likely to be staffed by ideologically committed social democrats and socialists who see union activity as one dimension of the working class's attempt at collective advancement and the transformation of society. In countries such as Britain, France, and Italy, for example, there are financial and ideological ties between the trade union movement and labor, socialist, and Communist parties. In America, in contrast, while labor unions are traditionally allied to the Democratic party, such unions do not see themselves as partaking in a collective transformation of society. Indeed, in the 1980 and 1984 elections major unions such as the Teamsters endorsed the Republican candidate for president.

In Europe, then, trade union education is frequently a politically contentious issue. Faculty teaching such courses are likely to be sympathetic to the union's role as socialist transformer of society and to be willing to branch out into curricular areas that go beyond the tasks and duties associated with the performance of specific union functions. In two studies of union education tutors in Britain, for example (Bright and Macdermott, 1981; Stuttard, 1974), the commitment of union tutors to engage in sensitive and controversial areas of study is noted. Furthermore, surveys of students in such courses (Titmus and Healy, 1976; McIlroy and Brown, 1980; Fatchett, 1982) record how such adult learners place their studies in the context of the political advancement of the working class. Titmus and Healy (1976) write that the members of the trade unionist group in their survey of working-class participants in adult education "were more aware of the collective dimension of adult education. . . . they esteemed it for its advantages to society, specifically the working class, criticized workers for their apathy towards it, and sought improvements which would encourage them to participate in order to make a better society" (p. 25). The other surveys note students' desire for courses on social, political, and economic issues (McIlroy and Brown, 1980) and the participation by students in political activism within the Labour party (Fatchett, 1982).

Universities, Polytechnics, and Community Colleges

One of the most significant developments in higher education in the last fifteen years has been the increasing number of adult students enrolled at universities, polytechnics, and community colleges. This trend has been discussed at length in major works, papers, and anthologies, such as those of Gould and Cross (1972), Houle (1973), Cross, Valley, and Associates (1974), Ellwood (1974), Harman (1976), Harrington (1977), Jones and Williams (1979), Charnley, Osborn, and Withnall (1980), Greenberg, O'Donnell, and Bergquist (1980), Heermann, Enders, and Wine (1980), Shriberg (1980), Apps (1981), Tight (1982), Campbell (1984), and Knapper and Cropley (1985). This trend has also been noted and explored in such major European reports and publications on lifelong education as those of Lengrand (1975), Dave (1976), Houghton and Richardson (1974), the Organization for Economic Cooperation and Development (1975), Himmelstrup, Robinson, and Fielden (1981), and Flude and Parrott (1979). For the purposes of the present discussion, however, the following comments will be restricted to adult student participation occurring within universities in the United States, Canada, and Britain, in polytechnics in Canada and Britain, and in community colleges in the United

States. These are all institutions of higher education established for the purpose of awarding degrees and certificates to students engaged in two to four years of full-time study, and until recently considered to be in the business of preparing those between eighteen and twenty-two years of age for the world of work.

That this situation has changed irrevocably is evidenced by a number of statistical sources, as well as by the observations of those who visit such campuses. Boaz (1978) estimated that 3.3 million adults were enrolled in university extension and continuing education courses in the United States, while another survey estimated that 7,160 different courses were being taken by adult participants in four-year colleges or universities (National Center for Education Statistics, 1982). This figure represented nearly 20 percent of the total number of courses (37,381) provided by all institutions and agencies and was exceeded only by courses provided by employers for employees (9,260). Apps (1981) reports that women aged thirty-five and over are the fastest-growing student group in colleges and universities, and the U.S. Bureau of the Census (1979) reported that 850,000 women and 460,000 men in this age group were enrolled in college. A national survey in the mid 1970s estimated that there were 4 million adult students participating in noncredit activities in community colleges, compared with 2.5 million in universities and 2 million in four-year colleges (National Center for Education Statistics, 1978). Other estimates of adult learners' participation in higher education are that in 1978 one-third of higher education students were aged twenty-five and over (U.S. Bureau of the Census, 1979), that 40 percent of students in higher education in 1977 attended part-time (Grant and Lind, 1979), and that 40 percent of adult learners who are involved in some formal program of education are enrolled in colleges and universities (National Advisory Council on Extension and Continuing Education, 1979). (For a review of these and other statistics, see Brodzinski, 1980.)

In the United Kingdom the same trend is discernible, but British universities and polytechnics seem to be more resistant to admitting older students than are their American counterparts. According to Jones and Williams (1979), 23.1 percent of all new entrants to undergraduate study in universities and polytechnics in 1977 were twenty-one or over. However, they note a decline in the number of part-time enrollments in universities from 3.2 percent of all undergraduate enrollments in 1965-66 to 1.5 percent in 1974-75. This should be placed in the context of the expansion of higher education generally in the 1960s and early 1970s, so that while the proportion of part-time students may have decreased, the actual numbers increased.

Tight (1982) estimates that 4,381 part-time students were enrolled in undergraduate courses in British universities in December 1979 (only 1.7 percent of the total). At the postgraduate level, 19.5 percent of students (9,938) were part-time, giving a total undergraduate part-time student population in universities of less than 15,000. Tight gives other figures, however, that are more heartening to educators of adults in universities. He estimates that 10,045 students were home study candidates for external degrees of the University of London in 1980. In extramural departments of universities (sometimes in conjunction with the WEA), 236,558 enrollments were recorded in 1979-80. Furthermore, 69,700 adult students were enrolled in Open University courses in February 1980 as undergraduate or postgraduate students, and 17,000 in short courses provided by the university. When the figures for part-time students in advanced, degree-level courses are added to the figures for universities and the Open University, a total of over 520,000 adult students were estimated to be engaged in higher education. In an analysis of continuing education in polytechnics and colleges of higher education, Wood (1982) quotes statistics that place the number of full-time equivalent students aged twenty-five and over as one-fourth of the total student population in polytechnics in 1979 and one-third of the population in colleges of higher education in 1977.

Notwithstanding the difficulties of gaining an accurate estimate of the numbers of adult students in higher education, it seems clear that adults now constitute a fast-growing client group for universities, polytechnics, community colleges, and other two- to four-year institutions of higher education. This

expansion in the number of adults in the student body has resulted in the provision of adult student counseling services
(Eisele, 1980; Payne, 1985; Shriberg, 1980; Butler, 1984), of
degree programs that emphasize the adult's capacity to undertake
independent study (Burgess, 1977; Percy and Ramsden, 1980;
Stephenson, 1981; Houle, 1973), of specialized programs for
adults preparing to enter higher education (Brookfield, 1981d;
Hutchinson and Hutchinson, 1979; Aird, 1980), and of courses
and services that help adults acquire learning-to-learn skills
(Smith, 1982a, 1983). It has also led to the use of learning contracts with adult students (Berte, 1975; Caffarella and Caffarella,
1983; Bauer, 1985a), the acknowledgment of adults' prior experiential learning (Moon and Hawes, 1980; Menson, 1982),
and the establishment of academic curricula deliberately oriented to take account of adult students' experiences (Shor,
1980; Cunningham, 1983; Hayenga and Isaacson, 1980; Payette, 1980).

Training in Business and Industry

The literature on adult education has generally been re-
luctant to become too engaged with the world of corporate
training, although there have been exceptions such as Kidd's
(1969) address on "Liberal Education for Business Leadership,"
Knowles's (1984) documentation of the application of andragogical principles in business and industry, and Nadler's (1984)
exploration and elaboration of human resource development.
This reticence of many college and university educators concerning corporate training is understandable. It springs from a
reluctance to equate education with the upgrading of skills
among employees so that greater profits can accrue to large
companies or multinational corporations.

There are good reasons, however, why educators should
become much more cognizant than they are of the world of
corporate training. First, there is a long tradition of companies
funding liberal studies programs in universities for management
personnel. The various Standard Oil companies, Ford Motor,
General Foods, General Electric, Proctor and Gamble, and

many others have established programs such as the University of Pennsylvania's Institute of Humanistic Studies for Executives (funded by the Bell Telephone Company in the 1950s).

Second, as a recent report on state policies and institutional practices on adult learning recognizes (Cross and McCartan, 1984), private industry is becoming a major provider of education for adults. The report lists four degree-granting institutions in Boston—a hospital, a manufacturer of computers, a consulting firm, and a banking institute—all of which are authorized by the state to grant associate, baccalaureate, and master's degrees. Corporate giants such as Xerox, IBM, American Telephone and Telegraph (AT&T), and McDonald's have established their own substantial training campuses. Dinkelspiel (1981) reports that 20,000 people attended the Xerox Leesburg, Virginia, campus in 1979. In 1982, AT&T spent over $6 million on remedial programs for 14,000 employees, many of these programs being concerned with basic academic skills. The Dale Carnegie Corporation (Mackey, 1983) has an annual enrollment of over 105,000 people in its courses. The American Society for Training and Development has 21,000 national members, with 20,000 additional local chapter members (Craig and Evers, 1981), and data collected by the 1978 U.S. Census estimated that 19 percent of all adult education courses were provided by businesses, industries, labor groups, and professional organizations ("U.S. Training Census . . . ," 1983).

The recent report by the Carnegie Corporation of New York on *Corporate Classrooms: The Learning Business* (Eurich, 1985) has focused the attention of educators and business trainers alike on what *Time* magazine called "a disconnected and poorly observed educational behemoth" ("Schooling for Survival," 1985, p. 75). This "behemoth"—the world of education and training organized and sponsored by firms and corporations —is estimated to involve eight million learners at any one time, along with an expenditure of some $60 billion per year. IBM alone is said to spend $700 million a year on employee education, and at least eighteen corporations nationwide have been authorized to grant academic credentials, ranging from associate degrees to doctorates. There is little doubt that as computer technology advances, the opportunities for corporations to offer individualized, computer-based training exercises will increase.

The wonder induced in many observers by the Carnegie report parallels in some respects the surprise prompted by the findings of investigators of self-directed learning, self-teaching, and independent learning in the 1960s and 1970s. At that time the educational world seemed almost shocked to learn that so many adults were engaged in informal learning efforts without the assistance of professional educators. Just as explorations of this generally unacknowledged adult learning iceberg (Tough, 1978) and parallel educational universe (Brookfield, 1981a) prompted a number of attempts to build strategies for encouraging self-directed learning into formal course offerings, so we can expect many adaptations of training techniques to be adopted by college and university educators in their own settings.

Third, a great many trainers, training managers, and educational consultants see themselves as educators, not simply as trainers, and draw from adult learning concepts and methods in designing training experiences. In my own institution, training managers from the corporate world and educational consultants working primarily with business and industry are regularly admitted to the doctoral program in adult education, and this situation is paralleled in most North American universities to the extent that the Commission of Professors of Adult Education voted at its 1984 business meeting to found a task force on human resource development. The academic world of adult education does not see the world of business as wholly alien, containing no educational dimensions. The fact that professors of adult education take seriously the theory and practice of human resource development is not surprising given the extent and vigor of many business and industry training programs and inservice development activities. The founding of this task force indicates just how seriously business and industrial training is taken as an adult educational activity by most academics in university departments of adult education.

Fourth, a number of concepts and methodological approaches developed within the corporate world have a good deal of relevance for educators of adults who work in nonbusiness settings. The field of evaluation, for example, draws heavily on models developed largely in industrial settings—for example, Kirkpatrick's (1967) hierarchy of evaluation. The concept of double-loop learning as developed by Argyris and Schön (1978), in which employees become critically aware of the norms and assumptions underlying organizational structures, is very close to the notion of critical reflectivity as explored by Mezirow (1985). The literature of team building (Dyer, 1977), of staff development (Laird, 1978; Lauffer, 1978; Seaman, 1981; Michalak and Yager, 1979), and of human resource development (Nadler, 1970, 1980, 1984) is of interest to educators of adults working in a variety of settings from voluntary organizations to CPE.

This last concept—that of human resource development (HRD)—is seen by Nadler as interchangeable with that of adult education (1984, p. xxvii). Nadler regards human resource development as a matter of organizing learning experiences that take place within a definite time period, increase the possibility of improving job performance, and result in individual and organizational growth (Nadler, 1984). Du Bois (1982) comes close to viewing the HRD specialist as an improved version of the adult educator. He writes that "the emerging role of the human resource developer encompasses much more than that of the traditional adult educator. This professional is a new professional on the educational scene; an adult educator with new and more expansive expertise, cognizant of the dynamics of human behavior and the workings of organizations" (p. 376).

In a study of 125 human resource development managers within business organizations, Shipp (1985) asked these managers to record the HRD activities in which they were involved in a specified period of time and to identify the amount of time spent on these activities. Typically, HRD managers were found to be engaged in HRD for four and a half hours each day and to divide this time among nine discrete functions. Program management and needs assessment were the most time-consuming activities, between them taking up 30 percent of most managers' time. The rest of their time was spent dealing with budgetary matters, writing or communicating reports, making evaluations, managing information, planning organizational change, forecasting future manpower needs, and supervising activities. As Shipp notes, "The traditional management skills of planning, budgeting, and business information processing assume far more importance for the HRD manager than the adult educators' instructional planning, instructing and meeting planning, and facilitating" (p. 73). He also points to a major difference in the evaluative criteria adopted by HRD managers and adult educators. He writes that "needs assessment and evaluation require a different orientation since HRD managers concern themselves with profit and costs, while adult educators concentrate on the growth and development of the individual" (p. 73).

Trying to decide whether human resource developers are improved adult educators is not particularly productive. But one important distinction is made by Du Bois (1982) when he points out that HRD specialists are integral elements of corporate cultures, committed to the goals of the organizations of which they are a part. These goals are, of course, to increase productivity and profit; and other aims, such as contributions to the cultural life of the community, are essentially by-products of this primary aim of achieving profit. Without an expanding economic base companies are not going to concern themselves with the cultural enrichment of society as a priority aim. But adult education centers, continuing education departments in universities and colleges, and school-based adult education programs, are not oriented to producing salable goods and services and making financial profits. A degree of financial stability is obviously necessary to their continuing existence, but the chief criteria by which their operations are judged are the quality, significance, and effectiveness of the learning undertaken by adults.

This is not to dismiss the world of business and industry, but simply to point out that the criteria used to judge the success of training initiatives within those settings will frequently be economic, not educational. A "good" training exercise will generally be one that helps trainees become more effective and, hence, more productive employees, not one in which employees become critically reflective and develop insights concerning their own lives, capacities, and relationships. Such organizational criteria of training success inevitably constrain the extent to which the principles of effective facilitation of learning can be exemplified. It will be much more difficult to use extended reflection on behaviors, to take the time to do collaborative needs assessments and curriculum building, or to generate negotiated evaluative criteria in a training setting where the emphasis is on quickly visible results in terms of increased efficiency and productivity.

It is self-defeating, however, for college and university educators to ignore the world of business and industry. At a very basic level, enormous numbers of adults are participating in training efforts in business and industry, and it is incumbent on educators working in these settings to ensure that these efforts are conducted humanely, respectfully, and carefully and that they incorporate collaborative and critically reflective elements. The identification by Peters and Waterman (1982) of precisely these collaborative and critically reflective elements as crucial to business success may result in an increased adoption of principles of effective facilitation in corporate training settings. Experiments such as the Westinghouse Corporation's Andragogical Executive Forum (Knowles, 1984) will become increasingly common in the next few years, and it is important that trainers ensure that such experiments do indeed incorporate principles of collaboration, respect for participants, and development of the ability to reflect critically on fundamental assumptions.

The literature on HRD and corporate training is predominantly American. In Britain, however, a growing number of college and university educators are seeking to understand the corporate environment without thereby suffering a loss of integrity through involvement with the world of business and industry. Parrott (1976) argues for the abandonment of the distinction between education and training, maintaining that "if education, broadly speaking, is concerned with helping people to a more highly developed awareness of self, that is, of their

potential for activity and social interaction, it is difficult today
to find training activities which do not contribute to this end
or which ought not to be made to contribute to this end" (p.
304). It is this last caveat that is particularly important and that
outlines one possible role for educators in the training process;
that is, the role of ensuring that training efforts do indeed help
participants become more aware of their own potential for self-
development.

A number of business training efforts said to be oriented
toward the self-development of participants are noted by Todd
(1984). He cites a program of management education that uses
a learning community approach (Huczynski and Boddy, 1978),
the use of experiential learning techniques (Boydell, 1976), and
the use of self-planned learning in the Continuing Education
Unit for Architectural Staff of the National Health Service
(Todd, 1982). Interestingly, another recently reported study of
organizational action as a component of health service architects' continuing education emphasized their use of job rotation, workplace rearrangement, office meetings, sabbaticals, and
job exchanges as self-educational activities (Harris, 1982). Harris reported these architects to be engaged in deuterolearning
(Argyris and Schön, 1978); in other words, they were investigating and reflecting upon their own learning styles. In discussing
the quality of learning occurring within training programs, Todd
(1984) advocates the use of peer teaching and small-group discussion, along with real life work problems as the basis for curriculum, and he argues that the trainer should serve as a non-
didactic facilitator. As he observes, work is an activity that is a
central life interest to most adults, a significant element in their
identity, and a source of considerable self-esteem. Hence, "the
potential to produce enjoyment, conviviality, competence, enhanced self-esteem, and the insights that support personal and
social change is not necessarily reduced because the learning
that is carried out is related to work. Rather, this depends upon
the educational process, and the extent to which it supports
these features" (p. 102).

Finally, a number of educators have been involved in taking the collaborative aspects of effective facilitation to their

logical outcome in the context of corporate education and industrial training, that is, to the development of worker-controlled cooperatives and the increase of workplace democracy. This is particularly the case with European educators who are used to experiments in workplace democracy, such as Volvo's in Sweden, and are familiar with worker cooperatives in France, England, and Italy. In Denmark, for example, Louis Pio advocated worker ownership that would allow workers to express their abilities and grant meaning to their lives through control over their work, until his expulsion from the country in 1871. Nineteenth-century English industrialists, social critics, and political theorists such as Robert Owen, William Morris, and John Ruskin were all vigorous experimenters with, or advocates for, a reorganization of factory production to allow for participatory worker management and profit sharing. Current experiments in worker cooperatives such as those in Scotland and Liverpool in the shipbuilding and motorbike industries therefore have a long tradition in British industrial life.

But the European educator historically most concerned with placing the education and training of adults squarely in the context of worker control over factory production was Antonio Gramsci. A founder member and later general secretary of the Italian Communist party, Gramsci was imprisoned by Mussolini in 1926. During the decade that he spent in prison, however, he was able to work out his ideas in notebooks and letters. Gramsci advocated a system of factory councils through which workers would control the workplace and production, and he had in fact been involved in creating such a system in Turin after the First World War. These factory councils were the media of industrial education, teaching the administrative and economic skills that workers would need to take effective control over the production process. During the occupation of factories in Turin in 1920, the factory councils maintained production at a normal (sometimes increased) level and imposed strict codes of discipline for leaving the factory, drinking, or pilfering. In his analysis of the role of unions and factory councils as the vehicles of worker control, adult learning, and the transformation of society, Gramsci has an obvious contemporary relevance to any discussion of adult learning in the workplace. Those readers interested in exploring his ideas further should consult Clark (1977), Davidson (1977), Entwistle (1979), Jackson (1981), and Lovett, Clarke, and Kilmurray (1983).

The contemporary Italian educator, Ettore Gelpi, has also placed his proposals for the transformation of societies within the sphere of the workplace and workers' education. Gelpi believes that "a new relationship between work and education is no longer a question of the access of workers to the educational institutions, rather the presence of workers as educators within these structures" (1979, p. 3). In his commentary on Gelpi's ideas, Ireland (1979) points out that Gelpi reinterprets workers' education not as vocational training but as the acquisition of skills and knowledge that will enable workers to experiment with self-management in factory production. Hence, vocational education to Gelpi is close to Gramsci's conception of such education since it includes attention to questions of ethics, esthetics, and the place of production in the wider society. Because Gelpi is head of the Division of Lifelong Education within UNESCO, his ideas concerning the need to expand union and workers' education to include techniques of worker management and the introduction of workplace democracy have had a considerable influence on contemporary European education.

That the connection between adult learning and the participation by workers in factory management and production has been understood in North America is evident from the response to conferences on the quality of working life in America and Canada (Cohen-Rosenthal, 1982). The American Society for Training and Development views the Quality of Working Life (QWL) movement as an extension of participatory management that is aimed at increasing organizational effectiveness. In this sense it is similar to the Japanese "quality circle," in which workers come together to analyze and suggest solutions to problems at the workplace. There are thousands of such circles now in existence in American industry (*The Learning Connection*, a monthly journal issued by the LERN organization, estimated that there were two to three thousand in 1981), and they exemplify the "theory Z" (Ouchi, 1981) of management, whereby Japanese principles of collective decision making are transferred to an American setting (Pascale and Athos, 1981). The United Automobile Workers have developed QWL programs at General Motors, Ford Motor, and Chrysler, and the United Steelworkers of America have negotiated "participation teams" with management in the industry. The Communications Workers of America have also negotiated a QWL program with AT&T. As Cohen-Rosenthal reports, "Worker participation can become a strategy for mass adult education" (1982, p. 5). Moreover, the principles of good practice identified in worker participation and in effective facilitation—collaborative methods and curriculum based on adults' experiences—are very similar. Commonly, QWL programs focus on the skills of problem solving, collective decision making, and leadership development.

Finally, some trainers and educators have also placed Freirean ideas and techniques in the context of industrial democracy and worker management. Wilson (1978) has documented the application of Freirean methods—particularly the generation of significant themes and the creation and exploration of word codes—in the Sheffield steel industry. In America, Frank Adams (letter to the author, May 3, 1984, p. 1) has recently posed several crucial questions: "How can worker-owners and adult educators establish the principles of appropriate learning out of labor's concrete experiences and cultural situation? How can worker-owners use adult education to foster the traits of cooperation and collective consciousness inherent in the democratic workplace into an ideology which gives cohesion to a movement for social change and a body of knowledge which expresses that movement? What are the characteristics of a pedagogy for economic literacy and worklife liberation?"

We can anticipate that greater numbers of trainers and educators will concentrate their attention on such questions as we move to the end of a century that has been distinguished by a faster rate of societal and technological change than any other period of human history. Indeed, it may be that increasing numbers of educators will come to believe, along with Lindeman, that "workers' education may henceforth become one of the most vital phases in the education system" (1944, p. 121), particularly as unions come to see workers not just as workers but also as citizens and human beings.

One of the most interesting initiatives in this regard in the United States is the Industrial Cooperative Association (ICA), which assists employee, union, and community groups to establish worker cooperatives. The ICA has been working since 1978 to provide advice and assistance for establishing worker cooperatives in response to plant closures, to aid ongoing small businesses to convert to cooperative ownership, and to assist in developing new cooperatives. It has been involved in providing help to such diverse activities as the Workers' Owned Sewing Company in North Carolina; the Stevens Paper Mill in Westfield, Massachusetts; the Moose Creek Construction Company in Burlington, Vermont; Extended Family Enterprises in Jonesboro, Arkansas; the Colonial Cooperative Press in Clinton, Massachusetts; and Family Homes Cooperative in Beckley, West Virginia. Other more familiar examples of businesses with elements of worker control in the United States include People Express airlines, Eastern Airlines, and the Weirton Steel Company in Pennsylvania.

The adult education dimension of worker cooperatives has, in fact, long been acknowledged in Canada and Britain, as well as in the United States. In Britain the workers' education movement has close ties with the cooperative movement, and the Cooperative College in the East Midlands is a major residential and nonresidential education center for working men and women, trade unionists, and activists in various community groups. One of the most renowned adult education enterprises in the history of Canada—the Antigonish movement (Coady, 1939)—focused on the need for educators to assist working men and women to establish some control over the means of production and distribution of their labor. Because Coady asserted as a fundamental principle that educational efforts should be rooted in the most pressing concerns of adults, he placed enormous emphasis on the teaching and learning transactions that occurred as workers sought to deal with bureaucracies and acquire skills and knowledge collaboratively that they could then apply to establishing cooperatives. As with Myles Horton, Coady saw an unbreakable link between economic democracy and political democracy, and he felt that educators working for democratic reforms had therefore to assist workers to create credit unions and cooperatives.

Conclusion: Contextual Distortions

The last two chapters have examined the nature and form of adult learning within eight common, but very diverse, practice settings: self-directed learning, adult literacy and basic education, continuing professional education, labor education, institutions of higher education, informal learning networks, training and human resource development within business and industry, and community action. Many other settings for practice could have been chosen, including correctional education, health education, and the military. The summaries of practice areas in the current chapter have of necessity been brief. It seemed important, however, to convey a sense of the multifarious forms and settings within which the principles of effective facilitation discussed in Chapter One are observable. Throughout the rest of this book specific and detailed case studies of practice are chosen to illustrate the application of these principles in the areas of teaching, andragogical practice, facilitating self-directed learning, and program development and evaluation. The case studies of implementation of practice are drawn from the eight areas already discussed. These eight were chosen for their diversity, and for the amount of documented material that is readily available on them, particularly to educators in the United States and Great Britain.

It is important to remember, however, that documented case studies of effective facilitation are context-specific descriptions of particular milieus in which groups of differing individuals are involved in achieving singular objectives. We should beware, therefore, of assuming that features of one model of program development, or techniques of needs assessment used with one client group, will be immediately replicable in other settings. Each practice initiative comprises a psychosocial drama in which available resources, the political ethos of the institution, the educator's personal philosophy of training or education, the expectations of clients, and the differing personalities of instructors, participants, administrators, and ancillary staff will all influence the form of the subsequent teaching-learning transaction. These contextual variables will determine the extent to which principles of good practice can be exemplified and will alter the form in which such principles are realized.

Facilitators of adult learning are, as Clark (1956) pointed out in a survey of continuing education settings in Southern California some thirty years ago, frequently in positions of marginality within their own institutions. This may enable them to experiment with innovative practices and to exploit their maverick status and professional ambiguity to good educational effect, particularly in times when the economy is expanding and educational funds are freely flowing. In the current era of monetaryism, supply-side economics, and the trickle-down theory of economic benefits, however, the reality is that these educators will generally find that their marginal status results in their being subject to the fluctuating preferences of political purse holders or the whims of administrative decision makers who are highly cost conscious. Financial and administrative constraints will, of course, serve to limit the extent to which principles of effective facilitation can be exemplified. At times it may be possible to build in collaborative elements in selecting methods but to have little opportunity for the renegotiation of curricula. At other times objectives, curricula, and methods may all be open to continuous revision and negotiation, but evaluative criteria that are applied to judging the success of the educational encounter may be in the hands of external decision makers. What may frequently occur is that facilitators may encourage learners to explore alternative interpretations of their experience and to consider different ways of thinking and living in their personal, occupational, political, and recreational worlds, but find that these adults are highly resistant to any suggestions that their long-cherished assumptions, values, and behaviors might in any way be flawed or contradictory.

Does the existence of the distorting factors identified

above, which may prevent the full realization of the six principles identified in Chapter One as illustrative of effective facilitation, mean that the subsequent encounters are not valuable or
valid examples of education? Obviously not. It is self-defeating
and unrealistic in the extreme to adopt some kind of purist pos-
ture whereby we only consider as valid education those instances in which all six principles are fully evident. The world
outside the pages of textbooks and manuals is one characterized
by contextuality, complexity, and ambiguity. To feel constantly guilty because one is not fully exemplifying all features of
effective facilitation is to crucify oneself on the cross of perfection. Such practitioners retire early, fall prey to ulcers, or retreat to eyries of relative isolation where they are not offended
daily by the chaotic unmanageability of the real world of practice.

It is just as dangerous, however, to have no sense of good
practice as to strive for impossible goals. Without some sense of
what is both effective and desirable, we may begin to shift with
whatever professional wind is blowing at the time or become
subject to the dictates of political officeholders who can use us
to achieve whatever ends they deem desirable. When we do possess a clear and reasoned idea about what constitutes effective
facilitation, however, we can present purse holders, politicians,
and administrators with a considered response to whatever
changes they suggest. We may not always be able to achieve all
our ends or to protect all aspects of our programs, but there will
most likely be a sense of unity and coherence informing our efforts, which will be observable to learners and administrators
alike. With such an observable and clear rationale of effective
practice, our professional status as facilitators of adult learning
is likely to be taken more seriously, and we are more likely to
be invited to advise on those aspects of the institution's operations in which adult learners are involved but for which we have
no direct professional responsibility. If we demonstrate that we
have a professional code of good practice, then we can expect
administrators of universities, polytechnics, community colleges, labor unions, professional associations, and training divisions in business to seek our assistance in dealing with counsel-

ing, teaching methods, curriculum building, and evaluation related to programs in which adults are involved. We can thereby ensure that the adult learners in such programs are treated with respect, that their sense of self-worth is enhanced rather than diminished, and that through participating in shaping the form of the educational activity in which they are involved, they will become more self-directed, critically aware adults capable of appraising and changing aspects of their personal relationships, occupational lives, political involvements, and recreational activities.

❦ 9 ❧

Program Development
for Adults

*Challenging
the Institutional
Approach*

One of the most frequently offered criticisms of programs of
professional preparation by graduates who subsequently inhabit
the "real world" of practice is that such programs are strong on
theory but weak on practical application. It is not unusual to
hear practitioners declare that their first few months of practice
were spent unlearning the lessons of graduate training programs.
Indeed, the low esteem and credibility granted to programs of
professional educator preparation is one of the most significant
commonalities of practitioners' attitudes that I have noticed
across the three countries in which I have worked as an educator and trainer of adults (Britain, America, and Canada). A common view is that one must attend university-sponsored programs of professional preparation and in-service development
because of licensing requirements and for the possibilities of
promotion and salary increases this brings. The idea that one
might become a more insightful or effective practitioner as a result of attendance at such courses is greeted with an amused
skepticism.

Nowhere is this theory-practice disjunction more evident than in the realm of program development for adult learners. As a professor who has taught many program development courses to educators and trainers of adults, I can attest to the frequency with which participants in these courses (who are mostly practitioners with several years of experience) state that they "break the rules of good practice" or "disregard theory for the *real* world of practice." It is as if such participants will tacitly agree to attend courses, conferences, and workshops on program development for the various career rewards this brings, but sit through such experiences only with a sustained suspension of belief. They give the appearance of battle-weary veterans of trench warfare; the skepticism with which they view neat textbook models of program development is grounded in their years of experience dealing with organizations in which personality conflicts, political factors, and budgetary constraints constantly alter neatly conceived plans of action. Hence, this chapter will examine the theory-practice disjunction produced by attempts to plan education and training programs for adults within organizations not strongly supportive of such activities.

Institutional Model of Program Development

As Thomas (1964) commented in his analysis of the concept of program, "No term or idea in adult education is quite so widely used, nor quite so elusive in meaning, as the term program" (p. 241). The word functions on several different levels of meaning, calls to mind a number of different associations, and is used in very different ways by different writers. Thomas observed that it was used to refer to activities, curricula, and courses, though he also noted that the three characteristics of series, order, and purpose seemed to be common to all definitions. Verner (1964) viewed an educational program as a series of learning experiences designed to achieve, in a delimited period of time, certain specific instructional objectives. He regarded the term as flexible enough to apply to the educational activities existing within a whole community, to those provided by a particular agency, or even to a particular class session. Schroeder

(1970) noted five common usages of the term, ranging from community-wide activities to single classes. Finally, Boyle and Jahns (1970) also viewed the term as covering a variety of providing agency activities. Some of these activities are specifically instructional, while others are directed toward maintaining the viability of the providing agency as a social entity.

Other writers have explored a more task-orientated concept of the term *program*. Niemi and Nagle (1979) regard the task of program planning as being to make explicit, prior to implementation, the specific combination of outcomes, processes, and inputs required for the educational program. The planner will identify instructional objectives, specify instructional, evaluative, and classroom management procedures, and outline required resources. In his analysis of program planning, Szczypkowski (1980) declares the setting of program objectives to be the most misunderstood and misapplied element in the planning process, yet no other aspect is deemed by him to be more crucial. In my own institution a list of necessary program development tasks has been compiled that identifies as essential to programming such diverse activities as survey research, needs assessment, conceptual analysis, committee management, prioritizing tasks, instructional design, classroom management, counseling, budgeting, administration, evaluation, public relations, and staff training. Burnham (1984), in his investigation of program planning as technology in a school district, community college, and university, identifies eighty-two discrete planning tasks. Finally, Simpson (1982) has outlined an interactive model of program development. He criticizes the excessive reliance on linear, sequential models and argues for greater attention to the procedures by which program rationales are crystallized and reference criteria are evolved. His model stresses the importance of recognizing the normative criteria adopted in the process of planning, the need to consult learners during planning, and the generally neglected significance of formative evaluation. Both planning and evaluation are seen as dynamic, generative, cyclic activities.

In all these attempts to conceptualize the notion of program, several features seem repeatedly to emerge. Prime among these is the notion of intent, deliberation, and purpose. Educational programs are viewed as intentionally purposeful activities. They are also thought to have order and sequence. Purpose is married to organization so that the separate elements in a program are somehow related to each other. Finally, there is a sense of finiteness built in to most definitions; programs are deemed to have clearly discernible beginning and end points. These three features—purpose, order, and finiteness—all characterize the model of program development most commonly adopted in facilitating adult learning. Over twenty years ago London (1960) observed that "there appears to be a remarkable consensus among adult educators as to the formal steps in successful program development" (p. 66). These steps were to determine the needs of constituents, enlist students' aid in planning, formulate clear objectives, design a program plan, and plan and carry out a system of evaluation.

These five stages of program planning are remarkably close to the model of curriculum planning first proposed by Tyler (1949) in his syllabus for Education 305. In fact, the Tylerian mode of program development has retained a conceptual preeminence in adult education since it was first adopted in the 1950s. Houle (1972) points out that most holders of graduate degrees in adult education in the United States obtained them in departments where Tyler's ideas were popular. Hence, it is not surprising that contemporary reviews of literature in program planning and evaluation (Apps, 1979; Brookfield, 1982; Stakes, 1981) conclude that this model is still in the ascendant.

A brief review of the program planning process as conceived in a number of program development books over the last twenty years demonstrates just how pervasive the influence of the institutional model of program development has been. Put briefly, the model comprises the following five stages: identify needs, define objectives (preferably in behavioral terms), identify learning experiences to meet these objectives, organize learning experiences into a plan with scope and sequence, and evaluate program outcomes in terms of the attainment of the behaviors specified in stage two. With some alterations, usually centering on the need to involve participants in planning the program format, this model has been adopted in nine major contributions to adult education literature. Thus, along with London's (1960) analysis, we have the work of Verner (1964), Bergevin, Morris, and Smith (1963), Boyle and Jahns (1970), Knowles (1980), Knox (1971), Houle (1972), Pennington and Green (1976), and Boyle (1981). Bergevin, Morris, and Smith, for example, advised educators to identify needs and interests, develop topics, set goals, select resources, select techniques, and outline activities to be accomplished. Verner saw educational program planning as a matter of determining a need, identifying educational goals, arranging learning tasks, and measuring achievement. To Boyle and Jahns a sequence of activities was to be arranged after examining the situation to be changed, translating the needs of the clientele group into objectives, designing learning activities to achieve these objectives, and designing an evaluation.

In *The Modern Practice of Adult Education*, however, Knowles prefaces the diagnosis of needs, formulation of objectives, design and management of learning, and evaluation with the setting of a climate for learning and the establishment of a mutual structure for planning. Knox also advises a preliminary appraisal of the situation before proceeding with needs identification and selection, development of the program plan, and implementation of the program. Houle's seven decision points and components of an educational planning framework fit cleanly into the institutional mode in that these steps focus on identifying an educational activity, deciding to proceed, clarifying objectives, designing a format, fitting the format into larger patterns of life, putting the plan into effect, and measuring and appraising results.

In their review of program development processes used by continuing educators in six fields from five campuses, Pennington and Green describe six clusters of program development activity. These are labeled originating the idea, developing the idea, making a commitment, developing the program, teaching the course, and evaluating the impact. Finally, Boyle proposes fifteen concepts that he considers important for educational program planning. However, although he does adopt some elements of the Tylerian model, particularly in his emphasis on an institutional framework for program development, he also identifies other significant concerns. Boyle feels, for example, that it is necessary to establish a philosophical basis for programming, to engage in the situational analysis of needs, to articulate criteria for establishing program priorities, to recognize contextual constraints, and to communicate the value of the program to politically powerful decision makers.

Shortcomings of the Model

Doubts concerning the viability of the institutional model have increased during my time as a professor of adult education. From graduate students in adult education in the United States, England, and Canada I have received the same message concerning the disjunction between theory as depicted in the major texts on program development and the real world of practice. These students (all of them practitioners in some kind of adult training or continuing education setting) declare that they are unable to recognize themselves in the pages of most program development manuals. The practitioners in these manuals seem to operate in contexts where adequate resources, congenial colleagues, supportive superiors, and a sympathetic political or institutional climate always exist. To myself, and to many of my graduate students, such a world is so unrealistic as to call seriously into question any practice injunctions given by these authors.

In the following paragraphs the institutional mode of program development will be examined critically, and some of this writer's most deeply felt misgivings about its usefulness and appropriateness will be voiced. Before doing so, however, it is important to recognize that for certain purposes this model is effective and appropriate. In those institutional settings where learners and teachers share a commitment to collaboratively defined objectives, and where a clear imbalance of expertise between teacher and taught exists, the model is suitable, even desirable. Indeed, no other model appears to have such a clearly articulated rationale where the short-term acquisition of well-defined proficiencies is concerned. It is also important to acknowledge that those adult education writers who have adapted the model for use with adults do add a collaborative, participatory dimension to it. They talk of enlisting learners' aid in planning, of establishing a mutual structure for planning, of appraising the situation, and of setting a climate for learning. Nowadays, few educators or trainers would publicly subscribe to any program development model that seemed to exclude adult learners from some kind of involvement in planning curricula or developing evaluative procedures.

The institutional model, nevertheless, still holds conceptual sway as the most effective means of organizing workshops, courses, conferences, and seminars. In the world of industrial training and management development it is often unchallenged. Time and again, members of my courses on program development in adult and continuing education turn in program designs that are direct translations of this model into their own practice settings. This despite the fact that the program development courses stress that the model is only one of a number of very different options. Deans of continuing education, staff trainers in business and industry, directors of in-service development in hospitals, and public school adult education directors all provide examples of their real world programs that consistently demonstrate that the institutional model is the only one they take seriously. Looking through papers submitted to my courses on program development over the last five years, I find virtually no reports of programs, or plans for future programs, that do not accept wholeheartedly the stepwise, sequenced, institutional model of program development. It is time, therefore, that the conceptual hegemony of this model be seriously challenged and that its claim to serve as the only realistic and available guide for practice be critically examined.

The critical comments that follow build on the analyses of Pennington and Green (1976), Apps (1979), Day and Baskett (1982), and Eisner (1985) in particular. Day and Baskett (1982) summarize their misgivings concerning the Tylerian, institutional model of program planning (which they call the "classical" model) as follows: "Focus on the attainment of predetermined objectives does not allow for natural or unanticipated learning during the course of the programmes and inadvertently leads the educator to view all learning in terms of demonstrable behavior (Apps, 1979: 117-122); and the tendency to interpret objectives behaviorally poses ethical questions as to whether one person should attempt consciously to modify the behavior of another" (p. 144).

Day and Baskett point out that attempts to develop collaborative, andragogical programs are frequently contradicted by institutional constraints and by "problems in matching states of learning readiness to course content and learning process" (p. 149). They also comment on the naiveté of presuming that textbook models of practice can be neatly replicated in the real world (p. 146).

> There are a variety of intervening factors such as work climate, motivation and organizational structure which suggest that educational input in the form of programmes is far too simplistic a solution and is based on a linear, unidirectional cause-effect model which does not realistically reflect the complexity of the world of the professional as a learner and doer. It may well be that no matter how careful we are in developing need-oriented programmes which meet all the criteria of programme planning, the exercise will be irrelevant because it will be unable to take into consideration the contextual variables of professional practice which are not under the educator's control.

These authors cite the work of Pratt (1979a), Knox (1979), and Sjogren (1979) as providing empirical illustration of the way in which program developers have become trapped within a narrow paradigm of thought and belief concerning the means by which programs for adult learners are best developed. This paradigm is inconsistent with the real world of professional practice, but, as in so many professional spheres, educational programmers rarely acknowledge the severe disjunctions that frequently arise when espoused theories (in which behavior is justified and explained) are tested against theories in use (actual behaviors that are effective in real life). This concept of theories in use will be examined further at a later point in this chapter. Put simply, a theory in use comprises a set of proven beliefs concerning effective practices that are appropriate to particular situations. Theories in use are often referred to as "playing hunches," "intuition," or "inspired guesswork" by practitioners, who are embarrassed about dignifying the creative improvisational aspects of their work with the term *theory*.

Before undertaking a more detailed critique of the Tylerian model, it is important to acknowledge that Tyler himself has significantly revised the ideas that he first set forth in the 1940s. He now urges a greater flexibility in formats of curriculum development than he did in *Basic Principles of Curriculum and Instruction* (1949) and admits that it may be seriously restrictive to argue in advance for too close a specification of predetermined educational objectives. In various seminars at adult education departments in the United States (Tyler, 1985; Carter, 1973), he has admitted that were he writing *Basic Principles of Curriculum and Instruction* now, he would not use the term *behaviors*, because this has been interpreted to mean a narrow concentration on performance behaviors. To Tyler, the term *behaviors* refers to feeling, perceiving, and thinking, not just to psychomotor behaviors.

In a collection of dialogues on facilitating learning with adults, Tyler had this to say about the usefulness of the concept of behavioral objectives: "I agree that if by behavioral objectives we have come to mean highly specific, only observable outcomes, then, in that sense, behavioral objectives do a disservice. But if you think of behavior as including thinking, and feeling, and acting, and you're talking about such things as what will help learners understand certain concepts—what principles they can follow; what kinds of problem-solving skills they can develop—then I think that the clarification of objectives can really be helpful to an adult educator" (quoted in Carter, 1973, p. 31). Tyler believes that it is Mager's (1975) work that has been most responsible for disseminating the view that all educational experiences must be judged by the extent to which learners exhibit specifically determined behavioral objectives, and he is critical of Mager's application of the shopfloor, industrial training methods developed at Litton Industries to all educational activities. Tyler asserts that it is much more helpful to think about clarity of objectives (that is, the intent of education) than constantly to worry about specific objectives.

Houle (1972) and Blaney (1974) refer to the institutional category of educational design and the institutional mode of curriculum development, respectively. The following comments rely particularly on Blaney's (1974, pp. 20-21): specification of selected educational program variables and their manifestation in the institutional mode:

- *Authority* is assumed by the educational institution and is largely external to learners.
- *Objectives* are determined prior to the educational encounter, and these provide the basis for program planning and evaluation. These objectives are consonant with the aims of the providing agency, although they may be revised by the teacher.
- *Methods of instruction* are chosen for their demonstrated effectiveness in achieving the previously determined objectives.
- *The teacher's roles* are those of instructional planner, manager of instruction, diagnostician, motivator, and evaluator.
- *The learner* assumes a dependent role regarding learning objectives and evaluative criteria; the learner's task is to achieve the prescribed objectives.
- *Evaluation* is criterion referenced, and criteria are based on the achievement of the prescribed objectives. The purpose of evaluation is to assess the effectiveness of instruction in assisting learners to achieve the prescribed objectives, to improve the program, and to diagnose learning difficulties.
- *Hard and soft technology* are both used in planning and conducting instruction.

Blaney concludes his specification of the institutional

mode by emphasizing the conditions of learning implicit in the model: that there are clearly explicated objectives determined prior to the program, that students have a knowledge of these, that students are given the opportunity for relevant practice, that they are provided with evaluative reaction to their performance, that they are motivated, and that learning opportunities are effectively organized.

Prespecified Learning Objectives. At the forefront of the institutional model is the specification by the providing agency or organizing educator of the learning objectives for the particular program, course, or class session. These objectives are the programmatic pivot; they serve as the reference point and focus for the design of instruction, the planning of course work, and the evaluation of program success. Any serious examination of this model, therefore, must begin with the preeminence it accords to predetermined objectives.

To Robinson and Taylor (1983), the question of "who decides what are to be the appropriate objectives for a course is at the root of the dichotomy between student-centered and teacher-directed approaches to learning" (p. 359). They argue that a student-centered approach emphasizes the constant renegotiation of goals through the exploration of processes of learning, whereas "the internal logic of an objectives model imposes a rigor incompatible with the unpredictability of a student-centered learning situation" (p. 359). They assert that the popularity of the teacher-directed mode of organizing educational experiences lies in its harmony with prevailing technological, rational modes of thought. Giroux (1983) has also noted how "the technological and behaviorist models that have long exercised a powerful influence on the curriculum were, in part, adapted from the scientific-management movement of the 1920s" (p. 44). Eisner (1985) links the rise in popularity of the behavioral objectives approach to the preeminence in the earlier part of this century of modes of thought focused on technical rationality in industry and on prediction and control of training outcomes in the military.

Several consequences flow from this emphasis on predetermined objectives in program development. First, because it is much easier to specify beforehand the acquisition of psycho-motor skills than it is to outline objectives regarding the development of affective, esthetic, or insightful capacities, these latter domains run the risk of being neglected in favor of more easily operationalized domains. It is difficult to outline in advance objectives that clearly relate to an adult's development of critical consciousness, to the internal mental rearrangement that follows from flash of insight, or to a growing appreciation of lyric poetry. To equate the development of artistic sensibility with the number of books read, the number of museums visited, or the number of concerts attended is simplistic and misconceived in the extreme. It is reductionist in the worst possible manner in that it attempts to reduce to a crude level of behavioral simplicity what are extremely complex mental operations.

In his discussion of the limitations of behavioral objectives, Eisner (1985) illustrates the absurdity of trying to outline the learning objectives for an educational interaction with much exactness. He asks how one would describe insight, integrity, perceptivity, or self-esteem when specifying these as learning outcomes, or how one would state the qualities of a late Beethoven quartet in precise, unambiguous, measurable terms. He asserts that "the point here is not an effort to inject the mystical into educational planning but rather to avoid reductionistic thinking that impoverishes our view of what is possible" (p. 115). Although Eisner's analysis is applied chiefly to school systems, his criticism of the view that the prespecification of goals is the rational way to proceed in curriculum planning in every instance is equally pertinent for adult learning encounters: "Life in classrooms, like that outside them, is seldom neat or linear. Although it may be a shock to some, goals are not always clear. Purposes are not always precise. As a matter of fact, there is much that we do, and need to do, without a clear sense of what the objective is. Many of our most productive activities take the form of exploration or play. In such activities, the task is not one of arriving at a preformed objective but rather to act, often with a sense of abandon, wonder, curiosity. Out of such activity rules may be formed and objectives created" (p. 116).

Indeed, one can make a convincing case that much reflective, complex learning—for example, the awareness of the contextuality and contingency of knowledge—are incapable of being specified too closely before its acquisition. This is not to say that we cannot recognize the existence of such forms of learning through observing alterations in behavior. Acts of learning that follow from traumatic events such as coming to terms with bereavement, illness, unemployment, or divorce will undoubtedly be reflected in behavioral changes. The point is that these behaviors cannot be specified beforehand as the performance behaviors around which a course should be structured.

The most fundamental flaw with the predetermined objectives approach, then, is its tendency to equate one form of adult learning—instrumental learning (how to perform technical or psychomotor operations more effectively)—with the sum total of adult learning. It neglects completely the domain of the most significant personal learning—the kind that results from reflection on experiences and from trying to make sense of one's life by exploring the meanings others have assigned to similar experiences. If asked on their death beds to identify their most important learning experience many people would probably speak of the insight and understanding of self that they had developed while trying to make sense of some calamitous event or unplanned experience. They would probably not single out some form of learning that had enabled them to perform a function better (important though this might be at different times).

It will often be the case, then, that the most significant personal learning adults undertake cannot be specified in advance in terms of objectives to be attained or behaviors (of whatever kind) to be performed. Thus, significant personal learning might be defined as that learning in which adults come to reflect on their self-images, change their self-concepts, question their previously uncritically internalized norms (behavioral and moral), and reinterpret their current and past behaviors from a new perspective. It is somewhat akin to perspective transformation (Mezirow, 1978) or "conscientization" (Freire,

1970b), though it may be less apocalyptic or staggeringly revelatory than that latter term implies.

Significant personal learning entails fundamental change in learners and leads them to redefine and reinterpret their personal, social, and occupational worlds. In the process, adults may come to explore affective, cognitive, and psychomotor domains that they previously had not perceived as relevant to themselves. But to establish a set of objectives where attainment determines the format and focus of the teaching-learning transaction is to make it impossible for learners to reformulate their goals and make them correspond more closely with their new perceptions of the world. One cannot specify in advance which changes one wishes to make when it is a question of redefining the self, reinterpreting past behaviors, or attempting to grant meaning to current or past experiences. This is one reason why the idea of continuous negotiation and renegotiation is stressed so strongly as a feature of effective practice. Only if this renegotiation is possible can one abandon previously formulated goals as these become demonstrably irrelevant and begin to formulate ones that will allow learners to explore new directions that appear to them to be more meaningful than those identified in advance by a facilitator, however perceptive he or she may be.

No one should conclude that these critical comments mean that we cannot specify course objectives for complex and sophisticated forms of learning. It is one thing to say that a set of behaviors cannot be specified in advance as the course objectives for a collection of individual adults engaged in complex mental operations. It is quite another to say that we should abandon altogether the concept of purpose. To this writer the concept of purpose remains central to our understanding of what constitutes education. However, general purposes need not always be translated into sets of closely specified objectives. In using the discussion method as a technique for facilitating learning, for example, it is crucial that the outcomes, direction, and purposes of such discussion activity be subject to constant negotiation. Such open and continuous negotiation is a defining characteristic of effective facilitation mentioned by Paterson

(1970b), Bridges (1979), and the Nottingham Andragogy Group (1983) in Chapter Six. Hence, we can have purposeful discussion without always seeking to specify exact cognitive outcomes for that discussion.

There is another potentially serious flaw with the specified objectives approach. Once specific course objectives are identified, whether by the teacher or collaboratively with learners, then those objectives become reified to a dangerous degree. They can become carved in stone, unchanging and unchallengeable. Their attainment comes to dominate every form of educational interaction, and attempts to pursue alternative avenues of inquiry or to reflect on the possibility of other forms of interaction are viewed as irrelevant or heretical. This has the effect of making the ends of education static and incapable of redefinition. In the name of establishing order or of introducing professionalism into educational planning, the proponents of the predetermined objectives approach may find that they are actually constraining the development of autonomous critical awareness among adult learners.

As both professor and student, nothing has proved more irksome to me than the insistence that for educational encounters to be valuable there must always be clearly specified learning objectives that are being assiduously pursued. This approach may be suitable in some settings—when it is a question, for instance, of acquiring the psychomotor skills needed to operate a new machine. It may also be well suited to some childhood educational settings, although even here the specified objectives may serve more as control mechanisms than as aids to intellectual development. Indeed, Jones (1982) and Robinson and Taylor (1983) both argue that the predetermined objectives approach represents an implicit alignment by educators with systems of control and authority in society. Because knowledge is socially constructed, the development of curricula for learners need to be informal, open-ended, and public. Jones regards the predefined objectives approach as "a process developed originally to constrain and control rather than to broaden and liberate" (p. 168). Apps (1973) has also criticized the inflexibility of the predetermined objectives approach. He points out that teacher adherence to a preplanned set of defined objectives precludes the alterations in curricular focus, usually as a result of participants' suggestions, so characteristic of adult education classes.

This is a crucial point. Readers of this book who have been members of adult learning groups as teachers or learners will probably recall many instances in which the intellectual direction of a course was changed as a result of learners' wishes. Such alterations, changes in direction, and continuous renegotiation of purposes for classes have been distinctive features of my own teaching career. Indeed, for the effective facilitation of learning as conceived in this book there can be no other alternative to this process of negotiation, change, and alteration. Through being encouraged to question accepted curricular formats and to suggest individually meaningful alternatives, learners come to view knowledge as socially constructed and to contemplate the possibility of arriving at a new definition of truth.

All this is not to say that the facilitator should have no agenda, should abdicate complete responsibility for a group's direction to participants, or should be totally nondirective in discussions. Chapter Six has already argued that this stance (in the name of democratic facilitation) represents an unwarranted retreat from the facilitator's true function. Not only is this stance morally questionable, however, it is also impossible to maintain in practice. It is impossible because no facilitator enters an educational situation without some (perhaps private) notions as to what constitutes important curricular concerns and desirable purposes. Just as grounded theory researchers cannot enter a research activity completely free of ideas regarding possible hypotheses, causal linkages, or substantive concerns, so facilitators cannot pretend that they are devoid of values, notions of what is important, or personal beliefs that will affect their pedagogy. To do so is tantamount to claiming to be a moral cipher. Hence, teachers of adults, or those responsible for program development, will always have purposes, intentions, and notions of educational importance, whether or not they choose to make these public. Throughout this book particular purposes for adult learning are proposed. The point is, however, that to insist on a close specification of these objectives prior to the educational experience is overly constraining.

Purposeful, enlightening, and personally significant discussion is not only possible without previously specified learning objectives, it actually requires that no such specifications be made. As Paterson (1970b) cogently argues, to engage in the collaborative exploration and interpretation of individual experience is the most meaningful form of discussion for adults. But such discussion cannot be tied to previously determined objectives. It must be open and subject to continuous negotiation. Teachers and learners will often hold conflicting beliefs, values, and notions of importance. The most illuminating encounter is one in which these beliefs, values, and notions are externalized and subjected to collaborative analysis and in which participants are always ready to alter their lines of inquiry on the basis of newly realized insights or interests.

My final criticism of previously defined objectives in program development for adults concerns the question of unplanned, incidental learning. If we use the attainment of previously specified learning objectives as the evaluative criterion for judging the success of an educational effort (as the institutional model proposes), then we must logically relegate unplanned, serendipitous, and incidental outcomes to a position of secondary importance. Indeed, we may consider such learning to have no real value at all. This idea, however, has proved so repugnant to some educational evaluators that a whole school of goal-free evaluation has developed as a counter to it. This school will be considered in Chapter Eleven. Here, we might simply note that several writers have questioned the idea that the only learning outcomes of any value are those that correspond to previously specified objectives. Apps (1979, p. 120) points out that it is impossible for educators to anticipate all the learning that will result from participation in adult education classes. Jones (1982) declares that "the unintended consequences of a learning situation are often much more important than the original restrictive catechism of goals which invariably assumes an instrumental role for learning" (p. 168).

Some empirical support for the view that learners may perceive the unplanned outcomes of course participation to be of considerable significance is presented by Fodor (1984). In her investigation of incidental learning occurring in structured educational experiences, she surveyed 246 adult accounting students in three different colleges (accounting students were chosen because courses in accounting are characterized by a uniformity of objectives). The study confirmed the ubiquity of incidentally learned information, skills, and attitudes in a set of circumstances designed for purposeful learning. Particularly important was the encouragement for such learning received from peers. Fodor advised adult teachers to arrange for informal interactions among peers as part of the course experience, to give greater attention to the cultivation of incidental learning in study skills courses, and to direct students to materials or resources that could help them develop independence and self-knowledge.

It is evident, then, that no programmer can predict the range of learning outcomes that are likely to arise from participation in one class session, let alone from membership in a course lasting several months. When the difficulties of trying to arrange learning outcomes for one adult are multiplied many times, the irrelevance of the predefined objectives approach for most programs becomes immediately apparent. That we still persist in using this approach to guide our program planning style irrespective of the nature of our clientele or our educational purposes is an extreme example of the "emperor's clothing" syndrome.

If, as programmers, we assume that the only valid learning is that which corresponds to some specific format we have previously arranged, then we are guilty of an unusually high degree of intellectual arrogance. Such arrogance is not uncommon, however. For example, if a learner leaves a program before the end of the course, such withdrawal is almost always regarded as symptomatic of failure—failure by the learner who did not apply his or her talents with sufficient industry or failure by the teacher who possessed inadequate pedagogic skills. An equally plausible interpretation, however, is that the learner feels that she has gained what was most valuable from the course and decides that, with limited time at her disposal, she would be better advised to pursue other avenues of learning. Indeed, withdrawal might sometimes be interpreted as a sign of the success of the course in that it has so animated a learner's interest in a field that she commits herself to a sustained and independent exploration of its boundaries.

It is timely to remind ourselves, then, that we cannot prescribe for our diverse clienteles the exact range, form, and number of learning outcomes that will result from their participation in our programs. Learners' perceptions of what is valuable learning may bear little relation to the previously determined objectives that we prescribe to determine instructional design, course content, and evaluative procedures. Learners will frequently take from course participation various skills, insights, and information that have nothing to do with the activities and outcomes initially intended by the educator.

In every learning group there may well be an optimal balance that can be attained among facilitators' purposes, participants' expectations, flexibility of format, and sense of overall direction. In the most satisfying of group transactions, this balance will be negotiated continually. This, of course, is not to advocate an abandonment of the concept of educational purpose, whether this be expressed in broad philosophical aims or in terms of specific behavioral or other performance objectives. Although various encounter or support groups may decide to meet for no other reason than to make contact with others of similar outlook and may be able to spend a great deal of time negotiating purposes, for many learning groups this will not be realistic. Community action groups, groups engaged in advocacy, work-study groups, groups seeking to acquire occupational skills, and groups meeting to undertake hard intellectual analysis will most likely not wish to spend more than a small part of their time engaged in an initial negotiation of purpose. They will probably benefit from a regular formative evaluation session, in which progress is discussed and fundamental purposes reiterated, but the majority of participants' time will be spent in purposeful learning.

The point is, however, that incidental learning, unplanned acquisition of skills and knowledge, or unanticipated insights should not be regarded by participants or facilitators as somehow innately less valid than previously specified learning outcomes. A sense of common purpose is probably a precondition of effective group interaction and development of a moral culture within a group. But it should not become reified to such an extent that deviations from the previously agreed-upon purpose are condemned as irrelevant even before they occur. This, in effect, may block off fruitful avenues of intellectual exploration and act against participants' making meaningful connections between learning activities and their own experiences.

The last comments on this question of behavioral objectives might profitably be left to Eisner (1985). As he remarks, "In thousands of ways, teachers draw on images of human virtue as criteria for the direction of their activity as teachers and for the directions they should take with their students. The storehouse of such images is large, and it needs to be. It is modulated according to the circumstances and context and with regard to the particular student with whom the teacher interacts" (p. 124). Why, then, should we regard it as unprofessional or irresponsible for facilitators to encourage learners to explore feelings, perceptions, and avenues of inquiry that were not originally specified as part of the learning group's activities? Arguably, the most exciting, memorable, and profound moments in learning are those in which individuals stumble into insights and perceptions of which they had previously been unaware. Such moments can rarely be planned beforehand in precise terms, though the facilitator can encourage a learning group culture that will make the likelihood of such moments occurring much stronger. A facilitator who can make unexpected connections between participants' contributions or who encourages learners to depart from the "script" of the session's activities to explore themes that were unanticipated but that engage and excite is the most valuable (and perhaps the rarest) of educators.

Satisfaction of Adults' Needs. With no exceptions, the program development models outlined earlier in this chapter place the determination of learners' needs at the forefront of their activities. The needs revealed by a needs assessment are what provide the goals and aims of a program, which are then translated into specific objectives, curricula, and evaluative criteria. Griffith (1978), however, has called the concept of need an adult education shibboleth in that the favored answer to questions concerning the function of an educational program is that it is meeting learners' needs, meeting adults' needs, or meeting the needs of the community.

The concept of need also functions as a "premature ultimate" in discussions concerning the proper role of education and training programs. A premature ultimate is a concept or term that provokes such reverence and contains such connotative potency that its invocation tends to silence any further discussion on a matter. Lawson (1979) points out that the term *need* functions in this manner when questions concerning the curricula of training and education programs are raised. Hence, to say that one is meeting needs in a program is to state a case rather than to argue a viewpoint. Discussion on the merits of the case comes to be seen as inappropriate. But to say that as a programmer one is meeting needs is somewhat akin to a politician's saying that an action or policy is democratic. In both instances the justification invoked for the decisions taken is ambiguous, while at the same time it forecloses further discussion. What is important to realize is that many different interpretations can be made of the concept of need and that the concept is irrevocably value laden.

The value-laden aspect of the concept has been discussed in several analyses (Griffith, 1978; Monette, 1977, 1979; Lawson, 1979; Brackhaus, 1984). As these writers all recognize, those who invoke the concept of need to justify their decisions should specify whether the needs in question are felt by learners or prescribed by educators. It is unpardonable to confuse the two, yet such confusion is frequently evident in the writings and conversations of educators and trainers. The difference between felt needs and prescribed needs has been discussed by the writers cited above and also by this writer (Brookfield, 1983a). Felt needs are equivalent to the wants, desires, and wishes of the learner. They are perceived and expressed by the learners themselves. Examples of commonly felt needs of adult learners might be how to use microcomputers, how to lose weight through aerobics, how to speak a foreign language, or how to cook in a certain style. Prescribed needs arise when an educator decides that an individual, group, or community falls short of some ideal identified by that educator. Monette (1977) calls such a need a normative need that entails three propositions on the part of the educator: "that someone is in a given state, that this state is incompatible with the norms held by some group or by society, and that therefore the state of that someone should be changed" (p. 118).

Felt needs, then, are expressions of preference or desire by learners. Prescribed needs are premised upon educators' beliefs concerning the skills, knowledge, behaviors, and values that they feel adults should acquire. To base education and training programs on a mix of felt and prescribed needs causes some educators to feel uncomfortable. It seems arrogant and authoritarian compared to the apparently democratic process of responding solely to the felt needs of learners. Nonetheless, it is my contention that a total subscription to a felt needs approach to program development condemns education to an adaptive, reactive mode and turns educators into mere providers of consumer goods. The exact form of these goods, according to this rationale, is to be determined by the market forces of expressed learner preferences. The educator becomes an automaton or functionary, a technician responding to expressed desires but with no responsibility for suggesting alternative curricula or activities. Such a view absolves the educator from ever having to make value choices or from having to prompt learners to consider the possibility of other ways of thinking, feeling, and behaving. This is entirely unacceptable as a way of viewing an educator's professional responsibilities. Those who behave in this manner and who equate the sum total of education with reacting to expressed learner needs are technicians, not educators.

The element of felt needs will determine some of the courses offered in every program. It would be hard for educators and trainers of adults to survive in most institutional settings if their programs did not clearly satisfy the felt needs of a reasonably large number of adults in the vicinity. Programs will frequently be mounted to attract large numbers of participants so as to allow programmers to engage in educationally crucial but economically unviable work. For example, the price of my running a free Educational Advisory Service for adults in the community (Brookfield, 1977a) was my arranging courses on popular subjects. The service was established to assist adults in charting a path through the bewildering range of formal educational opportunities open to them and to discuss general learning difficulties they were experiencing in their intellectual pursuits. No fee was paid for this service, and it was open to adults who were not enrolled in courses at my center, as well as those who were. Courses on yoga or on Vegetarian Cooking attracted large numbers of participants and made it easier for me to argue that the Educational Advisory Service should be continued, despite its not generating revenue for the college, since this was offset by the fees collected from yoga and cooking classes.

The danger, however, is that courses dictated by the felt needs rationale will come to comprise the total program offering. If this happens, then the programmer will be discouraged from engaging in provocative, controversial, or unpopular alternative programming. Encouraging adults to consider alternative ways of conceiving their world and acting within and upon it often involves a painful readjustment of perceptions. It is a threatening and traumatic experience to be prompted to reinterpret one's dearly held belief systems, value frameworks, and common behaviors from another perspective. We often bridle against being asked to consider the possibility that we might be operating under false assumptions or ignoring important realities.

A practical example may illustrate my point. It is my firm belief that every publicly funded adult education program should sponsor some kind of political discourse, whether by setting up a formal course or by providing resources for groups already engaged in such activity in the community. Adults would thereby be confronted with arguments, viewpoints, interpretations, and evidence that contradict and challenge their belief systems. To consider such contrary viewpoints and to admit that one's own belief system may be flawed or incomplete is uncomfortable. To those adults whose self-image is bound up with identification with a certain political doctrine granting that other belief systems have some validity is disturbing and at times painful. Under the pressure of operating according to a felt needs approach, however, the kind of programming outlined above might never be considered. Instead, the educator would probably seek institutional approval by offering a program that satisfied popular trends and expressed wishes. Such a program will be "successful" in terms of economic return, but if it never provides an opportunity for adults to consider alternatives to their present ways of thinking, feeling, and behaving, it will be an educational failure.

Sequencing of Educational Experiences. A central feature of the institutional model of program development is the organizing of identified learning activities into planned, ordered sequences. The model relies heavily on a predetermined sequencing of educational activities in which students are taken through operations of increasing levels of complexity. There are two problems with this assumption that educational programs should always exhibit order and sequence. The first is that adult groups, whether comprising a formal class or operating informally, have a tendency to change direction, to reformulate original purposes, and to alter evaluative criteria as they proceed. The work of Freire (1970b) provides a pedagogical rationale for proceeding in this way, as does the Nottingham Andragogy Group's (1983) reformulation of andragogy. Despite the best efforts of program planners and instructors, the adult groups under their influence frequently exhibit a tendency to diverge from the particular path of behavioral objectives charted for them. Second, adult learning groups (particularly those in noncredit settings) tend to operate on an open-entry basis. Participants in these courses are not typically screened for evidence of their past or current intellectual abilities. Hence, adult learning groups are often mixed-ability groupings. In such groups it is clearly inappropriate to expect all participants to proceed through a number of sequenced and previously specified operational stages. For the institutional model to work as it is supposed to, adult learners would have to be screened to ensure that they were roughly equal in ability. But such a selection procedure would be entirely counter to the open and democratic nature of many learning groups.

Contextual Factors in Program Development. It is clear that an awareness of contextuality—of the way in which bodies of knowledge, apparent givens, moral codes, beliefs, and behaviors are, at least partially, cultural products—is an important defining characteristic of adulthood. An awareness of the contextual and contingent aspects of the world is a necessary prelude to acting upon the world. In other words, before adults can change their personal and social worlds, they need to realize that such worlds are humanly constructed and can therefore be altered by human effort. Judged by this criterion of awareness of context, the writers of program development books seem to offend against one of the chief prescriptions regarding the recognition of adulthood. A startling feature of the literature noted by Pennington and Green (1976) is the abundance of models combined with the paucity of contextual awareness. The models are, of necessity, offered in a context-free manner. However, while proposing a model to guide practice, one might also take the time to counsel against the assumption that such models are easily transferable from setting to setting or that a fully supportive economic and political climate will always exist for their implementation.

Repeatedly, the participants in my courses on program development for adult learners have presented evidence of the manner in which contextual factors severely limit the extent to which models of practice can be introduced into their work. Having taught courses in program development to practitioners in both a Canadian and an American university and having also worked as a program developer for several years in Britain, I was continually struck by this theory-practice disjunction. Again and again course members reading the major works in this area would comment that "this is all very well in theory, but in practice. . . ." They would then proceed to describe the particular contextual features that made the adoption of certain apparently exemplary principles impossible.

Empirical corroboration for the crucial importance of

contextual variables is presented by Pennington and Green (1976). The fifty-two programmers who were interviewed for their comparative study admitted to planning programs "by the seat of the pants," (p. 20) and the authors identified four major areas of theory-practice disjunction. First, little comprehensive needs assessment was conducted, owing to lack of time, resources, and expertise. Lip service was paid to the principle of doing a needs assessment, but little actual evidence of this was discovered. Second, in determining the learning objectives by which programs were to be organized, programmers typically used only one source of evidence. Moreover, these objectives were not translated into specific cognitive, technical, or affective behaviors. Programmers reported that lack of expertise or institutional constraints prevented their consulting several sources of evidence before setting objectives or specifying the exact form of these behaviors.

Lack of time or expertise was also given as the reason for the third major theory-practice disjunction, namely, the failure to base learning methods on well-thought-out criteria such as learner characteristics, desired learning outcomes, or available resources. Finally, evaluation was conducted sporadically and through use of a limited number of methods. Pennington and Green concluded that the programmers they interviewed used the language of the institutional model of program development but that "as they describe their planning actions it becomes clear that personal values, environmental constraints, available resource alternatives, and other factors impinge on the program development process" (p. 22). They point out that these variables have received little attention in the literature but that they represent a major set of critical factors in program development.

Long (1983a) has recently commented on the failure of models of program development to address what he calls "the historical and broader social, psychological and technological variables in program planning" (p. 19). He urges planners to become aware of larger social issues, events, and trends and for them to be guided by philosophical concerns regarding the proper purpose and clientele for adult education. Schroeder

(1980) is one of the few writers who place adult education within a larger social context.

Several contextual variables seem to be ubiquitous in accounts of the program development process. Prime among these is the personality factor. Every education and training program comprises something of a psychosocial drama, a configuration of unique personalities. The personalities of the chief actors in this drama—the programmer, the administrators concerned, the support staff, the institutional head, the learners—all shape the form and process of the resultant program. An unsympathetic principal or personnel manager, support staff with whom the programmer has had previous conflict over working the late hours associated with training courses, or academic colleagues whose shortcomings have given the institution a poor reputation can all nullify the most carefully developed of programs. A janitor who insists on turning off heating an hour before groups finish their activities can wreck the most flawless effort at curriculum development.

Budgetary constraints or sudden changes in financial allocations imposed from above are also mentioned by students in program development courses as contextual factors of major importance. Since so many adult education programs are run on a cost-recovery basis, changes in financial allocation can visit enormous damage on the stability of these programs. This means that, in addition to being appreciative of the need to run courses that attract large enrollments, programmers also need to know how to adapt to unforeseen and unpredictable budgetary changes. In these circumstances it is easy to see how the most idealistic and well-intentioned educator can allow economic criteria to begin to dominate the form and content of a program.

Changes in economic arrangements obviously reflect political decisions. Under political administrations that favor balanced budgets, reduced government services, and cost-recovery programs, it is not surprising that economic criteria are used to determine educational decisions. What is surprising, however, is that the political source of these decisions is rarely acknowledged. Educators and trainers frequently develop, almost as a professional badge of identity, an air of weary but essentially accepting resignation about the marginality of their circumstances. They tend not to view their situation as politically created and hence politically alterable but rather as natural and immutable. The truth is, of course, that practitioners contribute to their condition of marginality by their ready acceptance of this situation. Because of a lack of political acumen, as well as a paucity of opportunities to act as advocates for their cause, practitioners can easily come to accept uncritically the demolition of programs in the name of cost-benefit analysis.

This is why courses of training for practitioners should always have some component that is concerned with tracing the connection between education and sociopolitical change. Educators and trainers should realize the way in which political decisions can come to influence their curricula, program formats, and evaluative standards. The chief element missing from my own professional preparation as an adult educator was the awareness that adult education programs were created in political situations, were open to alteration as a result of political decisions, and were dependent on a favorable political climate for their continuance. The importance of this awareness of the political dimensions to adult education program development was brought home sharply to me when, shortly after a general election in Great Britain, the funding for adult education in the region where I was working was cut savagely and my college was threatened with immediate closure. Despite three years of vigorous action against this prospect, public funding for the college was eventually removed. No more vivid illustration of the manner in which private troubles (in this case the imminent loss of my job and house) are inextricably related to public issues (in this case the election of a new national government) can be imagined.

There is a real danger that the marginality described by Clark (1956, 1958) as afflicting the education of adults may become accepted by professional practitioners, as well as by those with educational decision-making power, as a defining characteristic of adult education. In his case study of adult schools in California, Clark noted a strong service orientation, that is, programs were conducted in response to clientele expressions of need. This other-directed, service orientation was apparent, according to Clark, in the hiring and firing of teachers, in administrative roles, and in course curricula. Clark also noted that adult education had no constitutional mandate, that it was a secondary responsibility of administrators, that it had no separate plant or other fixed capital, and that various "watchdog" groups wanted to monitor major segments of the program.

The *enrollment economy* was the phrase that Clark used to characterize the workings of adult schools in California. Because adult education was financed from within high school and junior college districts, its budgetary support was derivative. The program had to be "sold" to other educators as well as to the public. Clark suggested that "the enrollment economy constitutes the basic complex of pressures operating upon the adult school. This is because organizational needs for survival and security are distinctly shaped in the adult education context by these factors" (1956, p. 62). Adult schools had to create clienteles by adapting to environmental factors. They had no specific mission to guide their operations, and this generality and diffuseness of purpose served to widen the discretion of administrators. With this lack of clearly defined purpose for adult education and the pressure of the enrollment economy, it was not surprising that "basic organizational needs [ruled] the day" (p. 65).

The picture of adult education painted by Clark is one familiar enough to present-day practitioners. It is a world characterized by diffuse efforts and by a lack of any clearly defined philosophical rationale to guide the formulation of mission statements or declarations of specific purposes. Furthermore, it is an adaptive, reactive enterprise, condemned by its desperate search for students to follow curricular fads and popular fancies irrespective of their educational merit. This search sometimes results in courses and programs of real educational merit in which felt learner needs are met. Often, though, it results in a superficially attractive program that has no lasting educational value.

The Chimera of Perfectability. The chimera of perfectability is present whenever manuals of practice prescribe exemplary behaviors or whenever idealized versions of reality are presented as the norm. Chapter Six noted a number of such exemplary prescriptions in the field of teaching adults. In similar fashion, the models of program development cited earlier in this chapter do not acknowledge that failure is possible. As they portray it, all the programmer has to do is follow the sequence of stages prescribed in the institutional mode. He or she conducts a full and revealing needs assessment, states clear objectives that are demonstrable in unambiguous performance behaviors, carefully designs appropriate instruction, and conducts complete evaluations.

As the work of Clark (1956, 1958) and Pennington and Green (1976) suggests, and as the experiences of many of my readers will confirm, however, such a picture of perfection bears little resemblance to the real world of education and training program development. But neophyte practitioners consulting these texts may well erect as a role model an imagined, exemplary professional. This exemplar will perform the tasks outlined earlier with panache and efficiency. A major task of those teaching courses in program development, therefore, must be to point to the departures from reality evident in these models. This does not mean that role models or exemplary behaviors should be completely abandoned; it means rather that professors and trainers should inject a healthy note of realism into discussions of such models and exemplary practices. If trainers point out this disjunction, practitioners will become aware of the contextuality of much program development. They will also realize that to be unable to put into practice the exemplary behaviors outlined in the manuals does not constitute professional failure. Those who graduate from programs of professional preparation bewitched by this chimera of "the perfect programmer" are doomed to a life of professional disenchantment. The reality described earlier, in which contextual variables serve continuously to alter practice and to redefine priorities, will represent an earthly professional purgatory for these unfortunate individuals. Graduate courses in adult education program development can serve no more humane function than to release aspiring practitioners from this doom.

Values and Program Development. My final misgivings on the dominance of the institutional mode of program development have to do with the way in which a concentration on technique comes to blur any consideration of the values underlying programmatic decisions. In an earlier work (Brookfield, 1983a), I discussed the value choices facing those educators who work with adults in nonformal settings. At that time I criticized the program-planning literature for its view of planning as "an applied skill which exists somehow independently of political and moral considerations," as well as for its view of the programmer as "a morally denuded automaton inhabiting an ethical vacuum" (p. 199). Subsequent experiences and reflection have only served to confirm these perceptions. The kinds of contextual variables mentioned earlier in this chapter influence the choices educators make when deciding which programs to sponsor. Limited resources in terms of budget, facilities, or manpower mean that programmers will constantly have to decide which of a variety of prescribed or felt needs should be met. Several factors will typically be taken into account when such decisions are made. Chief among these will be the institutional mission of the employing agency and the programmer's personal value system and priorities.

Many times the educator's sense of values will coincide neatly with the priorities of the institution. A specialist in adult basic education working for an affirmative action, social welfare agency will probably find that her preference for working with disadvantaged adults coincides perfectly with the priorities of the employing institution. But at other times this fit between individual and institution will not be so easy to arrange. Individual programmers will often find themselves wanting to devote energy and resources to programs not deemed especially important in institutional terms. Here, a conflict between the practitioner's own value system and the institutional ethos and mission is almost inevitable.

Few writers on program development in adult education address this point of conflict. Boyle (1981, p. 19), however, observes that in a well-developed program in continuing education the beliefs of those involved are consistent with the aims of the actual program. Although he does not himself propose explicit criteria to govern the operation of programs, he does discuss in general terms the four key issues identified by Apps (1973) as critical when deciding upon the purpose of education. As noted earlier, Long (1983a) has also recognized that philosophical concerns, particularly about the purpose of adult education, interact with contextual variables in the process of program development. There are, of course, no empirically provable arguments as to why one set of beliefs about the purpose of education should be preferred over any others as a guide to the development of programs. But one cannot make decisions about which programs to fund and sponsor solely on first-order grounds, that is, on grounds concerned with technical or administrative matters. The decision that one program is more deserving than another of one's time, energy, and budgetary allocation will result partly from second-order considerations, that is, from considerations having to do with the ethics, values, and moral stance of the educator. How programmers might begin to develop criteria that could help them choose among conflicting priorities is discussed in Chapter Twelve.

❦ 10 ❦

Structuring Programs
Around Learners' Needs
and Abilities

A major tenet of the rationale underlying the facilitation of learning is that educators should assist adults to speculate creatively on possible alternative ways of organizing their personal worlds. From an awareness of the contextuality of knowledge and of the culturally constructed nature of values, morals, and beliefs, it is argued, there will come a realization that it is possible to alter the circumstances of one's personal and social worlds. This rationale applies just as much to adults who happen to be organizers of educational programs for other adults, as it does to those adults who are enrolled in classes. Program developers should be made aware of the possibilities for program arrangements that do not conform to the sequenced institutional model. They should be made aware that this model is not an unchallangeable "given." It assumed its current preeminence as a result of both the rise of a scientific, technological consciousness among educators in the 1950s and the current political pressure to mount programs that are effective in cost-recovery terms.

Hence, those engaged in the professional preparation of future practitioners or in professional development for current workers in the field should stress the contextuality of the institutional model. Professional courses on program development, program planning, and evaluation should place the institutional model of practice in some socioeconomic context. Practitioners in these courses should come to realize that the dominant position of the model is not a result of its innate superiority or universal validity. The model should come to be seen as a cultural construct, a set of practical injunctions and assumptions that mirror the world view of certain behaviorist thinkers and that support the current institutional arrangements of employing agencies. In short, the popularity of the model comes in large measure from its ideological congruence with the self-financing, cost-recovery basis on which many education and training programs now operate.

In addition, the model is based upon procedural features that fit supremely well with the current institutional arrangements of many providing agencies. It allows for an institutional definition of needs, it cedes to institutional representatives the decisions concerning program format and content, and it allows for the placement and management of programs within previously designated, institutionally convenient time periods. As a consequence, educators and trainers of adults have come dangerously close to accepting uncritically a number of assumptions about the nature of learning derived from colleagues working in primary and secondary schools. It is obviously absurd to presume that adults learn only during two-hour blocks of time that occur on the same evening, between the same times, each week. And yet the organization of many adult education programs into weekly, two-hour blocks of instruction suggests the implicit acceptance of this bizarre assumption.

Those teaching training courses in program development, as well as writers of program development manuals, should critically redefine their operational assumptions, values, and expectations. Courses and textbooks should acknowledge the institutional model as but one available way of working, not as *the* one mode of program development for adults. And there are in fact some encouraging signs in current literature that this does occasionally happen. In issuing a critical challenge to programmers in adult education, London (1967) urged practitioners to "strive to develop a literature in adult education that provides a more critical appraisal of our programming" (p. 293). He advocated that program planners sponsor programs that would assist adults to undertake a critical analysis of their lives and environments. This would enable them to identify those conditions and circumstances that result in alienation and to understand those forces that serve to block their development as self-reliant persons. Such programs would have as their curricular focus "crucial problems and large human issues rather than tightly defined and restricted areas of subject matter" (p. 293).

Blaney (1974) identifies two particular modes of program formulation—the shared membership mode and the individual mode—that constitute alternatives to the institutional mode. In the shared membership mode, authority is shared between teacher and participants, objectives and purposes are collaboratively determined, and evaluation is formative and participatory. In the individual mode, the individual learner exercises authority over learning goals, methods, and evaluative criteria.

In his analyses of needs and needs assessment, Monette (1977, 1979) identifies the Tylerian rationale as preeminent in adult education and criticizes its lack of attention to values, its production line emphasis, and its avoidance of political, scientific, esthetic, and ethical dimensions. He also points out that graduate departments of adult education organize their courses in an institutional mode by focusing on pragmatic, administrative concerns. Monette posits an alternative approach based on the ideas of Freire. In this approach learners would be encouraged to examine critically the assumptions, values, and beliefs underlying their perceptions of the world. He points out that the felt needs approach is appropriate only with adults who are relatively sophisticated. This means that "the educator must be accountable for introducing others to things beyond their present comprehension and development and for bridging the worlds of private and public thought" (1979, p. 88). The connection between Monette's views and the injunctions contained within this book as to the need to present adults with alternative ways of interpreting the world and to help them connect private troubles and public issues hardly needs stating. Apps (1979) also discusses the use of Freire's ideas as a basis for program development. Although Apps does not advocate that a Freirean rationale replace the institutional mode, he does regard such a rationale as one viable alternative to the traditional model of program development.

There is ample evidence, then, that we need a radical rethinking of the assumption that the institutional mode is the natural mode of program development for adult learning. Central to a critical appraisal of the current preeminence of this model are several imperatives. At the very least, practitioners who are engaged in the process of arranging educational activities for adults should be presented with a range of alternative models of program development. They should be encouraged to consider the extent to which the institutional model is culturally produced and reflective of a certain intellectual era and orientation. They should be made aware of the contextual variables that call into question the replicability of the textbook models of practice. They should be helped to realize that, by using the felt needs approach, the educator may simply be abdicating responsibility for making value-based judgments concerning appropriate curricula.

Practitioners should also be encouraged to consider the extent to which the setting of predefined objectives and the sequencing of instructional events are appropriate approaches for ethnically diverse, multiability groups of adult learners. They should be made aware that programmatic decisions are not made in an ethical vacuum but that such choices reflect value orientations that practitioners derive from their own philosophies or from the institutional ethos of their employing agencies. They should also be weaned away from an unhealthy obsession with the chimera of perfectability and helped to realize that adjustments in practice and diversions from prescribed exemplary models in textbook manuals do not represent professional failure.

Finally, educators and trainers should be introduced to the literature, concepts, and practical accounts of program development for adults in contexts other than formal institutions. While there are any number of such models and initiatives available in such applied fields as counseling, community work, and social work, they are seldom considered in courses or textbooks on program development. For example, the models provided by community-based initiatives such as the Antigonish movement (Coady, 1939) in Nova Scotia, the work of community educators in the inner cities (Lovett, 1975), or living room learning experiments such as the Canadian Farm Forum (Conger, 1974) are rarely addressed in program development manuals or in courses on this topic. Yet there is a rich and substantial body of literature in existence that documents the many attempts of organizers, animateurs, and community workers to engage in educational work with adults outside institutions of formal education. And, while practitioners and trainers stay locked within the institutional mode, enterprising activists in community work and informal adult education are organizing free universities (Draves, 1980), study circles (Kurland, 1982; Osborne, 1981), learning exchanges (Lewis and Kinishi, 1977), educational brokering agencies (Hefferman, Macy, and Vickers, 1976), and educational counseling services for adults (Ironside and Jacobs, 1977; Osborn, Charnley, and Withnall, 1981), as well as developing the concept of the educative community (Hiemstra, 1982). Only occasionally, however, is this community action perspective considered in program development manuals (Knox, 1974; Nowlen, 1980).

Setting Priorities for Program Development

It has been argued that developing a clear philosophical rationale to guide practice is one way for programmers to determine which of a number of conflicting program possibilities to sponsor. In an analysis of priority setting Knox (1982a) writes that "it is important for administrators to realize that they have internalized value assumptions that produce the intuition upon which they depend for decision making" (p. 14). To him, the fundamental outcome of education and training should be the enhanced proficiency of adult learners, "enhanced proficiency" being defined as an increased capacity to perform effectively. As Knox acknowledges, however, his definition of what comprises effective performance is itself value based; hence, one can perform effectively according to someone else's agenda (such as becoming an obedient party member, uncritical bureaucratic functionary, or religious zealot) without ever developing the capacity for critical reflection on one's own actions or on the norms of the organization of which one is a part.

To many practitioners the use of such phrases as "organizational effectiveness," "the bottom line," or "cost effectiveness" represents the application of criteria of economic profitability to determine which forms of adult learning shall receive priority status. In their analysis of the bottom-line mentality among continuing educators at Kingsborough Community College in Brooklyn, Flanagan and Smith (1982) found that what comprised this most fundamental of criteria did, in fact, alter according to the context in which a program was developed. They argue against trying to develop some overall comprehensive framework for the analysis of conflicting priorities, maintaining instead that "the process of seeking—the reflection and debate in which practitioners engage—is an important endeavor in itself" (p. 45). They point out, for example, that debate concerning the future viability of certain programs frequently centers on the wider political importance of these programs or on their intrainstitutional significance, as much as on criteria of economic profitability. They cite with approval the work of Lindblom (1959) on "the science of muddling through." Lindblom maintained that attempts to erect stable hierarchies of values to guide decision making would inevitably lead to disappointment as a result of contextual distortions.

A number of attempts have been made, however, to erect procedural models for determining priorities in programs for adult learners. In his review of priority setting in professional literature, Sork (1979) reported that few practitioners provide any conceptual or theoretical foundation for their decision-making strategies, though two broad classifications do emerge, namely, the importance of meeting a need and the feasibility of doing so. Sork developed a procedural model that community education councils can use to determine the priority of adult learning needs. Its six criteria are as follows:

- *Contribution to goals.* How important are the goals to which the need relates, and how great is the contribution the need makes to the definition of the goal?
- *Magnitude of discrepancy.* How great is the measurable discrepancy between the current and future valued state of affairs?
- *Immediacy.* To what degree must the need be met immediately?
- *Instrumental value.* Will meeting the need have a positive or negative effect on meeting other needs?
- *Availability of resources.* Are resources to meet the need available?
- *Commitment to change.* Are "relevant publics" committed to meeting the need as defined?

Other attempts at erecting models for determining program priorities are those of Rauch (1972), Parker (1979), Kemerer (1981), Kemerer and Schroeder (1983), and Moore (1984). Parker (1979) develops what he calls a "mathematical programming model" designed to deal with conflict management in program selection. Kemerer (1981) assigns qualitative as well as quantitative dimensions to the concept of "importance" in determining which of many revealed needs educators should meet through program development. He relies on a "goal framework" model in which desired states are delineated in terms of specific attributes. Moore (1984) describes a project called Citizen's Viewpoint for which Pennsylvania State University designed a massive survey questionnaire. The questionnaire contained a list of program possibilities suggested by interviews with "experts," and a sample of over 14,000 individuals completed the questionnaire by rank ordering various program options.

In the Citizen's Viewpoint project educators ceded to learners some of the responsibility for determining needs, whereas the other models place greater stress on educators' awareness of the benefits, political importance, and feasibility of choosing to fund and sponsor certain programs. To many practitioners all these models for priority setting have an air of unreality

about them in that context distorts their applicability so greatly that it is sometimes better not to presume that any objectively valid, replicable model for determining priorities in program
development is possible. As Knox (1979) points out, most programs are planned within a certain organizational or community context; for most intents and purposes, therefore, the crucial criterion for determining which priorities are to be favored
in program development is the providing agency's institutional
mission. Procedural models will be of little relevance if practitioners are working within an institutional setting in which only
a limited range of program offerings are acceptable. It is to an
examination of some familiar distortions of context and theory-
practice disjunctions in program development for adult learners
that we now turn.

In the United States, Canada, and Britain a number of investigations into adult education program development have
documented the variety and importance of contextual distortions. The work of Pennington and Green (1976) has already
been discussed in the previous chapter. Other accounts are those
of Mee and Wiltshire (1978), Dohr, Donaldson, and Marshall
(1979), Venable (1981), Robbins (1981), Bina (1982), and
Yeshewalul and Griffith (1984). In a major study of adult education in England and Wales, Mee and Wiltshire (1978) paint a
picture of adult educators as autonomous professionals working
within the marginal sector of their employing institutions and
subject to a host of administrative and financial constraints in
their attempts to develop adult education programs. These writers conclude that much innovation in adult education can be explained in terms of the individual educator's energies and commitment. When educators find themselves in marginal positions,
they argue, their energy and commitment are probably the most
potent of all contextual variables in determining the format and
vigor of a program.

One particularly interesting aspect of Mee and Wiltshire's
survey is their application of role theory analysis to the understanding of adult education programmers' professional lives. In
this survey, and in a separate study by Mee (1980), these writers
describe the role conflicts typically experienced by adult educa-

tors. Many of the practitioners surveyed were running adult education programs on secondary school or community school premises and were required to spend a certain amount of time teaching schoolchildren during the day; as a result, they felt that their loyalties and energies were seriously divided. Adult educators were found to be prone to chronic overwork, as a result of their deep commitment to what they saw as an intrinsically valuable activity. Their professional lives frequently spilled over into their domestic arrangements, with some wives of male adult educators being deputed to serve as unpaid clerical assistants (there were no reports of the reverse).

In his follow-up analysis to this report, Mee (1980) discusses the most typical role conflicts experienced by adult educators. To begin with there are frequent conflicts between formal job expectations and individual personalities. In a profession where so much emphasis is placed on informality, personal warmth, flexibility of conduct, and sociability, it may be very difficult for some individuals both to satisfy the formal expectations of their jobs and to adjust to the informal mores of their group. While some individuals will welcome the ill-defined nature of many adult education positions and like the freedom to innovate that this allows, others will be inhibited by the lack of firm and unequivocal job descriptions. Conflict is also felt when employer expectations clash with educators' conceptions of their role. Mee records that practitioners frequently experience a great deal of frustration with the administrative and financial tasks that take away so much time from the "real" job of facilitating adult learning. However, those who deliberately attempt to change administrative procedures so as to allow time for encouraging adult learning are liable to be perceived as disruptive forces.

An extremely debilitating conflict results when the practitioner encounters persistent opposition to, or misunderstanding of, the adult educative function by professional colleagues in other educational sectors or by administrative staff. In multipurpose institutions administrative staff are frequently resentful of the extra work caused by dealing with adult education class enrollments, while teaching staff who work during the daytime accuse adult education staff of "disrupting" "their" rooms in their absence. Finally, as if the role conflicts experienced by institution-bound educators were not frustrating enough, Mee argues that the outreach worker who is acting as a change agent will spend a great deal of time trying to convince colleagues of the wisdom and viability of this work and attempting to secure money for program development. (I have discussed the limbo of the informal adult educator elsewhere. See Brookfield, 1983a.)

In the United States and Canada a number of smaller-scale inquiries have revealed the distorting effects of contextual variables on the development of adult education programs. In a triangulated investigation of program developers' orientations, Dohr, Donaldson, and Marshall (1979) identify three factors as chiefly responsible for program differences in apparently similar institutions—the programmer's individual belief system, the personal style of individual instructors, and the context of accountability affecting the providing agency. A study of over 100 Ohio adult education administrators in local school districts found a noticeable disparity between the literature and the practice of adult education; experienced administrators placed limited value on sixty-eight administrative behaviors identified in the literature as conducive to success in adult basic education programs (Bina, 1982). In their analysis of 153 agricultural extension agents in British Columbia, Idaho, and Washington State, Yeshewalul and Griffith (1984) identify a number of role conflicts afflicting these practitioners, though they do not make reference to Mee's (1980) analysis mentioned earlier. The fact that these workers feel that there are at least twice as many conflicts with their clients as with their employing organizations lead the authors of the study to conclude that "extension workers are more likely to conform to their employer's expectations than to those of their clientele" (Yeshewalul and Griffith, 1984, p. 205). Yeshewalul and Griffith speculate that conflict with clients might also arise because extension agents are frequently eager to lead and promote change, and this innovating zeal may cause them to violate the expectations of their clientele.

In only one survey (Robbins, 1981) is there any marked degree of congruence noted between theory and practice. In his research into sixty-four continuing education program planners in Florida, Georgia, and Tennessee, Robbins notes a consistency of opinions and approaches to program development among his respondents. He outlines a twelve-stage variant of the institutional mode of program development, and for each stage of the planning process he identifies three individuals or groups who might be involved in undertaking that stage—the continuing educator, other college staff, and clients and community members. Clientele and community members were found to be closely involved in the developmental process, and most sample members felt themselves to owe loyalties both to their clients and to their employing institutions. Robbins describes as "boundary spanning" the activities of involving clients and community members in planning, of maintaining strong links between the continuing education department and other college staff, and of ensuring that an employing institution's expectations concerning new program development are met. Continuing educators within employing agencies established for nonadult educational purposes are said to be boundary-spanning agents. These agents must be skilled at communicating with others, be able to understand and speak a number of different institutional and departmental languages, and be able to alter their behaviors with different individuals and agencies as appropriate.

The study concludes that "the use and sequence of planning steps, as well as the consistent involvement of clientele in planning, provide considerable support to popular professional literature" (Robbins, 1981, p. 181). Adult educators are found to function "as a linkage between persons with educational needs and organizations with educational resources" (p. 181), and Robbins suggests that programs of training for professional adult educators should concentrate on the preparation of practitioners for these boundary-spanning roles. It is, of course, precisely because adult educators have to become familiar with different organizational cultures, client groups, community members, and institutional expectations that the possibility for enormous role conflict exists. Because educators have to mediate between, and satisfy, the expectations of multifarious individuals, institutions, and groups, while at the same time remaining true to their own vision of adult education, it is not surprising that they exhibit the exhaustion, frustration, and sense of isolation documented by Clark (1956) and Mee (1980). Evidently, then, research into adult educators' role conflicts, and the cost of such conflicts to their personal lives, must be a priority for future investigations in this field.

The Facilitator as Practical Theorist

In recent years a useful framework of analysis that can be used to make some sense of the diverse and conflict-ridden world of program development for adults has been developed by theorists from the world of organizational psychology. Writers such as Schön (1983), Argyris (1982), Argyris and Schön (1974), and Carr and Kemmis (1983) have investigated the improvisational, problem-centered aspects of professional practice and have concluded that such creative patterns of action should be examined as valid and useful "theories-in-use" (Argyris and Schön, 1974). In their discussion of two contrasting paradigms of assumptions governing professional practice, Argyris and Schön argue that what they call "Model II" provides the most realistic abstraction of the actual experience of working professionals. In Model II, which they describe as theory-in-use, Argyris and Schön identify three governing variables that inform the design of professionally effective practice. According to this model, professionals who are effective in the real world base their practice on valid information (that is, information obtained from participants who are themselves involved in the professional activity); they exercise free and informed choice over practice activities; and they exhibit an internal commitment to their chosen course of action while constantly monitoring its implementation. Argyris and Schön urge practitioners to be sceptical of textbook models of exemplary practice, which they feel frequently represent distorted and highly abstract perceptions of the real world of practice.

Argyris and Schön suggest that the key to practitioner success is "developing one's own continuing theory of practice under real-time conditions" (1974, p. 157) rather than attempting to follow the neatly conceived models of practice found in manuals and textbooks. This requires the practitioner to be able to reflect on his or her own microtheories of action (that is, contextually specific ideas about what works in the real world) and to relate these microtheories to institutional norms and to client expectations. One's own theory of effective practice can be judged successful, according to these writers, by the degree to which it meets the following criteria (Argyris and Schön, 1974, p. 157):

- The theory permits detection of, and response to, its inconsistencies, ineffectiveness, and degree of obsolescence.
- The theory allows for mutual learning of client and practitioner.
- The theory allows the practitioner to seek out, identify, and respond to new kinds of clients.
- The theory should include attempts to transform other colleagues to adopting Model II type behaviors.
- The theory should help create a professional community which undertakes explicit, public, and cumulative learning.
- The theory should make professional practice compatible with self-actualization of the practitioner by setting "realistic yet challenging levels of aspiration to promote growth."

In the educational field Argyris and Schön note the disjunction between espoused theories of practice (for example, the use of team teaching) and effective theories-in-use. They also recognize that effective theories-in-use often cannot be translated into espoused theories of practice. For example, some professionals use informal analysis, experience, and insight in developing new programs that turn out to be enormously successful. When asked to reflect on the components of these effective theories-in-use, they frequently talk in terms of intuition, feeling, and "playing a hunch." If practitioners are helped to realize that they are, in effect, building theories of practice and if they are encouraged to reflect upon and make explicit the steps involved in this activity, then Argyris and Schön feel that the resultant dialogue and collaborative learning could lead to a dissemination of effective practice.

In an analysis of the reflective practitioner Schön (1983) argues that despite the growth of professional organizations and practitioner manuals, the last twenty years have been characterized by "lagging understandings, unsuitable remedies, and professional dilemmas" (p. 9), all of which have resulted in a crisis of confidence in the professions. He argues that practitioners currently perceive their professional knowledge as being "mismatched to the changing character of the situations of practice —the complexity, uncertainty, instability, uniqueness, and value conflicts which are increasingly perceived as central to the world of professional practice" (p. 14). In response to these conditions, competing conceptions of practice have emerged. Practitioners in a given field now hold highly conflictings views on the characteristics of a good practitioner, central practitioner values, and appropriate practice roles. Nonetheless, Schön believes that there is plenty of evidence to show that out of this multiplicity of conflicting views, many practitioners devise their own patterns of practice (theories-in-use) and consciously infuse their activities with intuitive, artistic elements.

At the heart of Schön's reformulation is his critique of the model of technical rationality, which he believes is the paradigm that until recently has determined our conceptions of practice. In Schön's view, "problem setting" (p. 40) is central to effective practice. Problem setting itself is not a technical exercise; rather, it is essentially intuitive and artistic, although the capacity to solve problems may involve technical knowledge and skills. In problem setting the practitioner identifies relevant situations to be addressed and frames the context in which exploration of these takes place. This is close to the concept of problem posing as developed by Freire (1973). Both problem setting and problem posing antedate problem solving and involve professionals in naming the situations they deem important and to which they will attend. Inherent in this capacity for problem setting (rather than problem solving, in which problems are frequently posed or set by others) is an appreciation and full understanding of the context for professional action. Schön describes the dynamic development of this understanding as "reflection-in-action" (p. 49).

The process of reflection-in-action is essentially artistic, that is, the practitioner makes judgments and exercises skills for which no explicit rationale has been articulated but in which she nevertheless feels an intuitive sense of confidence. When practitioners are faced with new and unfamiliar situations and have to react immediately to them, they call on their intuitive sense of professional correctness and their accumulated experience to introduce some order into their responses. These periods of trauma, surprise, and experimentation with new situations are frequently followed by idle speculation on the reasons why certain practices were intuitively chosen and found to be productive. Schön believes that in this process practitioners construct "a new theory of the unique case" (p. 68) in which reflection on a situation is married to experimentation and implementation. In urging practitioners to recognize the artistic elements in their activities and to understand how technical problem solving takes place in the broader context of reflective problem setting, Schön hopes to show "how reflection-in-action may be rigorous in its own right" and to "increase the legitimacy of reflection-in-action and encourage its broader, deeper, and more rigorous use" (p. 69).

One attempt to ground the process of training employees in an awareness and acknowledgment of context is Lefkoe's (1985) idea of "context training." Lefkoe argues that "if participants are able to create a new context for themselves, a new way of seeing themselves or of defining their roles in a work or social situation, they will take it upon themselves to do and learn most of the things required to operate within that new context" (p. 45). In this approach, the goal of training workshops in business and industry is no longer to impart information or to teach discrete skills but "to lead participants to discover that their job actually consists of (and has always consisted of) more than the mechanical tasks they have been performing" (p. 45). The central point of Lefkoe's is one well known to analysts of paradigm shifting and perspective transformation. Prior to teaching new skills to adults, one must encourage them to become familiar with the new context in which they are to operate. Once employees reinterpret their function and redefine the context within which they are working, then the identification of the skills necessary to function in that context will follow. Lefkoe believes that if "context shifting" can be induced and encouraged, most employees will find that they have in their current stock of skills those needed to operate successfully in the new context. The assumption is that if you are successful in changing adults' perceptions of the world in which they live, you will not need to *teach* adults to acquire new skills and knowledge—they will be eager to discover these for themselves.

The ideas of Schön are particularly relevant to the situation in which developers of adult learning programs find themselves. There can be few professional fields in which practitioners are required to be so consistently innovative and adaptive; but, as the previous chapter shows, the professional literature dealing with program development is generally loath to acknowledge the contextuality and individual creativity endemic to the process of reflection-in-action. This may be partly due to feelings of professional insecurity. Given that adult educators are frequently viewed as marginal to their employing agency's operations, it is not surprising if, rather than acknowledge the intuitive, improvisational aspects of their work, they emphasize its explicit technical rationality. But in the following section a case example *is* provided of one attempt to develop a professional development program using the inductive, intuitive, and improvisational aspects of what has been variously called "theories-in-use," "problem setting," "reflection-in-action," and "theories of the unique case."

Reflection-in-Action: A Case Study

What follows is a description of my attempt to devise a staff development workshop for high school principals and assistant principals. It is an account of a theory-in-use, in which an inductive, ground-upward approach was taken toward problem setting with a group of adult professionals. The setting for this activity was a one-day conference for over 1,000 principals and assistant principals in the High School Division of the New York Board of Education.

My workshop, which was titled "A Critical Look at Creating Staff Development Programs: From Needs Assessment Through Evaluation," was designed to introduce the staff development model to selected administrators who would then go back to their individual schools and construct their own staff development efforts by drawing on this model. The model was designed according to the principles of effective facilitation outlined at the outset of this book, and it was premised on the assumption that the teachers, principals, and assistant principals should be treated as adult learners. Apparently, one major difficulty with staff development efforts in New York City high schools up to that point was their tendency to follow the traditional pedagogic model employed by teachers in their own school classrooms. The typical staff development effort with teachers would take the form of a one- or two-hour lecture by an expert brought in from outside the school community to tell teachers at the school how they should be doing their jobs. This model of staff development contradicted the spirit and the form of effective facilitation. Teachers were not given the opportunity to take part in planning staff development activities; they were unable to identify with the content of the staff development effort; they did not feel that they were addressing issues and concerns that were meaningful to their own professional circumstances; and they had no opportunity to participate in the actual process of developing the program.

What follows is a more or less verbatim transcript of the document that was presented to principals and assistant principals at the opening conference as a guide for staff development. This guide centers on the concerns and issues of staffs, treats participants as adult learners, and emphasizes that each school constitutes a context-specific setting for staff development.

A CRITICAL LOOK AT CREATING
STAFF DEVELOPMENT PROGRAMS:
FROM NEEDS ASSESSMENT TO EVALUATION
Leader's Guide

The purpose of this document is to apply some principles of adult learning to the design of staff development programs in New York City schools. The emphasis throughout is on treating principals, assistant principals, and teachers as *adults* and, therefore, as *adult learners*. As adult learners, these individuals have clear ideas about what are the crucial problems, concerns, and issues in their own professional lives. Unless staff development efforts build upon these perceptions, feelings, and experiences, such efforts will be seen as irrelevant ways of taking up an hour or so of work time. For staff development to be successful where adult professionals are concerned, those individuals must feel an involvement in, commitment to, and responsibility for, the design, content, and conduct of this activity.

This guide also stresses that the circumstances, issues, and problems of each school in the city will have dimensions unique to that school. It is crucial, therefore, that realistic staff development be based on an accurate knowledge of the conditions obtaining at a particular school. This is why full involvement of all participants in the development effort is so important; not only will it reinforce participants' active commitment to the activity, but it will also ensure that the activity is focused on real life concerns and is therefore seen as immediately meaningful and relevant to participants.

General Principles

Make public the object of the training exercise, the criteria governing success, and the needs identified as important.
Involve staff members at all stages of the training process: in needs assessment, in the evolution of an inventory

of staff development needs, in the design of training exercises, and in the evaluation of course progress.

Always be flexible and adaptable. Don't presume there is one staff development model par excellence. No textbook model has any universally innate validity. Use whatever best fits your needs and circumstances and don't feel you have to follow a series of predetermined stages in some rigid manner.

Don't crucify yourself on the cross of perfection. Expect to be criticized, to make mistakes, to feel dissatisfied, and to be disappointed at times. Anyone who expects to please himself or herself and all trainees 100 percent of the time is heading for ulcers.

Ground your exercises in real life issues and concerns. Don't let anyone other than your trainees define what are important training needs. *They* are the ones on whom your time, effort, and funds are being expended. Accepting an outsider's definition of your staff's problems leaves you open to misunderstanding and a resentment of any training exercises offered.

Be your own methodologist. Don't be afraid to use a DIY approach (Do-It-Yourself).

Needs Assessment

The first, and most obvious, thing you need to do is to assess as accurately as possible the capabilities of your staff, their most pressing concerns, and the skills you need to develop or improve. Many techniques of needs assessment exist—administering questionnaires, conducting interviews, observing participants, consulting with experts—but most are extremely time consuming. One very useful, and quickly administered, method is that of "critical incidents." For effective staff development, a good first step is to ask all staff concerned to complete a critical incident exercise. This is a brief, written statement that forces participants to think about specific happenings. Many people find this easier than thinking more broadly or abstractly. The exercise will provide you with a series of one-paragraph statements from staff about their feelings and perceptions regarding the problems they face doing their jobs. You can then generalize on the basis of these individual statements.

Specimen Critical Incident Exercise

> Think back over the last six months and identify an incident you remember as one that caused you the greatest discomfort, pressure, or difficulty. Write down, in no more than half a page, the following details about the incident: (a) when and where it occurred; (b) who was involved (roles rather than personalities may be used here); and (c) what was so significant about the incident as to cause you problems.

You can adapt this exercise according to your needs. It can be used for individual faculty development or to identify broader organizational needs. Its importance lies in giving you as accurate a record as possible of the real concerns and feelings of your staff. You are also obtaining this information indirectly, rather than asking staff members to define their problems straight out. Such direct questions are often too embarrassing for respondents to answer publicly. By using a critical incident exercise, you will get a collection of brief but revealing private records of the concerns of your staff.

Inventory of Staff Development Needs

The next stage is to analyze these incidents and compile an Inventory of Staff Development Needs. This will synthesize and list the major concerns voiced by staff and will suggest both objectives and activities that might meet some of these needs. It is very important that the program's objectives include all perspectives; that is, not only what participants *want* but also what administrators feel they *need.* This way participants will "buy into" the training, and they will also come to realize what they don't know.

Specimen Inventory of Staff Development Needs

The critical incident exercise has revealed that the following problems are felt to be important by a significant number of you: misunderstanding of students from other cultures, lack of information concerning students' current ability levels, difficulty in promoting class interaction, and dropping out of students. Each of these represents a unique and different learning need. As a first step we might consider taking the following actions:

- *Misunderstanding of students from other cultures:* a series of one-hour workshops in which students and/or staff from other cultures represented in the student body will present some of the most common ideas, customs, cuisines, and art forms in their cultures.
- *Students' current ability levels:* a committee of four to six representatives from the major program areas to design a specimen Student Entry Evaluation Form to record, briefly and informally, information on student abilities. This to be circulated to all staff members and returned within three weeks. A one-hour meeting to be held to consider the feasibility of using adapted versions of such forms throughout the school.
- *Promoting class interaction:* a series of four one-hour training sessions in which we will practice and observe staff members' small-group leadership skills.
- *Dropping out of students:* a committee of three people to design a brief and simple survey instrument to be administered to students who have left classes. This to be distributed to staff and returned within three weeks. A one-hour meeting then to be held to discuss the feasibility of conducting a small-scale survey to identify reasons for dropping out.

From an inventory such as this, you can develop specific instructional objectives for your staff development program.

Determining Objectives/Content

The important point about the needs assessment exercise, the use of critical incidents, the compilation of an Inventory of Staff Development Needs, and the making public of perceived problems, objectives, and future activities is that all these stages are conducted with the full involvement of the staff who are to be the subject of the development efforts. As a teacher who has participated in staff development exercises for some ten years, I have found that the most annoying feature of such exercises is the way in which outside "experts" are brought in to identify *my* problems and then to suggest solutions *I* should undertake. The resentment caused by this external-diagnostic approach has proved to be such a block to any purposeful learning on my part as to make participation in staff development workshops of little value to me. In the guidelines proposed here, however, the staff who are to be the subjects of staff development play an active and participatory role in identifying concerns. The agenda and rationale for staff development efforts are made public, and staff are given several opportunities to suggest possible training activities and to comment on schemes proposed by trainers. The use of the critical incident exercise makes elaborate needs assessment procedures unnecessary and ensures that the time and money spent on staff development is cost effective. You will be devoting resources to deeply felt real needs and not falling into the trap of spending a great deal of time solving "problems" that *you* feel to be important as a staff developer but that are of little real significance to your staff.

Determining Methods

The specific format of any staff development effort will, of course, depend on the learning needs revealed by the critical incident exercise and presented in the Inventory of Staff Development Needs. As a rule, however, the following guidelines might apply:

1. Staff development exercises should concentrate on developing specific skills, not on acquainting participants with bodies of abstract knowledge. The skills to be improved or developed will be identified as a result of the critical incident exercise and will be published in the inventory.

2. The exercises should develop identified skills in real life settings. Two approaches are commonly used. First, games and simulations can be used to recreate common situations, and staff can attempt to deal with these situations while being observed by peers. All members can then discuss the individual's response to the simulation and suggest alternative approaches. Second, staff can agree to be observed in actual practice settings by inviting colleagues to observe, record, and comment on what appeared to be happening. This second approach is more ego threatening and, hence, less common. It should be tried only with the express prior consent of the individual staff member involved.

3. The training sessions should be participatory. "Participation" is not a fashionable phrase, a fad that will disappear in a few months or years. Research in education, management, and social science shows, over and over again, that the most effective training takes place when participants are actively involved in learning, not passive recipients of knowledge transmitted from above by "experts." This is crucial when dealing with adult learners.

4. The training exercise should allow for frequent, but informal, formative (that is, ongoing) evaluation. Trainers should be willing to be flexible and adaptive in reacting to changing priorities and concerns expressed by staff. If you feel threatened by criticism that you're not meeting learner needs, you shouldn't be doing staff development.

Evaluation

Evaluation is commonly conceived of as a final checking of the outcomes or results of a program. It happens *after* the training activity and assesses whether or not that activity has been successful in terms of the original statement of aims. For effective staff development such an approach is of little use.

What is much more useful is a regular checking of progress by encouraging participants to voice thoughts, feelings, impressions, and concerns. In a two-hour workshop this is probably unnecessary. For an exercise lasting several sessions, however, it is crucial. People develop and change as they undergo purposeful learning, and they often come to realize that what they thought were their main problems were perhaps masks for more deeply felt difficulties. If this happens, then the training exercise needs to be rethought.

Obviously at some point it becomes futile to engage in navel gazing without ever actually *doing* something. What tends to happen, however, is that trainers get a fixed idea regarding the format of training that must be adhered to, and this is pursued irrespective of how well it meets the needs of the learners. It is important in any extended training exercise to check regularly the perceptions of participants as to what they feel is happening. You may be unagreeably surprised at the degree of discrepancy between what you thought you were doing and what participants perceived as the object of the exercise.

Format of Evaluation

As with techniques of need assessment, a multitude of sophisticated data collection techniques are available for the evaluation of educational experiences. For the purposes of staff development in real life settings a formative style of evaluation is likely to be the most useful. Two informal approaches suggest themselves:

1. Completion of session evaluation sheets. A simple sheet could be designed for administration at the end of each session. It should take no more than five minutes to complete. The content of the sheet would be the participant's perceptions of the purpose of the session, the learning needs the session had addressed, the participant's perceptions of the skills and knowledge he or she felt had been acquired in the session, and the participant's views as to future issues and training needs raised by the session.

2. Collaborative evaluation through discussion. Unlike the completion of evaluation sheets, this second approach emphasizes a public (rather than private) assessment of the purposes and merits of the session. For ten to fifteen minutes at the end of each session, group members would compare notes as to the purpose, accomplishments, and future directions of the training sessions. Although these sessions would record individuals' perceptions of their own progress, a sense of a group endeavor would be more likely to result than with the first approach.

Both of these approaches stress participants' own perceptions of what is happening in the training exercises. They do not attempt to measure the success of the sessions by administering a checklist of previously specified performance behaviors and gauging the extent to which these have been exhibited. Instead, they take participants' own assessments of growth as the criterion of success, and they allow for the renegotiation of criteria of success by participants. This goal-free method of evaluation allows participants to feel in control of evaluation and assessment of the exercise.

Final Comments

The preceding guidelines have attempted to apply some of the most common research findings about how adults learn to the design of staff development programs for principals, assistant principals, and teachers in high schools. Throughout, the emphasis has been on making public the assumptions underlying the training process, its objectives, and the criteria applied to determining success. Participatory approaches have been advocated for their demonstrated utility, not because they are currently in fashion. Trainers have been urged to be courageous in adapting elements of different models and in designing their own formats. The principle underlying all these injunctions is that of *effectiveness*: Only if training exercises are grounded in real life concerns and real life settings will they be worthwhile. Since the concerns and settings of staff in your school are likely to be specific to that institution, you have to be brave enough to reject standardized models and design your own. This is not to say that the body of literature on techniques and formats is irrelevant. On the contrary, no one can be expected to design a range of specific exercises and data collection techniques on his or her own. The point is that the choice you make of which formats and techniques to use from the body of available material will be determined by your own specific circumstances.

The previous chapter repeatedly criticized excessive reliance on the institutional mode of program development. It might be useful, then, to summarize the features of effective program development for adult learning. Four themes appear to be particularly prominent, and it is these four themes that informed the preceding Leader's Guide.

The first of these concerns the underlying rationale of program development efforts. Programs that are based on learners' characteristics and engage learners in a dialogue about content, aims, and methods are likely to provide settings for meaningful learning. In contrast, programs in which organizational and institutional needs are the dominant ones in giving form and function to the program and in which learners' aspirations and experiences are not considered are likely to be much less successful in prompting personally significant learning.

Second, programmers should recognize that contextual distortion of neatly planned programs is likely to be a recurring feature of their professional practice. Acknowledging that contextual factors alter plans is the first step in practitioners' recognizing that imagined, exemplary role models of the perfect professional can be injurious to their self-esteem and their practice. Without a realization that context is crucial in affecting the possibilities and forms of practice, practitioners are likely to experience something close to despair each time a carefully planned program has to be altered because of some unforeseen eventuality.

Linked to this second point is a third one concerning the necessity of recognizing and encouraging the legitimacy of adaptive, improvisational practice. If practitioners come to realize that "playing hunches," "using intuition," "inspired guesswork," and improvisation are all acceptable, indeed valued, professional behaviors, then the theory-practice disjunction afflicting so many courses and workshops in adult education will be significantly reduced. The work of Argyris and Schön has prompted practitioners in a range of professional settings to realize that creative and improvisational activities are useful and legitimate aspects of professional performance. Those involved in developing programs for adult learners should be aware that altering program forms, methods, or content to take into account contextually specific features is not equivalent to an unprofessional deviation from plans for which they should feel guilty. Instead, they should learn to value their capacity to make programs more meaningful and relevant in terms of contextually specific features. Hence, improvisational ability should be recognized as crucial to successful practice.

Fourth, programmers should recognize the multiplicity of methods and techniques that might appropriately be used in program development. There is no single mode of program development suitable for the heterogenous universe of adult learners. Institutional, andragogical, self-directed, or Freirean approaches are probably used, at different times and in different degrees, in most programs. If teaching-learning encounters are genuinely transactional, then a diversity of methods will be required to meet the multiplicity of purposes that will inevitably arise.

A final note: Greater attention to the development of theories-in-use by practitioners is an evident research need. While the advantages of various program development modes are frequently touted, many practitioners will retreat to the professional security of publicly subscribing to textbook models of practice, while privately developing context-specific theories-in-use. As yet, studies that might illuminate our understanding of how practitioners do, in fact, develop programs for adult learners are comparatively rare. However, in a small-scale investigation in this area, Cole and Glass (1977) compared two groups of learners enrolled in in-service development programs at a North Carolina hospital. They concluded that "the group of adults who were given the opportunity to participate in program planning had higher achievement scores in regard to the course than did the adult group that did not have the opportunity to participate in program planning" (p. 87). This finding certainly supports what are now commonsense notions concerning the value of allowing learners to participate in planning their own education and training programs. It is also an example, however, of just how shaky is the empirical foundation for andragogical program-planning approaches. That only one study can be quoted to support the idea that involving learners in program planning is beneficial to their learning illustrates just how greatly current program development practice is based on intuition and assumption rather than on documented research.

❧ 11 ❧

Evaluating Learning and Its Facilitation

Attesting to the need for evaluation is somewhat akin to deciding to take exercise more regularly. Both are resolutions that are deemed important and necessary, but both are, for whatever reasons, rarely implemented. Just as needs assessment is viewed as the overture to the program development process, so evaluation becomes its final movement. There is a voluminous literature on evaluation, as well as a plethora of evaluative models available to the neophyte educator seeking to devise an instrument to evaluate a particular program. (There is also a widely held assumption that those educators who neglect to undertake this activity are guilty of dereliction of professional duty.)

As many readers already know, however, the reality is that pressures of time and money often militate against conducting systematic evaluations. More often than not, the programmer writes a brief report made up of a number of personal, mainly intuitive observations about the beneficial outcomes of the activity. Such observations may, of course, be extremely valuable. The accumulated intuitive insight of an educator who has been working to establish and implement a program can be of immense benefit for those seeking to offer similar programs elsewhere. Such observations are, however, inevitably open to accusations of distortion, subjectivity, and personal bias. Moreover, if the criteria used for making evaluative judgments regarding the success or achievements of a program are entirely personal, they are likely to have limited replicability. They will

261

reflect individualistic preferences and will be the product of contextual variables such as the sponsoring agency's mission, the institutional ethos as perceived by the educator, the financial climate of the time, and the programmer's personal philosophy. It is likely, for instance, that the criteria used by those organizing an in-service professional development program for health professionals or for business managers will differ from the criteria adopted by those organizing programs concerned with promoting personal liberation through literacy.

In these cases the criteria used to determine the success or achievements of programs will be chiefly situational. They will result from the interaction of the programmer's personal values and priorities with the institutional aims and the political ethos of the time. But it is impossible to use contextually based criteria to develop any general evaluative framework that might be applied to determine the effectiveness of a particular educational initiative. Hence, in this normative vacuum, evaluation becomes pragmatic, adaptive, and context specific.

One reason for the infrequency of systematic evaluation of adult learning is the absence of an evaluative model that derives its criteria and procedural features from the nature of the adult learning process. Evaluative models applied to adult learning tend to be drawn from secondary school or higher education settings and then adapted to the circumstances of adult learners. Rarely are they grounded in, or reflective of, the concepts, philosophies, and processes of adult learning. Stakes's (1981) review of evaluation models in adult education concluded that "if one had to assign adult educators to some school of evaluation thought, it would have to be one identified with goal attainment" (p. 23). As he pointed out, the emphasis throughout the literature is on the use of behaviorally stated objectives as criteria and indicators for evaluation. It seems, then, as if Tyler's school-based ideas are as predominant in the literature of evaluating adult learning as in the general literature of program development.

A study conducted by Buskey and Sork (1982) reveals that only five of ninety planning models reviewed in the literature fail to include evaluation as an important component of program planning. In their attempt to define adult education as an emerging field of university study, the American Commission of Professors of Adult Education set the tone for future work in this area when it accepted the notion of evaluation as coterminous with recording the extent to which previously defined performance behaviors were exhibited as the outcome of a program (Thiede, 1964). Within the succeeding twenty years a number of books and articles have reinforced this view.

Tenbrink (1974), moreover, found that teachers associate evaluation with tests, measurements, grades, unfairness, invasion of privacy, and judgment of achievement. This suggests, among other things, that the educational profession generally, and not just educators of adults, equates the act of evaluation with the assessment of previously specified performance behaviors. There are, however, a number of alternative evaluative frameworks. One school of writers stresses the use of evaluation for decision making (Cronbach, 1963; Alkin, 1969; Stufflebeam, 1968). Eisner (1976) advocates the critical judging of a program from an expert viewpoint. Gauging the community impact of a program and understanding the wider context in which a program operates are stressed by Knox (1979) and Parlett and Hamilton (1976). Stufflebeam and others (1971) and Scriven (1967) have argued that evaluation should be seen as a judgment of the merit, worth, and value of an activity. More recently Guba (1978), Guba and Lincoln (1981), and Lincoln and Guba (1985) have attacked the narrowly quantitative nature of most evaluation procedures and have proposed the use of qualitative data and the adoption of naturalistic evaluation. A number of the most significant of these models and approaches will be discussed later in this chapter.

In terms of a general concept of evaluation, I think the emphasis on the value-judgmental aspect of evaluation is the most fruitful. But it is particularly important to distinguish evaluation from assessment. These two terms are often used interchangeably, yet they are fundamentally different. The reason for their apparent interchangeability is that the institutional mode of evaluation stresses a value-free checking (assessment) of whether or not certain previously specified objectives have been attained. It is apparent that the term *assessment,* if applied to this latter activity, is being accurately used. Assessment is a value-free ascertainment of the extent to which objectives determined at the outset of a program have been attained by participants. Assessment of these objectives requires no value judgment as to their worthwhileness. It is simply a nonjudgmental checking as to whether or not certain purposes have been attained.

Evaluation, however, is inescapably a value-judgmental concept. The word *value* is at the heart of the term, with all the normative associations this implies. Scriven is the writer most associated with this viewpoint. In "The Methodology of Evaluation" (1967), he argues that even if all program objectives are achieved, the program itself cannot be considered successful unless the objectives attained are intrinsically worthwhile. Stufflebeam (1975) based his oft-quoted definition of evaluation on Scriven's thought: "Evaluation is the act of examining and judging, concerning the worth, quality, significance, amount, degree, or condition of something. In short, evaluation is the ascertainment of merit" (1975, p. 8). Even in discussions of the highly technical cost-benefit approach to evaluation, it has been recognized that value questions are central to the activity. In a review of cost-benefit analysis, for instance, Steele (1971) comments that scientifically "pure" data is of little validity unless it can be applied in settings where individuals are able to relate it to value components. She declares that "the adult educator cannot escape valuing by burrowing into data" (p. 11). Interestingly, the emphasis on the value basis of evaluation contained within the writings of Scriven, Stufflebeam, and Steele parallels the insistence of analytic philosophers of education such as Peters (1965), Lawson (1979), and Paterson (1979) that activities can only be considered properly educational if what is taught and learned is regarded as worthwhile.

Before looking at various models of evaluation, it is important to note that the political dimensions of the evaluative act have, in general, been ignored in textbooks on the subject. In much the same way that program development manuals ignore the contextual variables of institutional climate and the political ethos of the time, evaluation texts fail to recognize the political nature of evaluation. The most important exception to this is Guba and Lincoln (1981), who emphasize the importance of identifying stakeholders in the audiences that are the focus of the evaluation.

Stakeholders, according to Guba and Lincoln, are those individuals and groups who have a stake (an investment) in securing a favorable evaluation for a certain program. They will attempt to provide the evaluator with information that shows the program is successful and is accomplishing the goals for which it was established. Since evaluations are frequently undertaken to decide whether or not a program's funding should be continued, the evaluator is likely to be wooed, flattered, cajoled, nudged, and stroked into providing an overall favorable verdict.

Conscious of the fact that livelihoods are at stake in such circumstances, evaluators are likely to err on the side of fulsomeness rather than on that of understatement. They may do this from a broad sympathy for the program's goals rather than from a genuinely felt belief in the empirically proven accomplishments of the program. And individuals who themselves work as free-lance or consultant evaluators for their livelihoods will also be under pressure to provide favorable evaluations. Since their opportunities for employment depend to a great extent on an informal referral system, they will not wish to acquire reputations as "hard" evaluators. Providing too many negative evaluations that result in reductions in funding will ensure that the evaluator concerned will be avoided by many program administrators. Evaluators, therefore, are under many pressures to suspend rigorous, critical scrutiny when they examine program accomplishments.

It is important that external evaluators who enter a program setting to conduct a review of its accomplishments be aware of the political dimensions of such activity. Evaluators need to clarify what their employers see as the evaluative role. Employers' expectations concerning the "proper" focus for evaluation efforts need to be made explicit. The institutional goals and mission must be fully understood by the prospective

evaluator. He or she should also know something of the interpersonal conflicts present in the institution being reviewed. It is
not uncommon, for example, for an evaluation of a department
or experimental program to be called for because of some personal animosity between an institution's director and the program head. The external evaluator therefore needs to spend
considerable time (if possible before accepting a contract) investigating the interpersonal conflicts, hidden institutional agendas,
and covert purposes that may have surrounded the decision to
call for an evaluation. Every adult education program is a
unique psychosocial drama. The cast of characters will never be
exactly the same from one program to another, and the publicly
stated reasons for conducting an evaluation may bear little relation to the private agendas possessed by the actors in the drama.

Models of Evaluation

At this point, it would be useful to review, if only briefly,
some of the major models of evaluation that are current in the
field of continuing professional education, as well as in staff
training in business and industry, health education, and so
forth. Most formal evaluations of adult learning programs tend
to adapt one of the frameworks identified below.

Predetermined Objectives Approach. As already noted,
the most influential writer in the field of evaluating adult learning is Ralph Tyler. It is salutary to reflect, therefore, that the
approach to evaluation now so preeminent in many adult education programs, in business and industrial training, and in the
health professions was initially applied to a school-based setting.
This means that thousands of trainers and educators now working with adults in a variety of settings regard as natural and appropriate a method of evaluation devised for use with pupils in
high schools.

In 1932 Tyler was made director of an eight-year study in
which student performance under progressive high school curricula was compared to that under conventional curricula. He
insisted that the curricula be organized around objectives and
that these objectives serve as the basis for planning instruction.

These objectives would also represent evaluative criteria; that is, a program would be judged successful according to the extent to which these objectives had been attained. Tyler (1949) wrote that "the process of evaluation is essentially the process of determining to what extent the educational objectives are actually being realized. . . . since educational objectives are essentially changes in human beings, . . . then evaluation is the process for determining the degree to which these changes in behavior are actually taking place" (p. 106).

As Guba and Lincoln have acknowledged (1981), this view of evaluation as the measurement of predetermined behaviors is systematic, formal, precise, and internally logical. For these reasons, it has prevailed in all fields of educational endeavor. Its apparent scientism has provided an aura of legitimation for the field of educational evaluation, and its precision and system have proved invaluable to educators and trainers. Faced with the inchoate confusion and ambiguity of practitioner reality, they can turn to the model and its presentation of an ideal type of practice. Its unequivocal, unambiguous character inspires a certain kind of confidence in the programmer's ability to give form and order to course offerings where instructors, participants, and institutional priorities are uncertain. Hence, the model functions as a navigational device to assist seasick practitioners to chart a course through the storm-tossed waters of daily practice.

Some of the criticisms applied to the predetermined objectives approach as a general model for program development for adult learners dealt with in Chapter Nine also apply to this approach to evaluation. It is school based, it does not allow for unintended outcomes, it is authoritarian, it encourages a reification of program objectives, it discourages flexibility, and it takes no account of differences in students' experiences, interests, and abilities. To this extent it is unsuitable as a general purpose model of evaluation for adult learning. Depending on how it is employed, it may contradict many of what are deemed to be central principles of effective practice in facilitating learning—a democratic ethos, the collaborative determination of curricula, flexibility of format and direction, and the encouragement of self-direction among learners. The predefined objectives approach is useful in certain training courses and other settings where its specificity and a predefinition of methods and purposes are necessary. As a general rationale for the evaluation of adult learning, however, it is flawed.

Goal-Free Evaluation. In the mid 1960s a respected philosopher of social science, Michael Scriven, turned his attention to the field of evaluation. He insisted that value questions were at the heart of evaluation, he formulated the frequently cited distinction between formative (ongoing) and summative (final) evaluation, and he proposed a form of goal-free evaluation. In a paper on goal-free evaluation (Scriven, 1972) he criticized the separation of goals and side effects in evaluation reports. Because of the uncritical acceptance of the predetermined objectives approach, any events other than those contributing to the acquisition of specified objectives were deemed to be unimportant and irrelevant. Thus, behaviors, events, and accomplishments not related to the program's declared objectives were generally termed side effects, incidental outcomes, or unanticipated consequences. Scriven criticized this equating of the unplanned aspects of a program with unimportant events or achievements. To call such behaviors and events "side effects" or "accidental results" implied their innate inferiority, when in fact they might frequently represent the most important achievements of a program.

As an antidote to preoccupation with the attainment of previously specified objectives, Scriven proposed the idea of goal-free evaluation. In this approach the evaluator would be external to the program under study and would deliberately be unaware of the program's intended goals. In the absence of declared terminal objectives, program goals, or institutional criteria for determining success, the evaluator would simply record what seemed to be the major effects, achievements, and consequences of the program. Those employing the evaluator could then compare his or her report with their original purposes for the program.

It is, of course, unrealistic to expect an external evaluator to be completely unaware of the official aims and purposes of the program being studied. Indeed, the importance of the evaluator's determining hidden institutional agendas and covert assumptions has already been stressed. Just as a researcher using the most open-ended variant of grounded theory will always have some suspicions, intuitions, and expectations concerning what he or she will find, so an evaluator will always have some awareness of a program's declared purposes. For educators and trainers, however, the goal-free model is important in that it acknowledges the significance of the unplanned results of education. Since many adult learners frequently claim the "accidental" or "unofficial" aspects of their participation in a program to be the most important ones (changes in their self-image or the development of resource networks, for example), the goal-free approach has great relevance for adult learning.

An example from practice may make this clearer. Adult literacy staff may calculate improvements in the reading or writing abilities of their students according to some standard measure. Or, they may adopt various evaluative indexes to gauge the program's success—for example, changing levels of newspaper readership, book purchase, or library borrowing. As Charnley and Jones (1979) have made clear, however, learners' criteria of success are less clear. There is a strong affective dimension to the way in which they gauge their achievements. They will talk of feelings of increased confidence, better familial relationships, a new sense of purpose, and a changed self-concept. Increased book readership or job acquisition are obvious external indicators of a program's success, but just as significant to many students will be feelings of enhanced self-esteem and improved personal relationships. A goal-free evaluation would uncover this affective dimension and record that participants in the program held it to be a significant aspect of their participation. Were the evaluation to focus only on previously specified objectives, this aspect of the program would have been discounted. In this manner goal-free evaluation gives learners' perceptions and estimates of value a credibility that is missing from the Tylerian approach. This is directly in accordance with a democratic, learner-centered ethos.

CIPP Model of Evaluation. Scriven's response to the perceived constrictions of the Tylerian approach was to abandon official declarations of program purpose and to concentrate on recording as accurately as possible *all* program outcomes. A somewhat different reaction to Tyler's work has been explored by Stufflebeam (1971, 1975). Stufflebeam objects to the Tylerian preoccupation with the terminal outcomes of an educational program as placing undue emphasis on summative evaluation. To Stufflebeam, evaluation of a program should include scrutiny of the program's origins, implementation, and continuing operations, as well as its final achievements. In this approach formative evaluation is regarded as being of equal importance to summative evaluation.

Stufflebeam (1971) proposes an overall model of evaluation—the CIPP model—in which attention is given to studying the *C*ontext of the program, *I*nput into the program, *P*rocess within the program, and the program's *P*roduct. This model requires evaluators to study the effectiveness and feasibility of the initial policy decisions that gave rise to the program, as well as the program's actual operation. In this emphasis on contextual factors surrounding program development the CIPP model makes a useful contribution to the attempt to develop an evaluation model grounded in practitioner concerns. In any evaluation undertaken according to this model, the influence of institutional priorities, the impact of individual personalities, and the importance of the prevailing political climate would receive due acknowledgment. At present, many evaluations lack this critical contextual component.

The chief difficulty with the CIPP model, as has been recognized by Worthen and Sanders (1973) and Knox (1979), concerns the cost and time such an evaluative effort would require. To conduct an evaluation of all stages of a program's development may consume more time and energy than that expended in actually executing the program. But the value of the model lies in its recognition of the need to study the context surrounding the establishment of a program and in its shifting of attention away from the Tylerian preoccupation with the terminal outcomes of a program.

Kirkpatrick Hierarchy of Evaluation. In much the same

way as Stufflebeam's work emphasizes the importance of the contextual factors surrounding a program's origins, Kirkpatrick's (1967) hierarchy of evaluation places at its apex the community impact of a program. Put briefly, the Kirkpatrick hierarchy is comprised of four levels of evaluation. At the lowest level the reaction of program participants is obtained, and some overall estimate of learner satisfaction is made. The second level of the hierarchy is concerned with the actual learning that has occurred. At this level the evaluator collects data on the new knowledge and skills learners are able to demonstrate. The third level of evaluation is concerned with the transference of behaviors learned in the classroom to real life settings. Kirkpatrick is chiefly concerned with the learning of new job skills by workers and whether these are later demonstrated in the workplace, but the principle applies in any number of settings. Finally, the highest level of evaluation is concerned with the broad impact of the program on the wider community. The following table gives three examples of the application of the hierarchy to different program evaluation settings:

Kirkpatrick maintains that many evaluations stop at the first level (reaction), so that a recording of expressions of satisfaction or dissatisfaction becomes equated with the complete evaluation. Such an evaluation will have little or no value, particularly if the program evaluator and program developer are one and the same person. It is hard to imagine that trainees would express dissatisfaction with their employer's training efforts. Again, since many participants are likely to view some minimal acquisition of knowledge and skill as better than nothing, they are more likely to express satisfaction than disappointment. Finally, learners expressing dissatisfaction may do so because the program has caused them to engage in a difficult and possibly painful examination of the unquestioned assumptions by which they are living or working. In this last example, the practitioner might regard as evidence of real success (prompting learners to examine their value systems, beliefs, and behavioral codes) precisely those factors that cause the learners to express dissatisfaction.

The Kirkpatrick hierarchy is cast firmly within a pre-

Table 1. Kirkpatrick's Hierarchy of Evaluation.

Levels of Evaluation	Job Training	Nutrition Education	Adult Literacy
4. *Results* (Community impact)	Does output rise?	Do hospital admissions fall?	Does public library usage increase?
3. *Behavior* (Transference of skills)	Are skills used in work?	Do food-purchasing habits change?	Do learners read at home?
2. *Learning*	Do trainees demonstrate their acquisition of skills?	Do participants show knowledge of good diet?	Do learners show mastery of reading and writing skills?
1. *Reaction*	Do trainees express their satisfaction with the program?	Do participants express their satisfaction with the program?	Do learners express their satisfaction with the program?

determined objectives mode in that the criteria for success are clearly and closely specified from the outset. These criteria are set by those in positions of power and are, generally, unalterable. In this regard it may seem strange to look upon the Kirkpatrick hierarchy as a model with relevance for adult learners. Nonetheless, the model does have the virtue of emphasizing evaluative criteria other than learners' simple expressions of satisfaction. Also, it places at the apex of its evaluative framework some change in community structures or behaviors. It does not regard as the most important indicator of success some intrainstitutional factor. The hierarchy is particularly suitable for adaptation to community education evaluations or for any programs that are concerned with outreach projects.

Naturalistic Evaluation. The last general approach to evaluation that has some relevance to adult learning was developed by Egon Guba. In a monograph (Guba, 1978) and in two major texts (Guba and Lincoln, 1981; Lincoln and Guba, 1985), he has launched an attack on what he regards as a national scandal, namely, the failure to use evaluation findings to improve practice in any significant degree. Guba and Lincoln (1981) declare traditional evaluation approaches to be bankrupt and to be doomed to failure "because they do not begin with the concerns and issues of their actual audiences and because they produce information that, while perhaps statistically significant, does not generate truly worthwhile knowledge" (p. ix). To replace this approach, Guba proposes what he calls naturalistic evaluation. The crucial feature of naturalistic evaluation regarding the evaluation of facilitation is that it takes into account participants' definitions of key concerns and issues. It seeks to use language and modes of presenting findings that are accessible to those being evaluated. In this way naturalistic evaluation is somewhat similar to participatory research as proposed by the International Council for Adult Education (Hall, 1975). Present in both approaches is the desire to use subjects' definitions of importance as the criteria for deciding the research focus, to communicate research findings in as accessible a manner as possible, and to ensure that evaluation results are used to benefit those being studied.

Proponents of naturalistic inquiry advocate the use of qualitative rather than quantitative modes of data collection. They argue that evaluators cannot obtain a real understanding of their subjects' concerns and what they consider important through quantitative, survey research methods. Likely to be of much greater value are such methods as participant observation and open-ended interviews, as well as life histories, journals, and letters. Naturalistic evaluation also acknowledges the political dimensions of evaluation and the need to be wary of the competing claims of stakeholders in the evaluation. In its acknowledgment of context, its emphasis on allowing subjects to set the investigative agenda and to determine criteria for evaluation, and its concern that results be disseminated clearly, naturalistic evaluation is clearly a school of evaluation with great relevance for educators and trainers of adults.

Developing an Evaluative Approach to Adult Learning

There are, then, several major evaluative approaches current in the literature that, with some adaptation, might be used to evaluate adult learning. The importance of acknowledging learners' definitions of significance is stressed in the goal-free evaluation approach and in naturalistic evaluation. The CIPP model focuses attention on contextual factors surrounding the establishment of a program, as does the naturalistic approach. The importance of the extrainstitutional impact of a program on the surrounding community is emphasized in the Kirkpatrick hierarchy.

Grotelueschen (1980) suggests that any evaluative framework adopted by educators should be compatible with democratic and naturalistic approaches. I would agree and suggest we resist the temptation to adapt in a wholesale manner evaluative frameworks prepared by professionals from other fields for nonadult educational purposes. As Stakes (1981) and I (Brookfield, 1982), have acknowledged, there is a broad acceptance of Tyler's work among writers on the evaluation of adult learning. Thiede (1964) is typical of such writers, declaring as he did that the task orientation displayed by adult learners meant that only the Tylerian approach was feasible. He noted that most adult education programs were short term and informal and that this made careful external evaluation difficult. He also lamented the fact that since courses were framed in response to idiosyncratic and widely varying learner objectives, valid replicable evaluative indexes were hard to devise.

One can argue, however, that informality and flexibility are not necessarily handicaps to valid evaluation but, rather, that they can be used as guidelines for framing distinctively adult educational evaluative procedures. Such an approach is implicit in the work of Beder (1979) and Ruddock (1981), both of whom make a virtue of necessity in stressing the need for adaptability and flexibility in evaluations of adult learning. Beder, for example, stresses the criterion of appropriateness as the one that should govern the choice of evaluative methods. He discusses the manner in which at different times one could use such different evaluative methods as experimental design, measurement of objectives, descriptive analysis, input-output analysis, expert opinion, the free market approach, and informal feedback.

Ruddock (1981) employs a photographic metaphor to

emphasize the different levels of detail and interpretative orientations that can coexist in evaluative efforts. Like Beder, Ruddock outlines a range of different methods that can be used in evaluations. He advocates that educators pay more attention to the question of appropriateness and reviews how and when evaluators can use the methods of experiential analysis, statistical analysis, panels, sociometric analysis, participant observation, illumination evaluation, critical incidents, role analysis, depth interviews, life histories, document analysis, and participatory research. Central to Ruddock's analysis is an emphasis on the inescapable philosophical and political issues facing all evaluators, as well as an emphasis on basic questions of value. Knox (1969) echoes this attention to questions of value in his declaration that the first purpose of any evaluation must be to make explicit the rationale underlying an educational program.

Instances of the acceptance of the Tylerian rationale as appropriate for evaluating adult learning are evident in the work of the Committee on Program Evaluation of the Adult Education Association of the U.S.A. (1952), Miller and McGuire's (1961) analysis of liberal adult education, Boyle and Jahns' (1970) essay in the decennial *Handbook of Adult Education,* Verduin's (1980) evaluation of adult education curriculum building, and the recent report on *Principles of Good Practice in Continuing Education* published by the Council on Continuing Education Unit (1984). An oddity among these efforts is the work of Miller and McGuire (1961) who attempt, under the sponsorship of the Center for the Study of Liberal Adult Education, to specify a host of content and behavioral objectives for assessing adult education programs that deal with political, social, moral, and ethical questions. Their attempts to measure the development of moral discrimination using standardized test items represent a somewhat tortuous exercise in forcing the evaluation of complex and sophisticated mental shifts into a framework of predetermined objectives. That Miller and McGuire tried to adapt the Tylerian method to the evaluation of liberal adult education is signaled by the fact that Tyler himself authored the preface to the work.

But if we judge the previously specified objectives approach to evaluating adult learning to be too constraining and unrealistic, what can we propose as an alternative? What is needed is an evaluative framework that is grounded in, and derived from, some central features of adult learning. The three models that appear most likely to qualify as candidates for a uniquely adult educational evaluation framework are participatory evaluation, perspective discrepancy assessment, and andragogy. It is to a consideration of each of these that we now turn.

Participatory Evaluation. The idea that adults should be involved at all stages in the teaching-learning process is, of course, one of the most fundamental principles of facilitation. As an alternative to the Tylerian preoccupation with the summative evaluation of outcomes according to institutionally designated criteria of success, the idea of allowing adult learners to assume control for the evaluation of their learning appears both logical and humanistic. Such an idea was certainly at the heart of one of the last papers authored by Lindeman (1955). Arguing from the premise that evaluation methods must exhibit the same sense of freedom and democracy that characterize the learning process itself, Lindeman concluded that adults must learn how to evaluate their own success. He suggested that they would display a high degree of flexibility in the evaluative methods they chose and that they would use as a principal criterion of success the extent to which they felt themselves to be cohering into a true group. Hence, "all of our past and future experiments in evaluation are founded upon the assumption that adult learners must become participant observers" (p. 20).

In a critique of the disjunction between evaluation theory and the actual evaluations practiced in the real world of adult education, Forest (1976) rejected the behavioral objectives approach to evaluation as impractical and as neglectful of the value of programs to the participants themselves. As an alternative, Forest proposed a framework in which accountability would be to students, criteria would be individual and varied, data collection would be subjective, and control would rest with students. Kinsey (1981) claimed a formidable list of advantages for ensuring a degree of participatory involvement in evaluation. Participation was held to increase the accuracy of data, to prompt learning of staff and students, to improve awareness and communication, to increase the commitment of program members, and to develop external support for the program. As Kinsey points out, however, it is all too easy to express a simple preference for participation while giving no thought to the questions of who is to participate and what is to be the focus and manner of this participation. He proposed a middle course that would recognize the contextual constraints placed by institutions on comprehensive participation but would also acknowledge the need for some measure of participation.

The logic of participatory evaluation is compelling and attractive. It is also dangerous in that it may seduce us into adopting a felt needs rationale. The danger of a full-fledged participatory evaluation lies in the possibility that participants will generate criteria of educational evaluation that have little intrinsic educational worth. Participants may judge a program to be successful if it results in their meeting a potential marriage partner, if it increases their earning capacity, if it allows them to impress superiors with newly gained knowledge, and so forth. The educator who abrogates responsibility for setting evaluative criteria to participants is as guilty of professional misconduct as the teacher who refuses to take a value stance on controversial matters, or the programmer who abdicates responsibility for curricular offerings to those clients who shout the loudest and longest for particular courses.

Perspective Discrepancy Assessment. One evaluative model designed specifically for use with adult learners is perspective discrepancy assessment (PDA). Developed by a team of researchers at Columbia University's Teachers College, PDA is premised on the assumption that "the educational process can best be understood by examining how those involved perceive and understand the process and themselves in relation to it" (Mezirow, 1978, p. 52). The model is qualitative in nature and draws on the countenance model of evaluation (Stake, 1967), as well as on the phenomenological tradition of social analysis. PDA presumes that educational endeavors are context specific and that evaluations of particular programs cannot always be undertaken using a standardized, summative approach. The model concentrates on identifying key decision areas and the crucial questions facing those involved in decision making. Individuals answer questions (through questionnaires or interviews) on their perceptions of current and intended practice. From their responses it is possible to identify major discrepancies in their perceptions of the underlying assumptions, actual practice, and future efforts of those involved in the program. Detailed descriptions of the methodology of PDA are found in Mezirow (1978), Spencer (1980), and Smalley (1984).

A number of research efforts have used the perspective discrepancy approach to try to understand the interactive mechanisms evident in particular programs. As Spencer (1980) points out, however, the model is not to be standardized and applied in a mechanistic manner. Its emphasis is on appreciating the context-specific aspects of programs; directors, administrators, and policy makers should adapt the model to fit the circumstances of their own settings. It is quite likely that key decision areas will differ widely from program to program. Nonetheless, the central elements of the model—the identification of discrepancies in the perceptions of key personnel regarding current and future practice within the program—can be adapted to a variety of settings and used for both formative and summative evaluation purposes. Examples of the application of PDA to the evaluation of particular programs have been recorded with adult basic education (Mezirow, Darkenwald, and Beder, 1975), women's reentry programs (Mezirow and Rose, 1977), community adult education (Spencer, 1979), community colleges (Flanagan, 1979), nursing programs (Bailey, 1979), four-year colleges (Gardner, 1984), vocational programs for women (Higgins, 1980), and Dale Carnegie instructional programs (Mackey, 1977).

It is, of course, quite likely that several discrepancies in perceptions will exist among actors in a program, but this should not be a cause for concern. Indeed, it may be essential for the development of a thriving program that different personnel have different viewpoints and adopt varying approaches. A lively range of views and interpretations could be a sign of organizational health, rather than a cause for alarm. What is a problem, however, is if the key actors in a drama of program development are playing their roles according to different scripts. In other words, confusion, ambiguity, and ineffectiveness will be the likely result if deans, administrators, instructors, and learners hold contradictory ideas concerning the fundamental purpose of a program. Conducting a PDA would help to make explicit the covert assumptions and private agendas that significantly influence practice but are not publicly displayed or shared.

Andragogy and Collaborative Modes of Evaluation. The evaluative framework adumbrated by the Nottingham Andragogy Group (1983) has already been mentioned earlier in this book. In many ways, this model is much less impressive than the participatory evaluation approach or the PDA. The group offers no examples of data collection techniques, and neither does it outline any methodological procedures for implementing its praxis evaluation approach. What it does offer, however, are a number of provocative ideas concerning a subjective, dialogic approach to evaluation. It suggests that changing relationships among group members can be examined through a detailed analysis of verbal interchanges. This would not be a simple sociometric analysis of the origin and direction of statements and comments but rather would attend to the subtleties of meaning contained within those exchanges. The group advocates observing how the educator hands over power and responsibility for managing the group process to members, though it offers no specific guidelines on how this might be accomplished. It also emphasizes the need to encourage group members to reflect on their participation and to record the extent and nature of the changes they have undergone as a result of group participation.

Beyond suggesting that adult learners (including the facilitator) should engage in frequent reflection on these matters, the group recommends no specific approaches. What is significant about the group, however, is that it spells out the criteria it employs to evaluate the educational worth of a particular activity. Whereas the participatory evaluation approach and PDA offer a range of sophisticated data collection techniques, they do not outline fundamental evaluative criteria that can be applied to assessing the educational value of various efforts. Participatory evaluators in large measure place responsibility for generating evaluative criteria on learners. Those using a PDA model are more concerned with identifying significant disjunctions in outlook among actors in a program than with establishing criteria by which its success can be measured.

The Nottingham Andragogy Group, however, offers a fundamental criterion that we might apply to any teaching-learning transaction in order to make some judgments about its worth. An activity is an example of effective facilitation, the group argues, to the extent to which it enables participants who initially saw themselves as passive recipients of transmitted knowledge to begin to take responsibility for managing the group process, for controlling their own learning, and for pushing back the boundaries of knowledge and experience in the group.

Several attempts to instigate andragogical, collaborative modes of evaluation are included in a recent volume of case studies (Deshler, 1984). In it, a number of evaluation specialists document how they developed formative and participatory evaluative frameworks for a variety of adult client groups. It is Deshler's contention that formative evaluations are most appropriate when educators are seeking to improve existing programs, to contribute to social learning, and to give guidance on active interventions in programs when the educational context is constantly changing. Moreover, such approaches are applicable in many different settings, as demonstrated by case studies of their use in voluntary organizations (Eggert, 1984), with the elderly (H. W. Brown, 1984), and in management training and organizational development (Whitcomb, 1984).

Deshler also documents two interesting attempts to involve citizens, adult education participants, and volunteers in evaluative efforts. In the Reflective Appraisal of Programs approach used by the Cornell Cooperative Extension in New York State (Bennett, 1982), the emphasis is placed on "perceptions," or "reflective" evidence, from program participants who estimate in interviews by volunteers the extent to which the program has brought about a change in their lives or in the community" (Deshler, 1984, p. 16). Again, in Lancaster County, Pennsylvania, a volunteer citizen committee makes site visits to evaluate mental health/mental retardation programs. Members of these citizen teams include mental health consumers, and no team members may be paid employees of the program evaluated (Kastner and Olds, 1983).

These case studies of formative, participatory evaluation are important for a number of reasons. First, the criteria for evaluation, and the substantive focuses for data collection, are based on participants' and clients' notions of relevance, as well as on the providing agencies' specifications of valuable practice. Considerable credence is given, therefore, to the client perspective as a variable in determining the format of the evaluation. Second, the methods used in these case studies are, for the most part, qualitative. The most frequent data collection techniques used by contributors to the Deshler volume are interviews and observational methods. Third, the evaluation activities themselves are frequently carried out by teams of volunteers, who may well be clients of the service being evaluated. Finally, the case studies all acknowledge the context-specific nature of evaluative efforts. They exemplify the pertinence of Deshler's (1984) observation that "it is now widely recognized that appropriate selection of models to match requirements of particular situations produces the evaluation results that are most likely to be useful for specific purposes. It is no longer acceptable for practitioners or evaluators to apply to everything the one model with which they are familiar" (p. 12).

As the qualitative approaches to evaluation advocated by such writers as Guba and Lincoln (1981), Lincoln and Guba (1985), and Patton (1980) are increasingly granted intellectual credibility and practical utility by educators and trainers, we can expect many more attempts to use these approaches in developing a body of formative-participatory evaluation models, all of which can be dismantled and adapted as appropriate. That this is already happening is clear from the use of value audits (Smith, 1984), the use of rating scales developed by the Syracuse Rating Group (Cameron, 1983), the use of educational technology for formative evaluation (Huber and Gay, 1984), and the adaptation of collaborative evaluation through group interviews and group analyses of experience. The next ten years will most likely witness a major growth in the development of, and experimentation with, qualitative techniques in the search for an evaluative approach that incorporates principles of effective facilitation with adults.

This kind of collective effort is greatly needed. Without a fundamental notion of what constitutes excellence, programs will be evaluated according to criteria chosen by those funding the evaluations. Some acceptance of these criteria is inevitable; no agency is likely to employ an evaluator who ignores the agency's purposes and produces an evaluation based on criteria unconnected to these. It is important, though, that whenever we evaluate adult education activities (whether our own or those of others), we operate from some common understanding of what comprises good practice. Without such a common framework of concepts and assumptions we will be unable to speak to each other with any degree of accuracy or authenticity concerning the relative value of various programs. Some suggestions regarding the form of the framework which can be applied to judging good practice are presented in the next chapter.

✣ 12 ✣

Facilitating Learning

Toward Guidelines for Good Practice

Specifying Criteria

As a conclusion to this book, I want to present an evaluative rationale that readers can adopt, perhaps partially, perhaps
wholly, to guide their evaluations. The rationale is derived from
my philosophy of adult education, and it is a brief elaboration
of this philosophy that ends my book. The critical evaluative
rationale, therefore, is based on the extent to which certain
philosophical dimensions are evident in the facilitation of adult
learning. Briefly stated, this critical philosophy regards the facilitation of learning as a value-laden activity in which curricular
and programmatic choices reflect normative preferences. It sees
adult education as a socialization agent of some force, capable
of confirming values and behaviors uncritically assimilated in
earlier periods or of prompting adults to challenge the validity
of their received ideas and codes.

Developing in adults a sense of their personal power and
self-worth is seen as a fundamental purpose of all education and
training efforts. Only if such a sense of individual empowerment
is realized will adults possess the emotional strength to challenge behaviors, values, and beliefs accepted uncritically by a
majority. Both causally antecedent to, and concurrent with,

283

this developing sense of self-worth in the individual comes an awareness of the contextuality of knowledge and beliefs. The task of the educator, then, becomes that of encouraging adults to perceive the relative, contextual nature of previously unquestioned givens. Additionally, the educator should assist the adult to reflect on the manner in which values, beliefs, and behaviors previously deemed unchallengeable can be critically analyzed. Through presenting alternative ways of interpreting and creating the world to adults, the educator fosters a willingness to consider alternative ways of living.

These criteria are offered for consideration by educators as fundamental indicators by which they may judge the worth of a formal or informal effort to facilitate learning. In real life, of course, all adults will not develop a sense of self-worth, an awareness of the contextuality of knowledge, a willingness to speculate on alternatives, and a capacity to re-create their personal and social worlds, according to the neatly sequenced stages described in the previous paragraph. Some adults will come to appreciate the contextuality of knowledge or learn to speculate on alternatives, without having the sense of self-worth and personal power needed to realize those alternatives. Others will have the internal strength to alter certain peripheral features of their lives (their attitudes to other cultures, their susceptibility to advertisements, and so forth) but will be unable to change the patterns that govern their significant personal relationships. Still others may consider social alternatives and even imagine new political forms, but lack the techniques, skills, or collective support needed to effect change. This does not mean, however, that we should abandon attempts to specify as clearly as possible the criteria we are adopting to determine the success of our efforts.

Such criteria will, inevitably, take the form of abstractions. They will be oversimplifications of reality. The real world of social encounters is sufficiently chaotic to make the detection of whether or not these criteria have been satisfied a correspondingly haphazard and often messy enterprise. Nevertheless, if we make no attempt to specify criteria, we will be unable to assign value and worthwhileness to different activities. All educational encounters will then exist in some kind of moral vacuum, and we will be unable to judge whether a lecture in which a religious or political dogma is fervently and uncritically expounded is more or less educational than a discussion of the ethical assumptions underlying communism and capitalism.

If we are to wear the mantle of "educator," we must, at some minimum level, make explicit the criteria by which we determine the educational worth of our efforts. Not to do so is unthinking or dishonest, and it is to consign ourselves to being adaptive and reactive satisfiers of whatever consumer learning needs happen to capture our attention. But it is to the means for determining whether or not these criteria are actually being met in an educational activity that we must now turn our attention.

The preceding chapters have been concerned chiefly with matters of practice—facilitating adult learning through self-directed modes, using andragogical methods, teaching adults through discussion groups, developing programs for adult learners, and evaluating effective practice. Implicit in these discussions of practice, however, has been a concept of facilitation somewhat different from that held by many practitioners. In this final chapter it is important that the philosophical assumptions on which this concept is based be stated clearly. As has been repeatedly argued, practical expertise that exists in a moral vacuum can be a dangerous thing. Practitioners can become technically proficient but find that without a firm philosophical rationale to guide the application of their skills, they are devoting their efforts to programs and purposes that are morally dubious.

The concept of facilitation informing this book was discussed initially in Chapter One in terms of the six characteristics of effective facilitation. Contained in these characteristics are features that will be familiar to those who know the literature of humanistic psychology and psychotherapy—a respect for participants in the teaching-learning transaction, a commitment to collaborative modes of program development, and an acknowledgment of the educational value of life experiences. Also contained in this concept of facilitation, however, is an element of critical analysis that may not be quite so familiar.

Stated briefly, this analytic component requires that facilitators and practitioners prompt learners to consider alternative perspectives on their personal, political, work, and social lives. Hence, effective facilitation means that learners will be challenged to examine their previously held values, beliefs, and behaviors and will be confronted with ones that they may not want to consider. Such challenges and confrontations need not be done in an adversarial, combative, or threatening manner; indeed, the most effective facilitator is one who can encourage adults to consider rationally and carefully perspectives and interpretations of the world that diverge from those they already hold, without making these adults feel they are being cajoled or threatened. This experience may produce anxiety, but such anxiety should be accepted as a normal component of learning and not as something to be avoided at all costs for fear that learners will leave the group. There are forms of fulfillment that are quite unlike those produced by a wholly joyful encounter with a new form of knowledge or a new skill area. It is this dimension of increased insight through critical reflection on current assumptions and past beliefs and behaviors that is sometimes ignored in treatments of adult learning. One purpose of this book is to place the prompting of this form of learning at the heart of what it means to be a good facilitator.

It is important to state, however, that because teaching-learning transactions are collaborative, the prompting of critical reflection may not always be done by the participant designated as the facilitator. In the most effective learning groups, facilitating behaviors are assumed by various members of these groups at different times. One feature of the leaderless groups discussed in Chapter Six—women's consciousness-raising groups, quality circles, political advocacy groups, and so on—is that the member who is responsible for the initial formation of these groups does not have to assume full responsibility for facilitating learning. As a group culture develops, various members will challenge others to examine their current ways of thinking and living, and this activity will be seen as wholly appropriate. As a recent study of self-concept change among black women students at college points out (Meyer, 1985), one of the valued characteristics of good facilitators as identified by these women is a readiness to challenge learners.

Building a Critical Philosophy of Practice

The public articulation of a philosophy of effective practice is an activity viewed with apparent indifference or distaste by many educators and trainers of adults. Such educators might appear to an outsider to be bereft of any rationale for their practice. This is rarely the case. In reality, most practitioners accept employing agency mission statements as general definitions of purpose or declare good practice to be the satisfaction of felt and expressed needs. These positions in themselves exemplify a philosophical rationale—that of pragmatism.

Acceptance of this pragmatic rationale is perhaps most evident in the tendency to equate the design of effective program-planning models with the sum total of effective practice. According to this argument, the education of adults is a matter of designing, conducting, and evaluating educational experiences so as to meet the felt needs of adults. Hence, practitioner effectiveness becomes defined in terms of processes and activities—the ability to design, conduct, and evaluate programs for learners—rather than in terms of fundamental purposes or curriculum. But if we view effective practice solely as the improvement of ever more refined practice skills and regard facilitator roles and responsibilities as being primarily those of technicians of design, we denude practice of any philosophical rationale, future orientation, or purposeful mission. There exists no philosophical yardstick in terms of criteria of success, notions of purpose, or appropriate curricula against which the effectiveness of such facilitation can be judged. Furthermore, if we accept the view that we should serve only felt needs, then our priorities, purposes, and primary functions will be wholly determined by others. Our curriculum will be devised in response to demands made by those who can best attract our attention and are most articulate in presenting their case.

To counter this danger that facilitation will become solely a responsive, reactive activity, it is important that practitioners develop a philosophical rationale, or what Apps (1982) calls a belief system, to grant their practice order and purpose. They need to identify those characteristics by which the fundamental worth of any attempt to facilitate adult learning can be judged.

This does not mean that such a philosophy must be exemplified to its fullest degree in every educational encounter with adults. Such an insistence would be so intimidating to practitioners as to prevent *any* attempt to implement a philosophy. We should regard this rationale rather as a variable that can be realized to a greater or lesser extent at different times, in different settings, with different groups. Even within one class session the extent to which this philosophy is realized will vary with the nature of the individuals concerned, the exercises pursued, and the educator's conduct. Nonetheless, it is vital that a clear rationale be articulated so that practitioners may have a benchmark for judging the extent to which their activities exemplify fundamental purposes, principles, and practice. Without a coherent rationale (even if full implementation is not always possible), practice will be condemned to an adaptive, reactive mode. Practitioner activities will be determined by current curricular trends (whether these be for aerobics, computer literacy, or peace education) or by the ability of certain individuals and groups to make themselves heard and their demands felt.

Several writers have indeed warned of the dangers of succumbing to a reactive and pragmatic rationale. Lawson (1979) and Monette (1979) have both condemned the insidious influence of the service rationale on programs for adult learners. According to this rationale, practitioners are technicians whose function is to cater to the expressed needs of their clients in as effective a manner as possible. These writers point out that by responding to felt needs, the educator does not have to make value judgments concerning the relative merits of different curricular offerings. Only rarely is there any acknowledgment in the literature of the moral and professional requirement that the educator act in accordance with value choices.

Crabtree (1963) has also condemned the manner in which the idea of "customer service" comes to determine the form of the curriculum for adult learners. Similarly, Powell (1964) warned against the importing of a business rationale into adult education and expressed his concern at the growing tendency to let a preoccupation with needs assessments and marketing procedures replace the setting of fundamental goals for a program. Seduction of the programmer by evidence of a strong and immediate demand for a certain course offering was also recognized by Herring (1953), who blamed the galloping mediocrity he saw in many programs for adult learners on the institutionally prescribed need to increase enrollments. Herring lamented the tendency of program planners to avoid social and political issues that they thought were too serious or too contentious to draw large numbers of participants.

In adult education, however, we seem currently to be in danger of becoming preoccupied with refining techniques to the exclusion of any consideration of the rationale underlying those techniques. We are philosophically numb, concerned with the design of ever more sophisticated needs assessment techniques, program planning models, and evaluative procedures. It seems not to have occurred to us that the perfection of technique can only be meaningful when placed within a context of some fundamental human or social purpose. Technique is, after all, only a means to broader ends. When technique is worshipped to the exclusion of the human or social purposes it is meant to serve, then it is easy for us to become dazzled by the convolutions of the latest shaman of procedure and by the pronouncements of those who flaunt commonsense ideas regarding teaching and learning under the guise of presenting a revolutionary paradigm of practice.

In contrast, this chapter attempts to comment on the fundamental nature and proper purpose of facilitating learning by outlining a philosophy of practice that comprises three fundamental elements. First, there should be offered a clear definition of the activity concerned. Second, from this definition there should be derived a number of general purposes for the field. Finally, on the basis of this definition and this general statement of purpose there should be formulated a set of criteria by which the success of various practitioner efforts can be judged. Such criteria would allow us to reflect on our own practice and to examine the activities of others in terms of their effectiveness.

This definition, statement of purposes, and explication of criteria should be firmly and avowedly prescriptive. A philosophy of practice should, at the most fundamental level, be concerned with the resolution of second-order questions, that is, questions that cannot be answered by recourse to the empirical world. In other words, we cannot conduct a survey to determine in some objectively empirical sense what should be the purpose of our efforts. We can conduct assessments of present levels of competence and declare certain populations to be in states of educational need with regard to some previously defined standard. Such assessments are only objective, however, to the extent that they are based on a normatively defined standard of competence. Similarly, by conducting a Delphi survey of adult education professors, we can determine their views on the proper purposes of facilitation. This survey will not answer for us, however, the fundamental question concerning what should be the purpose of educating adults, for this is a question that is explored in a quite separate area of intellectual discourse. The domain of discourse surrounding such a question is one of prescriptive preferences, moral commitments, and categorical imperatives. We will come to construct our philosophy of practice on the basis of the personal and social imperatives we feel to be most potent. In the course of this construction we will admittedly be cognizant of the opinions of those intellectual leaders we respect. Such opinions cannot grant to our philosophy its internal power and commitment, however, since this will be derived from our experience of the world and from our personal belief system concerning the most desirable and meaningful aspects of this experience.

Implementing the Rationale

A philosophy of practice should allow considerable scope for operationalization. In an activity such as facilitating learning, statements of fundamental purpose are of limited value if they cannot be realized in terms of practice. Concomitant with this outline of a philosophical rationale, therefore, should be some guidance in regard to teaching method, curriculum development, program planning, and evaluation. But such techniques will not exist in their own right; they will be grounded in, and derived from, a carefully explicated rationale. This rationale—from which are derived various practical injunctions in terms of planning, teaching, curriculum development, and evaluation—will serve as a yardstick against which the effectiveness and worth of a particular effort can be judged. This philosophy and its concomitant operationalizations should serve as a benchmark and as a guide by which practice can be mapped.

The philosophy of practice proposed within this last chapter centers on the notion of the adult's developing sense of control and autonomy. Such autonomy is not to be equated with atomistic isolation; rather, it is realized in personal relationships, in sociopolitical behavior, and in intellectual judgment. The purpose of facilitation is to assist individuals to begin to exercise control over their own lives, their interpersonal relationships, and the social forms and structures within which they live. This is not to say that facilitation will enable adults to exert complete control over all aspects of their worlds. However, it is possible to envisage existences that are more or less meaningful and authentic to the individuals involved, according to the degree to which they feel they have some proactive role in creating their worlds.

It is proposed that all involved in teaching-learning transactions assist each other to identify the external sources and internalized assumptions framing their conduct and to be ready to assess these critically. Such critical awareness will involve an appreciation of the contextual, provisional, and relative nature of truth, public knowledge, and personal beliefs. When a disjunction becomes evident between adults' individual aspirations and the socially received codes, value frameworks, and belief systems informing their behavior, then autonomy is reflected in a jettisoning of received assumptions. Occurring along with this abandonment of assumptions perceived as irrelevant and inauthentic will be the transformation of individual and collective circumstances. Such a transformation will be manifest in renegotiations of personal relationships, attempts to re-create the conditions of work so as to imbue these with some sense of personal significance, and attempts to alter social forms.

All human interactions alter the consciousness of those

involved to a greater or lesser extent. Teaching-learning transactions are no exceptions to this rule; indeed they possess an unusual degree of potency in that the facilitator's statements and comments are typically granted a high degree of credibility and significance by learners. Learners grant authority to interpretations, generalizations, and statements of preference made by the facilitator, even though he or she may avow this equality of status with learners and emphasize that they are partners in a collaborative endeavor. Facilitators may profoundly dislike this role, particularly those of a democratic, egalitarian temper. To be the beneficiary of imputations of moral as well as intellectual superiority by learners is confining and often even embarrassing. However, inasmuch as most adults received an initial education that encouraged them to see teachers as authority figures, it is hardly surprising if they prove incapable, at least at first, of viewing the facilitator as a partner and intellectual collaborator.

This ascribed authority places facilitators in an uncomfortable position, particularly if they subscribe to andragogical principles. It also makes the adoption of an ethical code of practice—a requirement of first importance in any profession —doubly necessary. Any position of authority, whether ascribed or prescribed, carries within it the possibility of abuse. This potential will be reduced if facilitators seek, as rigorously as possible, to submit all assertions (including their own) to critical scrutiny. Facilitators will cite appropriate evidence for any generalizations they make and will treat all theories, explanatory systems, standards of esthetic discrimination, conceptual constructs, and criteria of excellence as provisional and relative.

Aside from viewing theoretical systems or explanations as provisional, the facilitator should also present alternative interpretations and possibilities to students. Such alternatives may be esthetic, cognitive, or sociopolitical. Hence, a course on craft skills should encourage inquiries into the origins of standards of excellence and not concentrate only on the development of psychomotor skills exemplifying those standards. A similar requirement also holds for courses dealing with bodies of cognitive knowledge. These should submit central concepts and theoretical frameworks to critical review. Criteria of intellectual excellence should be viewed as humanly contrived, not divinely ordained, and all statements and assertions should be regarded as provisional. With regard to those courses dealing with behavioral phenomena—for example, role training, interpersonal skill development, or counseling techniques—the twin canons of relativity and provisionality also pertain.

In fields such as health education, administrative studies, or personnel management, training courses can only qualify as examples of effective facilitation if the behavioral paradigms presented in them are subjected to critical scrutiny. Moreover, if such courses are to be seen as involving education and not simply training, they must incorporate a willingness to consider alternatives to the popularly prevailing norms governing correct professional behaviors. Participants in such courses would learn to be skeptical of definitive sets of principles of practice and to view conventionally accepted wisdom or apparently exemplary behaviors as relative and provisional.

The chief argument proposed here is that effective facilitation is present when adults come to appreciate the relative, provisional, and contextual nature of public and private knowledge and when they come to understand that the belief systems, value frameworks, and moral codes informing their conduct are culturally constructed. It is also evident when adults are enabled to create meaning in their personal worlds through a continual redefinition of their relationships with others. Following on from this exhibition of personal autonomy and the realization that individual circumstances can be consciously altered comes the insight that it is possible, in concert with others, to change cultural forms, including attitudinal sets, role expectations, conventions, and folkways, as well as social structures.

This concept of facilitation is obviously prescriptive; that is to say, the outcomes identified in the preceding paragraph are given in the form of stipulative preference statements. This is not to imply that adults can become adept at critical reflectivity in some final, static manner. Rather, it is to say that adults should be encouraged to engage in the continuous critical analysis of received assumptions, commonsense knowledge, and conventional behaviors. The state of adulthood can never be fully realized, and it is not a question of an adult's acquiring a set of fixed competencies. Adult education as a transactional encounter is essentially a process. Central to this process is a continual scrutiny by all involved of the conditions that have shaped their private and public worlds, combined with a continuing attempt to reconstruct those worlds. This praxis of continual reflection and action might be accurately viewed as a process of lifelong learning.

It is important to realize that philosophical prescriptions painstakingly derived from impeccably developed rationales are going to be contradicted daily in the real world of practice. Teaching-learning transactions are, after all, dynamic interactions—psychosocial dramas in which unforeseen eventualities, serendipitous circumstances, and individual idiosyncrasies constantly distort our neatly planned visions of how our learning groups should function. Educators employed within formal educational institutions daily contradict their own prescriptions concerning how best to foster learners' freedom and individuality.

An example drawn from my own practice may illustrate what I mean. In a course I teach on the philosophy and theory of adult education, I generally invite group members to identify within this same course any elements of "banking education" (Freire, 1970b) practices that they may perceive. ("Banking education" refers to the system whereby knowledge is seen as deposited by experts in the vaults that are learners unformed minds. The educator retains total control over the goals, content, and evaluative criteria of the educational activity.) Very often, as the learning group reviews the curriculum, format of meetings, and evaluative procedures of the last few weeks or months, it becomes evident that a familiar dynamic has operated, despite all our best intentions to the contrary. According to this dynamic, I have begun by emphasizing the collaborative nature of the course and then, with the apparently unwitting connivance of course members, have proceeded to assume major responsibility for the most important decisions concerning course content and format. Although all members of the group (myself included) pay frequent testimony to the need to draw on individual participants' own experiences, to ground curricula in their concerns, and to evolve a collaborative format, we fall easily and unthinkingly into a pattern of interaction whereby I begin to expound on adult education from an expert standpoint and they passively receive my distilled wisdom. Participants and I have been socialized to such an extent into a banking education mode that we fall easily into our respective roles of authority figure and inexperienced learners, no matter what our resolutions to the contrary. Educators of adults, as much as learners, uncritically assimilate various assumptions, norms, beliefs, and values, and it is a genuinely humbling experience to ask participants in a learning group to point out the disguised authoritarianism in one's own practice.

What must never be lost sight of, however, is the need to develop a clear rationale for practice, even though that rationale may be contradicted or only partially realized in the day-to-day practitioner reality of facilitating learning. Without such a rationale we are little more than reactive automatons—ciphers through whom are channeled the latest curricular or methodological fads, irrespective of any consideration of their innate validity. While a healthy skepticism regarding the possibility of continually exemplifying such a philosophy of practice is essential to the sanity of facilitators, the necessity to develop such a philosophy should be regarded as fundamental to good practice.

Educators of adults have grown accustomed to living with organizational and professional contradictions. They probably became facilitators because they saw that as a way of increasing individuals' fulfillment, happiness, and sense of control, yet organizational criteria for their success are frequently antithetical to these motivations. In colleges and universities, for example, educators are encouraged to develop curricula and to arrange classrooms so as to attract the largest possible number of learners. The reason for this is not only to add to the sum total of human happiness and enlightenment, but also to make money. Educational institutions, particularly in an era dominated by supply side economics, are viewed by politicians, trustees, administrators, and sometimes even faculty partly as educational enterprises partly as business operations. Hence, the greater the numbers of students that can be attracted, the greater the revenues for the educational institution. In business and industrial settings, these economic criteria are applied quite openly to determining the success of training initiatives. While trainers may hope that workshops and seminars will enable adults to make sense of themselves and their worlds, their success as trainers will be judged by whether or not productivity rises as a consequence of attendance at the training sessions.

Furthermore, most educators and trainers of adults sub-scribe to a professional code that acknowledges the value of democratic collaboration and the inequity of forcing students to learn. Yet in their daily practice they repeatedly encounter a set of contextual constraints that force them into precisely the behaviors that they criticize in philosophical terms. Institutional timetables, economic necessities, standardized curricula, and un-official norms of "what works in the *real* world" all conspire to nudge the educator into more didactic, authoritarian attitudes and behaviors than he or she might wish. The conspiracy of con-textual constraints becomes all the more compelling when learn-ers repeatedly declare that they wish for more direction from facilitators or that they want facilitators to "put more of them-selves" into the learning encounter. Learners, as much as facilita-tors, have been socialized into a view of education as an authori-tarian-based transmission of information, skills, and attitudinal sets from teacher to taught. Under these circumstances, it will often be hard for educators to stand firm against the temptation to take more control over the learning encounter. Yet to give in to this temptation is to reaffirm precisely those patterns of dependency that prevent adults from becoming empowered, self-directed learners.

Given the force of these organizational constraints and professional expectations, it is not surprising that facilitators re-vert, with only an occasional twinge of conscience, to patterns of behavior they observed in their own teachers. How, then, can they break these patterns and begin to assume the kinds of fa-cilitation roles outlined in this book? My answer is, only by developing a thoughtful rationale to guide their practice. Possessed of such a rationale, facilitators are more likely to stand firm against organizational and professional imperatives that exert pressure on them to dominate learners under the guise of "providing structure" or "clarifying ambiguities." Without such a rationale it is likely that most facilitators will sooner or later fall unthinkingly into patterns of facilitation that support structures of organizational convenience and confirm learners' patterns of dependency learned in the school classroom but have little to do with assisting adults to create, and re-create, their personal, occupational, and political worlds.

Abbreviations

❧ ❧ ❧ ❧

ABE—adult basic education
AERC—Adult Education Research Conference
AEGIS—Adult Education through Guided Independent Study
API—Andragogy in Practice Inventory
AT&T—American Telephone and Telegraph Company
BBC—British Broadcasting Company
CIPP—Context of . . . , Input into . . . , etc.
CPE—continuing professional education
ESL—English as a Second Language
GED—General Educational Development (exam)
HRD—human resource development
IBM—International Business Machines
ICA—Industrial Cooperative Association
ILO—International Labor Office
MCE—mandatory continuing education
NECs—national executive committees
OECD—Organization for Economic Cooperation and Development
PALS—Principles of Adult Learning Scale
PDA—Perspective Discrepancy Assessment
QWL—Quality of Working Life (movement)

SBPFC—South Bronx People for Change
SDLRS—Self-Directed Learning Readiness Scale
TLE—The Learning Exchange
TSI—Training Style Inventory
TUC—Trades Union Congress
UNESCO—United Nations Educational, Scientific, and Cultural
      Organization
WEA—Workers' Educational Association

References

Adams, F. "Highlander Folk School: Getting Information, Going Back and Teaching It." *Harvard Educational Review,* 1972, *42* (4), 497-520.

Adams, F. *Unearthing Seeds of Fire: The Idea of Highlander.* Winston-Salem, N.C.: Blair, 1975.

Adult Education Association of the United States. *How to Teach Adults.* Washington, D.C.: Adult Education Association of the United States, 1955.

Advisory Council for Adult and Continuing Education. *A Strategy for the Basic Education of Adults.* Leicester, England: Advisory Council for Adult and Continuing Education, 1979.

Advisory Council for Adult and Continuing Education. *Continuing Education: From Policies to Practice.* Leicester, England: Advisory Council for Adult and Continuing Education, 1982.

Aird, E. "NOW Courses and the Changing Pattern of Adult Education." *Studies in Adult Education,* 1980, *12* (1), 30-44.

Aldred, D. "The Relevance of Paulo Freire to Radical Community Education in Britain." *International Journal of Lifelong Education,* 1984, *3* (2), 105-113.

Alkin, M. C. "Evaluation Theory Development." *Evaluation Comment,* 1969, *2* (1), 2-7.

301

Allan, D. M. E., Grosswald, S. J., and Means, R. P. "Facilitating Self-Directed Learning." In J. S. Green, S. J. Grosswald, E. Suter, and D. B. Walthall III (eds.), *Continuing Education for the Health Professions: Developing, Managing, and Evaluating Programs for Maximum Impact on Patient Care.* San Francisco: Jossey-Bass, 1984.

Allerton, T. D. "Selected Characteristics of the Learning Projects Pursued by Parish Ministers in the Louisville Metropolitan Area." Unpublished doctoral dissertation, Department of Adult Education, University of Georgia, 1974.

Amison, P. *The Attleborough Experiment: A Handbook.* Cambridge, England: National Extension College, 1982.

Anderson, M. L., and Lindeman, E. C. *Education Through Experience.* New York: Workers Education Bureau, 1927.

Anderson, R. A., and Darkenwald, G. G. *Participation and Persistence in American Adult Education.* New York: College Entrance Examination Board, 1979.

Apps, J. W. *Toward a Working Philosophy of Adult Education.* Syracuse, N.Y.: Syracuse University Publications in Continuing Education, 1973.

Apps, J. W. *Problems in Continuing Education.* New York: McGraw-Hill, 1979.

Apps, J. W. *The Adult Learner on Campus: A Guide for Instructors and Administrators.* New York: Cambridge Books, 1981.

Apps, J. W. "Developing a Belief System." In C. Klevins (ed.), *Materials and Methods in Adult and Continuing Education.* Canoga Park, Calif.: Klevens Publications, 1982.

Argyris, C. *Reasoning, Learning, and Action: Individual and Organizational.* San Francisco: Jossey-Bass, 1982.

Argyris, C., and Schön, D. A. *Theory in Practice: Increasing Professional Effectiveness.* San Francisco: Jossey-Bass, 1974.

Argyris, C., and Schön, D. A. *Organizational Learning: A Theory of Action Perspective.* Reading, Mass.: Addison-Wesley, 1978.

Arms, D., Chenevy, B., Karrer, C., and Rumpler, C. H. "A Baccalaureate Degree Program in Nursing for Adult Students." In M. S. Knowles and Associates, *Andragogy in Action: Ap-*

plying Modern Principles of Adult Learning. San Francisco: Jossey-Bass, 1984.

Armstrong, D. "Adult Learners of Low Educational Attainment: The Self-Concepts, Backgrounds, and Educative Behavior of Average and High Learning Adults of Low Educational Attainment." Unpublished doctoral dissertation, Department of Adult Education, University of Toronto, 1971.

Armstrong, K. A. *Masters of Their Own Destiny: A Comparison of the Work of Coady and Freire.* Vancouver: Centre for Continuing Education, University of British Columbia, 1977.

Ash, C. R. "Applying Principles of Self-Directed Learning in the Health Professions." In S. Brookfield (ed.), *Self-Directed Learning: From Theory to Practice.* New Directions for Continuing Education, no. 25. San Francisco: Jossey-Bass, 1985.

Aslanian, C. B., and Bricknell, H. M. *Americans in Transition: Life Changes as Reasons for Adult Learning.* New York: College Entrance Examination Board, 1980.

Atkins, S. "Law and the Challenge to Patriarchy." In *Women, Class, and Adult Education.* Southampton, England: Department of Adult Education, University of Southampton, 1981.

Austin, E. K. *Guidelines for the Development of Continuing Education Offerings for Nurses.* East Norwalk, Conn.: Appleton-Century-Crofts, 1981.

Bailey, P. S. "Assessment of the Needs of the Adult Learner in Baccalaureate Nursing Programs." Unpublished doctoral dissertation, Department of Nursing Education, Teachers College, Columbia University, 1979.

Baillie, S. "Limits of the Process Perspective." In J. Warden (ed.), *Process Perspectives: Community Education as Process.* Charlottesville, Va.: Mid-Atlantic Community Education Consortium, 1979.

Barndt, D. *Just Getting There: Creating Visual Tools for Collective Analysis in Freirean Education Programmes for Migrant Women in Peru and Canada.* Toronto: International Council for Adult Education, n.d.

Barton, G. E. *Ordered Pluralism: A Philosophic Plan of Action for Teaching.* Notes and Essays on Education for Adults, no.

42. Chicago: Center for the Study of Liberal Education for Adults, 1964.

Bauer, B. A. "Self-Directed Learning in a Graduate Adult Education Program." In S. Brookfield (ed.), *Self-Directed Learning: From Theory to Practice.* New Directions for Continuing Education, no. 25. San Francisco: Jossey-Bass, 1985a.

Bauer, B. A. "The Adult Education Guided Independent Study (AEGIS) Program: An Administrative Case Study." Unpublished doctoral dissertation, Department of Adult Education, Teachers College, Columbia University, 1985b.

Beder, H. W. "Program Evaluation and Follow-Up." In P. D. Langerman and D. H. Smith (eds.), *Managing Adult and Continuing Education Programs and Staff.* Washington, D.C.: National Association for Public Continuing and Adult Education, 1979.

Beder, H. W., and Darkenwald, G. G. "Differences Between Teaching Adults and Preadults: Some Propositions and Findings." *Adult Education* (U.S.A.), 1982, *32* (3), 142-155.

Beder, H. W., Darkenwald, G. G., and Valentine, T. "Self-Planned Professional Learning Among Public School Adult Education Directors: A Social Network Analysis." *Proceedings of the Adult Education Research Conference,* no. 24, Montreal: Concordia University/University of Montreal, 1983.

Bennett, C. F. *Reflective Appraisal of Programs (RAP): An Approach to Studying Clientele-Perceived Results of Cooperative Extension Programs—Rationale, Guide, Workbook.* Ithaca, N.Y.: Media Services, Cornell University, 1982.

Benson, F. B. "Learning Projects of Selected Administrators in Tennessee Colleges and Universities." Unpublished doctoral dissertation, Department of Adult Education, University of Tennessee, 1974.

Bergevin, P. *A Philosophy for Adult Education.* New York: Seabury Press, 1967.

Bergevin, P., McKinley, J., and Smith, R. M. "The Adult Education Activity: Content, Processes, and Procedures." In G. Jensen, A. A. Liveright, and W. C. Hallenbeck (eds.), *Adult Education: Outlines of an Emerging Field of University Study.* Washington, D.C.: Adult Education Association of the U.S.A., 1964.

Bergevin, P., Morris, D., and Smith, R. M. *Adult Education Procedures: A Handbook of Tested Patterns for Effective Participation.* New York: Seabury Press, 1963.

Berte, N. A. (ed.). *Individualizing Education by Learning Contracts.* New Directions for Higher Education, no. 10. San Francisco: Jossey-Bass, 1975.

Bina, J. V. "Administrative Behaviors Deemed Important by Local Adult Basic Education Administrators for Program Success." *Proceedings of the Adult Education Research Conference,* no. 23. Lincoln: University of Nebraska, 1982.

Blaney, J. "Program Development and Curricular Authority." In J. Blaney, I. Housego, and G. McIntosh (eds.), *Program Development in Education.* Vancouver: Centre for Continuing Education, University of British Columbia, 1974.

Bligh, D. A. *What's the Use of Lectures?* Harmondsworth, England: Penguin Books, 1972.

Bloch, F. S. "The Andragogical Basis of Clinical Legal Education." *Vanderbilt Law Review,* 1982, *35* (2), 321-353.

Blondin, M. "Animation Sociale." In J. A. Draper (ed.), *Citizen Participation: Canada.* Toronto: New Press, 1971.

Boaz, R. L. *Participation in Adult Education, Final Report 1975.* Washington, D.C.: National Center for Education Statistics, 1978.

Bock, L. A. *Teaching Adults in Continuing Education.* Champaign-Urbana: Office of Continuing Education and Public Service, University of Illinois, 1979.

Bode, R. L. "Living Room Learning." In G. Burch (ed.), *Accent on Learning: An Analytical History of the Fund for Adult Education's Experimental Discussion Project, 1951-1959.* Washington, D.C.: Fund for Adult Education, 1960.

Boone, E. J., Shearon, R. W., White, E. E., and Associates. *Serving Personal and Community Needs Through Adult Education.* San Francisco: Jossey-Bass, 1980.

Booth, N. "Information Resource Utilization Patterns and the Learning Efforts of Low-Income Urban Adults." *Proceedings of the Adult Education Research Conference,* no. 20. Ann Arbor: University of Michigan, 1979.

Borgstrom, L., and Olofsson, L. "Participation in Study Circles and the Creation of Individual Resources." *Proceedings of the Adult Education Research Conference,* no. 24. Montreal: Concordia University/University of Montreal, 1983.

Boshier, R. "Motivational Orientations of Adult Education Participants: A Factor Analytic Exploration of Houle's Typology." *Adult Education* (U.S.A.), 1971, *21* (2), 3-26.

Boshier, R. "The Development and Use of a Dropout Prediction Scale." *Adult Education* (U.S.A.), 1972, *22* (2), 87-99.

Boshier, R. "Educational Participation and Dropout: A Theoretical Model." *Adult Education* (U.S.A.), 1973, *23* (4), 255-282.

Boud, D. J. (ed.). *Developing Student Autonomy in Learning.* London: Kogan Page, 1981.

Boud, D. J., and Prosser, M. T. "Sharing Responsibility: Staff-Student Cooperation in Learning." *British Journal of Educational Technology,* 1980, *11* (1), 24-35.

Boud, D. J., and Prosser, M. T. "Sharing Responsibility for Learning in a Science Course-Staff Student Cooperation." In M. S. Knowles and Associates, *Andragogy in Action: Applying Modern Principles of Adult Learning.* San Francisco: Jossey-Bass, 1984.

Boydell, T. *Experiential Learning.* Manchester Monographs in Adult Education, no. 5. Manchester, England: University of Manchester, 1976.

Boyle, P. G. *Planning Better Programs.* New York: McGraw-Hill, 1981.

Boyle, P. G., and Jahns, I. R. "Program Development and Evaluation." In R. M. Smith, G. F. Aker, and J. R. Kidd (eds.), *Handbook of Adult Education.* New York: Macmillan, 1970.

Brackhaus, B. "Needs Assessment in Adult Education: Its Problems and Prospects." *Adult Education Quarterly,* 1984, *34* (4), 223-239.

Bradford, L. P. "The Teaching-Learning Transaction." In C. Verner and T. White (eds.), *Adult Learning.* Washington, D.C.: Adult Education Association of the USA, 1965.

Brew, J. M. *Informal Education: Adventures and Reflections.* London: Faber and Faber, 1965.

Bridges, D. *Education, Democracy, and Discussion.* Windsor,

England: National Foundation for Educational Research, 1979.

Bright, D., and Macdermott, T. "Trade Union Tutors and Job Satisfaction." *Adult Education* (U.K.), 1981, *54* (3), 236-240.

Brill, N. I. *Working with People: The Helping Process.* (2nd ed.) Philadelphia: Lippincott, 1978.

Brockett, R. "Facilitator Roles and Skills." *Lifelong Learning: The Adult Years,* 1983a, *6* (5), 7-9.

Brockett, R. "The Relationship Between Life Satisfaction and Self-Directedness Among Older Adults." In *Lifelong Learning Research Conference Proceedings,* no. 5. College Park: Department of Agriculture and Extension Education, University of Maryland, 1983b.

Brockett, R. "Methodological and Substantive Issues in the Measurement of Self-Directed Learning Readiness." Paper presented at 25th annual meeting of the Adult Education Research Conference, Raleigh, N.C., Apr. 1984a.

Brockett, R. "Program Planning at the Adult Level" (course outline), 1984b.

Brockett, R., and Hiemstra, R. "Bridging the Theory-Practice Gap in Self-Directed Learning." In S. D. Brookfield (ed.), *Self-Directed Learning: From Theory to Practice.* New Directions for Continuing Education, no. 25. San Francisco: Jossey-Bass, 1985.

Brodzinski, F. R. "Adult Learners—The New Majority: A Demographic Reality." In A. Shriberg (ed.), *Providing Student Services for the Adult Learner.* New Directions for Student Services, no. 11. San Francisco: Jossey-Bass, 1980.

Brookfield, S. D. "Educational Advice for Adults." *Education and Training,* 1977a, *19* (5), 137-139.

Brookfield, S. D. "A Local Correspondence Tuition Service." *Adult Education* (U.K.), 1977b, *50* (1), 39-43.

Brookfield, S. D. "Individualizing Adult Learning: An English Experiment." *Lifelong Learning: The Adult Years,* 1978a, *1* (7), 18-20.

Brookfield, S. D. "Learning to Learn: The Characteristics, Motivations, and Destinations of Adult Study Skills Students." *Adult Education* (U.K.), 1978b, *50* (6), 363-368.

Brookfield, S. D. "Supporting Autonomous Adult Learning Groups." *Adult Education* (U.K.), 1979a, *51* (6), 366-369.

Brookfield, S. D. "Adult Study Problems." *Journal of Further and Higher Education,* 1979b, *3* (1), 91-96.

Brookfield, S. D. "Independent Adult Learning." Unpublished doctoral dissertation, Department of Adult Education, University of Leicester, 1980.

Brookfield, S. D. "Independent Adult Learning." *Studies in Adult Education,* 1981a, *13* (1), 15-27.

Brookfield, S. D. "The Adult Learning Iceberg: A Critical Review of the Work of Allen Tough." *Adult Education* (U.K.), 1981b, *54* (2), 110-118.

Brookfield, S. D. "Overcoming Culture-Specific Limitations on Interviewing." *Proceedings of the Adult Education Research Conference,* no. 22. DeKalb: Northern Illinois University, 1981c.

Brookfield, S. D. "Preparing Students for Entry to Higher Education: Continuing Education Initiatives in the U.K." *Canadian Journal of University Continuing Education,* 1981d, *8* (1), 4-9.

Brookfield, S. D. "Evaluation Models and Adult Education." *Studies in Adult Education,* 1982, *14*, 95-100.

Brookfield, S. D. *Adult Learners, Adult Education, and the Community.* Milton Keynes, England: Open University Press, 1983a.

Brookfield, S. D. "Adult Education and the Democratic Imperative: The Vision of Eduard Lindeman as a Contemporary Charter for Adult Education." *Studies in Adult Education,* 1983b, *15*, 36-46.

Brookfield, S. D. "The Contribution of Eduard Lindeman to the Development of Theory and Philosophy in Adult Education." *Adult Education Quarterly,* 1984a, *34* (4), 185-196.

Brookfield, S. D. "The Meaning of Adult Education: The Contemporary Relevance of Eduard Lindeman." *Teachers College Record,* 1984b, *85* (3), 513-524.

Brookfield, S. D. "Self-Directed Learning: A Critique of Research and Theory." *Proceedings of the Adult Education Research Conference,* no. 25. Raleigh: North Carolina State University, 1984c.

Brookfield, S. D. (ed.). *Self-Directed Learning: From Theory to Practice.* New Directions for Continuing Education, no. 25. San Francisco: Jossey-Bass, 1985a.

Brookfield, S. D. "Discussion as an Effective Educational Method." In S. Rosenblum (ed.), *Involving Adults in the Educational Process.* New Directions for Continuing Education, no. 26. San Francisco: Jossey-Bass, 1985b.

Brostrom, R. "Training Style Inventory." In *Annual Handbook for Group Facilitators.* La Jolla, Calif.: University Associates, 1979.

Brown, C. D. "Reappraising the Professionalism of Adult Education." *Adult Education Quarterly,* 1984, *34* (2), 97-104.

Brown, G. *Microteaching: A Programme of Teaching Skills.* London: Methuen, 1975.

Brown, H. W. "Formative Evaluation of Program Goals and Purposes." In D. Deshler (ed.), *Evaluation for Program Improvement.* New Directions for Continuing Education, no. 24. San Francisco: Jossey-Bass, 1984.

Brundage, D. H., and Mackeracher, D. *Adult Learning Principles and Their Application to Program Planning.* Toronto: Ministry of Education, Ontario, 1980.

Brunner, E. de S., and others. *An Overview of Adult Education Research.* Chicago: Adult Education Association of the U.S.A., 1959.

Bryson, L. *Adult Education.* New York: American Book Company, 1936.

Burge, E. J. (ed.). "Adult Learners, Learning, and Public Libraries." *Library Trends,* 1983, *31* (4), (entire issue).

Burgess, T. *Education After School.* Harmondsworth, England: Penguin Books, 1977.

Burkitt, A. "Trade Union Education and Its Relationship to Adult Education in England and Wales." *International Journal of Lifelong Education,* 1982, *1* (1), 63-76.

Burnham, B. "Program Planning as Technology in Three Adult Education Units." *Proceedings of the Adult Education Research Conference,* no. 25. Raleigh: North Carolina State University, 1984.

Buskey, J. H., and Sork, T. J. "From Chaos to Order in Program Planning: A System for Selecting Models and Ordering

Research." *Proceedings of the Adult Education Research Conference,* no. 23. Lincoln: University of Nebraska, 1982.

Butcher, H., Collis, P., Glen, A., and Sills, P. *Community Groups in Action: Case Studies and Analysis.* Boston: Routledge & Kegan Paul, 1980.

Butler, L. *Case Studies in Educational Guidance for Adults.* Leicester, England: Advisory Council for Adult and Continuing Education, 1984.

Buttedahl, K. "Living Room Learning." In J. R. Kidd and G. Selman (eds.), *Coming of Age: Canadian Adult Education in the 1960s.* Toronto: Canadian Association for Adult Education, 1978.

Buzzell, M., and Roman, O. "Preparing for Contract Learning." In D. Boud (ed.), *Developing Student Autonomy in Learning.* London: Kogan Page, 1981.

Caffarella, R. S., and Caffarella, E. P. "Self-Directedness and Learning Contracts in Graduate Education." Paper presented at annual meeting of the Commission of Professors of Adult Education, Philadelphia, Nov. 1983.

Callaway, H. "Women's Perspectives: Research as Re-vision." *Convergence,* 1981, *14* (4), 34–43.

Cameron, S. W. "The Perry Scheme: A New Perspective on Adult Learners." *Proceedings of the Adult Education Research Conference,* no. 24. Montreal: Concordia University/ University of Montreal, 1983.

Campbell, D. D. *Adult Education as a Field of Study and Practice: Strategies for Development.* Vancouver: Centre for Continuing Education, University of British Columbia, 1977.

Campbell, D. D. *The New Majority: Adult Learners in the University.* Edmonton: University of Alberta Press, 1984.

Campbell, D. M. "Community Education for Group Growth." In R. D. Boyd, J. W. Apps, and Associates, *Redefining the Discipline of Adult Education.* San Francisco: Jossey-Bass, 1980.

Carlson, R. A. "Professionalization of Adult Education: An Historical-Philosophical Perspective." *Adult Education* (U.S.A.), 1977, *28* (1), 53–63.

Carp, A., Peterson, R., and Roelfs, P. "Adult Learning Interests and Experiences." In K. P. Cross, J. R. Valley, and Associates, *Planning Non-Traditional Programs: An Analysis of the Issues for Postsecondary Education.* San Francisco: Jossey-Bass, 1974.

Carr, D. "Self-Directed Learning in Cultural Institutions." In S. Brookfield (ed.), *Self-Directed Learning: From Theory to Practice.* New Directions for Continuing Education, no. 25. San Francisco: Jossey-Bass, 1985.

Carr, W., and Kemmis, S. *Becoming Critical: Knowing Through Action Research.* Victoria, Australia: Deakin University Press, 1983.

Carter, G. L. *Facilitating Learning with Adults: What Ralph Tyler Says.* Madison: Division of Program and Staff Development, University of Wisconsin-Extension, 1973.

Cervero, R. M., and Rottet, S. "Analyzing the Effectiveness of Continuing Professional Education: An Exploratory Study." *Adult Education Quarterly,* 1984, *34* (3), 135–146.

Chadwick, A. F. *The Role of the Museum and Art Gallery in Community Education.* Nottingham, England: Department of Adult Education, University of Nottingham, 1980.

Charner, I. *An Untapped Resource: Negotiated Tuition-Aid in the Private Sector.* Washington, D.C.: National Manpower Institute, 1978.

Charnley, A. H. *Paid Educational Leave.* St. Albans, England: Hart-Davis Educational, 1975.

Charnley, A. H., and Jones, H. A. *The Concept of Success in Adult Literacy.* London: Adult Literacy and Basic Skills Unit, 1979.

Charnley, A. H., Osborn, M., and Withnall, A. *Mature Students.* Review of Existing Research in Adult and Continuing Education, Vol. 1. Leicester, England: National Institute for Adult Continuing Education, 1980.

Charters, A. N. "Continuing Education for the Professions." In R. M. Smith, G. F. Aker, and J. R. Kidd (eds.), *Handbook of Adult Education.* New York: Macmillan, 1970.

Chené, A. "The Concept of Autonomy in Adult Education: A Philosophical Discussion." *Adult Education Quarterly,* 1983, *34* (1), 38–47.

Christensen, F. "Equipping Faculty to Serve Lifelong Learners." In B. Heerman, C. C. Enders, and E. Wine (eds.), *Serving Lifelong Learners*. New Directions for Community Colleges, no. 29. San Francisco: Jossey-Bass, 1980.

Clark, B. R. *Adult Education in Transition: A Study of Institutional Insecurity*. Berkeley: University of California Press, 1956.

Clark, B. R. *The Marginality of Adult Education*. Chicago: Center for the Study of Liberal Education for Adults, 1958.

Clark, M. *Antonio Gramsci and the Revolution That Failed*. New Haven, Conn.: Yale University Press, 1977.

Clark, M. "Meeting the Needs of the Adult Learner: Using Nonformal Education for Social Action." *Convergence*, 1978, *11* (3-4), 44-53.

Clyne, P. *The Disadvantaged Adult: Educational and Social Needs of Minority Groups*. New York: Longman, 1973.

Coady, M. M. *Masters of Their Own Destiny*. New York: Harper & Row, 1939.

Coady, M. M. "Adult Education in Action." *Learning*, 1979, *2* (4), 6.

Coe, M., Rubenzahl, A., and Slater, V. "Helping Adults Reenter College." In M. S. Knowles and Associates, *Andragogy in Action: Applying Modern Principles of Adult Learning*. San Francisco: Jossey-Bass, 1984.

Coffin, L. "Holland College Models the Future of Adult Learning." *The Learning Connection*, 1983, *4* (4), 10-11.

Cohen, R. D. "Assisting the Adult Learner in 'Settling-In.' " In A. Shriberg (ed.), *Providing Student Services for the Adult Learner*. New Directions for Student Services, no. 11. San Francisco: Jossey-Bass, 1980.

Cohen-Rosenthal, E. "Participation as Pedagogy: Quality of Working Life and Adult Education." *Convergence*, 1982, *15* (1), 5-16.

Cole, J. W., and Glass, J. C. "The Effect of Adult Student Participation in Program Planning on Achievement, Retention, and Attitude." *Adult Education* (U.S.A.), 1977, *27* (2), 75-88.

Committee on Program Evaluation of the Adult Education Association of the USA. *Program Evaluation in Adult Education.* Washington, D.C.: Adult Education Association of the U S A, 1952.

Conchelos, G., and Kassam, Y. "A Brief Review of Critical Opinions and Responses on Issues Facing Participatory Research." *Convergence,* 1981, *14* (3), 52-64.

Confer, S. H. "Organized Labor." In L. Nadler (ed.), *The Handbook of Human Resource Development.* New York: Wiley, 1984.

Conger, D. S. *Canadian Open Learning Systems.* Prince Albert, Canada: Saskatchewan Training Research and Development Station, Department of Manpower and Immigration, 1974.

Connelly, H. W. "An Exploratory Investigation of the Effects of Microlab Activities and Instrumental Exercises on Selected Outcomes of Participation Training." Unpublished doctoral dissertation, Department of Adult Education, Indiana University, 1970.

Conti, G. J. "Rebels with a Cause: Myles Horton and Paulo Freire." *Community College Review,* 1977, *5* (1), 36-43.

Conti, G. J. "Principles of Adult Learning Scale: An Instrument for Measuring Teacher Behavior Related to the Collaborative Teaching-Learning Mode." Unpublished doctoral dissertation, Department of Adult Education, Northern Illinois University, 1978.

Conti, G. J. "Principles of Adult Learning Scale." *Proceedings of the Adult Education Research Conference,* no. 20. Ann Arbor, University of Michigan, 1979.

Conti, G. J. "Principles of Adult Learning Scale: Follow-Up and Factor Analysis." *Proceedings of the Adult Education Research Conference,* no. 24. Montreal: Concordia University/University of Montreal, 1983.

Conti, G. J. "Does Teaching Style Make a Difference in Adult Education?" *Proceedings of the Adult Education Research Conference,* no. 25. Raleigh: North Carolina State University, 1984.

Conti, G. J. "Assessing Teaching Style in Adult Education: How and Why." *Lifelong Learning: The Adult Years,* 1985, *8* (8), 7-11, 28.

Coren, E. H. *The Easy-To-Use Concise Teaching Handbook for Part-Time Non-Teachers.* Mamaroneck, N.Y.: Coren Associates, 1983.

Cortwright, R., and Brice, E. W. "Adult Basic Education." In R. M. Smith, G. F. Aker, and J. R. Kidd (eds.), *Handbook of Adult Education.* New York: Macmillan, 1970.

Costello, N., and Richardson, M. (eds.). *Continuing Education for the Post-Industrial Society.* Milton Keynes, England: Open University Press, 1982.

Council on Continuing Education Unit. *Principles of Good Practice in Continuing Education.* Silver Spring, Md.: Council on Continuing Education Unit, 1984.

Crabtree, A. P. "A Vision of Greatness." *Adult Leadership,* 1963, *12* (6), 162-164, 189-190.

Craig, R. L., and Evers, C. J. "Employers as Educators: The 'Shadow Educational System.' " In G. G. Gold (ed.), *Business and Higher Education: Toward New Alliances.* New Directions for Experiential Learning, no. 13. San Francisco: Jossey-Bass, 1981.

Cronbach, L. J. "Course Improvement Through Evaluation." *Teachers College Record,* 1963, *64* (8), 672-683.

Cross, K. P. "Adult Learners: Characteristics, Needs, and Interests." In R. E. Peterson and Associates, *Lifelong Learning in America.* San Francisco: Jossey-Bass, 1979.

Cross, K. P. *Adults as Learners: Increasing Participation and Facilitating Learning.* San Francisco: Jossey-Bass, 1981.

Cross, K. P., and McCartan, A. *Adult Learning: State Policies and Institutional Practices.* ASHE-ERIC Higher Education Research Report, no. 1. Washington, D.C.: Association for the Study of Higher Education, 1984.

Cross, K. P., Valley, J. R., and Associates. *Planning Non-Traditional Programs: An Analysis of the Issues for Postsecondary Education.* San Francisco: Jossey-Bass, 1974.

Cunningham, P. M. "Contradictions in the Practice of Non-Traditional Continuing Education." In S. B. Merriam (ed.), *Linking Philosophy and Practice.* New Directions for Continuing Education, no. 15. San Francisco: Jossey-Bass, 1982.

Cunningham, P. M. "Helping Students Extract Meaning from

Experience." In R. M. Smith (ed.), *Helping Adults Learn How to Learn.* New Directions for Continuing Education, no. 19. San Francisco: Jossey-Bass, 1983.

Cunningham, P. M., and Hawking, J. "Literature Review of Research on MCE for Professionals." In T. Heaney (ed.), *Task Force on Voluntary Learning Report.* Chicago: Adult Education Association of the U.S.A., 1980.

Dadswell, G. "The Adult Independent Learner and Public Libraries: A New Perspective for the Library Service." *Adult Education* (U.K.), 1978, *51* (1), 5-11.

Dale, S. "The Adult Independent Learning Project: Work with Adult Self-Directed Learners in Public Libraries." *Journal of Librarianship,* 1979, *11,* 83-106.

Dale, S. "Another Way Forward for Adult Learners: The Public Library and Independent Study." *Studies in Adult Education,* 1980, *12* (1), 29-38.

Daloisio, T., and Firestone, M. "A Case Study in Applying Adult Learning Theory in Developing Managers." *Training and Development Journal,* 1983, *37* (2), 73-78.

Danis, C., and Tremblay, N. "Critical Analysis of Adult Learning Principles from a Self-Directed Learner's Perspective." *Proceedings of the Adult Education Research Conference,* no. 26. Tempe: Arizona State University, 1985.

Darkenwald, G. G. "Program Development in Adult and Continuing Education" (course outline). Department of Higher and Adult Education, Teachers College, Columbia University, 1976.

Darkenwald, G. G., and Merriam, S. B. *Adult Education: Foundations of Practice.* New York: Harper & Row, 1982.

Darnell, J. T. "How to Train Quality Circle Leaders: A Training System That Works." Paper presented at annual conference of the International Association of Quality Circles, St. Louis, Mar. 1-4, 1982.

Dave, R. H. (ed.). *Foundations of Lifelong Education.* Elmsford, N.Y.: Pergamon Press, 1976.

Davenport, J., and Davenport, J. A. "A Chronology and Analysis of the Andragogy Debate." *Adult Education Quarterly,* 1984, *35* (3), 152-159.

Davidson, A. *Antonio Gramsci: Toward an Intellectual Biography.* London: Merlin Press, 1977.

Davis, A. "A Preparation Course for Adults Intending to Study at University." *Adult Education* (U.K.), 1984, *57* (1), 36–43.

Davis, J. A. *Great Books and Small Groups.* New York: Free Press, 1961.

Day, C., and Baskett, H. K. "Discrepancies Between Intentions and Practice: Reexamining Some Basic Assumptions About Adult and Continuing Professional Education." *International Journal of Lifelong Education,* 1982, *1* (2), 143–155.

Day, M. "On Behalf of Voluntary Adult Education." In T. Heaney (ed.), *Task Force on Voluntary Learning Report.* Chicago: Adult Education Association of the U.S.A., 1980.

De Bono, E. *The Use of Lateral Thinking.* Harmondsworth, England: Penguin Books, 1971.

Department of Adult Education, University of Southampton. *Women, Class, and Adult Education.* Southampton, England: Department of Adult Education, University of Southampton, 1981.

De Paula, Z. S. "Teaching English as a Second Language to Immigrant Community College Students." In M. S. Knowles and Associates (ed.), *Andragogy in Action: Applying Modern Principles of Adult Learning.* San Francisco: Jossey-Bass, 1984.

Deshler, D. (ed.). *Evaluation for Program Improvement.* New Directions for Continuing Education, no. 24. San Francisco: Jossey-Bass, 1984.

Dewey, J. *Democracy and Education.* New York: Macmillan, 1916.

Dickinson, G. *Teaching Adults: A Handbook for Instructors.* Don Mills, Ont.: General Publishing, 1973.

Dinges, R. F. "The Degrees of Utilization of the Collaborative Teaching-Learning Mode by Adult Basic Education Teachers in Illinois." Unpublished doctoral dissertation, Department of Adult Education, Southern Illinois University, 1980.

Dinkelspiel, J. R. "Education and Training Programs at Xerox." In P. B. Doeringer (ed.), *Workplace Perspectives on Education and Training.* Hingham, Mass.: Kluwer Nijhoff, 1981.

Dohr, J. H., Donaldson, J. F., and Marshall, M. "Relationship of Programmer's Planning Orientations to Program Development." *Proceedings of the Adult Education Research Conference*, no. 20. Ann Arbor: University of Michigan, 1979.

Douglas, J. A., Carnochan, S., and Leslie, D. "Return to Study: Access Point to Continuing Education?" *Adult Education* (U.K.), 1984, *57* (2), 131-134.

Douglass, J. F. "An Analysis of the Relationship Between Professional Training in Adult Education and Orientation to the Collaborative Teaching-Learning Mode in Washington State Hospital and the Washington State Cooperative Extension Service." Unpublished doctoral dissertation, Department of Adult Education, Indiana University, 1982.

Draves, W. A. "The Free University Network." *Lifelong Learning: The Adult Years*, 1979, *3* (4), 4-5, 30.

Draves, W. A. *The Free University: A Model for Lifelong Learning*. New York: Cambridge Books, 1980.

Draves, W. A. *How to Teach Adults*. Manhattan, Kan.: Learning Resources Network, 1984.

Drennan, A. P. "Adult Basic Education and English as a Second Language: A Critique." In E. J. Boone, R. W. Shearon, E. E. White, and Associates, *Serving Personal and Community Needs Through Adult Education*. San Francisco: Jossey-Bass, 1980.

Dubin, S., and Okun, M. "Implications of Learning Theories for Adult Instruction." *Adult Education* (U.S.A.), 1973, *24* (1), 3-19.

Du Bois, E. E. "Human Resource Development: Expanding Role." In C. Klevens (ed.), *Materials and Methods in Adult and Continuing Education*. Canoga Park, Calif.: Klevins Publications, 1982.

Durkheim, E. *Suicide: A Study in Sociology*. Boston: Routledge & Kegan Paul, 1952. (Originally published 1897.)

Dwyer, R. "Workers Education, Labor Education, Labor Studies: An Historical Delineation." *Review of Educational Research*, 1977, *47* (1), 179-207.

Dwyer, R., and Torgoff, C. "A Labor College." In H. Stack and C. M. Hutton (eds.), *Building New Alliances: Labor Unions and Higher Education.* New Directions for Experiential Learning, no. 10. San Francisco: Jossey-Bass, 1980.

Dyer, W. G. *Team Building: Issues and Alternatives.* Reading, Mass.: Addison-Wesley, 1977.

Eggert, J. D. "Formative Evaluation as Model Building." In D. Deshler (ed.), *Evaluation for Program Improvement.* New Directions for Continuing Education, no. 24. San Francisco: Jossey-Bass, 1984.

Eisele, G. R. "Counseling for Development." In B. Heermann, C. C. Enders, and E. Wine (eds.), *Serving Lifelong Learners.* New Directions for Community Colleges, no. 29. San Francisco: Jossey-Bass, 1980.

Eisenberg, S., and Delaney, D. M. *The Counseling Process.* (2nd ed.) Skokie, Ill.: Rand McNally, 1977.

Eisner, E. W. "Educational Connoisseurship and Criticism: Their Form and Functions in Educational Evaluation." *Journal of Aesthetic Education,* 1976, *10* (3-4), 135-150.

Eisner, E. W. *The Educational Imagination: On the Design and Evaluation of School Programs.* (2nd ed.) New York: Macmillan, 1985.

Elias, J. M. "Andragogy Revisited." *Adult Education* (U.S.A.), 1979, *29* (4), 252-255.

Ellwood, C. *Adult Learning Today: A New Role for the Universities?* Beverly Hills, Calif.: Sage, 1974.

Elsdon, K. T. *Training for Adult Education.* Nottingham, England: Department of Adult Education, University of Nottingham, 1975.

Elsey, B. "Voluntary Organizations and Adult Education." *Adult Education* (U.K.), 1974, *46* (6), 391-396.

Elsey, B. "Mature Students' Experiences of University." *Studies in Adult Education,* 1982, *14,* 69-77.

Elsey, B., and Gibbs, M. *Voluntary Tutors in Adult Literacy.* Nottingham, England: Department of Adult Education, University of Nottingham, 1981.

Elsey, B., Hall, D., Hughes, I., and Laplace, C. *Volunteers in Adult Education.* Leicester, England: Advisory Council for Adult and Continuing Education, 1983.

Ely, M. L. (ed.). *Adult Education in Action.* New York: American Association for Adult Education, 1936.

Ely, M. L. (ed.). *Handbook of Adult Education in the United States.* New York: Bureau of Publications, Teachers College, Columbia University, 1948.

Employment and Immigration Canada. *Learning a Living in Canada.* Vols. 1 and 2. Toronto: Minister of Supply and Services Canada, 1983.

Enright, C. "Paulo Freire and the Maiden City." *Adult Education* (U.K.), 1975, 47 (6), 352-356.

Entwistle, H. *Antonio Gramsci: Conservative Schooling for Radical Politics.* Boston: Routledge & Kegan Paul, 1979.

Essert, P. L. "The Discussion Group in Adult Education in America." In M. L. Ely (ed.), *Handbook of Adult Education in the United States.* New York: Teachers College Press, 1948.

Eurich, N. P. *Corporate Classrooms: The Learning Business.* Princeton, N.J.: Princeton University Press, 1985.

Even, M. J. "Adapting Cognitive Style Theory in Practice." *Lifelong Learning: The Adult Years,* 1982, 5 (5), 14-16, 27.

Fabian, B. S., and Mink, B. "Line Managers as Learning Facilitators at an Equipment Manufacturer." In M. S. Knowles and Associates, *Andragogy in Action: Applying Modern Principles of Adult Learning.* San Francisco: Jossey-Bass, 1984.

Fair, J. "Teachers as Learners: The Learning Projects of Beginning Elementary School Teachers." Unpublished doctoral dissertation, Department of Adult Education, University of Toronto, 1973.

Faris, R. *The Passionate Educators: Voluntary Associations and the Struggle for Control of Adult Educational Broadcasting 1919-1952.* Toronto: Peter Martin, 1975.

Farquharson, A. "Learning Through Teaching Among Undergraduate Social Work Students." In M. S. Knowles and Associates, *Andragogy in Action: Applying Modern Principles of Adult Learning.* San Francisco: Jossey-Bass, 1984.

Fatchett, D. "What Happens to Trade Union Day-Release Students?" *Adult Education* (U.K.), 1982, 55 (1), 39-42.

Fawcett-Hill, W. M. *Learning Thru Discussion: Guide for Leaders and Members of Discussion Groups.* (2nd ed.) Beverly Hills, Calif.: Sage, 1977.

Feinstein, O., and Angelo, F. *To Educate the People: An Experimental Model for Urban Higher Education for the Work-*

ing Adult. Detroit: Center for Urban Studies, Wayne State University, 1977.

Ferguson, M. *The Aquarian Conspiracy.* Los Angeles: Tarcher, 1980.

Ferrier, B., Marrin, M., and Seidman, J. "Student Autonomy in Learning Medicine: Some Participants' Experiences." In D. Boud (ed.), *Developing Student Autonomy in Learning.* London: Kogan Page, 1981.

Fingeret, A. "Social Network: A New Perspective on Independence and Illiterate Adults." *Adult Education Quarterly,* 1983, *33* (3), 133-146.

Fingeret, A. *Adult Literacy Education: Current and Future Directions.* Information Series, no. 284. Columbus, Ohio: ERIC Clearinghouse on Adult, Career, and Vocational Education, 1984.

Finlay, L. S., and Faith, V. "Illiteracy and Alienation in American Colleges: Is Paulo Freire's Pedagogy Relevant?" *Radical Teacher,* 1979, *16,* 28-37.

Fisher, F. "Resource Exchange Networking: Metaphorical Inventions in Response to Differentiated Human Needs in a Collectivist-Oriented Society." *Journal of Voluntary Action Research,* 1983, *12* (1), 50-64.

Flanagan, G. F. "A Process for Assessing the Perspectives of Key Community College Personnel Who Have an Impact on Continuing Education/Community Service Function." Unpublished doctoral dissertation, Department of Higher and Adult Education, Teachers College, Columbia University, 1979.

Flanagan, G. F., and Smith, F. B. "What's the Bottom Line? Continuing Educators Discuss Priorities and Values." In S. B. Merriam (ed.), *Linking Philosophy and Practice.* New Directions for Continuing Education, no. 15. San Francisco: Jossey-Bass, 1982.

Flanders, N. A. *Analyzing Teacher Behavior.* Reading, Mass.: Addison-Wesley, 1970.

Fletcher, C. "Community Studies as Practical Adult Education." *Adult Education* (U.K.), 1980, *53* (2), 73-78.

Fletcher, C. "Adult Education and Community Needs: Towards a Distinctive University Extra-Mural Contribution." *Studies in Adult Education,* 1983, *15,* 60-66.

Flude, R., and Parrott, A. *Education and the Challenge of Change.* Milton Keynes, England: Open University Press, 1979.

Fodor, J. H. "Incidental Learning in the Intentional and Structured Learning Experiences of Adult Students." *Proceedings of the Adult Education Research Conference,* no. 25. Raleigh: North Carolina State University, 1984.

Fordham, P., Poulton, G., and Randle, L. *Learning Networks in Adult Education: Non-Formal Education on a New Housing Estate.* Boston: Routledge & Kegan Paul, 1979.

Forest, L. B. "Program Evaluation for Reality." *Adult Education* (U.S.A.), 1976, *26* (3), 167–177.

Fox, J. "Criteria for Evaluation of Adult Teaching." *Studies in Adult Education,* 1975, 7 (2), 117–127.

Fox, R. D. "Formal Organizational Structure and Participation in Planning Continuing Professional Education." *Adult Education* (U.S.A.), 1981, *31* (4), 209–226.

Frandson, P. E. (ed.). *Power and Conflict in Continuing Education.* Belmont, Calif.: Wadsworth, 1980.

Freire, P. *Cultural Action for Freedom.* Cambridge, Mass.: Harvard Educational Review and Center for the Study of Development and Social Change, 1970a.

Freire, P. *Pedagogy of the Oppressed.* New York: Herder and Herder, 1970b.

Freire, P. *Education for Critical Consciousness.* New York: Seabury Press, 1973.

Freire, P. *The Politics of Education.* South Hadley, Mass.: Bergin and Garvey, 1985.

Fried, E. "Factory Workers and the Humanities." In H. Stack and C. M. Hutton (eds.), *Building New Alliances: Labor Unions and Higher Education.* New Directions for Experiential Learning, no. 10. San Francisco: Jossey-Bass, 1980.

Fromm, E. *The Fear of Freedom.* Boston: Routledge & Kegan Paul, 1942.

Gagné, R. M. "Learning Research and Its Implications for Independent Learning." In R. A. Weisgerberger (ed.), *Perspectives in Individualized Learning.* Itasca, Ill.: Peacock, 1971.

Galbraith, M. W., and Gilley, J. W. "Using Self-Directed Learning Contracts to Improve Performance and Instruction." *Performance and Instruction Journal,* Oct. 1984, pp. 9–10.

Gardner, L. J. S. "An Assessment of Programs for Part-Time Students at a Selective Admissions College." Unpublished doctoral dissertation, Department of Higher and Adult Education, Teachers College, Columbia University, 1984.

Gayfer, M. "Women Speaking and Learning for Ourselves." *Convergence,* 1980, *13* (1-2), 1-13.

Gelpi, E. *A Future for Lifelong Education.* 2 vols. Manchester, England: Department of Adult and Higher Education, University of Manchester, 1979.

Gibb, J. R. "Learning Theory in Adult Education." In M. S. Knowles (ed.), *Handbook of Adult Education in the United States.* Washington, D.C.: Adult Education Association of the U.S.A., 1960.

Gibbs, G. *Teaching Students to Learn.* Milton Keynes, England: Open University Press, 1981.

Giroux, H. A. *Theory and Resistance in Education: A Pedagogy for the Opposition.* South Hadley, Mass.: Bergin and Garvey, 1983.

Godbey, G. C. *Applied Andragogy: A Practical Manual for the Continuing Education of Adults.* College Park: Pennsylvania State University, 1978.

Goldschmid, M. " 'Parrainage': Students Helping Each Other." In D. Boud (ed.), *Developing Student Autonomy in Learning.* London: Kogan Page, 1981.

Gonnella, J. S., and Zeleznik, C. "Strengthening the Relations Between Professional Education and Performance." In S. M. Grabowski (ed.), *Strengthening Connections Between Education and Performance.* New Directions for Continuing Education, no. 18. San Francisco: Jossey-Bass, 1983.

Gorham, J. "A Current Look at 'Modern Practice': Perceived and Observed Similarities and Differences of the Same Teachers in Adult and Pre-Adult Classrooms." *Proceedings of the Adult Education Research Conference,* no. 25. Raleigh: North Carolina State University, 1984.

Gould, S. B. (ed.). *Diversity by Design.* San Francisco: Jossey-Bass, 1973.

Gould, S. B., and Cross, K. P. (eds.). *Explorations in Non-Traditional Study.* San Francisco: Jossey-Bass, 1972.

Gouldner, A. *Enter Plato.* Boston: Routledge & Kegan Paul, 1967.

Graham, T. B., and others. *The Training of Part-Time Teachers of Adults.* Nottingham, England: Department of Adult Education, University of Nottingham, 1983.

Grant, N. "Innovations in Eastern Europe." In *Learning Opportunities for Adults.* Vol. 2: *New Structures, Programmes and Methods.* Paris: Organization for Economic Cooperation and Development, 1979.

Grant, W. V., and Lind, C. G. *Digest of Education Statistics, 1979.* Washington, D.C.: U.S. Government Printing Office, 1979.

Gray, L. *The American Way of Labor Education.* Reprint Series 184. New York: New York State School of Industrial and Labor Relations, Cornell University, 1966.

Green, G. M. "Product Training for Customers at Du Pont." In M. S. Knowles and Associates, *Andragogy in Action: Applying Modern Principles of Adult Learning.* San Francisco: Jossey-Bass, 1984.

Green, J. S., Grosswald, S. J., Suter, E., and Walthall, D. B., III (eds.). *Continuing Education for the Health Professions: Developing, Managing, and Evaluating Programs for Maximum Impact on Patient Care.* San Francisco: Jossey-Bass, 1984.

Greenberg, E. "Designing Programs for Learners of All Ages." In E. Greenberg, K. O'Donnell, and W. Bergquist (eds.), *Educating Learners of All Ages.* New Directions for Higher Education, no. 29. San Francisco: Jossey-Bass, 1980.

Greenberg, E., O'Donnell, K., and Bergquist, W. (eds.). *Educating Learners of All Ages.* New Directions for Higher Education, no. 29. San Francisco: Jossey-Bass, 1980.

Griffith, W. S. "Educational Needs: Definition, Assessment, and Utilization." *School Review,* May 1978, pp. 382–394.

Grotelueschen, A. D. "Program Evaluation." In A. B. Knox and Associates, *Developing, Administering, and Evaluating Adult Education.* San Francisco: Jossey-Bass, 1980.

Guba, E. G. *Toward a Methodology of Naturalistic Inquiry in Educational Evaluation.* SE Monograph Series in Evaluation, no. 8. Los Angeles: Center for the Study of Evaluation, University of California, 1978.

Guba, E. G., and Lincoln, Y. S. *Effective Evaluation: Improving the Usefulness of Evaluation Results Through Responsive and Naturalistic Approaches.* San Francisco: Jossey-Bass, 1981.

Guglielmino, L. M. "Development of the Self-Directed Learning Readiness Scale." Unpublished doctoral dissertation, Department of Adult Education, University of Georgia, 1977.

Gulley, H. E. *Discussion, Conference, and Group Process.* New York: Holt, Rinehart & Winston, 1965.

Habermas, J. *Knowledge and Human Interests.* Boston: Beacon Press, 1971.

Hall, B. L. "Participatory Research: An Approach for Change." *Convergence,* 1975, *8* (2), 24–31.

Hall, B. L. "Participatory Research: Breaking the Academic Monopoly." In J. A. Niemi (ed.), *Viewpoints on Adult Education Research.* Information Series, no. 171. Columbus, Ohio: ERIC Clearinghouse on Adult, Career, and Vocational Education, 1979.

Hanna, I. "A Socio-Psychological Survey of Student Membership of Adult Education Classes in Leeds and Changes in the Adult Student Population since 1945." Unpublished master's thesis, Department of Adult Education, University of Leeds, 1964.

Harden, R. M., Stoane, C., Dunn, W. R., and Murray, T. S. "Learning at a Distance: Evaluation at a Distance." In G. T. Page and Q. Whitlock (eds.), *Educational Technology to the Year 2000.* London: Kogan Page, 1979.

Hargreaves, D. *Adult Literacy and Broadcasting: The BBC's Experience.* London: Frances Pinter, 1980.

Harman, D. (ed.). *Expanding Recurrent and Nonformal Education.* New Directions for Higher Education, no. 14. San Francisco: Jossey-Bass, 1976.

Harri-Augstein, E. S., and Thomas, L. F. "Developing Self-Organized Learners: A Reflexive Technology." In R. M. Smith (ed.), *Helping Adults Learn How to Learn.* New Directions for Continuing Education, no. 19. San Francisco: Jossey-Bass, 1983.

Harrington, F. H. *The Future of Adult Education: New Responsibilities of Colleges and Universities.* San Francisco: Jossey-Bass, 1977.

Harris, S. "The Fourth Arena—Organizational Action as a Component of Architects' Continuing Education." *Studies in Adult Education*, 1982, *14*, 30-41.

Hartree, A. "Malcolm Knowles's Theory of Andragogy: A Critique." *International Journal of Lifelong Education*, 1984, *3* (3), 203-210.

Haverkamp, K. "The Orientation Experience for the Adult Learner." In R. M. Smith (ed.), *Helping Adults Learn How to Learn*. New Directions for Continuing Education, no. 19. San Francisco: Jossey-Bass, 1983.

Hayenga, E. S., and Isaacson, H. B. "Competence-Based Education for Adult Learners." In B. Heermann, C. C. Enders, and E. Wine (eds.), *Serving Lifelong Learners*. New Directions for Community Colleges, no. 29. San Francisco: Jossey-Bass, 1980.

Heaney, T. W. " 'Hanging On' or 'Gaining Ground': Educating Marginal Adults." In C. E. Kasworm (ed.), *Educational Outreach to Selected Adult Populations*. New Directions for Continuing Education, no. 20. San Francisco: Jossey-Bass, 1983.

Heath, L. L. "Role Models of Successful Teachers of Adults." In A. B. Knox (ed.), *Teaching Adults Effectively*. New Directions for Continuing Education, no. 6. San Francisco: Jossey-Bass, 1980.

Heermann, B., Enders, C. C., and Wine, E. (eds.). *Serving Lifelong Learners*. New Directions for Community Colleges, no. 29. San Francisco: Jossey-Bass, 1980.

Hefferman, J. M., Macy, F. U., and Vickers, D. F. *Educational Brokering: A New Service for Adult Learners*. Syracuse, N.Y.: National Center for Educational Brokering, 1976.

Hendrickson, A. "Adult Learning and the Adult Learner." *Adult Leadership*, 1966, *14* (8), 254-256, 286-287.

H.M. Stationery Office. *Adult Education: A Plan for Development*. London: H.M. Stationery Office, 1973.

Herring, J. W. "Adult Education: Senior Partner to Democracy." *Adult Education* (U.S.A.), 1953, *3* (2), 53-59.

Heynemann, S. P., and Loxley, W. A. "The Effect of Primary-School Quality on Academic Achievement Across Twenty-Nine High and Low Income Countries." *American Journal of Sociology*, 1983, *88* (6), 1162-1194.

Heywood, C. L. "Broadcasting Adult Education Half a Century Ago." *Adult Education* (U.K.), 1981, *54* (3), 242-245.

Hiemstra, R. "The Educative Community in Action." *Adult Leadership,* 1975, *24* (3), 82-85.

Hiemstra, R. *The Educative Community: Linking the Community, Education, and Family.* (2nd ed.) Baldwinsville, N.Y.: HiTree Press, 1982.

Higgins, D. "An Assessment Model for a Technology Program Designed for Women." Unpublished doctoral dissertation, Department of Higher and Adult Education, Teachers College, Columbia University, 1980.

Hills, P. J. *The Self-Teaching Process in Higher Education.* New York: Wiley, 1976.

Himmelstrup, P., Robinson, J., and Fielden, D. (eds.). *Strategies for Lifelong Learning: A Symposium of Views from Europe and the U.S.A.* Esbjerg, Denmark: University Centre of South Jutland/Association for Recurrent Education, 1981.

Hirshon, S. *And Also Teach Them to Read.* Westport, Conn.: Hill, 1983.

Hohmann, L. "Professional Continuing Education: How Can the Professional Associations and Other Providers Best Interact?" In P. E. Frandson (ed.), *Power and Conflict in Continuing Education.* Belmont, Calif.: Wadsworth, 1980.

Holmes, J. "Thoughts on Research Methodology." *Studies in Adult Education,* 1976, *8* (2), 149-163.

Holtzman, W. H. "Cross Cultural Comparisons of Personality Development in Mexico and the United States." In D. A. Wagner and H. W. Stevenson (eds.), *Cultural Perspectives on Child Development.* New York: W. H. Freeman, 1982.

Hostler, J. "The Art of Teaching Adults." *Studies in Adult Education,* 1982, *14,* 42-49.

Houghton, V., and Richardson, K. *Recurrent Education: A Plea for Lifelong Learning.* London: Ward Lock Educational/Association for Recurrent Education, 1974.

Houle, C. O. *The Inquiring Mind: A Study of the Adult Who Continues to Learn.* Madison: University of Wisconsin Press, 1961.

Houle, C. O. *The Design of Education.* San Francisco: Jossey-Bass, 1972.

Houle, C. O. *The External Degree.* San Francisco: Jossey-Bass, 1973.

Houle, C. O. *Continuing Learning in the Professions.* San Francisco: Jossey-Bass, 1980.

Huber, V. L., and Gay, G. "Uses of Educational Technology for Formative Evaluation." In D. Deshler (ed.), *Evaluation for Program Improvement.* New Directions for Continuing Education, no. 24. San Francisco: Jossey-Bass, 1984.

Huczynski, A., and Boddy, D. "The Learning Organization: An Approach to Management Education and Development." *Studies in Higher Education,* 1978, *4* (2), 211-222.

Hughes, M., and Kennedy, M. "Breaking Out—Women in Adult Education." *Women's Studies International Forum,* 1983, *6* (3), 261-269.

Hunter, C. S., and Harman, D. *Adult Illiteracy in the United States.* New York: McGraw-Hill, 1979.

Hutchinson, E., and Hutchinson, E. *Learning Later: Fresh Horizons in English Adult Education.* Boston: Routledge & Kegan Paul, 1979.

Illich, I. *Deschooling Society.* New York: Harper & Row, 1970.

Ilsley, P. J., and Niemi, J. A. *Recruiting and Training Volunteers.* New York: McGraw-Hill, 1981.

Imhoff, K. J. "Professionalization: Implications for Canadian Adult Education." *Proceedings of the Adult Education Research Conference,* no. 21. Vancouver, Canada: University of British Columbia, 1980.

Ingalls, J. D. *A Trainer's Guide to Andragogy.* (Rev. ed.) Washington, D.C.: U.S. Department of Health, Education, and Welfare, 1973.

International Labor Office. *Worker's Education and Its Techniques.* Geneva: International Labor Office, 1975.

Ireland, T. D. *Gelpi's View of Lifelong Education.* Manchester, England: Manchester Monographs, no. 14, Department of Adult and Higher Education, University of Manchester, 1979.

Ironside, D. J., and Jacobs, D. E. *Trends in Counselling and Information Services for the Adult Learner.* Toronto: Ontario Institute for Studies in Education, 1977.

Jackson, K. "Adult Education and Community Development." *Studies in Adult Education,* 1970, *2* (2), 165-172.

Jackson, T. "The Influence of Gramsci on Adult Education: An Essay Review." *Convergence,* 1981, *14* (3), 81–86.

James, W. B. "An Analysis of Perceptions of the Practices of Adult Educators from Five Different Settings." *Proceedings of the Adult Education Research Conference,* no. 24. Montreal: Concordia University/University of Montreal, 1983.

Jarvis, P. *Adult and Continuing Education: Theory and Practice.* London: Croom Helm, 1983a.

Jarvis, P. *Professional Education.* London: Croom Helm, 1983b.

Jarvis, P. "Andragogy: A Sign of the Times." *Studies in the Education of Adults,* 1984, *16,* 32–38.

Jennings, B. *Adult Education in United Kingdom.* Prague: European Centre for Leisure and Education, 1981.

Jennings, B. "The Open-Door University: A Strategy for Continuing Education Leading to Degrees." *Studies in Adult Education,* 1983, *15,* 47–59.

Jensen, G. E. "The Nature of Education as a Discipline." In G. Jensen (ed.), *Readings for Educational Researchers.* Ann Arbor, Mich.: Ann Arbor Publishers, 1960.

Jensen, G. E. "Socio-Psychological Foundations of Adult Learning." In I. Lorge, H. Y. McClusky, G. E. Jensen, and W. C. Hallenbeck (eds.), *Psychology of Adults.* Washington, D.C.: Adult Education Association of the U.S.A., 1963.

Johns, W. E. "Selected Characteristics of the Learning Projects Pursued by Practicing Pharmacists." Unpublished doctoral dissertation, Department of Adult Education, University of Georgia, 1974.

Johnson, V., Levine, H., and Rosenthal, E. L. *Learning Projects of Unemployed Adults in New Jersey.* New Brunswick, N.J.: Labor Education Center, Rutgers University, 1977.

Johnstone, J. W. C., and Rivera, R. J. *Volunteers for Learning: A Study of the Educational Pursuits of Adults.* Hawthorne, N.Y.: Aldine, 1965.

Jones, H. A., and Charnley, A. H. *Adult Literacy: A Study of Its Impact.* Leicester, England: National Institute for Adult Continuing Education, 1978.

Jones, H. A., and Williams, K. E. *Adult Students and Higher Education.* Leicester, England: Advisory Council for Adult and Continuing Education, 1979.

Jones, R. K. "The Dilemma of Educational Objectives in Higher and Adult Education: Do We Need Them?" *Adult Education* (U.S.A.), 1982, *32* (3), 165-169.

Kastner, R., and Olds, M. L. *Citizen Evaluation Using Program Analysis of Service Systems.* Lancaster, Pa.: Lancaster County Mental Health/Mental Retardation, Drugs/Alcohol, 1983.

Kasworm, C. E. "An Exploratory Study of the Development of Self-Directed Learning as an Instructional/Curriculum Strategy." In *Lifelong Learning Research Conference Proceedings,* no. 3. College Park: Department of Agriculture and Extension Education, University of Maryland, 1982.

Kathrein, M. A. "A Study of the Self-Directed Continued Professional Learning Activities of Members of the Illinois Nurses Association." In *Lifelong Learning Research Conference Proceedings,* no. 3. College Park: Department of Agriculture and Extension Education, University of Maryland, 1982.

Kaye, A., and Harry, K. *Using the Media for Adult Basic Education.* London: Croom Helm, 1982.

Keddie, N. "Adult Education: An Ideology of Individualism." In J. L. Thompson (ed.), *Adult Education for a Change.* London: Hutchinson, 1980.

Kellaway, J. "Part-Time Learning." In *Women, Class, and Adult Education.* Southampton, England: Department of Adult Education, University of Southampton, 1981.

Kelley, N. E. "A Comparative Study of Professionally Related Learning Projects of Secondary School Teachers." Unpublished master's thesis, Department of Adult Education, Cornell University, 1976.

Kelly, T. A. *A History of Adult Education in Great Britain.* (2nd ed.) Liverpool, England: Liverpool University Press, 1970.

Kemerer, R. W. "A Procedural Model for Determining the Relative Importance of Community-Wide Needs." *Proceedings of the Adult Education Research Conference,* no. 22. DeKalb: Northern Illinois University, 1981.

Kemerer, R. W., and Schroeder, W. L. "Determining the Importance of Community-Wide Adult Education Needs." *Adult Education Quarterly,* 1983, *33* (4), 201-214.

Kennedy, W. B. "Highlander Praxis: Learning with Myles Horton." *Teachers College Record,* 1981, *83* (1), 105-119.

Kidd, J. R. (ed.). *Learning and Society*. Toronto: Canadian Association for Adult Education, 1963.

Kidd, J. R. *Education for Perspective*. Toronto: Peter Martin, 1969.

Kidd, J. R. "Adult Education, the Community and the Animateur." In J. A. Draper (ed.), *Citizen Participation: Canada*. Toronto: New Press, 1971.

Kidd, J. R. *How Adults Learn*. New York: Cambridge Books, 1973.

Killeen, J., and Bird, H. *Education and Work: A Study of Paid Educational Leave in England and Wales*. Leicester, England: National Institute for Adult Continuing Education, 1980.

Kilpatrick, A. C., Thompson, K. H., Jarrett, H. H., and Anderson, R. J. "Social Work Education at the University of Georgia." In M. S. Knowles and Associates, *Andragogy in Action: Applying Modern Principles of Adult Learning*. San Francisco: Jossey-Bass, 1984.

Kinsey, D. "Participatory Evaluation in Adult and Nonformal Education." *Adult Education* (U.S.A.), 1981, *31* (3), 155-168.

Kirkpatrick, D. L. "Evaluation of Training." In R. Craig and L. Bittel (eds.), *Training and Development Handbook*. New York: McGraw-Hill, 1967.

Klevins, C. (ed.). *Materials and Methods in Adult and Continuing Education*. Canoga Park, Calif.: Klevens Publications, 1982.

Knapper, C. K., and Cropley, A. J. *Lifelong Learning and Higher Education*. London: Croom Helm, 1985.

Knoll, J. "New Approaches in Post-Secondary Education in Germany." In *Learning Opportunities for Adults*. Vol. 2: *New Structures, Programmes and Methods*. Paris: Organization for Economic Cooperation and Development, 1979.

Knott, E. S. "A Philosophical Consideration of the Relevance of Paulo Freire for the Education of Older Adults." In *Lifelong Learning Research Conference Proceedings*, no. 4. College Park: Department of Agriculture and Extension Education, University of Maryland, 1983.

Knowles, M. S. (ed.). *Handbook of Adult Education in the*

United States. Chicago: Adult Education Association of the U.S.A., 1960.

Knowles, M. S. *Self-Directed Learning: A Guide for Learners and Teachers*. New York: Cambridge Books, 1975.

Knowles, M. S. *A History of the Adult Education Movement in the United States*. (2nd ed.) Melbourne, Fla.: Krieger, 1977.

Knowles, M. S. *The Modern Practice of Adult Education: From Pedagogy to Andragogy*. (2nd ed.) New York: Cambridge Books, 1980.

Knowles, M. S. *The Adult Learner: A Neglected Species*. (3rd ed.) Houston, Tex.: Gulf, 1984.

Knowles, M. S., and Associates. *Andragogy in Action: Applying Modern Principles of Adult Learning*. San Francisco: Jossey-Bass, 1984.

Knox, A. B. "Continuous Program Evaluation." In N. Shaw (ed.), *Administration of Continuing Education*. Washington, D.C.: National Association for Public School Adult Education, 1969.

Knox, A. B. *In-Service Education in Adult Basic Education*. Tallahassee: Florida State University Press, 1971.

Knox, A. B. "Life-Long Self-Directed Education." In R. J. Blakely (ed.), *Fostering the Growing Need to Learn*. Rockville, Md.: Division of Regional Medical Programs, Bureau of Health Resources Development, 1974.

Knox, A. B. "Helping Adults to Learn." In R. M. Smith (ed.), *Adult Learning: Issues and Innovations*. DeKalb, Ill.: ERIC Clearinghouse in Career Education, 1976.

Knox, A. B. *Adult Development and Learning: A Handbook on Individual Growth and Competence in the Adult Years*. San Francisco: Jossey-Bass, 1977.

Knox, A. B. (ed.). *Assessing the Impact of Continuing Education*. New Directions for Continuing Education, no. 3. San Francisco: Jossey-Bass, 1979.

Knox, A. B. (ed.). *Teaching Adults Effectively*. New Directions for Continuing Education, no. 6. San Francisco: Jossey-Bass, 1980.

Knox, A. B. (ed.). *Leadership Strategies for Meeting New Chal-*

lenges. New Directions for Continuing Education, no. 13. San Francisco: Jossey-Bass, 1982a.

Knox, A. B. "Organizational Dynamics in University Continuing Professional Education." *Adult Education* (U.S.A.), 1982b, *32* (3), 117-129.

Knox, A. B. "Epilog: Further Strategies for Strengthening Continuing Education for the Health Professions." In J. S. Green, S. J. Grosswald, E. Suter, and D. B. Walthall III (eds.), *Continuing Education for the Health Professions: Developing, Managing, and Evaluating Programs for Maximum Impact on Patient Care.* San Francisco: Jossey-Bass, 1984a.

Knox, A. B. "Response to Woll's Critique of Houle's *Continuing Learning in the Professions.*" *Adult Education Quarterly,* 1984b, *35* (1), 51-54.

Knox, A. B., and Associates. *Developing, Administering, and Evaluating Adult Education.* San Francisco: Jossey-Bass, 1980.

Knox, A. B., Grotelueschen, A., and Sjorgen, D. D. "Adult Intelligence and Learning Ability." *Adult Education* (U.S.A.), 1968, *18* (3), 188-196.

Knox, A. B., and Sjorgen, D. D. "Research on Adult Learning." *Adult Education* (U.S.A.), 1965, *15* (3), 133-137.

Kolb, D. A. *The Adaptive Style Inventory.* Form B481. Cleveland: David KOLB, 1980.

Kordalewski, J. B. *The Regional Learning Service: An Experiment in Freeing Up Lives.* Syracuse: Regional Learning Service of Central New York, 1982.

Kozol, J. *Prisoners of Silence: Breaking the Bonds of Adult Illiteracy in the United States.* New York: Continuum, 1980.

Kozol, J. *Illiterate America.* New York: Doubleday, 1985.

Kulich, J. "Lifelong Education and the Universities: A Canadian Perspective." *International Journal of Lifelong Education,* 1982, *1* (2), 123-143.

Kurland, N. "The Scandinavian Study Circles: An Idea for the United States?" *College Board Review,* 1979, *114,* 20-23.

Kurland, N. "The Scandinavian Study Circle: An Idea for the U.S." *Lifelong Learning: The Adult Years,* 1982, *5* (5), 24-7, 30.

Laidlaw, A. F. *The Campus and the Community: The Global Impact of the Antigonish Movement.* Montreal: Harvest House, 1961.

Laird, D. *Approaches to Training and Development.* Reading, Mass.: Addison-Wesley, 1978.

Langerman, P. D., and Smith, D. H. *Managing Adult and Continuing Education Programs and Staff.* Washington, D.C.: National Association for Public Continuing and Adult Education, 1979.

Lasker, H., and Moore, J. "Current Studies of Adult Development: Implications for Education." In H. Lasker, J. Moore, and E. L. Simpson, *Adult Development and Approaches to Learning.* Washington, D.C.: National Institute of Education, 1980.

Lauffer, A. *The Practice of Continuing Education in the Human Services.* New York: McGraw-Hill, 1977.

Lauffer, A. *Doing Continuing Education and Staff Development.* New York: McGraw-Hill, 1978.

Lawson, K. H. *Philosophical Concepts and Values in Adult Education.* (Rev. ed.) Milton Keynes, England: Open University Press, 1979.

Lawson, K. H. *Analysis and Ideology: Conceptual Essays on the Education of Adults.* Nottingham, England: Department of Adult Education, University of Nottingham, 1983.

Leahy, R. "Teaching: Through a Spectrum of Styles." *Lifelong Learning: The Adult Years,* 1977, *1* (4), 14-16, 22.

Leann, C., and Sisco, B. *Learning Projects and Self-Planned Learning Efforts Among Under-educated Adults in Rural Vermont.* Washington, D.C.: National Institute of Education, 1981.

Lefkoe, M. "Shifting Context: A Better Approach to Training?" *Training,* 1985, *22* (2), 43-47.

Legge, D. "Relationships Within Adult Classes." In M. D. Stephens and G. W. Roderick (eds.), *Teaching Techniques in Adult Education.* Newton Abbot, England: David and Charles, 1971.

Legge, D. *The Education of Adults in Britain.* Milton Keynes, England: Open University Press, 1982.

Lengrand, P. *An Introduction to Lifelong Education.* London: Croom Helm, 1975.

Lenz, E. *The Art of Teaching Adults.* New York: Holt, Rinehart & Winston, 1982.

Lewis, G. R., and Kinishi, D. R. *The Learning Exchange.* Evanston, Ill.: Learning Exchange, 1977.

Lewis, O. *Children of Sanchez: Autobiography of a Mexican Family.* New York: Random House, 1961.

Lincoln, Y. S., and Guba, E. G. *Naturalistic Inquiry.* Beverly Hills, Calif.: Sage, 1985.

Lindblom, C. E. "The Science of Muddling Through." *Public Administration Review,* 1959, *19,* 79-88.

Lindeman, E. C. *The Meaning of Adult Education.* New York: New Republic, 1926.

Lindeman, E. C. "Adult Education." *Encyclopedia of the Social Sciences.* New York: Macmillan, 1930.

Lindeman, E. C. "New Needs for Adult Education." *Annals of the American Academy of Political and Social Sciences,* 1944, *231,* 115-122.

Lindeman, E. C. "World Peace Through Adult Education." *Nation's Schools,* 1945, *35* (3), 23.

Lindeman, E. C. "Adults Evaluate Themselves." In *How to Teach Adults.* Washington, D.C.: Adult Education Association of the U.S.A., 1955.

Lipnack, J., and Stamps, J. *The First Report and Directory of Networking.* New York: Doubleday, 1982.

Lipsett, L., and Avakian, N. A. "Assessing Experiential Learning." *Lifelong Learning: The Adult Years,* 1981, *5* (2), 19-22.

Little, D. "Adult Learning and Education: A Concept Analysis." In P. Cunningham (ed.), *Yearbook of Adult and Continuing Education, 1979-1980.* Chicago: Marquis Academic Media, 1979.

Liveright, A. A., and Haygood, N. (eds.). *The Exeter Papers.* Chicago: Center for the Study of Liberal Education for Adults, 1969.

Lloyds Bank of California. "Self-Directed Learning on the Job at Lloyds Bank of California." In M. S. Knowles and Associates, *Andragogy in Action: Applying Modern Principles of Adult Learning.* San Francisco: Jossey-Bass, 1984.

London, J. "Program Development in Adult Education." In M. S. Knowles (ed.), *Handbook of Adult Education in the United States.* Washington, D.C.: Adult Education Association of the U.S.A., 1960.

London, J. "Perspective on Programming in Adult Education: A Critical Challenge." *Adult Leadership,* 1967, *15* (8), 258-260, 291-293.

Long, H. B. *Adult and Continuing Education: Responding to Change.* New York: Teachers College Press, 1983a.

Long, H. B. *Adult Learning: Research and Practice.* New York: Cambridge Books, 1983b.

Lotz, J. "The Antigonish Movement: A Critical Analysis." *Studies in Adult Education,* 1973, *5* (2), 79-112.

Lotz, J. *Understanding Canada: Regional and Community Development in a New Nation.* Toronto: N.C. Press, 1977.

Lotz, J., and Welton, M. R. "Knowledge for the People: The Historical and Social Setting of the Antigonish Movement." Unpublished paper, Department of Adult Education, Dalhousie University, 1984.

Lovett, T. *Adult Education, Community Development, and the Working Class.* London: Ward Lock Educational, 1975.

Lovett, T. "Adult Education and Community Action." In J. L. Thompson (ed.), *Adult Education for a Change.* London: Hutchinson, 1980.

Lovett, T. "A New Initiative in Community Education." *Peace by Peace,* Sept. 9, 1983, p. 5.

Lovett, T. "Ulster People's College." *Community Education Network,* 1984, *4* (6), 6.

Lovett, T., Clarke, C., and Kilmurray, A. *Adult Education and Community Action.* London: Croom Helm, 1983.

Luckham, B. "Television and the Family—A Self-Programming Discussion Group Project." *Adult Education* (U.K.), 1983, *56* (2), 123-130.

Lynton, E. A. *The Missing Connection Between Business and the Universities.* New York: Macmillan, 1984.

McCatty, C. "Patterns of Learning Projects Among Professional

Men." Unpublished doctoral dissertation, Department of Adult Education, University of Toronto, 1973.

McCullough, K. O. "Andragogy and Community Problem Solving." *Lifelong Learning: The Adult Years,* 1978, *2* (2), 8-9, 31.

Macdonald, C. "A University Introduction to Study." *Adult Education* (U.K.), 1982, *55* (1), 7-11.

McElroy, M. *The Nature of Cooperation Between Public Libraries and Free Universities/Learning Networks.* Manhattan, Kan.: Free University Network, 1980.

Macfarlane, J. "Coal Miners at University—A Second Chance in Education." *Adult Education* (U.K.), 1975, *48* (2), 81-87.

McIlroy, J. A., and Brown, J. "Giving the Workers What They Want—The WEA and Industrial Education." *Adult Education* (U.K.), 1980, *53* (2), 91-95.

McKeachie, W. J. "Psychological Characteristics of Adults and Instructional Methods in Adult Education." In R. G. Kuhlen (ed.), *Psychological Backgrounds of Adult Education.* Syracuse, N.Y.: Syracuse University Publications in Continuing Education, 1970.

Mackenzie, J. R. "Labor Education." In E. J. Boone, R. W. Shearon, E. E. White, and Associates, *Serving Personal and Community Needs Through Adult Education.* San Francisco: Jossey-Bass, 1980.

McKenzie, L. "The Issue of Andragogy." *Adult Education* (U.S.A.), 1977, *27* (4), 225-229.

Mackenzie, N., Postgate, N., and Scupham, R. *Open Learning: Systems and Problems in Postsecondary Education.* Paris: UNESCO Press, 1975.

Mackey, P. J. "Assessment of Instruction in the Dale Carnegie Course." Unpublished doctoral dissertation, Department of Higher and Adult Education, Teachers College, Columbia University, 1977.

Mackey, P. J. "Change Strategies Used by a Proprietary School: The Dale Carnegie Organization." In S. M. Grabowski (ed.), *Strengthening Connections Between Education and Performance.* New Directions for Continuing Education, no. 18. San Francisco: Jossey-Bass, 1983.

Mackie, K. *The Application of Learning Theory to Adult Teaching.* Nottingham, England: Department of Adult Education, University of Nottingham, 1981.

McKinley, J. *Group Development Through Participation Training.* New York: Paulist Press, 1980.

McKinley, J. "Training for Effective Collaborative Learning." In R. M. Smith (ed.), *Helping Adults Learn How to Learn.* New Directions for Continuing Education, no. 19. San Francisco: Jossey-Bass, 1983.

McLeish, J., Matheson, W., and Park, J. *The Psychology of the Learning Group.* London: Hutchinson, 1973.

Mager, R. F. *Preparing Instructional Objectives.* Belmont, Calif.: Fearon, 1975.

Manley, M. J. "A Delphi Study of Adult Learning Principles." Unpublished paper, Center for Adult Education, Teachers College, Columbia University, 1984.

Mansbridge, A. *The Kingdom of the Mind.* London: Dent, 1944.

Margolis, F. H. "Teaching Technical Skills in a National Accounting Firm." In M. S. Knowles and Associates, *Andragogy in Action: Applying Modern Principles of Adult Learning.* San Francisco: Jossey-Bass, 1984.

Marienau, C. A. "Adults in Higher Education: From Theory to Practice." *Proceedings of the Adult Education Research Conference,* no. 23. Lincoln: University of Nebraska, 1982.

Martens, K. H. "Self-Directed Learning: An Option for Nursing Education." *Nursing Outlook,* Aug. 1981, pp. 472-477.

Mee, G. *Organization for Adult Education.* New York: Longman, 1980.

Mee, G., and Wiltshire, H. *Structure and Performance in Adult Education.* New York: Longman, 1978.

Meltsner, M., and Schrag, P. "Report from a CLEPR Colony." *Columbia Law Review,* 1976, *76,* 584-587.

Meltsner, M., and Schrag, P. "Scenes from a Clinic." *University of Pennsylvania Law Review,* 1978, *127,* 32-33.

Menson, B. (ed.). *Building on Experiences in Adult Development.* New Directions for Experiential Learning, no. 16. San Francisco: Jossey-Bass, 1982.

Meyer, S. B. "An Investigation of Self-Concept Change in Black Reentry Women." Unpublished doctoral dissertation, Department of Higher and Adult Education, Teachers College, Columbia University, 1985.

Mezirow, J. *Education for Perspective Transformation: Women's Reentry Programs in Community Colleges.* New York: Center for Adult Education, Teachers College, Columbia University, 1978.

Mezirow, J. "A Critical Theory of Adult Learning and Education." *Adult Education* (U.S.A.), 1981, *32* (1), 3-27.

Mezirow, J. "A Critical Theory of Self-Directed Learning." In S. Brookfield (ed.), *Self-Directed Learning: From Theory to Practice.* New Directions for Continuing Education, no. 25. San Francisco: Jossey-Bass, 1985.

Mezirow, J., Darkenwald, G. G., and Beder, H. W. *Evaluation of Adult Education in the State of Iowa.* New York: Center for Adult Education, Teachers College, Columbia University, 1975.

Mezirow, J., Darkenwald, G. G., and Knox, A. B. *Last Gamble on Education: Dynamics of Adult Basic Education.* Washington, D.C.: Adult Education of the U.S.A., 1975.

Mezirow, J., and Rose, A. *An Evaluation Guide for College Women's Re-Entry Programs.* New York: Center for Adult Education, Teachers College, Columbia University, 1977.

Michalak, D. F., and Yager, E. G. *Making the Training Process Work.* New York: Harper & Row, 1979.

Miller, H. L. *Teaching and Learning in Adult Education.* New York: Macmillan, 1964.

Miller, H. L., and McGuire, C. H. *Evaluating Liberal Adult Education.* Chicago: Center for the Study of Liberal Education for Adults, 1961.

Miller, N. "Teachers and Non-Teaching Professionals as Self-Directed Learners." Unpublished master's thesis, Department of Adult Education, Cornell University, 1977.

Mills, C. W. *The Sociological Imagination.* Oxford, England: Oxford University Press, 1959.

Minkler, M., and Cox, K. "Creating Critical Consciousness in Health: Applications of Freire's Philosophy and Methods to the Health Care Setting." *International Journal of Health Services,* 1980, *10* (2), 311-322.

Minzey, J. D., and LeTarte, C. *Community Education: From Program to Process to Practice.* Midland, Mich.: Pendell, 1979.

Monette, M. L. "The Concept of Educational Need: An Analysis of Selected Literature." *Adult Education* (U.S.A.), 1977, *27* (2), 116-127.

Monette, M. L. "Need Assessment: A Critique of Philosophical Assumptions." *Adult Education* (U.S.A.), 1979, *29* (2), 83-95.

Moon, R. G., Jr., and Hawes, G. (eds.). *Developing New Adult Clienteles by Recognizing Prior Learning.* New Directions for Experiential Learning, no. 7. San Francisco: Jossey-Bass, 1980.

Moore, A. B. "Learning and Teaching Styles of Adult Education Teachers." *Proceedings of the Adult Education Research Conference,* no. 23. Lincoln: University of Nebraska, 1982.

Moore, D. E. "Determining Priorities for Adult Education: An Example of Statewide Needs Assessment." In S. V. Martorana and W. E. Piland (eds.), *Designing Programs for Community Groups.* New Directions for Community Colleges, no. 45. San Francisco: Jossey-Bass, 1984.

Moore, M. G. "Toward a Theory of Independent Learning." *Journal of Higher Education,* 1973, *44* (12), 661-679.

Moore, M. G. "Independent Study." In R. D. Boyd, J. W. Apps, and Associates, *Redefining the Discipline of Adult Education.* San Francisco: Jossey-Bass, 1980.

Moriarty, P., and Wallerstein, N. "Student/Teacher/Learner: A Freire Approach to ABE/ESL." *Adult Literacy and Basic Education,* Fall 1979, *3* (1), 193-200.

Morris, J. F. "The Planning Behavior and Conceptual Complexity of Selected Clergymen in Self-Directed Learning Projects Related to Their Continuing Professional Education." Unpublished doctoral dissertation, Department of Adult Education, University of Toronto, 1977.

Mouton, J. S., and Blake, R. R. *Synergogy: A New Strategy for Education, Training, and Development.* San Francisco: Jossey-Bass, 1984.

Nadler, L. "Business and Industry." In R. M. Smith, G. F. Aker, and J. R. Kidd (eds.), *Handbook of Adult Education.* New York: Macmillan, 1970.

Nadler, L. "Human Resource Development for Managers." In E. J. Boone, R. W. Shearon, E. E. White, and Associates, *Serving Personal and Community Needs Through Adult Education.* San Francisco: Jossey-Bass, 1980.

Nadler, L. (ed.). *The Handbook of Human Resource Development.* New York: Wiley, 1984.

National Advisory Council for Adult Education. *Terms, Definitions, Organizations, and Councils Associated with Adult Learning.* Washington, D.C.: National Advisory Council for Adult Education, 1980.

National Advisory Council on Extension and Continuing Education. *A Special Report to the President and to the Congress of the United States.* Washington, D.C.: U.S. Government Printing Office, 1979.

National Association for Public Continuing and Adult Education. *When You're Teaching Adults.* Washington, D.C.: National Association for Public Continuing and Adult Education, 1959.

National Association for Public Continuing and Adult Education. *Tested Techniques for Teachers of Adults.* Washington, D.C.: National Association for Public Continuing and Adult Education, 1972.

National Association for Public Continuing and Adult Education. *You Can Be a Successful Teacher of Adults.* Washington, D.C.: National Association for Public Continuing and Adult Education, 1974.

National Center for Education Statistics. *Statistics of Trends in Education: 1966-67 to 1976-77.* Washington, D.C.: Office of Education, U.S. Department of Health, Education, and Welfare, 1978.

National Center for Education Statistics. *Preliminary Data: Participation in Adult Education, 1978.* Washington, D.C.: Office of Education, U.S. Department of Health, Education, and Welfare, 1980.

National Center for Education Statistics. *Participation in Adult*

Education, May 1981. Washington, D.C.: U.S. Department of Education, 1982.

National Institute of Adult Education. "Adequacy of Provision." *Adult Education* (U.K.), 1970, *42* (6), (entire issue).

Neill, A. S. *Summerhill.* New York: Hart, 1960.

Neufeld, V. R., and Barrows, H. S. "The 'McMaster Philosophy': An Approach to Medical Education." *Journal of Medical Education,* 1974, *49* (11), 1040-1050.

Niemi, J. A., and Anderson, D. *Adult Education and the Disadvantaged Adult.* Syracuse, N.Y.: ERIC Clearinghouse on Adult Education, 1970.

Niemi, J. A., and Nagle, J. M. "Learners, Agencies, and Program Development in Adult and Continuing Education." In P. D. Langerman and D. H. Smith (eds.), *Managing Adult and Continuing Education Programs.* Washington, D.C.: National Association for Public Continuing and Adult Education, 1979.

Noble, P. *Formation of Freirian Facilitators.* Chicago: Latino Institute, 1983.

Nottingham Andragogy Group. *Toward a Developmental Theory of Andragogy.* Nottingham, England: Department of Adult Education, University of Nottingham, 1983.

Nowlen, P. M. "Program Origins." In A. B. Knox and Associates, *Developing, Administering, and Evaluating Adult Education.* San Francisco: Jossey-Bass, 1980.

Organization for Economic Cooperation and Development. *Recurrent Education: Trends and Issues.* Paris: Organization for Economic Cooperation and Development, 1975.

Organization for Economic Cooperation and Development. *Learning Opportunities for Adults.* Vol. 1. Paris: Organization for Economic Cooperation and Development, 1979.

Osborn, M., Charnley, A. H., and Withnall, A. *Educational Information, Advice, Guidance, and Counseling for Adults.* Leicester, England: National Institute for Adult Continuing Education, 1981.

Osborne, K. Q. "Informal Learning and Public Policy Issues." In H. W. Stubblefield (ed.), *Continuing Education for Community Leadership.* New Directions for Continuing Education, no. 11. San Francisco: Jossey-Bass, 1981.

Osinski, F. W. W., Ohliger, J., and McCarthy, C. *Toward Gog and Magog Or?: A Critical Review of the Literature of Group Discussion.* Syracuse, N.Y.: Syracuse University Publications in Continuing Education, 1972.

Ouchi, W. G. *Theory Z.* Reading, Mass.: Addison-Wesley, 1981.

Parker, L. G. "A Mathematical Programming Model to Recognize Conflict in Adult Education Program Selection." *Proceedings of the Adult Education Research Conference,* no. 20. Ann Arbor, University of Michigan, 1979.

Parlett, M., and Hamilton, D. "Evaluation as Illumination: A New Approach to the Study of Innovative Programs." In G. V. Glass (ed.), *Evaluation Studies Review Annual,* Vol. 1. Beverly Hills, Calif.: Sage, 1976.

Parrott, A. "Lifelong Education and Training." *Adult Education* (U.K.), 1976, *48* (5), 301-307.

Participatory Research Group. *Participatory Research Group Information Leaflet.* Toronto: International Council for Adult Education, 1980.

Pascale, R. T., and Athos, A. G. *The Art of Japanese Management.* New York: Warner Books, 1981.

Paterson, R. W. K. "Social Change as an Educational Aim." *Adult Education* (U.K.), 1970a, *45* (3), 353-359.

Paterson, R. W. K. "The Concept of Discussion: A Philosophical Approach." *Studies in Adult Education,* 1970b, *1* (2), 28-50.

Paterson, R. W. K. *Values, Education, and the Adult.* Boston: Routledge & Kegan Paul, 1979.

Patton, M. Q. *Qualitative Evaluation Methods.* Beverly Hills, Calif.: Sage, 1980.

Payette, D. L. "The Adult Learner and Student Programming." In A. Shriberg (ed.), *Providing Student Services for the Adult Learner.* New Directions for Student Services, no. 11. San Francisco: Jossey-Bass, 1980.

Payne, J. "Educational Guidance Services and the Provision of Adult Education." *International Journal of Lifelong Education,* 1985, *4* (1), 35-54.

Pearson, T. G. "Managerial Philosophy and Adult Learning Principles: Training and Development Professionals as Managers of Collaborative Learning." Unpublished doctoral dissertation, Department of Adult Education, Northern Illinois University, 1980.

Penland, P. R. *Self-Planned Learning in America.* Pittsburgh: Book Center, Graduate School of Library and Information Science, University of Pittsburgh, 1977.

Pennington, F., and Green, J. "Comparative Analysis of Program Development Processes in Six Professions." *Adult Education* (U.S.A.), 1976, *28* (1), 13-23.

Percy, K., and Ramsden, P. *Independent Study: Two Examples from English Higher Education.* Guildford, England: Society for Research into Higher Education, University of Surrey, 1980.

Perraton, H. "I Sat in H. G. Wells' Chair." *Teaching at a Distance,* 1978, *13,* 1-4.

Perry, W. *The Open University: History and Evaluation of a Dynamic Innovation in Higher Education.* Milton Keynes, England: Open University Press, 1977.

Perry, W. G. *Forms of Intellectual and Ethical Development in the College Years.* New York: Holt, Rinehart & Winston, 1970.

Peters, R. S. "Education as Initiation." In R. D. Archambault (ed.), *Philosophical Analysis and Education.* Boston: Routledge & Kegan Paul, 1965.

Peters, T. J., and Waterman, R. H. *In Search of Excellence: Lessons from America's Best Run Companies.* New York: Harper & Row, 1982.

Petersen, C. H., Adkins, D., Scott, M., and Tzuk, R. "Adult Problem Solving Training: An Experimental Investigation of Andragogical Counseling Techniques." In *Proceedings of the Adult Education Research Conference,* no. 22. DeKalb: Northern Illinois University, 1981.

Peterson, D. A. *Facilitating Education for Older Learners.* San Francisco: Jossey-Bass, 1983.

Peterson, R. E., and Associates. *Lifelong Learning in America: An Overview of Current Practices, Available Resources, and Future Prospects.* San Francisco: Jossey-Bass, 1979.

Powell, J. W. "Adult Education: A Philosophy of Communication." *Adult Leadership,* 1964, *12* (7), 194-196, 217, 222.

Pratt, C. C. "Evaluating the Impact of Training on the World of

Practice." In P. P. Le Breton (ed.), *The Evaluation of Continuing Education for Professionals: A Systems View.* Seattle: University of Washington Press, 1979a.

Pratt, D. D. "Instructor Behavior and Psychological Climate in Adult Learning." *Proceedings of the Adult Education Research Conference,* no. 20. Ann Arbor: University of Michigan, 1979b.

Pratt, D. D. "Teacher Effectiveness—Future Directions for Adult Education." *Studies in Adult Education,* 1981, *13* (2), 112–119.

Pratt, D. D. "Andragogical Assumptions: Some Counter-Intuitive Logic." *Proceedings of the Adult Education Research Conference,* no. 25. Raleigh: North Carolina State University, 1984.

Rauch, D. B. (ed.). *Priorities in Adult Education.* New York: Macmillan, 1972.

Reed Ash, C. "Applying Principles of Self-Directed Learning in the Health Professions." In S. Brookfield (ed.), *Self-Directed Learning: From Theory to Practice.* New Directions for Continuing Education, no. 25. San Francisco: Jossey-Bass, 1985.

Reimer, E. *School Is Dead: Alternatives in Education.* New York: Doubleday, 1971.

Rivera, W. M., Patino, H., and Brockett, R. G. "Conceptual Framework for Program Development." In C. Klevins (ed.), *Materials and Methods in Adult and Continuing Education.* Canoga Park, Calif.: Klevens Publications, 1982.

Robbins, J. N. "Boundary-Spanning Roles of Continuing Education Program Planners." *Proceedings of the Adult Education Research Conference,* no. 22. DeKalb: Northern Illinois University, 1981.

Robinson, J. J., and Taylor, D. "Behavioural Objectives in Training for Adult Education." *International Journal of Lifelong Education,* 1983, *2* (4), 355–369.

Robinson, R. D. *An Introduction to Helping Adults Learn and Change.* Milwaukee: Omnibook, 1979.

Rockhill, K. "Professional Education Should Not Be Mandatory." In B. W. Kreitlow and Associates, *Examining Controversies in Adult Education.* San Francisco: Jossey-Bass, 1981.

Rockhill, K. "Mandatory Continuing Education for Professionals: Trends and Issues." *Adult Education* (U.S.A.), 1983, *33* (2), 106–116.

Roderick, G., Bell, J., and Hamilton, S. "Unqualified Mature Students in British Universities." *Studies in Adult Education,* 1982, *14,* 59–68.

Rogers, C. R. *On Becoming a Person: A Therapist's View of Psychotherapy.* Boston: Houghton Mifflin, 1961.

Rogers, C. R. *Freedom to Learn.* Westerville, Ohio: Merrill, 1969.

Rogers, J. "Independent Learning in the Post-Compulsory Sector in the United Kingdom." In *Learning Opportunities for Adults, Vol. 2: New Structures, Programmes and Methods.* Paris: Organization for Economic Cooperation and Development, 1979.

Rogin, L. "Labor Unions." In R. M. Smith, G. F. Aker, and J. R. Kidd (eds.), *Handbook of Adult Education.* New York: Macmillan, 1970.

Rossman, M. H., Fisk, E. C., and Roehl, J. E. *Teaching and Learning Basic Skills: A Guide for Adult Basic Education and Developmental Education Programs.* New York: Teachers College Press, 1984.

Ruddock, R. *Perspectives on Adult Education.* (2nd ed.) Manchester, England: Manchester Monographs, no. 2, Department of Adult and Higher Education, University of Manchester, 1980.

Ruddock, R. *Evaluation: A Consideration of Principles and Methods.* Manchester, England: Manchester Monographs, no. 18, Department of Adult and Higher Education, University of Manchester, 1981.

Ruyle, J., and Geiselman, L. A. "Non-Traditional Opportunities and Programs." In K. P. Cross, J. R. Valley, and Associates, *Planning Non-Traditional Programs: An Analysis of Issues for Postsecondary Education.* San Francisco: Jossey-Bass, 1974.

Rymell, R. G. "Learning Projects Pursued by Adult Degreed Engineers." Unpublished doctoral dissertation, Department of Adult Education, North Texas State University, 1981.

Sarason, S. B., and Lorentz, E. *The Challenge of the Resource*

Exchange Network: From Concept to Action. San Francisco: Jossey-Bass, 1979.

Sarason, S. B., and others. *Human Services and Resource Networks: Rationale, Possibilities, and Public Policy.* San Francisco: Jossey-Bass, 1977.

Savoie, M. L. "Continuing Education for Nurses: Predictors of Success in Courses Requiring a Degree of Learner Self-Direction." Unpublished doctoral dissertation, Department of Adult Education, University of Toronto, 1980.

Sawyers, L. L. "Learning Contracts: Education for the Self-Directed." *Alert,* 1985, *14* (4), 21-23.

Schmidt, S. D. "Examining the Learning Styles of Returning Adult Students: Emerging Elements of Best Practice with Implications for Teaching Styles." *Proceedings of the Adult Education Research Conference,* no. 25. Raleigh: North Carolina State University, 1984.

Schön, D. A. *The Reflective Practitioner: How Professionals Think in Action.* New York: Basic Books, 1983.

"Schooling for Survival." *Time,* Feb. 11, 1985, p. 75.

Schroeder, W. L. "Adult Education Defined and Described." In R. M. Smith, G. F. Aker, and J. R. Kidd (eds.), *Handbook of Adult Education.* New York: Macmillan, 1970.

Schroeder, W. L. "Typology of Adult Learning Systems." In J. M. Peters and Associates, *Building an Effective Adult Education Enterprise.* San Francisco: Jossey-Bass, 1980.

Schuster, D. C., and Berner, A. J. "The Role of the Adult Student Resource Center." In A. Shriberg (ed.), *Providing Student Services for the Adult Learner.* New Directions for Student Services, no. 11. San Francisco: Jossey-Bass, 1980.

Scottish Education Department. *Adult Education: The Challenge of Change.* London: H. M. Stationery Office, 1975.

Scriven, M. "The Methodology of Evaluation." In R. M. Gagné, M. Scriven, and R. W. Tyler (eds.), *Perspectives on Curriculum Evaluation.* AERA Monograph, no. 1. Skokie, Illinois: Rand McNally, 1967.

Scriven, M. "Pros and Cons About Goal Free Evaluation." *Evaluation Comment,* 1972, *3* (4), 1-4.

Seaman, D. F. *Working Effectively with Task-Oriented Groups.* New York: McGraw-Hill, 1981.

Severinsen, H. "A New Approach in Danish Adult Education." In *Learning Opportunities for Adults,* Vol. 2: *New Structures, Programmes and Methods.* Paris: Organization for Economic Cooperation and Development, 1979.

Shaw, N. C. *Administration of Continuing Education.* Washington, D.C.: National Association for Public Continuing and Adult Education, 1969.

Shipp, T. R. "The HRD Professional: A Macromotion Study." In *Lifelong Learning Research Conference Proceedings,* no. 6. College Park: Department of Agriculture and Extension Education, University of Maryland, 1985.

Shipp, T. R., and Mckenzie, L. "Adult Learners and Non-Learners: Demographic Characteristics as an Indicator of Psychographic Characteristics." *Adult Education* (U.S.A.), 1981, *31* (4), 187-198.

Shor, I. *Critical Teaching and Everyday Life.* Boston: South End Press, 1980.

Shriberg, A. (ed.). *Providing Student Services for the Adult Learner.* New Directions for Student Services, no. 11. San Francisco: Jossey-Bass, 1980.

Sibley, J. C. "Faculty of Health Sciences, McMaster University, Canada—The 1977 Perspective." *Medical Education,* 1978, *12* (5), 15-19.

Sim, A. R. *Canada's Farm Radio Forum.* Paris: UNESCO Press, 1954.

Simpson, E. L. "Adult Learning Theory: A State of the Art." In H. Lasker, J. Moore, and E. L. Simpson (eds.), *Adult Development and Approaches to Learning.* Washington, D.C.: National Institute of Education, 1980.

Simpson, E. L. "Program Development: A Model." In C. Klevins (ed.), *Materials and Methods in Adult and Continuing Education.* Canoga Park, Calif.: Klevens Publications, 1982.

Sinclair, C., and Skerman, R. "Management Development at a Public Service Board." In M. S. Knowles and Associates, *Andragogy in Action: Applying Modern Principles of Adult Learning.* San Francisco: Jossey-Bass, 1984.

Sjogren, D. D. "Issues in Assessing Educational Impact." In
A. B. Knox (ed.), *Assessing the Impact of Continuing Educa-
tion.* New Directions for Continuing Education, no. 3. San
Francisco: Jossey-Bass, 1979.

Smalley, J. "Perspective Discrepancy Assessment." Unpublished
paper, Department of Higher and Adult Education, Teachers
College, Columbia University, 1984.

Smith, D. C. "Program Improvement Through Value Audits."
In D. Deshler (ed.), *Evaluation for Program Improvement.*
New Directions for Continuing Education, no. 24. San Fran-
cisco: Jossey-Bass, 1984.

Smith, R. M. "The New Professional: Professor or Facilitator?"
In B. Heermann, C. C. Enders, and E. Wise (eds.), *Serving
Lifelong Learners.* New Directions for Community Colleges,
no. 29. San Francisco: Jossey-Bass, 1980.

Smith, R. M. *Learning How to Learn: Applied Learning Theory
for Adults.* New York: Cambridge Books, 1982a.

Smith, R. M. "Some Programmatic and Instructional Implications of the Learning How to Learn Concept." *Proceedings
of the Adult Education Research Conference,* no. 23. Lincoln: University of Nebraska, 1982b.

Smith, R. M. (ed.). *Helping Adults Learn How to Learn.* New
Directions for Continuing Education, no. 19. San Francisco:
Jossey-Bass, 1983.

Smith, R. M., Aker, G. F., and Kidd, J. R. (eds.). *Handbook of
Adult Education.* New York: Macmillan, 1970.

Smith, R. M., and Haverkamp, K. K. "Toward a Theory of
Learning How to Learn." *Adult Education* (U.S.A.), 1977,
28 (1), 3-21.

Snyder, R. E., and Ulmer, C. *Guide to Teaching Techniques for
Adult Classes.* Englewood Cliffs, N.J.: Prentice-Hall, 1972.

Solomon, D., Bezdek, W. E., and Rosenberg, L. *Teaching Styles
and Learning.* Chicago: Center for the Study of Liberal Education for Adults, 1963.

Solomon, D., and Miller, H. L. *Explorations in Teaching Styles.*
Chicago: Center for the Study of Liberal Education for
Adults, 1961.

Somerton, M. *Trade Union Education: Why We Need More.*

Hull, England: Occasional Papers Series, Industrial Studies Unit, Department of Adult Education, University of Hull, 1979.

Sork, T. J. "Development and Validation of a Normative Process Model for Determining Priority of Need in Community Adult Education." *Proceedings of the Adult Education Research Conference,* no. 20. Ann Arbor, University of Michigan, 1979.

Spencer, B. B. "A Program Evaluation Model for Community Adult Education." Unpublished doctoral dissertation, Department of Higher and Adult Education, Teachers College, Columbia University, 1979.

Spencer, B. B. "Perspective Discrepancy Assessment: A Qualitative Evaluation Approach." Paper presented at the Adult Education Research Conference at the University of British Columbia, Vancouver, May 1980.

Spender, D. "Learning to Create Our Own Knowledge." *Convergence,* 1980, *13* (1-2), 14-23.

Squires, G. D. "The Learning Exchange: An Innovation in Adult Education." *Adult Leadership,* 1974, *23* (4), 98, 109.

Squires, G. "Innovations in Higher Education and Their Implications for Adult Education." In *Learning Opportunities for Adults,* Vol. 2: *New Structures, Programs and Methods.* Paris: Organization for Economic Cooperation and Development, 1979.

Stack, H., and Pascal, O. "The University Studies and Weekend College Program: Beyond Access." In H. Stack and C. M. Hutton (eds.), *Building New Alliances: Labor Unions and Higher Education.* New Directions for Experiential Learning, no. 10. San Francisco: Jossey-Bass, 1980.

Stake, R. E. "The Countenance of Educational Evaluation." *Teachers College Record,* 1967, *68* (7), 523-540.

Stakes, R. L. "Conceptualizing Evaluation in Adult Education." *Lifelong Learning: The Adult Years,* 1981, *4* (8), 4-5, 22-23.

Steele, S. M. *Cost Benefit Analysis and the Adult Educator: A Literature Review.* Syracuse, N.Y.: ERIC Clearinghouse on Adult Education, 1971.

Stephens, M. D., and Roderick, G. W. (eds.). *Teaching Techniques in Adult Education*. Newton Abbott, England: David and Charles, 1971.

Stephenson, J. "Student Planned Learning." In D. Boud (ed.), *Developing Student Autonomy in Learning*. London: Kogan Page, 1981.

Stephenson, J. "Higher Education: School for Independent Study." In M. Tight (ed.), *Adult Learning and Education*. London: Croom Helm, 1983.

Stern, M. P. (ed.). *Power and Conflict in Continuing Professional Education*. Belmont, Calif.: Wadsworth, 1983.

Strong, M. "The Autonomous Adult Learner." Unpublished master's thesis, Department of Adult Education, University of Nottingham, 1977.

Stufflebeam, D. L. *Evaluation as Enlightenment for Decision-Making*. Columbus: Evaluation Center, Ohio State University, 1968.

Stufflebeam, D. L. "Evaluation as a Community Education Process." *Community Education Journal*, 1975, *5* (2), 7-12, 19.

Stufflebeam, D. L., and others. *Educational Evaluation and Decision-Making in Education*. Itasca, Ill.: Peacock, 1971.

Stuttard, G. "Industrial Tutors—A Case Study of a Society." *Adult Education* (U.K.), 1974, *46* (5), 301-306.

Suanmali, C. "The Core Concepts of Andragogy." Unpublished doctoral dissertation, Department of Higher and Adult Education, Teachers College, Columbia University, 1981.

Sullivan, R. "Introducing Data Processing at an Insurance Company." In M. S. Knowles and Associates, *Andragogy in Action: Applying Modern Principles of Adult Learning*. San Francisco: Jossey-Bass, 1984.

Szczypkowski, R. "Objectives and Activities." In A. B. Knox and Associates, *Developing, Administering, and Evaluating Adult Education*. San Francisco: Jossey-Bass, 1980.

Taaffee, T., and Litwak, E. "A Union Campus." In H. Stack and C. M. Hutton (eds.), *Building New Alliances: Labor Unions and Higher Education*. New Directions in Continuing Education, no. 10. San Francisco: Jossey-Bass, 1980.

Tan, J. S. "Education for Empowerment." Unpublished doctoral dissertation, Department of Higher and Adult Education, Teachers College, Columbia University, 1984.

Taylor, F. J. "Educational Leave and Retirement Education in France." *Adult Education* (U.K.), 1980, *53* (4), 237-241.

Taylor, R., and Ward, K. "Extra-Mural Work: Different Settings, Common Themes." *Adult Education* (U.K.), 1984, *54* (1), 12-18.

Tenbrink, T. D. *Evaluation: A Practical Guide for Teachers.* New York: McGraw-Hill, 1974.

Thiede, W. "Evaluation and Adult Education." In G. Jensen, A. A. Liveright, and W. C. Hallenbeck (eds.), *Adult Education: Outlines of an Emerging Field of University Study.* Washington, D.C.: Adult Education Association of the U.S.A., 1964.

Thiel, J. P. "Successful Self-Directed Learners' Learning Styles." *Proceedings of the Adult Education Research Conference,* no. 25. Raleigh: North Carolina State University, 1984.

Thomas, A. "The Concept of Program." In G. Jensen, A. A. Liveright, and W. C. Hallenbeck (eds.), *Adult Education: Outlines of an Emerging Field of University Study.* Washington, D.C.: Adult Education Association of the U.S.A., 1964.

Thompson, J. L. (ed.). *Adult Education for a Change.* London: Hutchinson, 1980.

Thompson, J. L. "Second Chance for Women." In *Women, Class and Adult Education.* Southampton, England: Department of Adult Education, University of Southampton, 1981.

Thompson, J. L. *Learning Liberation: Women's Response to Men's Education.* London: Croom Helm, 1983.

Thompson, V. "Adult Learning in a Resource Exchange Network: A Case Study of the Westchester Resource Exchange Network." Unpublished doctoral dissertation, Department of Higher and Adult Education, Teachers College, Columbia University, 1984.

Thorne, E. H., and Marshall, J. L. "Managerial Skills Development: An Experience in Program Design." *Personnel Journal,* Jan. 1976, pp. 15-38.

Thornton, A. H., and Bayliss, F. J. *Adult Education and the In-dustrial Community.* London: National Institute for Adult Education, 1965.

Thresher, J. "Public Libraries Are Natural Homes for Brokering Services, but Are Librarians 'Natural' Brokers?" *National Center for Educational Brokering Bulletin,* 1979, *4* (5), 1-2.

Tight, M. *Part-Time Degree Level Study in the United Kingdom.* Leicester, England: Advisory Council for Adult and Continu-ing Education, 1982.

Titmus, C. *Strategies for Adult Education: Practices in Western Europe.* Milton Keynes, England: Open University Press, 1981.

Titmus, C., and Healy, C. G. "Collective and Individual Dimen-sions in the Adult Education of Working People." *Studies in Adult Education,* 1976, *8* (1), 15-28.

Todd, F. "Fostering the Development of Professional Skills: The Work of the Continuing Education Unit for Architec-tural Staff." *British Journal of Educational Technology,* 1982, *13* (2), 129-136.

Todd, F. "Learning and Work: Directions for Continuing Pro-fessional and Vocational Education." *International Journal of Lifelong Education,* 1984, *3* (2), 89-104.

Tough, A. M. "The Assistance Obtained by Adult Self-Teach-ers." *Adult Education* (U.S.A.), 1966, *17* (1), 30-37.

Tough, A. M. *Learning Without a Teacher: A Study of Tasks and Assistance During Adult Self-Teaching Projects.* Educa-tional Research Series, no. 3. Toronto: Ontario Institute for Studies in Education, 1967.

Tough, A. M. *Why Adults Learn: A Study of the Major Reasons for Beginning and Continuing a Learning Project.* Toronto: Ontario Institute for Studies in Education, 1968.

Tough, A. M. "Major Learning Efforts: Recent Research and Future Directions." *Adult Education* (U.S.A.), 1978, *28* (4), 250-263.

Tough, A. M. *The Adult's Learning Projects: A Fresh Approach to Theory and Practice in Adult Learning.* Toronto: Ontario Institute for Studies in Education, 1979.

Tough, A. M. *Intentional Changes: A Fresh Approach to Helping People Change.* New York: Cambridge Books, 1982.

Trenaman, S. J. M. "Attitudes to Opportunities for Further Education in Relation to Educational Environment and Background in Samples of the Adult Population." Unpublished baccalaureate thesis, Oxford University, 1957.

Turner, J. C. "Labor and Continuing Education." In *Proceedings of the Invitational Conference on Continuing Education, Manpower Policy, and Lifelong Learning.* Washington, D.C.: National Advisory Council on Extension and Continuing Education, 1977.

Tyler, R. W. *Basic Principles of Curriculum and Instruction.* Chicago: University of Chicago Press, 1949.

Tyler, R. W. "Instructional Strategies" (seminar). Department of Adult and Community College Education, North Carolina State University, Raleigh, Feb. 1985.

U.S. Bureau of the Census. "Population Profile of the United States: 1978." Current Population Reports, ser. P-20, no. 336. Washington, D.C.: U.S. Government Printing Office, 1979.

"U.S. Training Census and Trends Report, 1983." *Training,* 1983, *20* (entire issue).

Valley, J. R. "External Degree Programs." In S. B. Gould and K. P. Cross (eds.), *Explorations in Non-Traditional Study.* San Francisco: Jossey-Bass, 1972.

Valley, J. R. "Local Programs: Innovations and Problems." In R. E. Peterson and Associates, *Lifelong Learning in America: An Overview of Current Practices, Available Resources, and Future Prospects.* San Francisco: Jossey-Bass, 1979.

Venable, W. R. "The Urban Community Education Director." *Proceedings of the Adult Education Research Conference,* no. 22. DeKalb: Northern Illinois University, 1981.

Verduin, J. R. *Curriculum Building for Adult Learning.* Carbondale: Southern Illinois University Press, 1980.

Vermilye, D. W. (ed.). *Lifelong Learners—A New Clientele for Higher Education: Current Issues in Higher Education 1974.* San Francisco: Jossey-Bass, 1974.

Verner, C. "Definition of Terms." In G. Jensen, A. A. Liveright, and W. C. Hallenbeck (eds.), *Adult Education: Outlines of an Emerging Field of University Study.* Washington, D.C.: Adult Education Association of the U.S.A., 1964.

Waniewicz, I. *Demand for Part-Time Learning in Ontario.* Toronto: Ontario Institute for Studies in Education, 1976.

Warden, J. W. *Process Perspectives: Community Education as Process.* Charlottesville, Va.: Mid-Atlantic Community Education Consortium, 1979.

Warren, V. B. *How Adults Can Learn More—Faster.* Washington, D.C.: National Association for Public School Adult Education, 1961.

Warren, V. B. *The Second Treasury of Techniques for Teaching Adults.* Washington, D.C.: National Association for Public Continuing and Adult Education, 1970.

Watts, O. F. "Adult Education at a Distance: The Box Scheme in Western Australia." *Studies in Adult Education,* 1978, *10* (1), 14-27.

Weathersby, R. P. "Education for Adult Development: The Components of Qualitative Change." In E. Greenberg, K. O'Donnell, and W. Bergquist (eds.), *Educating Learners of All Ages.* New Directions for Higher Education, no. 29. San Francisco: Jossey-Bass, 1980.

Weathersby, R. P., and Tarule, J. M. *Adult Development: Implications for Higher Education.* ASHE-ERIC-Higher Education Research Report, no. 4. Washington, D.C.: American Association for Higher Education, 1980.

Wenden, A. L. "The Processes of Self-Directed Learning: A Case Study of Adult Language Learners." Unpublished doctoral dissertation, Department of Higher and Adult Education, Teachers College, Columbia University, 1982.

Westbrook, R., and Whitehouse, J. "TUC Representative Training." *Industrial Tutor,* 1978, *2* (8), 5-22.

Westwood, S. "Adult Education and the Sociology of Education: An Exploration." In J. L. Thompson (ed.), *Adult Education for a Change.* London: Hutchinson, 1980.

Whale, B. W. "The Community as a Place to Learn." In H. B.

Baker (ed.), *The Teaching of Adults Series*. Saskatoon: University of Saskatchewan Press, 1976.

Whitcomb, D. B. "Applications in Management Training and Organizational Development." In D. Deshler (ed.), *Evaluation for Program Development*. New Directions for Continuing Education, no. 24. San Francisco: Jossey-Bass, 1984.

White, T. J. "The United States: A Review of Higher Education Degree Programmes Specially Designed for Adults." In *Learning Opportunities for Adults*, Vol. 2: *New Structures, Programmes and Methods*. Paris: Organization for Economic Cooperation and Development, 1979.

Wiley, K. "Effects of a Self-Directed Learning Project and Preference for Structure on Self-Directed Learning Readiness." *Nursing Research*, 1983, *32* (3), 181-185.

Williams, G. L. "Adults Learning About Adult Learning." *Adult Education* (U.K.), 1980, *52* (6), 373-377.

Wilson, J. P. "Can We Improve Research on Competencies Required of Adult Instructors?" *Proceedings of the Adult Education Research Conference*, no. 20. Ann Arbor: University of Michigan, 1979.

Wilson, W. *Toward Industrial Democracy in Britain*. Manchester, England: Department of Adult Education, University of Manchester, 1978.

Wiltshire, H. W. "The Role of the University Adult Education Department." *Studies in Adult Education*, 1983, *15*, 3-10.

Witkin, H. A. "The Nature and Importance of Individual Differences in Perception." *Journal of Personality*, 1949, *18*, 145-170.

Witkin, H. A. "Individual Differences in Ease of Perception of Embedded Figures." *Journal of Personality*, 1950, *19*, 1-15.

Witkin, H. A., and Berry, J. W. *Psychological Differentiation in Cross-Cultural Perspective*. Princeton, N.J.: Educational Testing Service, 1975.

Woll, B. "The Empty Ideal: A Critique of *Continuing Learning in the Professions* by Cyril O. Houle." *Adult Education Quarterly*, 1984, *34* (3), 167-177.

"Women and Adult Education." *Convergence,* 1980, *13* (entire issue).

Wood, D. *Continuing Education in Polytechnics and Colleges: Perceptions and Policies in the Provision of Continuing Education in Nonuniversity Institutions of Higher Education in England and Wales.* Nottingham, England: Nottingham Studies in Continuing Education in Higher Education, Department of Adult Education, University of Nottingham, 1982.

Worthen, B. R., and Sanders, J. R. (eds.). *Educational Evaluation: Theory and Practice.* Belmont, Calif.: Wadsworth, 1973.

Yarnit, M. "150 Hours: Italy's Experiment in Mass Working-Class Adult Education." In J. L. Thompson (ed.), *Adult Education for a Change.* London: Hutchinson, 1980a.

Yarnit, M. "Second Chance to Learn, Liverpool: Class and Adult Education." In J. L. Thompson (ed.), *Adult Education for a Change.* London: Hutchinson, 1980b.

Yeshewalul, A., and Griffith, W. S. "Agricultural Extension Workers' Roles in Canada and the United States." *Adult Education Quarterly,* 1984, *34* (4), 197-212.

Zerges, R. A. "Instructional Behaviors Valued by Adult Continuing Education Students Related to Student Personality Type." *Proceedings of the Adult Education Research Conference,* no. 25. Raleigh: North Carolina State University, 1984.

Name Index

357

Cohen, R. D., 312
Cohen-Rosenthal, E., 194, 195, 312
Cole, J. W., 260, 312
Collis, P., 158, 310
Conchelos, G., 113, 313
Confer, S. H., 179, 181, 313
Conger, D. S., 15, 156, 237, 313
Connelly, H. W., 313
Conti, G. J., 34-36, 38, 39, 132, 163, 313
Corbett, N., 155
Coren, E. H., 127, 314
Cortwright, R., 167, 314
Costello, N., 171, 314
Cox, K., 174, 338-339
Crabtree, A. P., 288, 314
Craig, R. L., 187, 314
Cronbach, L. J., 263, 314
Cropley, A. J., 183, 330
Cross, K. P., 3, 5, 62, 90-91, 96, 101, 183, 187, 314, 322
Cunningham, P. M., 88, 175, 186, 314-315

D

Dadswell, G., 80, 315
Dale, S., 80, 315
Daloisio, T., 103, 315
Danis, C., 45, 99, 121, 315
Darkenwald, G. G., 3, 5, 6, 31, 129, 147, 152-153, 166, 179, 278, 302, 304, 315, 338
Darnell, J. T., 315
Dave, R. H., 183, 315
Davenport, J., 120, 315
Davenport, J. A., 120, 315
Davidson, A., 194, 316
Davis, A., 316
Davis, J. A., 15, 156, 316
Day, C., 90, 95, 96, 120, 207-208, 316
Day, M., 174, 316
De Bono, E., 316
Delaney, D. M., 63, 318
De Paula, Z. S., 174, 316
Deshler, D., 280, 281, 316
Dewey, J., 15, 122, 162, 316
Dickinson, G., 127, 316
Dinges, R. F., 35, 316

Dinkelspiel, J. R., 187, 316
Dohr, J. H., 240, 242, 317
Donaldson, J. F., 240, 242, 317
Douglas, J. A., 317
Douglass, J. F., 35, 101, 317
Draves, W. A., 127, 134, 153-154, 237, 317
Drennan, A. P., 167, 317
Dubin, S., 25, 129, 130, 317
Du Bois, E. E., 189, 190, 317
Dunn, W. R., 174, 324
Durkheim, E., 94, 317
Dwyer, R., 179, 182, 317-318
Dyer, W. G., 189, 318

E

Eggert, J. D., 280, 318
Eisele, G. R., 186, 318
Eisenberg, S., 63, 318
Eisner, E. W., 207, 211, 212, 220, 263, 318
Elias, J. M., 93, 96, 120, 318
Ellwood, C., 183, 318
Elsdon, K. T., 138, 318
Elsey, B., 149, 167, 318
Ely, M. L., 147, 318-319
Enders, C. C., 183, 325
Enright, C., 168, 319
Entwistle, H., 194, 319
Erikson, E. H., 93
Essert, P. L., 137, 319
Eurich, N. P., 187, 319
Even, M. J., 41-42, 129, 130, 319
Evers, C. J., 187, 314

F

Fabian, B. S., 103, 319
Fair, J., 149, 319
Faith, V., 17, 320
Faris, R., 156, 319
Farquharson, A., 174, 319
Fatchett, D., 181, 183, 319
Fawcett-Hill, W. M., 139, 319
Feinstein, O., 182, 319-320
Ferguson, M., 151, 320
Ferrier, B., 79, 174, 320
Fielden, D., 183, 326

Subject Index

❧ ❧ ❧ ❧

A

Adaptive Style Inventory, 43, 130
Adult basic education: adult learning in, 166-170; and learning instrument, 35; and teaching styles, 132; and voluntarism, 167-168
Adult Education Act of 1966, 166
Adult Education Association of the United States, 126, 275, 301, 312-313
Adult Education Research Conference, 153
Adult Education Through Guided Independent Study, xiii, 73-77, 83, 85
Adult Independent Learning Project, 80
Adult learners: as accommodators, 43; autonomy for, 291; characteristics of, 5; concept of, 5; educational needs of, 123-125; learning styles of, 128-133; pluralistic nature of, 127-128; and previous educational attainment, 5-6
Adult learning: in adult basic education, 166-170; agencies for, 4;

analysis of motives and implications of, 1-24; background on, 1-3, 123-126; in business and industry, 186-197; commonalities in, 2-3; in community action groups, 158-165; concept of, 93; contextual distortions of, 197-200; in continuing professional education, 170-177; criteria for, 283-286; defined, 5; discussion method for, 135-143; enrollment economy in, 229; evaluation for, 273-283; exemplary practices in, 133-135; facilitator's role in, 22-24, 62-69, 123-146, 284; formal settings for, 166-200; guidelines for, 283-297; in higher education institutions, 183-186; informal settings for, 147-165; in labor education, 177-183; models for, 126-128; non-participation in, 6-8; participants in, 3-9; participatory techniques in, 12; philosophy of, 287-290; principles of effective practice in, 9-20; purpose of, 283-284; settings for, 147-148; teaching out-